Making the Voyageur World

France Overseas:
Studies in Empire and Decolonization

SERIES EDITORS:
Philip Boucher, A. J. B. Johnston,
James D. Le Sueur, and Tyler Stovall

Making the Voyageur World

Travelers and Traders in the North American Fur Trade

Carolyn Podruchny

UNIVERSITY OF NEBRASKA PRESS • LINCOLN AND LONDON

Parts of chapter 3 were previously published in a different form as "Baptizing Novices: Ritual Moments among French Canadian Voyageurs in the Montreal Fur Trade, 1780–1821," in *Canadian Historical Review* 83, no. 2 (2002): 165–95. Copyright © 2002 by the University of Toronto Press. Reprinted by permission of University of Toronto Press Incorporated.

Parts of chapter 3 were also previously published as "*Dieu, Diable* and the Trickster: *Voyageur* Religious Syncretism in the *Pays d'en haut*, 1770–1821," in *Western Oblate Studies* 5, Proceedings of the Fifth Symposium on the History of the Oblates in Western and Northern Canada, edited by Raymond Huel and Gilles Lesage, Winnipeg: Presses Universitaires de Saint-Boniface, 2000, 75–92. Reprinted with permission.

Parts of chapter 5 were previously published as "Unfair Masters and Rascally Servants? Labour Relations among Bourgeois, Clerks and Voyageurs in the Montréal Fur Trade, 1780–1821," in *Labour / Le travail: Journal of Canadian Labour Studies* 43 (Spring 1999): 43–70. Reprinted with permission.

Parts of chapter 9 were previously published as "Un homme-libre se construit une identité: Voyage de Joseph Constant au Pas, de 1773 à 1853," in *Cahiers franco-canadienes de l'Ouest* 14, nos. 1 and 2 (2002): 33–59. Reprinted with permission.

Set in Quadraat by Kim Essman.
Designed by R. W. Boeche.
Image on title page
© Christine Balderas/ iStockphoto.

Library of Congress Cataloging-in-Publication Data
Podruchny, Carolyn.
Making the voyageur world : travelers and traders in the North American fur trade / Carolyn Podruchny.
p. cm.—(France overseas)
Includes bibliographical references and index.
ISBN-13: 978-0-8032-8790-7 (pbk. : alk. paper)
ISBN-10: 0-8032-8790-9 (pbk. : alk. paper)
1. French-Canadians—North America—History. 2. Fur trade—North America—History. 3. Fur trade—New France—History. 4. Fur traders—North America—History. 5. Fur traders—New France—History. 6. Métis—North America—History. 7. Indians of North America—History. 8. North America—Description and travel. 9. Saint Lawrence River Valley—Description and travel. 10. Frontier and pioneer life—North America.
I. Title. II. Series.
E49.2.F85P63 2006
970'.004114—dc22
2006013379

Contents

Illustrations, Maps, and Tables

Illustrations

Maps

Tables

Fig. 1. Canoe cup, Great Lakes region, ca. 1775–1825. Private collection. Courtesy of the Donald Ellis Gallery, Dundas, Ontario.

Preface

The voyageur's canoe cup shown in figure 1 represents a fascinating nexus of values held by French Canadian voyageurs who worked in the fur trade as paddlers and laborers in the eighteenth and nineteenth centuries. Voyageurs carried cups, secured with string to their belts or sashes, to easily quench their thirst during their arduous trips along rivers, streams, portages, and lakes. Carved out of wood into the shape of a turtle shell with the name "Pierre Anthoine" engraved on the bottom, this particular cup shows how voyageurs' identities blended influences of their French Canadian homes in the St. Lawrence valley with Aboriginal worlds they encountered in the continental interior. The turtle shell is a common symbol of the earth among Algonquian-speakers and Iroquoian-speakers. Many origin stories speak of one or more people falling from the sky onto the back of a turtle in a primordial sea, and various animals diving to the bottom of the sea for soil to place on the turtle's back to create land. A naked man, serving as the cup handle, appears to be holding up the land or earth. This symbol is reminiscent of the famous Greek tale of Atlas, Titan leader and ancestor of the Trojans, condemned by Zeus to hold up the heavens. Although trapped in pressing servitude, Atlas is a symbol of male strength and recognized as the god of daring thoughts. The naked figure may also represent the idea that voyageurs had to lug the world around with them while they worked as porters in the fur trade. What looks like a wild boar is engraved above the name on the bottom of the cup. Boars were indigenous to the forests and grasslands of Europe and the Mediterranean countries and were the ancestors of domesticated pigs. In medieval and early modern Europe, wild boars were hunted both for their meat, considered a delicacy, and to mitigate the damage they cause to crops and forests. In Greek, Roman, and Celtic traditions, a boar represented power, ferocity, and strength. One of the twelve labors of Hercules was hunting a wild boar. The boar was a common charge in both English and French heraldry. Although pigs were brought to North America by the earliest colonists, wild boars did not become widespread there until the late nineteenth century. It is likely that the carved boar on the canoe cup represented a heraldic charge brought to the St. Lawrence valley by a French settler. Even if the cup's carver did not belong to the family with the crest, he may have borrowed the image to convey his prowess in hunting. The centrality of the boar on the cup reflects the importance of food to voyageurs, whose occupation demanded intense physical labor. The carver of this cup seemingly felt free to draw widely on symbolic vocabularies from European and Aboriginal traditions, even if he was unaware of the full extent of their connections and meanings. The message embedded in the unique design of this canoe cup suggests that although Pierre-Anthoine felt the burden of his indentured servitude while serving in the trade, he was proud of his occupation, which required strength and bravery. This book explores the complex and varied values, like those reflected in the canoe cup, that developed among French Canadian voyageurs, who formed a mainstay of labor in the fur trade, a major European-based economy in early North America.

My interest in voyageurs began with a desire to contribute to the history of plebeian peoples who did not leave a documentary record yet who had a significant impact on the social and cultural landscape of early North America. French Canadian voyageurs traveled vast distances over the continent and left a significant legacy. French was one of the main languages among Europeans and European Americans in the Montreal fur trade until the mid-nineteenth century, and its presence today is reflected in placenames across the continent. Many voyageurs formed kinship ties with Aboriginal people and settled in the Northwest to raise their families. A large portion of métis people had French ancestry. Dozens of Francophone communities exist in northwestern North America today, and a large part of these descended from fur trade families. Today voyageurs are highly visible as colorful caricatures in popular culture and history, but they have rarely been the subject of serious study. The fragmented nature of sources on voyageurs and their subjugation in commercial and political arenas has confined them to the peripheries of most historical narratives. This book places French Canadian voyageurs squarely in the center of historical narrative as serious people with compelling stories and lasting consequences. The book devotes considerable attention to Aboriginal and mixed-blood, or métis, peoples, but only in the context of their relationship to French Canadian voyageurs.

Several key terms used extensively throughout the book—*voyageurs*, *freemen*, *bourgeois*, *métis*, *pays d'en haut*, and *Aboriginal*—require some clarification. In its most general sense, the term *voyageur* has referred to travelers, to contracted servants (*engagés*), or to small-scale independent fur traders, who worked alone or in small groups, with some financial backing from merchants. I use the criteria of labor status to distinguish these categories. Thus in this book the term *voyageur* refers to engagés, servants, and workers. Independent traders, including those who traded illegally without licenses, are designated as *coureurs de bois*. *Freemen* refers to former voyageurs who chose to go on living in the pays d'en haut independently, relying on a variety of means to survive, including trading, trapping, hunting, fishing, and engaging in short labor contracts with fur trading companies. After the end of the Seven Years' War (also known as the French and Indian War) in 1763, the fur trade operating out of Montreal was reorganized under the direction of Scottish, English, American, and a few French Canadian managers. These men, who included company partners, those in charge of districts, and the occasional senior clerk, called themselves *bourgeois*. One bourgeois, Alexander Ross, suggested that the term originated with the voyageurs themselves and was a holdover from the New France fur trade. Partnerships of bourgeois hired voyageurs mainly from parishes around Montreal and Trois-Rivières. Along with French Canadians, Iroquoian men from Kahnewake were hired to work as voyageurs in the trade, but their numbers never reached beyond 10 percent of the total servants. Their experiences working in the trade were distinct from those of French Canadian men, and I have not explored them in this book. This book refers to *métis* as people who are descended from both Aboriginal and European ancestors, and to *Métis* as a specific ethnic identity that emerged around the Great Lakes in the seventeenth century. It was often not easy to distinguish between French Canadian and métis voyageurs (the sons of European traders and Aboriginal women). By the early nineteenth century, métis voyageurs came to occupy a significant place in the fur trade labor pool. Their unique heritage and cultural development, especially where Métis was recognized as a distinct ethnicity, merit close and dedicated study, which is beyond the scope of this project.

Literally translated as "the country up there," or "upper country," the term *pays d'en haut* referred to areas "upriver" where French speakers from the St. Lawrence valley trapped and traded furs. In the early years of New France, the term referred to the area north of the St. Lawrence River, in present-day Quebec, and west of Montreal, in present-day Ontario. By the late seventeenth century, the term came to be widely used for the fur-trading territory mainly around the Great Lakes. After the mid-eighteenth century, the boundaries of the pays d'en haut moved farther west and north, following the reaches of the fur trade to the prairies around the Mississippi, the Missouri, and the Assiniboine rivers; to the northern parkland along the Saskatchewan River; and even to the subarctic around Lake Athabasca. In this book the term is used to designate any area where voyageurs were sent to trade and carry goods.

Because there is no universal term to refer to indigenous peoples living in North America, the book employs *Aboriginal*, *Aboriginal peoples*, and *Indians* in hopes of appealing to the broadest audience and to minimize confusion. The American terms *American Indians* and *Native Americans* are cumbersome and confusing to many non-Americans, especially when they refer to indigenous peoples living outside the current borders of the United States. Likewise, the Canadian term *Native peoples* may confuse Americans who refer to those born in the United States as Natives. The popular term *First Nations* implies a European sense of nations that is not easily translated to Aboriginal identities. I am uncomfortable with *First peoples* because it seems imprecise, and with *Amerindians* because its usage is not widespread among English speakers. The term *Aboriginal* is clear, precise, and widespread, and despite its colonial baggage, the term *Indian* works well in this book because of its common usage in the historic sources and its long history in North America.

Abbreviations of names have been silently expanded, such as "Frs" to "François" and "Antne" to "Antoine."

Acknowledgments

This book began its life as a doctoral dissertation written at the University of Toronto, and I am grateful to the lively intellectual atmosphere of the community of scholars in Toronto. Its subsequent transformation into a book has benefited from equally stimulating environments at the University of Winnipeg's Centre for Rupert's Land Studies, the Newberry Library, Western Michigan University, and York University.

Financial assistance has been generously provided by the Social Sciences and Humanities Research Council of Canada, the Imperial Order of Daughters of the Empire, the International Council of Canadian Studies, the Ontario Ministry of Education, and the University of Toronto's Department of History and School of Graduate Studies. Many archivists welcomed me to their collections and assisted me in finding sources. In particular I thank Judith Hudson Beattie, Anne Morton, and Leslie Clark at the Hudson's Bay Company Archives; Gilbert Comeau at the Provincial Archives of Manitoba; the late Alfred Fortier, Gilles Lesage, and William Benoit at the Société historique de Saint-Boniface; Pam Miller at the McCord Museum of Canadian History; Luc Lepine, Estelle Brisson, and Evelyn Kolish at the Archives nationales de Québec à Montréal; Karen Bergsteinson and Leon Warmsky at the Ontario Archives; and the staffs of the Rare Books and Special Collections Division of McGill University Libraries, the Library and Archives Canada (and especially Ghislain Malett for last-minute reference queries), the Minnesota Historical Society, the Thomas Fisher Library (University of Toronto), the Baldwin Room at the Toronto Metropolitan Reference Library, the Newberry Library, and the British Library. I also thank the Inter-Library Loan offices at the University of Toronto, the University of Winnipeg, and Western Michigan University. Linnea Fredrickson at the University of Nebraska Press and Barb Wojhoski worked hard to help me prepare the manuscript for publication.

I thank those who answered my many questions and shared their sources and knowledge with me, including Peter Bakker, Robert Bringhurst, Edith Burley, Dale Cockran, Gilbert Comeau, Donald Fyson, Konrad Gross, Richard Hoffman, Joe Holtz, George Lang, Pam Logan, Hugh MacMillan, Ian S. MacLaren, Bryan Palmer, Ellen Paul, Katherine Pettipas, Patrick Schifferdecker, and especially Sylvia Van Kirk, who gave me copies of her decoded transcriptions of George Nelson's journals. I thank members of the Toronto Area Early Canada and Colonial North America Seminar Series and of the Newberry Library colloquia; the audiences at the meetings of the American Society for Ethnohistory, the Algonquian Conferences, the Canadian Historical Association, and Omohundro Institute of Early American History and Culture; and anonymous reviewers for many helpful suggestions. In addition friends and colleagues provided suggestions and sources and created intellectual environments that have helped me write this book. These include Darlene Abreu-Ferierra, Rebecca Bach, Jerry Bannister, Judith Hudson Beattie, Carl Benn, Bob Berkhofer, Louis Bird, Heidi Bohaker, José-Antonio Brandaõ, Tina Chen, Michael Chiarappa, Luca Codignola, Matt Cohen, Alicia Colson, Juanita De Barros, Heather Devine, Fay Devlin, Harry W. Duckworth, Hilary Earl, Matthew Evenden, Magda Fahrni, Nora Faires, the late Alfred Fortier, John Gay, Peter Geller, Marion (Buddy) Gray, Mark Guertin, Sally Hadden, Karl Hele, Catherine Heroux, Tobie Higbie, Catherine Julien, Gilles Lesage, Maureen Matthews, Anne Morton, Susanne Mrozik, James Muir, Sasha Mullally, Lucy Eldersveld Murphy, Laura Murray, Tamara Myers, John Nichols, Trudy Nicks, Jan Noel, Jean O'Brien, Ian Radforth, Roger Roulette, Myra Rutherdale, Nicole St.-Onge, Bethel Saler, Theresa Schenck, Nancy Shoemaker, Susan Sleeper-Smith, Judith Stone, Helen Hornbeck Tanner, Robert Vézina, Bruce White, Cory Wilmont, Chris Wolfart, and Takashi Yoshida. The inspiration behind this book has come from my intellectual guides: Jennifer S. H. Brown, Sarah Carter, Allan Greer, Toby Morantz, Laura Peers, Arthur J. Ray, Sylvia Van Kirk, and Germaine

Warkentin. Several people deserve a special acknowledgment for reading the whole or parts of the manuscript: José-Antonio Brandaõ, Allan Greer, Theodore Karamanski, Magda Fahrni, and Myra Rutherdale. I am deeply indebted to Jennifer S. H. Brown, Susanne Mrozik, and Germaine Warkentin, who went over the whole manuscript with a fine-tooth comb. Despite their best efforts, all errors are my own.

I reserve the final thanks for my family. My sister, Heather Podruchny, believed in this project and in me. My parents, Thomas Podruchny and Sonia Podruchny, provided me with support in too many ways to list here. My grandparents, Frances Zatylny, Rose Bilowus, and especially Michael Bilowus inspired me to become an academic. This book is dedicated to their memories.

Note on Sources

Most materials on which this book is based are the writings of fur trade bourgeois and clerks and of travelers passing through fur trade communities in the period after the Seven Years' War, which ended in 1763, and before the 1821 merger of the Hudson's Bay Company and the North West Company. Bourgeois and clerks wrote post journals, letters, and memoirs and published accounts of their experiences working in the trade, and the resulting documents can be found in libraries and archives spread across the continent. The best single concentration of North West Company and XY Company material is the Masson Collection, divided evenly between the Rare Books and Special Collections Division of McGill University Libraries in Montreal and the Library and Archives Canada in Ottawa. The collection had its origins in Roderick McKenzie's long efforts to collect material on the Montreal fur trade to document its history. Sometime in the first several years of the nineteenth century, McKenzie sent a circular letter asking all bourgeois and clerks in the trade to send him surveys of regions under their control, and their post journals, letters and notes. In 1889–90, L. R. Masson published a small part of this collection in *Les Bourgeois de la Companie du Nord-Ouest*. A second collection rich in Montreal fur trade material is the world-renowned Hudson's Bay Company Archives in Winnipeg. The Hudson's Bay Record Society has published parts of this vast collection. A small but very rich collection is the writings of George Nelson, housed in the Toronto Metropolitan Reference Library, parts of which have been published by Jennifer S. H. Brown, Robert Brightman, Laura Peers, and Theresa Schenck. His coded journals have been decoded by Sylvia Van Kirk.

Material in this book is not confined to these collections nor to this time period. I consulted additional fur trade material in the Archives nationales de Québec à Montréal, the Rare Books and Special Collections Division of McGill University Libraries, the McCord Museum of Canadian History, the Bibliotheque municipales, and the Archives de la chancelleries de L'Archevèche de Montréal in Montreal; the Library and Archives Canada in Ottawa; the Ontario Archives, the Thomas Fisher Library, and the Baldwin Room at the Toronto Metropolitan Reference Library in Toronto; the Newberry Library in Chicago; the Société historique de Saint-Boniface, the Provincial Archives of Manitoba, and the Hudson's Bay Company Archives in Winnipeg; the Minnesota Historical Society in St. Paul; the Municipal Reference Library in Vancouver, British Columbia; and the British Library in London. The Canadian Institute for Historic Microreproductions has issued on microfiche most of the published primary material I consulted.

In a very few sources I was able to come close to the voices of the voyageurs. These included court cases, where voyageurs were plaintiffs, defendants, or witnesses; their engagements; and letters (I found only sixteen) written from voyageurs' friends and families to them while they were in the service. I found one letter written by a voyageur (Jean Mongle) to his wife. L'abbé Georges Dugas's biography of the voyageur Jean-Baptiste Charbonneau, published seventy years after Charbonneau retired from the service, provided much insight into voyageurs' mental world. But the writings of the literate members of the fur trade proved to be the most useful; some recorded long passages quoting voyageurs on their attitudes and describing their customs and rituals.

Abbreviations

ANQM	Archives nationales de Québec, dèpot de Montréal
CPCM	Cours des plaidoyers communs du district de Montréal
DCB	*Dictionary of Canadian Biography*
HBC	Hudson's Bay Company
HBCA	Hudson's Bay Company Archives (Winnipeg)
JR	*Jesuit Relations* (edited by R. G. Thwaites)
LAC	Library and Archives Canada (Ottawa)
MC	Masson Collection
MHS	Minnesota Historical Society
MRB	Rare Books and Special Collections Division of McGill University Libraries (Montreal)
NWC	North West Company
NWCC	North West Company Collection
OA	Ontario Archives (Toronto)
PAM	Provincial Archives of Manitoba (Winnipeg)
PRO	Public Record Office
TBR	Toronto Metropolitan Reference Library Baldwin Room
XYC	XY Company (or New NWC)

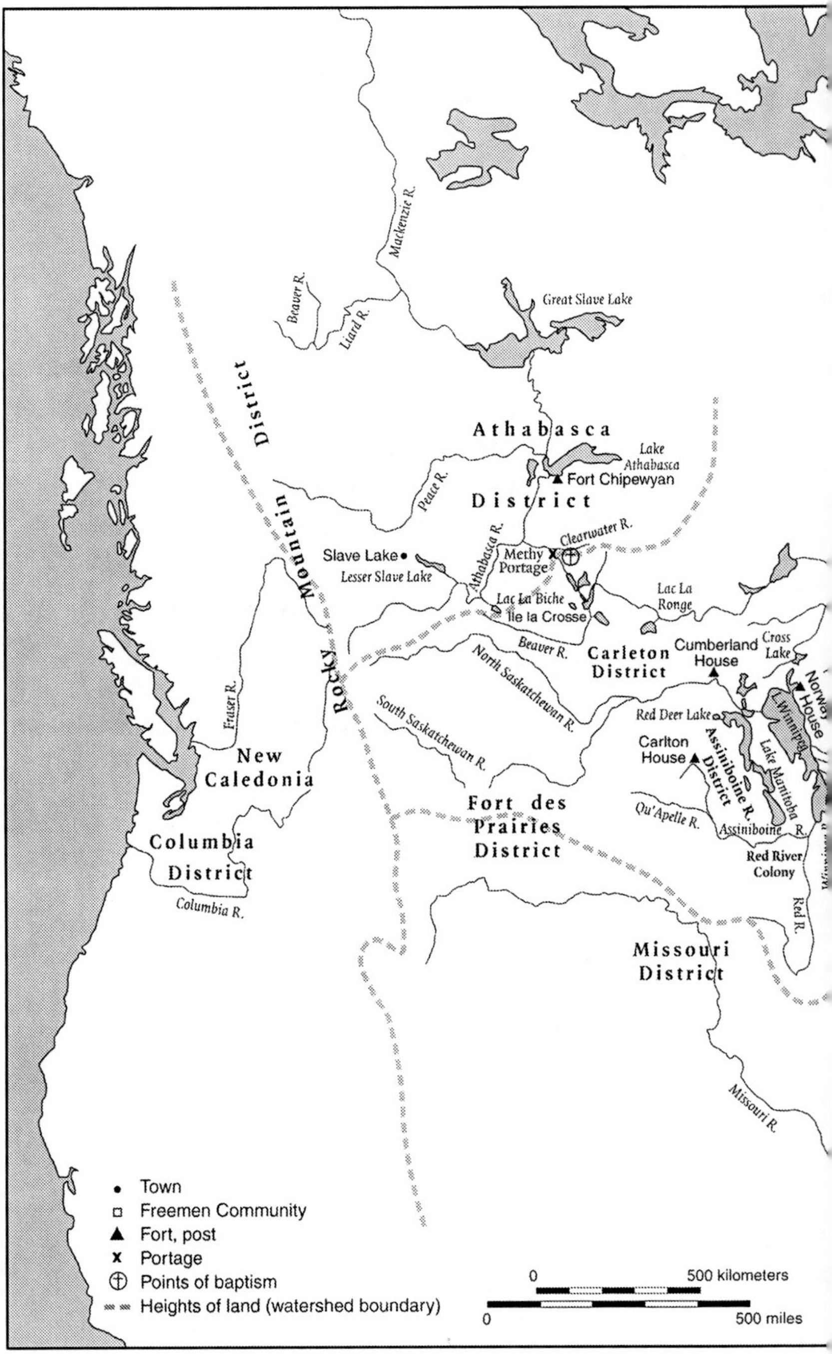

Map 1. The voyageurs in North America

Hudson Bay
Churchill R.
Nelson R.
Hayes R.
York Factory
James Bay
ort Alexander (Bas de la Riviere)
Lake Nipigon
Lake of the Woods
Fort William
Grand Portage
ac La Pluie
Rainy Lake
ost
L. Superior
ond du Lac
Great Lakes
S.Ste. Marie
Georgian Bay
Michilimackinac
Minnesota Territory
Folle Avoine District
Michigan Terr.
L. Huron
Mississippi R.
L. Michigan
Detroit
L. Erie
York
(Toronto)
L. Ontario
Kingston
Upper Canada
Lower Canada
Montreal
Ottowa R.
Quebec City
St. Lawrence R.
St. Louis

Making the Voyageur World

1. Introduction

Sons of the Farm, the Trade, and the Wilderness

And as it may be interesting to the reader to know something of the character of these super-annuated sons of the wilderness, we shall sketch them.[1]

Stereotypes

In his 1855 book, *Fur Hunters of the Far West*, trader Alexander Ross used these words to introduce a section describing French Canadian voyageurs and, in so doing, helped initiate a long history of stereotyping. Voyageurs are idealized and romanticized in North American history and popular culture. In the northern United States, they figure alongside rugged mountain men and rough-hewn farmers as hardy men who conquered the wilderness and settled the frontier. In Canada voyageurs occupy a central place in the mythology of nation building; by being friends of Aboriginal peoples and learning the skills necessary to thrive in the wilderness, they opened the way for later settlers. In both countries pictures of voyageurs adorn the labels on beer bottles, the sides of U-Haul vans, and advertisements for canoe vendors, summer camps, and wilderness tourism. Winter festivals in Manitoba and Minnesota commemorate them. Voyageurs National Park in Minnesota is "named for the . . . French-Canadian canoe-men who traveled these waters in their birch-bark canoes from the Great Lakes to the interior of the western United States and Canada."[2] A major Canadian bus company goes by the name of Voyageur Corporation.[3]

The image of the voyageur evokes ruggedness, joie de vivre, and the ability to transport goods quickly and efficiently. The popular Canadian writer

Peter C. Newman describes voyageurs as "a remarkable ragbag of magnificent river rats" and "cockleshell heroes on seas of sweet water," who held together a fur trade empire with their raw muscle. Surpassing even his own usual rhetorical excesses, Newman declares, in a series of vivid and inconsistent tropes,

> *Unsung, unlettered and uncouth, the early fur-trade voyageurs gave substance to the unformed notion of Canada as a transcontinental state. . . . Their eighteen-hour paddling days were more wretched than many men then or now could survive. They were . . . galley slaves, and their only reward was defiant pride in their own courage and endurance. Because they could boast of their exploits to no one but themselves, the voyageurs, like a wild and worn-out professional hockey team perpetually on the road, had to concoct their own sustaining myths. No voyageur ever reported meeting a small bear, a tame moose or a wolf that wasn't snarling with blood-lust.*[4]

Even in more erudite venues, voyageurs were both idolized and simplified. Grace Lee Nute's *Voyageur* (1931) opens with the elegy, "His canoe has long since vanished from the northern waters; his red cap is seen no more, a bright spot against the blue of Lake Superior; his sprightly French conversation, punctuated with inimitable gesture, his exaggerated courtesy, his incurable romanticism, his songs, and his superstitions are gone."[5] Harold Adams Innis, the grandfather of fur trade and Canadian economic history, remarked in *The Fur Trade in Canada* (1930) that the work of the voyageurs opened the path to Canadian confederation.[6] Like comic-book heroes, voyageurs have a highly visible reputation, building the Canadian nation with their Herculean strength, while singing, laughing, leaping over waterfalls, and paddling faster than speeding arrows.

These representations of voyageurs as merry workhorses have a long history that begins with the writings of their superiors.[7] In 1815 North West Company clerk Daniel Harmon described the voyageurs he had gotten to know over fifteen years as:

> *ficle & changeable as the wind, and of a gay and lively disposition. . . . they make Gods of their bellies, yet when necessity obliges them . . . they will endure all the fatigue and misery of hard labour & cold weather &c. for several Days following without much complaining. . . . They are People of not much veracity. . . . Therefore there is little dependence to be placed on what they say and they are much given to pilfering and will even steal when favourable opportunities offer. . . . . by flattering their vanities (of which they have not a little) they may be made to go through fire and water.*[8]

Who were these brave and untrustworthy men? Why have they received so little attention as ordinary men working in difficult conditions and yet so much attention as colorful caricatures? This book looks past the stereotypes of voyageurs to their lives, world-views, values, and unique situation as fur trade workers navigating the vast distances—physical, social, and cultural—between their homelands and those of the Aboriginal peoples who surrounded them in the continental interior. Fur traders and voyageurs called their new home "Indian Country" or the pays d'en haut, meaning the country that lay beyond the St. Lawrence valley.

Silences

Despite their highly visible profile in popular culture and history, voyageurs have received little scholarly attention. The fur trade has been subject to intensive inquiry since Harold Adams Innis's monumental study *The Fur Trade in Canada*, but the sole monograph devoted to voyageurs was published by Grace Lee Nute in 1931. Fur trade scholars have been exemplary in illuminating the everyday lives of ordinary people in the past by paying close attention to Aboriginal peoples, both men and women.[9] Yet most major works have focused on elites. Even though the labor system of the fur trade was built largely on indentured servitude, scholars have lumped together French Canadian voyageur servants with their mostly British and American masters, and voyageurs are usually described in only a single paragraph in textbooks of Canadian history.[10] Other groups of European and European American laborers in the fur trade have recently come to the attention of scholars, especially working people in the New France fur trade, the Hudson's Bay Company, and the American Fur Company.[11] Those who have turned their attention to voyageurs have been constrained by the limited information that could be gleaned from their labor contracts, such as their parishes of origin, their numbers, and their economic contributions to New France and Lower Canada. Heather Devine's recent *The People Who Own Themselves: Aboriginal Ethnogenesis in a Canadian Family 1660–1900* (2004) situates the importance of voyageurs' occupation within family and ethnic contexts. Yet, the world of voyageurs has remained shrouded in mystery.[12]

The voyageurs were the "proletarians" of the Montreal fur trade from the 1680s until the 1870s. As indentured servants, voyageurs transported—primarily by canoe—vast quantities of furs and goods between Montreal and posts in the far western and northern reaches of North America and traded with many different Aboriginal people, primarily in Aboriginal lodges and hunting camps. At their peak in the decade before 1821, up to three thousand French Canadian servants worked in the trade at any given moment. It is impossible to measure their precise numbers because their contracts signed in Montreal have not all survived, nor were contracts made in the pays d'en haut collected in a systematic manner. Based on signed contracts, Gratien Allaire calculated a steady climb in the number of engagements issued to workers in the fur trade between 1701 and 1745, peaking at 380 in 1738.[13] This number represents between one-third and one-fifth of all men working in the trade, because their engagements lasted three to five years. Table 1 lists some estimates of numbers of voyageurs working in the trade after the 1763 conquest.

The estimates listed in this chart are problematic for a number of reasons and are probably on the low side. Aside from Heriot, the commentators do not specify whether they are referring only to French Canadian servants from the St. Lawrence valley, or whether they are also including Iroquois from Kahnewake (the Sault St. Louis Christian reserve just outside Montreal), métis born in the pays d'en haut, or Aboriginal people indentured at the interior posts.[14] The reported estimates probably only refer to one com-

Table 1. Numbers of Voyageurs Working in the Trade

Year	Number	Commentary	Source
1784	500 voyageurs	"In 1784 the NWC employed 500 men in the service, whom they divided into two equal sets. The first set of 250 men transported goods from Montreal to the administrative center at western tip of Lake Superior in canoes capable of carrying about four tonnes, requiring eight to ten men to operate. The other set of 250 men transported goods from Lake Superior to the posts in the interior country, some as far as 3,000 miles distant."	Letter of Benjamin and Joseph Frobisher to General Haldimand, October 4, 1784, in Wallace, *Documents* 73–74.
1790s	1,150 voyageurs	"The number of people usually employed in the north-west trade, and in the pay of the company, amounts, exclusive of savages, to 1,270 or 1,280 men, 30 of whom are clerks, 71 interpreters and under clerks, 1,120 are canoe-men, and 35 are guides."	Heriot, *Travels through the Canadas*, 107.
1801	1,120 voyageurs	In his brief 1801 history of the fur trade, Alexander Mackenzie asserted that usually the NWC employed in one year 50 clerks, 71 interpreters and clerks, 1,120 canoe-men, and 35 guides. Of these, 5 clerks, 18 guides, and 350 canoe-men worked on the Great Lakes run.	Mackenzie, "General," 33.
1802	1,500 voyageurs	Simon McTavish reported approximately 1,500 French Canadian servants working for the NWC.	London, PRO, Board of Trade Papers, Lt. Governor Milnes to Hobart, Oct. 30, 1802, List of Depts in the NWC supplied by McTavish, Frobisher & Co.
1816	2,000 voyageurs	"The number of voyageurs in the service of the North-West Company cannot be less than 2,000."	T. Douglas, *Sketch of the British Fur Trade*, 39.

pany working out of Montreal (the largest was the NWC). The estimates do not specify whether they refer to the number of contracts signed in one year, or whether they take into consideration the numbers of voyageurs in the middle of their contracts. They omit informal contracts made at interior trading posts (to the best of my knowledge bourgeois did not keep a clear record of these cases). The Montreal companies did not have the same tradition of meticulous recordkeeping as did the HBC. Many partnerships with limited life spans did not preserve their records, even though large collections of voyageur contracts can be found in the archival collections of Canadian notaries.[15] My estimate of three thousand voyageurs working in the trade at one time is a conservative approximation based on reported numbers and speculations about unreported numbers.

Voyageurs were primarily nonliterate and left few records. It is difficult to uncover their lives and voices. Only one document authored by a voyageur is presently known. John Mongle, a voyageur from the parish of Maskinongé, wrote to his wife in 1830 to tell her that he missed her. The quality of the letter's penmanship and the absence of any other writing by Mongle suggest that he had the help of a clerk. Sixteen letters written by voyageurs' families and friends to them help to portray the strains of families pulled apart when voyageurs entered the service. Voyageurs' voices sometimes also speak in court cases in which they were plaintiffs, defendants, or witnesses; and through their engagements (labor contracts), which outlined the terms of their service. One biography of a voyageur, Jean-Baptiste Charbonneau, written by L'abbé Georges Dugas and published seventy years after Charbonneau retired from the service, also provides insight into voyageurs' world-views.

One of the most useful surviving sources are the writings of the literate members of the fur trade, primarily the clerks and the bourgeois, who left post journals, letters, memoirs, and published accounts of their working experiences (see the Note on Sources for a full description). Some long passages quote voyageurs; other passages extensively describe their attitudes, customs, and rituals. In addition, northern explorers passing through the fur trade social world produced a wealth of surprisingly detailed and nuanced reflections on voyageurs.

Yet viewing voyageurs through the eyes of these others generates a host of methodological problems. These texts contain layers of multiple meanings and multiple perspectives. We must "read beyond the words" in these written sources and take up the challenge to see beyond their biases.[16] Without these records, historians would have few and narrow views of voyageurs.

I use the term *bourgeois* loosely to refer to all men who were not laborers, but the literate masters of the fur trade were not a cohesive, homogenous group by any means. They ranged from clerks to partners and shareholders, with different ethnic backgrounds, salaries, and status, but the men tended to form similar assumptions about social hierarchy, gender, race, and age. They all had a vested interest in making the trade profitable and in viewing voyageurs as subordinates. Bourgeois cast voyageurs as "other" in their efforts to construct themselves as serious, industrious, and successful men. The representations of voyageurs varied in different contexts. When describing their adventures in the wild and harsh Northwest, bourgeois portrayed voyageurs as part of the exotic landscape, as a source of additional tribulation and a test of their power and patience. Voyageurs added to the colorful and dangerous background of bourgeois adventures, as recounted, for example, in the elite setting of the Beaver Club in Montreal, open to bourgeois who had spent at least one winter west of Lake Superior.[17] However, in commercial contexts, where the bourgeois reported on their success in the fur trade, they wrote about voyageurs' great strength, ability, and suitability to fur trade work, emphasizing their obedience and loyalty. Bourgeois Alexander Mackenzie remarked in his general history of the fur trade (1801), "[Voyageurs] always show the greatest respect to their employers, who are comparatively but few in number, and beyond the aid of any legal power to enforce due obedience. In short, a degree of subordination can only be maintained by the good opinion these men entertain of their employers which has been uniformly the case, since the trade has been formed and conducted on a regular system."[18] In this commercial context, Mackenzie portrayed the workers as loyal and hardworking in order to bolster the sense of success in trade and the authority and might of the bourgeois. One strategy to penetrate the biases in the bourgeois writings is to understand that the varying contexts in which bourgeois described voyageurs determined how they represented them.

A second strategy in overcoming the bias in the written record is to read widely in the writings of the bourgeois to discern broad patterns. "Repeating evidence" or incidents and behaviors that emerge frequently in a broad array of bourgeois writings reflect both widespread patterns and practices that were thought to be remarkable. At the interior posts the bourgeois repeatedly remarked on every animal that was killed by their servants, which reveals concerns about securing food but also that voyageurs spent much of their time hunting. Determining the variety of incidents and behaviors reflects the edges of "permissibility" in voyageur culture or the widest range of acceptable behaviors, rather than reflecting a "norm." Thus, when the bourgeois wrote of voyageurs bullying or playing cruel tricks on one another, these were probably not common occurrences but reflect fractures in relationships and acceptable means of expressing tensions. Voyageur behavior can also be determined from a few particularly observant bourgeois and clerks who wrote much about them. General behavior can be inferred from specific instances described in great detail.

A third strategy in overcoming the difficulty in fur trade sources is to "read against their grain," or to read around the overt intentions of the bourgeois. Fur trade sources contain many voices and perspectives, but some are more difficult than others to hear. Mikhail Bakhtin's concept of *heteroglossia* has aided scholars in hearing a multitude of intentions and perspectives within the writing of a single person.[19] In *Clues, Myths, and the Historical Method*, which uses inquisitorial records to discover information about the world-views of peasants, Carlo Ginzburg commented that "[w]hile reading the inquisitorial trials, [he] often felt as if [he] was looking over the judges' shoulders, dogging their footsteps, hoping . . . that the alleged offenders would be talkative about their beliefs."[20] The passage from Daniel Harmon quoted earlier in this chapter portrays voyageurs as thoughtless and childlike "others" who were guided by the base lusts of their bellies, loins, passions, and vanities. Yet Harmon's colored view of the voyageurs sometimes contained a glint or glimmer of a voyageur voice. He notes that voyageurs worked hard in difficult circumstances, valued generosity, and cared about "faire L'Homme," or making the man. Harmon laments, as an Anglophone, that he often felt alienated and alone, but that even if he could have spoken French fluently, "what conversation would an illiterate ignorant Canadian be able to keep up. All of their chat [was] about Horses, Dogs, Canoes and Women, and strong Men who can fight a good battle."[21] Harmon's dismissal of voyageurs in fact illuminated their interest in dogs, canoes, women, wrestling, and racing. Incidental descriptions of voyageurs' activities, rather than the bourgeois' moral preaching about them, can be very revealing. A bourgeois might have casually mentioned that his crew canoed for twenty-five songs or five pipes. His intention was to record the distance the crew traveled, but he also disclosed that distances were measured by voyageurs' work rituals.

A fourth strategy for reading beyond the words of the bourgeois is to unpack the meaning in voyageur rituals. Rituals were often described by bourgeois in tones of amusement or derision, but their "texts" offer valuable readings of the mental world of the voyageurs. Rituals produced and maintained community solidarity and thus were key to group solidarity.[22] Celebrations in Montreal and at fur trade posts during the departures and arrivals of trading brigades were not simply quaint and sentimental customs. Their descriptions convey the importance of the voyageurs to their families and fellow workers, an acknowledgment of the danger during voyages, and markers of specific social worlds.

The sources are so fragmentary that it is rare to find much commentary about voyageurs at any one time and place. Because voyageurs were a mobile workforce, covering a vast area in the Northwest, and because northern fur trade posts were usually temporary and frequently moved, no large community of voyageurs could be found in any one area for an extended period of time. To capture the fluid and far-flung character of voyageurs' lives, I have drawn widely from the many temporary post journals, correspondence, and travel narratives of the constantly moving bourgeois as well the chronicles of other travelers. I have hoped to glimpse their broad contours by casting my net as widely as possible and by illuminating the lives of some individuals that appear in detail in the documentary record.

Canoes, Horses, Dogs, Courage, Risk, Women, and Freedom

In 1855 former NWC clerk Alexander Ross wrote about a group of aged voyageurs who had worked most of their lives in the fur trade and whom he hired to take him from Norway House to the Red River colony. This group of "sons of the wilderness," as Ross called them, was talkative, high-spirited, independent, and had long yarns to tell about their lives. The eldest voyageur, who acted as the leader of his crew, shared with Ross some reflections on his life, which Ross tried to recount in the voyageur's own words. He bragged that he had been in Indian country for forty-two years. Although he was old, he could do anything requested of him: steer, row, or sail, proclaiming that he had been "brought up to voyage." For twenty-four years he was a "light canoe-man" and hardly slept, easily paddling for fifty songs a day. He announced that no portage was too long for him, and the end of his canoe never touched the ground. He saved the lives of his bourgeois and was always the favorite, because he never paused at rapids or even waterfalls, claiming "No water, no weather, ever stopped the paddle or the song." This aged voyageur also bragged about other accomplishments: he had had twelve wives, fifty horses, and six running dogs. He claimed:

> *"No Bourgeois had better-dressed wives than I; no Indian chief finer horses; no white man better-harnessed or swifter dogs. I beat all Indians at the race, and no white man ever passed me in the chase. I wanted for nothing; and I spent all my earnings in the enjoyment of pleasure. Five hundred pounds, twice told, have passed through my hands; although now I have not a spare shirt to my back, nor a penny to buy one. Yet, were I young again, I should glory in commencing the same career again. . . . There is no life so happy as a voyageur's life; none so independent; no place where a man enjoys so much variety and freedom as in Indian country."*[23]

This passage is full of revelations about voyageur values. Tools of the transporting occupation—canoes, horses, and dogs—held a significant place as prized possessions. They were coveted, well cared for, and decorated. These tools reflected voyageurs' masculine virtues, therefore canoes, dogs, and horses had to be tough, fast, and strong, just like their owners. The old voyageur whom Ross recorded measured his prowess against Aboriginal men, his bourgeois, and his fellows. The voyageur reflected that he was usually an obedient servant, but he wanted to show that he was stronger and more capable than his bourgeois. A true test of strength was to "beat all Indians at the race," to live in the wilderness as an Indian better than the Indians could themselves. Many voyageurs' values converged with or were adopted directly from Aboriginal peoples, such as being stoic and cheerful in the face of hardship, yet voyageurs distinguished themselves from Aboriginal peoples by wanting to be better than them. Aboriginal women were thus often treated as prize trophies, for there was no better demonstration of success in being a "son of the wilderness" than to possess one of its daughters as a bride. Winning the hearts of Aboriginal women signified a space for sexual and romantic pleasure, where perhaps both exploitation and love flourished. It also meant that voyageurs could attempt to live among Aboriginal communities if they wished. But because women usually sought men who could meet their economic needs, the pride in having wives also signified that men valued wealth for what it could buy, as opposed to wealth for its own sake. Finally, key values for the old man quoted here included freedom and independence. Voyageurs were indentured servants, working under the control of their masters and in a foreign land where Aboriginal peoples often controlled life and death. To counter their vulnerable position, voyageurs proclaimed their desire to be free. In his biography of the voyageur Jean-Baptiste Charbonneau, l'abbé Georges Dugas writes, "It was their desire to enjoy the unlimited freedom that they believed they would find in the deserts of the West."[24] By overcoming the dangerous landscape through strength, the voyageurs could claim a stronger manhood than their British masters and Aboriginal neighbors. They carved out a social space to assert their distinct identity, a space in which canoes, horses, dogs, courage, risk, women, and freedom were central.

Voyageurs' lives were shaped by three major influences. First, because the overwhelming majority of voyageurs were from the parishes surrounding Montreal and Trois-Rivières, their French Canadian peasant roots were clearly visible. Many voyageurs thought of themselves as habitants (peasants) working only temporarily in the trade to earn extra money for their farms and families, and they returned after only a few seasons in the service. These men never seriously abandoned their primary identity as habitants. Yet unlike some sojourning workers, voyageurs did not transplant their French Canadian communities to their new place of work. They rarely maintained kin, neighbor, or parish ties in the interior. No particular parishes seem to be associated with interior posts, and most posts were made up of men from many different parishes.[25] Rather, voyageurs formed new friendships and relationships in the context of work. This is not surprising considering the structure of the service. Usually only one sibling in a family became a voyageur. Men signed individual labor contracts rather than group contracts. The bourgeois determined the location of voyageurs' postings. Voyageurs moved around frequently and were often reposted from year to year. Voyageurs entered "Indian country" as French Canadian peasants and underwent rituals to mark the beginning of their new occupational identity and which laid out new cultural values and meanings. The longer voyageurs stayed in the interior, the more they adapted to the distinct voyageur way of life. Regardless, their identities were always French Canadian in some way, and many of them maintained connections to French Canada. The labor force, including men who devoted most of their lives to the service and indeed most people involved in the trade, spoke French. They sang French songs, practiced Roman Catholic rites, and maintained the values and cosmology of their French Canadian home.

Yet voyageurs also entered the social domain of Aboriginal peoples. They traveled great distances over plains, parklands, forests, mountains, and tundra and met speakers of Iroquoian, Algonquian, Athapaskan, Siouan, Salishan, and Wakashan languages, and even Inuit. This second major influence on voyageurs, that of Aboriginal peoples, can be seen most obviously in material culture. Voyageurs had to adopt Aboriginal technologies to survive the harsh conditions of living in the pays d'en haut. They ate Aboriginal food, dressed in Aboriginal clothing, and used Aboriginal tools along with their own. Aboriginal peoples also came to influence their notions of property, wealth, and independence. The connections formed between voyageurs and Aboriginal peoples provided conduits for an exchange in social and moral values. Working in the fur trade, and especially coming into close contact with Aboriginal people, offered voyageurs a new kind of life unknown to habitants in the St. Lawrence valley. Some voyageurs chose to leave French Canadian society altogether to live with Aboriginal people.[26] However, they left one social system to enter another, with as many rules and boundaries on behavior. Voyageurs idealized freemen, men who left indentured servitude, remained in the Northwest interior, and independently traded and lived off the land on the margins of both fur trade and Aboriginal societies.[27] These men lived simply within small family units or joined together to form diverse communities, such as The Pas, Swan River, Turtle Mountain, Pembina, and Lesser Slave Lake.[28] Although many voyageurs became freemen and joined Aboriginal families or emerging métis communities, their occupational culture remained distinct from these groups.

The third influence on the voyageurs was the workplace itself. Voyageurs worked under the hegemonic rule of their primarily British masters and yet outnumbered them in the pays d'en haut. They were also an all-male group of sojourners, alienated from French Canadian women. Like sailors and lumbermen, this community of men made masculinity, rather than family life, the central social principle in their lives. Their expressions of masculinity resembled what some scholars have labeled "rough culture" among other groups of all-male sojourners, encompassing behaviors such as drinking, gambling, and fighting and valuing strength and risk.[29] Garnering symbolic, social, and cultural capital became ways to measure masculine success. Taking risks, such as running rapids, and competing with one another in canoe races, gambling, and boxing matches provided ways for voyageurs to earn "masculine capital" and bolster their reputations. Contests and gaming were common at the interior posts. Play was a forum in which new social behaviors could emerge. Annual celebrations and parties at arrivals and departures helped voyageurs cope with the centrifugal forces caused by the mobility of the job and the transience of individuals. Dancing and music became sites where voyageurs combined French Canadian customs with Aboriginal customs. The liminal spaces of the fur trade particularly encouraged jokes and trickery. These provided a means for voyageurs to release tensions, and they sometimes served as sites of cultural connection with Aboriginal communities.

Voyageurs measured their masculinity against male "others." Resisting bourgeois hegemony was a way to stand up to the master. The central tenet of the master and servant relationship was the legal contract that bound voyageurs to loyalty and obedience in exchange for food, clothing, and wages. A social contract developed around the legal obligations, in which masters and voyageurs tried to negotiate the edges of their rights and duties. Voyageurs engaged in a "theater of resistance" that included working slowly, stealing provisions, free-trading, and deserting the service. In this way they sought to control the workplace to some degree and pressure their masters for better working conditions. By demonstrating their physical superiority to their masters in canoeing, portaging, and hunting, voyageurs earned "symbolic capital" that they could spend in negotiations with their masters. Being more Indian than the Indians was another means by which voyageurs sought to earn masculine capital.

Journeys

Voyageurs lived in a state of liminality, literally a "threshold." Liminality is an in-between site where transitions occur.[30] Most scholars who use liminality as a metaphor focus simply on the small space and time of transition within a ritual. My work, however, suggests that while voyageurs worked in the fur trade their lives were characterized by transitions. As voyageurs traveled from their homes in French Canada to the Aboriginal interior, they underwent continuous transformations in identity and cultural association.[31] My use of the term *liminality* does not strictly refer to the act of passage but rather characterizes an entire cultural space. The process of continual movement in the fur trade workplace made it a liminal space, one where voyageurs traveled between the European colony in the St. Lawrence valley through foreign landscapes and Aboriginal worlds to isolated bastions and fragments of European society at the fur trade posts. They journeyed between cultures, on the margins of French Canadian society, on the thresholds of Aboriginal societies, and under the authority of their predominantly British masters. In this liminal space they created an incipient and fluid social order that was neither static nor homogenous, but embodied a range of values and beliefs that helped voyageurs order their world.[32]

Voyageurs sustained their world-views and values not primarily through familial reproduction but through the arrivals of new men entering the vocation. Chain migration occurred in a few cases, such as in the Desjarlais family, described by Heather Devine.[33] Although many voyageurs married Aboriginal women in the interior, and some of their children were raised as voyageurs and initiated into the occupation at very young ages, the practice was not widespread enough to generate the high numbers of voyageurs who were needed to work in the service. Men who married Aboriginal women frequently left the fur trade service to live with their wives' families, to live as independent freemen, or to settle around the Great Lakes or Red River in emerging métis societies.[34] Other voyageurs abandoned their Aboriginal families when they decided to leave fur trade service, and their children usually left posts to join their mothers' relatives. Voyageurs' values and world-views were thus maintained by "immigrants" or new employees, who were sometimes relatives and descendents of those already working in the trade. These men had to be initiated into the voyageur world and taught new ways of living, working, and playing.

Traveling in the exotic and adventurous "Indian country" opened voyageurs to new cultural beliefs and practices. The liminality of the workplace led to fluidity, inventiveness, and an openness to different cultural practices. Rituals became a way for voyageurs to express and maintain their beliefs. The canoe journey out of Montreal and into the pays d'en haut became the point of transition into voyageur life and was a social space for the teaching of new values. The "cultural performance" of mock baptisms at designated sites along fur trade routes signified the thresholds crossed by French Canadian laborers as they entered a new occupational and cultural identity as well as new stages of manhood. The religico-magical rites practiced by voyageurs were modified in the interior to emphasize the dangerous and frequent tragedies in their jobs. In addition, voyageurs imprinted themselves and their history on the social and physical landscape of the pays d'en haut by (re)naming lakes, rivers, rapids, and portages.

The metaphor of "the voyage" provides an ideal way to organize this cultural history of voyageur identity. This group of all-male sojourners were labeled as "travelers," first among French speakers and after the 1763 conquest among English-speaking clerks and bourgeois. Although the *Oxford English Dictionary* dates the first usage of *voyageur* in an English-language text as trader John McDonell's 1793 chronicle of a journey from Montreal to Grand Portage, the sense of the word was widespread among participants in the Montreal trade throughout its history. The term underscored not only the geographical distance voyageurs journeyed but also the social and cultural distances. This book follows an archetypical voyage, which will portray both the drama of their lives and the performative aspects of their culture. In chapter 2 the opening scene is set on a farm just outside Montreal, where voyageurs left their families to join the fur trade for extra money. The chapter outlines the organization of the trade, contracts, and wages and discusses the means by which voyageurs conceptualized their Canadian homes while in the interior. Chapter 3 explores voyageurs' understanding of their time and place in the cosmos, focusing on their religious practices and beliefs, which were a blend of Roman Catholicism, peasant "magic," and Aboriginal animism. The chapter also examines liminal moments, or points of transition, which included ritual baptisms along the routes, competitions of strength between the men, battles with ferocious animals and storms, marriages *à la façon du pays* (in the custom of the country) with Aboriginal women, and funeral rites for voyageurs who died in the service. Chapter 4 describes the organization of servants at Lachine, the first leg of their journey to the western tip of Lake Superior, rates of travel, paying toll fees to Aboriginal groups along the route, provisioning, positions in a canoe, and the mechanics of paddling, shooting rapids, tacking, and portaging. The workplace was dominated by paternalism, but as in many early modern labor settings, workers engaged in a theater of misrule. Chapter 5 is devoted to sketching the contours of the master and servant relationship, servant disobedience, and the performative aspects of cultural hegemony. The meeting of western and eastern brigades at the western tip of Lake Superior in midsummer was a time of celebration, respite, and planning. The annual rendezvous was the biggest party in fur trade society, a time when *carnivale* reigned. The rendezvous, a site of cultural transformation, symbolizing the distinctiveness of life in the trade, is discussed in chapter 6, as well as the annual calendar of festivals, which mimicked the calendar of Catholic feasts observed by habitants in the St. Lawrence valley. Chapter 7 looks at fur trade life beyond Lake Superior. Space and work are illuminated through routes, ideas of landscape, and social geography. Work at interior posts was divided into the four categories of construction and artisanal crafts, provisioning, sending mail and messages, and trading. Voyageurs had direct and extended contact with Aboriginal peoples when they were sent out to trade *en dérouine*, or with a small complement of goods to trade with Aboriginal people at their lodges. Voyageurs often spent winters in Aboriginal lodges. Chapter 8 examines the strong ties many voyageurs formed with Aboriginal women, with whom they had sexual and emotional relationships. Many voyageurs married Aboriginal women and had long-lasting families, but the dominant pattern of fluid monogamy was shaped by the fact that voyageurs and Aboriginal women traveled constantly in the interior. Voyageurs were often reposted to different forts from one year to the next. Aboriginal women followed annual cycles of travel to harvest seasonal economic resources. Although many unions became serious and monogamous, they were not usually long-term. The bonds formed between voyageurs and Aboriginal women were important to trading alliances, but they were often impermanent. Chapter 9 examines what voyageurs did after they left fur trade service, focusing on the idealization of freedom embodied in "freemen."

2. Leaving Home

Family and Livelihood in French Canada and Beyond

Ma tres cher Epousse
Cest avec boucoup d'annuit que j'ai attandu L'occasions qui Se presante Par les voyageur[s] qui vont a Moreal [Montreal], pour vous informé L[']état de de [repetition] Ma Santé qui est tres bonne Grace a Dieu jusqu[']o [au] presant. Dieu veuille que La presante lettre vous trouve jouissant du meme bonneur [bonheur], je croit qui [qu'il] N'est Rien de plus sansible que d'etre Separé du Person aussi cher que Son Epousse[.] aussite je vous assur que Rien ne peut Retardé Mon retoure apres mon tems finis.

My very dear Wife,
It is with a deep longing that I awaited the occasion which presents itself by the voyageurs going to Montreal, to let you know the state of my health, which is very good so far, thanks be to God. I pray God that the present letter will find you enjoying the same happiness, I think that there is nothing more painful than to be separated from someone as dear as a wife. Also I assure you that nothing can delay my return once my time is up.[1]

This excerpt is taken from a letter written on April 12, 1830, by Jean Mongle, posted at Fort Colville, to his wife Marie St. Germain, living in the parish of Maskinongé in the St. Lawrence valley. It is the only known surviving document to have been written by a French Canadian voyageur. The only known information about Jean Mongle and his family is contained in a few disparate documents.[2] Mongle was probably born around 1800 in the district of Maskinongé, located a few miles west of Trois-Rivières, on the north shore of the St. Lawrence River. His parents may have been the peasants Andres Mongle (appears as Mongal in the Maskinongé Parish register), who was a Hessian soldier with the Hanau Chasseurs, and Marie-Judith Panneton.[3] Jean Mongle first entered the fur trade service in 1814 or 1816 and was employed by the North West Company for three years as a *milieu*, or middleman, who helped paddle the canoe.[4] From 1819 to 1821 he does not appear in fur trade records. He may have decided to farm in the St. Lawrence valley during these years and marry his first wife, Marie Caret or Comette. Mongle reappears as a middleman in 1821, when he signed on for another three years with the newly constituted Hudson's Bay Company after its 1821 merger with the NWC.[5] Despite his many years working in the trade, Mongle maintained close connections to his home parish of Maskinongé. Presumably his first wife passed away, because he married Marie St. Germain there in 1827.[6] Mongle once again joined the HBC in 1829, this time as a *boute*, or "end," which means he was a steersman or foresman in the canoe and was paid more than his previous milieu's salary.[7] Sadly, Mongle did not live long enough to enjoy his higher wages. He drowned in the Columbia River on October 25, 1830.[8]

His April 1830 letter to his wife presents a mystery. Voyageurs were typically nonliterate, and there is no reason to believe Mongle was exceptional. If he had been able to write, no doubt a HBC officer would have remarked on it, and Mongle might have been encouraged to become a clerk in the HBC. The grammar and spelling of the letter are poor, but it was written with beautiful penmanship. Mongle probably dictated the letter to an English speaker, perhaps a clerk or a missionary who spelled words phonetically with the English alphabet. In the letter Mongle asks his wife if she had received an earlier letter, sent in the fall of 1829, instructing her to claim a part of his wages at the HBC office, probably in Montreal. He regrets that the rest of his wages must be paid directly to him, but he would try in the future to ensure that they would be paid to her. Mongle asks if his wife is still a boarder in the same house and pleads with her to remain there until his return. Mongle records his hopes that his letter would be passed along somehow through voyageurs to his wife in the St. Lawrence valley. The letter's journey to her would have probably taken six months to a year.

Like her husband, Marie St. Germain also tried to reach out to her spouse across vast distances. In a remarkable coincidence, she wrote a letter to her husband on April 20, 1830, only eight days after he wrote to her.[9] She informed him of her good health, reported on news in the extended family, told him that she missed him, and asked him to send home more of his wages and some pairs of shoes (perhaps moccasins). Unfortunately, the letter was never delivered because Mongle had passed away in October 1830.[10] Fortunately for us, however, both of these letters have survived. In January 1832 St. Germain sent the letter written by her husband to the HBC as proof of her marriage when she was claiming Mongle's wages.

St. Germain's anxiety must have increased as months passed without news of her husband. Probably sometime late in 1831, a Monsieur Morin, perhaps another voyageur, informed St. Germain of her husband's death. On January 13, 1832, she wrote to the HBC, first to confirm Jean Mongle's death, and second, to ask for her husband's wages.[11] She wrote that her "great misery, under obligation to everyone," obliged her "to ask [their] honours to have the goodness to examine the accounts to see whether something is owed to him, with the sole purpose of assisting [her] and at the same time to beg [their] honours to have some regard for [her] misery."[12]

What can these three letters tell us about voyageurs participating in the fur trade? Why would men like Mongle choose to enter the fur trade and work far away from their families in a risky occupation? Mongle's story resonates with those of thousands of other families in the St. Lawrence valley from the 1680s until well into the 1830s. Sons and husbands decided to leave their families to join the fur trade for extra money mainly because their farms were producing very little above subsistence and feudal tithes.[13] They met with recruiting agents and signed contracts, or *engagements*, to work in the summer months transporting goods and furs between Montreal and the western tip of Lake Superior or to work year-round in the trade far away in the pays d'en haut. The newly recruited voyageurs bid goodbye to parents, children, wives, girlfriends, and neighbors as they set off, no doubt hoping they would return home again but also fearing a fate like Jean Mongle's.

This chapter addresses the question of how and why French Canadian peasants entered the fur trade and shows the connections between individual family strategies and the continental scope of the vast mercantile system of the fur trade. In its simplest terms, the fur trade required the labor provided by voyageurs, and French Canadian peasants required the money provided by working in the fur trade service. The pull of adventure and desire for freedom also influenced many men's decision to enter and stay in the fur trade service, despite its high risk. In addition, this chapter looks at labor recruitment, contracts or *engagements*, wages, and the close ties that many voyageurs maintained with their families in the St. Lawrence valley, even when they had traveled thousands of miles and had been away for years.

Organization of Labor: The Continental Context

When Jean Mongle entered the fur trade for the first time in 1816, he may not have realized the vast reaches of this mercantile commerce, but he would probably have been aware of the central role the fur trade played in the development of his home community. The quest for furs was one of the reasons for European settlement in the St. Lawrence valley in the seventeenth century. Europeans set up outposts on the Atlantic coast of northern North America first to acquire fish and later furs for trade in Europe, which would increase the fortunes of colonial empires as well as of individual merchants.[14] In 1608 French colonizer Samuel de Champlain established the first permanent fur trade post in the St. Lawrence valley to trade goods for furs with Iroquoian and Algonquian peoples in the region. The fur trade became the central economic enterprise in the colony of New France and remained important until the first quarter of the nineteenth century; the trade was expanded far into the continent not simply for profit but also to meet political aims. The colonial expansion in North America planned by Louis XIV of France was intended to confine English colonies to the south of the Atlantic seaboard.[15]

The practice of hiring indentured servants to work in the trade began in Montreal in the 1690s. Initially the fur trade was open to most habitants, provided they pay fees to join a company and taxes on their returns. Most habitants traded for pelts with Aboriginal peoples visiting the island of Montreal. In the 1660s specialized merchants, called coureurs de bois, began making trading journeys to the Great Lakes region. These men borrowed capital, purchased outfits of trade goods, and traveled to the interior to trade with Aboriginal peoples. In 1681 the French minister of marine, Jean-Baptiste Colbert, inaugurated the license, or congé, system, in which the New France government granted a limited number of licenses and quotas every year to merchants trading in the interior. Many coureurs de bois traded illegally without licenses, so the total volume of trade is difficult to gauge.[16] By this time merchants who had specialized to the point of forming small partnerships of two, three, or four parties began to hire servants, or engagés, to transport the goods and furs back and forth between Montreal and the interior.[17] Historian Louise Dechêne asserts that the "trend towards concentration in the early eighteenth century was no temporary phenomenon but presaged the gradual proletarianization of the men employed in the fur trade."[18] These engagés gradually became known as voyageurs, and the option of entering the fur trade became an important strategy to increase the livelihood of families such as that of Jean Mongle.

The strongest rival to the fur trade in the St. Lawrence valley was established far to the north in Hudson Bay. In 1660 Pierre Esprit Radisson and Médard Chouart des Groseilliers learned of a vast region rich in beavers to the north that was most easily accessed from the shores of Hudson Bay. After they failed to find support for a sea route to the bay from the French Canadians or the French, Prince Rupert of England, cousin of King Charles II, supported their trading venture in 1668. The success of this venture led Charles II to proclaim a royal charter in 1670 for "The Governor and Company of Adventurers Trading into Hudson's Bay." The Hudson's Bay Company, as it became known, was granted exclusive trading rights to Rupert's Land, which included all the lands draining into Hudson Bay, a vast territory that stretches into six modern Canadian provinces and territories as well as four U.S. states. Hudson Bay and Rupert's Land became a new arena for the ongoing struggles between the British and the French. Unlike the small partnerships in the St. Lawrence valley, the HBC was a hierarchical and conservative joint stock company that established trading posts only on the shores of the bay. Only in the 1770s, after the competition mounted by Canadian traders moving far into the west and north developed, did the HBC begin to set up inland posts.[19]

In the St. Lawrence valley the system of small partnerships financing and outfitting themselves and hiring voyageurs continued essentially intact through the eighteenth century. After the Seven Years' War (1756–63), when the French abandoned North America to the British and the Spanish, the St. Lawrence valley became a colony in British North America. A few administrative changes ensued. The congé system was dismantled, and trade in Montreal was opened to everyone, which led to a significant expansion of the trade beyond the Great Lakes, north, south, and west. Despite the American Revolution, trade extended south along the Mississippi, with St. Louis emerging as a major depot.[20] People from Scotland, England, and the United States slowly replaced the French Canadian fur trade bourgeois.[21] Small partnerships began to merge into larger ones. In 1779 the NWC was created out of nine partnerships and underwent significant reorganization in the ensuing three decades.[22] In 1798 some disgruntled NWC bourgeois formed the "New North West Company," which came to be known as the XY Company, because they marked "XY" on their shipping bales to distinguish them from those of the NWC. The XYC competed directly with the NWC and located small posts adjacent to NWC posts, including Grand Portage. In 1804 the two companies merged because the bitterness in their competition was diminishing profits for both and because one of the major protagonists in the feud between the two companies, Simon McTavish, died.[23] Voyageurs would probably have had mixed views of these companies. Competition between fur trade companies created more jobs and raised the level of wages, but it also increased the risks of working in the service. All companies, including the HBC, were often hostile; men from opposing companies harassed and intimidated one another in their efforts to prevail in the trade, and incidents could escalate into violence. In 1802 at Ring Lake, north of Lake Athabasca, a NWC engagé, Jean-Baptiste Adam, assaulted an XYC engagé named Menard in a fight over furs.[24]

In the meantime the Jay Treaty of 1794 determined that land south of the Great Lakes would belong to the United States, and in 1818 the forty-ninth parallel was established as the northern boundary of the Louisiana Purchase, separating the United States from what would become Canada up to the Rocky Mountains. Although British and American traders were allowed to trade on either side of this border, with the provision of duties or taxes, American traders attempted to drive away Canadian traders from the areas immediately south of the line in order to maximize their own profits.[25] The wealthy New York fur merchant John Jacob Astor formed the American Fur Company in 1808 to compete with the NWC and the HBC. With the cooperation of some Canadian merchants, Astor's early operations around the Great Lakes were carried out under a subsidiary, the South West Company. In 1810 he established another subsidiary, the Pacific Fur Company, to compete in the fur trade in the Columbia River valley on the Pacific coast. The War of 1812 destroyed both companies, and in 1813 the NWC purchased the Pacific Fur Company. An 1817 act of Congress excluded foreign traders from U.S. territory, after which the American Fur Company dominated the U.S. trade until its demise in 1850.[26]

In 1821 a significant shift occurred among traders to the north. The NWC merged with the HBC (the new company continued to be called the HBC) because competition was making the trade untenable for both companies. Profits were diminishing, and instances of violence between the companies had increased. Although the coalition between the two companies was a union of equals, the center of the trade shifted to Hudson Bay, and York Factory became the major site of fur shipments to Europe.[27] The merger did not have an immediate impact on the number of French Canadian men entering the trade. We have seen that Jean Mongle continued his pattern of contracting with the new HBC in 1821 and again in 1829. Many French Canadians began to turn away from working in the trade, however, because the new contracts reduced their wages and stipulated that voyageurs provide their own equipment.[28] After the mid-1830s supplies of willing servants and levels of hiring began to diminish in parishes surrounding Montreal and Trois-Rivières.[29]

Although all the companies hired French Canadian servants, most voyageurs worked for Montreal partnerships and for the NWC, which dominated the Montreal trade until its 1821 merger with the HBC. In 1784 the NWC employed 500 men who carried out two distinct sets of tasks. One group of 250 transported goods from Montreal to Grand Portage, the administrative center at the western tip of Lake Superior. They used canoes capable of carrying about four tonnes, and each required eight to ten men to operate. These seasonally employed summer men were known as *mangeurs de lard*, or pork eaters. The other group of 250 men transported goods from Lake Superior to the posts in the interior country, some as far as three thousand miles distant. These men who wintered in the interior were referred to as northmen, or *hommes du nord*.[30] Jean Mongle graduated from pork eater to northman after his first year(s) in the trade. In 1817 he was posted at Nipigon, about twenty-five miles north of Lake Superior, and in 1819 he was posted much farther west at Lake Winnipeg.[31]

The fur trade labor force grew substantially over the next fifteen years, as table 1 in the first chapter shows. In 1790 traveler George Heriot reported that 350 paddlers, 18 guides, and 5 clerks were usually employed every year to run the cargo between Montreal and Grand Portage.[32] In 1801 Alexander Mackenzie asserted that the NWC employed 50 clerks, 71 interpreters and clerks, 1,120 canoe men, and 35 guides.[33] In 1802 Simon McTavish reported approximately fifteen hundred French Canadian servants working for the NWC.[34] Later estimates of voyageurs employed in the interior reach as high as two thousand.[35] These numbers were augmented by voyageurs hired by partnerships and firms that were not a part of the NWC and may have reached as high as three thousand.

When he first entered the fur trade, Jean Mongle would have traveled to the departure point at Lachine, west of Montreal, in May and joined a crew of about a dozen men in the large Montreal canoes. The provisions carried on board would be consumed by the time they reached the western end of

Lake Huron. At this midway point brigades stopped to purchase additional supplies for themselves, for servants at the Lake Superior administrative post, and for the canoes heading out into the interior. Brigades could go to Sault Ste. Marie, a post between Lake Huron and Lake Superior, or Fort Michilimackinac, a major post between Lake Michigan and Lake Huron that was transferred to Mackinac Island in the 1780s.[36] Sloops (a type of sailing ship) were employed to assist in transporting goods from Michilimackinac or Sault Ste. Marie to the western tip of Lake Superior. Speed was of the essence; goods had to reach the Lake Superior administrative post by early July so that the interior canoes had enough time to load and return to their posts. The interior canoes were smaller than Montreal canoes, required only four to five men to operate, and were generally loaded with two-thirds trade goods and one-third provisions. The supplies were rarely sufficient for the journeys, and the men had to procure provisions along the way from Aboriginal peoples. Crews generally ran the risk of starvation—more so on the spring voyage, when resources were scantier.[37]

The Lake Superior administrative centers of Grand Portage and later Fort William were the sites of transition between these two main transportation systems. The center was a place of bustling activity as very large numbers of people came together during the summer rendezvous. By 1800 as many as five hundred people could be found coming from and going to Grand Portage. Small independent traders set up shop to sell goods to the engagés. These businesses were quite successful, as the voyageurs were often paid their wages at Grand Portage and Fort William.[38] Fort William would have been where Jean Mongle made his transition from a pork eater to a northman in his first year(s) of fur trade service.

Although the crews in these two transportation systems were considered distinct, overlap occurred in personnel and the substance of their jobs. Men who initially signed on to become northmen while still in the St. Lawrence valley worked the first leg of their journey with crews of pork eaters.[39] At the Lake Superior administrative center, pork eaters and northmen came into contact with each other while they were exchanging the goods from the Montreal canoes with the furs from the interior canoes. Men were reequipped once the ladings were exchanged.[40] Also at the Lake Superior post, travel parties and exploration expeditions exchanged their canoes for smaller ones.[41] An administrative center was set up at Rainy Lake (Lac La Pluie), west of Lake Superior, because Athabasca brigades often could not make it all the way to Grand Portage or Fort William within the short ice-free season. At this center Athabasca ladings were exchanged with the Montreal ladings, and fatigued crews could be exchanged for fresh ones.[42] The voyage between Grand Portage and Rainy Lake usually took a month, and a group of pork eaters at Lake Superior was selected from among the Montreal brigades to make this additional journey.[43] The experience gained by the pork eaters from this extra run helped many of them to make the transition to northmen and work in the interior. About one-third of the pork eaters went on to become northmen.[44]

The Montreal Fur Trade in the Late Eighteenth Century: The Rural Context

Given the hardships of the work, it is surprising that so many men became voyageurs. Life in the St. Lawrence valley, however, could make the life of a voyageur seem like an attractive alternative. Farming in the St. Lawrence valley was dominated by the feudal regime of the seigneurial system, which shaped land distribution and occupation and lasted from 1627 to 1854. The French Crown granted parcels of land to seigneurs, or feudal lords, who in turn granted land to peasant farmers, also called habitants and *censitaires*. In return for the seigneurie, seigneurs were obliged to ensure that the land was cultivated and had to establish courts of law, operate mills, and organize communes. Habitants were obliged to pay their seigneurs various forms of rent.[45] In a close economic and social study of three Quebec parishes—Sorel, St. Denis and St. Ours—from 1740 to 1840, historian Allan Greer asserts that their farms were self-sufficient but suffered under a feudal burden that prevented them from accumulating capital.[46] Habitant families raised some money through trading grain to purchase supplies they could not produce themselves, such as salt, sugar, and tea, and hardware such as iron goods and barrels, and most habitants accumulated debt while clearing land and purchasing their farms.[47] Local merchants supplied the parish families with retail goods and accepted payments in farm produce, usually wheat. When habitant families could not produce enough surplus wheat beyond their own needs and seigneurial dues, they became anxious to find another source of tradable products or a source of cash income, and they found it in the fur trade.

In the early part of the eighteenth century, the majority of voyageurs were recruited from the immediate vicinity of Montreal and to a lesser extent Trois-Rivières. Gratien Allaire found that between 1701 and 1745 almost 50 percent of all engagés were from the island of Montreal, 34 percent were from parishes on the south shore of the St. Lawrence, while only 16 percent came from the north shore.[48] Beginning in the latter part of the eighteenth century, merchants turned increasingly to the distant countryside to recruit a workforce because in Montreal the fur trade partnerships had to compete with urban employers.[49] Greer explains that the traders thought these men would be "cheap and docile." Habitant farmers could supply the large numbers of canoemen that were needed intermittently and sustain themselves between stints of working in the trade. Fur trade companies could access experienced men without having to pay them a "living wage." Peasant laborers were less likely to form "combinations," or strikes, against their employers than were urban workers because they were scattered throughout the countryside much of the time and were seldom close to complete poverty.[50]

Beginning in the 1790s, rural parishes such as Maskinongé and others in the western part of the St. Lawrence valley saw their young men enter the fur trade in droves. Families sent their sons and husbands into the trade to earn extra cash. Usually only poorer parishes around Montreal and Trois-Rivières became "voyageur parishes."[51] Unfortunately no one has yet identified voyageur parishes in the period after the 1740s, except for Greer, who has closely examined the voyageur parish of Sorel, located on the south shore of the St. Lawrence and approximately fifteen miles southwest of Maskinongé. Between the 1790s and 1820s, large numbers of Sorel men entered the fur trade, amounting to well over a third of the adult male population, while in the neighboring parishes of St. Ours and St. Denis, very few men entered the trade.[52] Sorel was approximately fifty miles northeast of Montreal and was far enough away from the city not to be influenced by the urban labor market that demanded higher wages and better working conditions. Parish habitants would have gained experience in boat travel because Sorel had many islands where the St. Lawrence River enters Lake St. Pierre.[53] Sorel habitants were also accustomed to wage work. During the American Revolution many of them were drafted for transportation duties for the large British military camp located in the parish. The most important factor, however, was that Sorel's soil was sandy and poor and its agricultural productivity low. By the late eighteenth century wheat could not be productively cultivated.[54] Wages earned in the fur trade became a suitable replacement for wheat that was traded to merchants for retail goods. Fur trade wages more than made up for Sorel's agricultural deficiencies as the parish grew prosperous.[55]

Like Sorel parts of Maskinongé contained poor soil and impoverished habitants. Because it was located on the north shore of the St. Lawrence east of Sorel, approximately seventy-five miles from Montreal, its geography was shaped by the riverbed. Soil closest to the river was rich in minerals, but land farther from the river became rocky and steep. Those who lived close to the river became prosperous farmers, while those far away from the river became poor.[56] The term *maskinongé* (muskellunge in English) was adapted from an Algonquian word and refers to a species of fish, sometimes mistaken for a large pike. Presumably habitants close to the rivers in Maskinongé depended on this fish for livelihood. Did poor soil in the higher regions drive habitants, specifically Jean Mongle, into the trade? Or was there a shortage of fish?

To the best of my knowledge no qualitative descriptions of habitants deciding to leave the family farm have survived in documentary evidence.[57] Some scholars have found that service in the fur trade was an occupation handed down through generations—if the father served in the trade, then so would one of his sons and some of his grandsons.[58] In other cases it seems that working as a voyageur was a common practice in the parish and not limited to individual families.[59] In some cases being a voyageur may have become a family or parish tradition, and tales of the pays d'en haut may have been passed down from generation to generation among community members. Working in the trade came to occupy a prominent position in the cultural history of the colony because at various times up to 12 percent of some parish male populations did so.[60]

Why were particular habitants drawn to a life of working in the trade? There was certainly a multitude of reasons, earning money being one of the primary motivations. Income from the fur trade had a significant economic impact on the financial fortunes of a parish and family, and voyageurs made enough money to attract them back to the service year after year.[61] This seemed to be the case for Jean Mongle, who probably did not have his own farm because his wife lived as a boarder while he worked in the trade. The question of money was addressed in their surviving correspondence. Yet many men did not make money in the trade. Clerk George Nelson mused that what drew all men, voyageurs and bourgeois alike, into the fur trade was the "deluded" belief that they could make large fortunes. He contended that "the lack of reflection by friends, relations, and themselves, their own blind ambition almost never fail[ed] to lead them to their ruin."[62] Although Nelson's warning probably reflected his failure to further his own fur trade career beyond that of a clerk, his comments should be seriously considered.[63]

Nelson contended that what also drew traders and voyageurs into the service was their desire to lead an adventurous and licentious life, free of restraint. Some chose to go to the pays d'en haut "where they [were thought] to be unknown to every body" and "prefer[ed] a great deal passing the remainder of their lives in this brute Country than ever to return."[64] Former NWC clerk Alexander Ross similarly commented: "In the various arrangements from year to year there is generally contentment and satisfaction among all classes. This arises as much from that variety of scene, that love of freedom of which man is so universally fond, and which he here so fully enjoys, as from anything else. There are pleasures at times in wild and savage countries as alluring as those in gay cities and polished circles; and on the whole, few ever leave the scenes of the wilderness without deep regret."[65] Does this picture of the "free" Northwest reflect more than just romantic stereotyping by ostentatious rhetoricians? Ironically, when they entered the service of the fur trade, voyageurs relinquished a significant amount of freedom. Although habitants paid dues to their seigneur and felt the feudal burden, they essentially worked for themselves. Heads of households decided when and what to plant and controlled their means of production.[66] Voyageurs were usually sons of still-living fathers and thus subject to their fathers' will, but their "familial servitude" was not particularly onerous or restricting. In the fur trade service, voyageurs were contracted to be loyal and obedient to their masters, and although they had a fair amount of autonomy on the job, the bourgeois defined what the job was. The hierarchy of power and authority was underscored by the fact that the bourgeois gave the orders and worked separately from the voyageurs (paternalism in the master and servant relationship will be addressed in chapter 5). Yet many writers have commented on the "love of freedom" that drew men into the trade. Leaving the restrictive confines of close-knit families and parishes provided men with social freedom, an opportunity to explore new behaviors and create new identities. The theme of freedom and independence appears widely in commentary on the voyageurs. The old voyageur that Alexander Ross met on Lake Winnipeg, discussed in the first chapter, attested, "There is no life so happy as a voyageur's life; none so independent; no place where a man enjoys so much variety and freedom as in Indian country."[67]

Recruitment

Once Jean Mongle had decided to try working in the fur trade to earn extra cash, how did he enter the service? In most cases voyageurs would have to travel to Montreal to meet with a fur trade recruiter, but in some cases recruiters were sent directly to voyageur parishes to find men to fill their labor quota. Most Montreal-based fur trade companies, including the NWC and XYC, were coproprietorships, so engagements were made in the names of the various firms and individuals that comprised the shareholders and partnerships.[68] Each of these individuals and partnerships had their own recruitment agents working in Montreal. Some of the agents had previously been foremen in the trade, and some went on to become merchants supplying either voyageurs or the companies with goods.[69] Agents were stationed in Montreal and at the major interior administrative posts, such as Grand Portage, Fort William, and Michilimackinac. At the end of autumn, they recruited both novices and experienced men in the returning brigades. Engagements were also drawn up throughout the winter, and contracts made in the Northwest interior or rural parishes were sent to Montreal headquarters up to March and April. Only rarely were engagements made in the summer months.[70]

Recruiters, especially former voyageurs, frequently hired men from their own parish. Sometimes certain brigades would be composed of men from one parish. John McDonell's 1793 brigade was made up of men from the parish of Berthier, all recruited by Joseph Faignant. Faignant, described by McDonell as "a faithful servant and favorite of Jos. Frobisher Esq., for many years in the North west," worked his way up to the position of recruiter.[71] He had entered the service at least by 1781, working for J. E. Waddens in Lac La Ronge. By 1785 Faignant was working as a Grand Portage guide, and by 1786 he acted as a "voyageur agent" in the transfer of money to Canada. Jean Mongle would have probably entrusted a voyageur like Faignant with delivering letters and money to his wife in Maskinongé. In the winter of 1791-92, NWC bourgeois John Gregory commissioned "St. Cir & Faignant" to engage winterers for the company and wrote in a letter to Simon McTavish, "Fainiant is to Go Through the Different Parishes Round Him." Faignant then accompanied the brigade of Montreal crews that he had recruited all the way to Grand Portage.[72] The bourgeois also directed recruiters to look beyond their own parishes to what they deemed suitable places to find "stout lads," as bourgeois Joseph Frobisher ordered St. Cir to do. Recruiters were paid a commission for every man whom they signed on for the service. For example, bourgeois Joseph Frobisher paid his agent St. Cir five shillings for every man he hired to "come and go" (pork eaters), one guinea for each winterer, and all St. Cir's traveling expenses. However, St. Cir assumed the risk for any wages he advanced to the men.[73] One of the partnerships at the center of the NWC, McTavish and Frobisher, hired both a local notary and a local voyageur in 1797 to recruit Sorel men to work in the trade. In later years both the American Fur Company and the HBC sent outside agents to Sorel to recruit fur trade labor, but HBC governor George Simpson instructed the recruiter to look for men who had the same family names as "favored" voyageurs.[74]

Engaging was a regular part of business at the major administrative posts. When northmen arrived at Grand Portage or Fort William in the middle of the summer, those who had not yet entered into agreements during the winter signed contracts.[75] Men were engaged at Michilimackinac, St. Louis, Detroit, St. Joseph's Island, Sault Ste. Marie, and Kingston.[76] Voyageurs also frequently signed engagements at the interior posts (discussed in chapter 7).

It was not always easy for agents to fill the quotas of men needed for each year's complement. Men were unwilling to engage when the price of wheat was high and farming profitable.[77] It was difficult to find men during the summer months because experienced voyageurs were already employed, while other laborers worked on the St. Lawrence boats that traveled between Montreal and Quebec.[78] During other times of the year, labor shortages could pose problems. For example, in 1791 Joseph Frobisher gave instructions to his agents in Montreal, St. Cir and Faignant, to begin hiring men in late November, providing them with an advance "to Run about the Country from his Parish to Quebec," guaranteeing that all traveling expenses would be paid by Frobisher.[79] John Gregory of the same partnership reported a month and a half later:

> *[W]e Come On Very Slowly with the Engaging our Men, Though Every Pains are Taken for that purpose, at Foot you Have An account of What are Engaged Here. St Cir, Faniant, & Tranchemontaigne, I Expect Will Each Compleat their Brigades, Besides Some Good Wintering Men, I Think I Never Saw the Men So Backward as This Year, & Shoud they Stand of Much Longer, it Will Be Ab-*

> *solutely Necessary We Shoud Make a Small Augmentation to the Men to Go & Come, the Outfit is Making Up as Fast as Possible, the Holidays are Now at an End, and I intend Beginning to Bale up After to Morrow, & Expect the Latter End of the Month to Have the Greatest Part at La chine.*[80]

Joseph Frobisher thought that the difficulty they had in meeting their recruitment goals was due to the mild winter, which prevented the river from freezing and thus made travel difficult. He was encouraged enough to remark, "[A]ll our old Men that has made their appearance in Town we have hired." Yet as late as February the bourgeois were alarmed at the low recruitment levels and were willing to pay larger advances to the "old hands" to ensure their engagements. The "old hands" were generally preferable to novices. The number of winterers was seventy at that point, but the bourgeois wished to engage surplus men as insurance against sickness or desertion and to avoid relying on greenhorns.[81] It was also difficult to hire replacement voyageurs along the canoe routes if one of their men became injured or deserted.[82] Smaller crews slowed a brigade's progress as the men had to stop more frequently to rest.[83]

The bourgeois also had problems with labor shortages at the interior posts.[84] This was especially common during the summer months, when most of the men were busy transporting goods and furs between the interior posts and the administrative centers on Lake Superior. Few men were left at the interior posts to continue trading and work on construction projects.[85]

Wages

If Jean Mongle left his dear wife in Maskinongé and journeyed far into the pays d'en haut for the money, it is worth taking a close look at voyageur wages. Like most forms of eighteenth-century labor systems, the Montreal fur trade labor system was organized around indentured servitude.[86] When men were recruited into the fur trade service, they signed three- to five-year contracts that legally bound them to their masters. They agreed to be obedient and loyal in exchange for food, shelter, and wages.

Engagements signed by the voyageurs usually listed their name, parish of origin, destination in the Northwest, job position, length of term, age on entering the service, and, of course, their wages. Scholars have studied some of these patterns in voyageurs' engagements, and combined with parish and other notarial records, they have examined voyageur mortality rates, marriage patterns, and the extent to which joining the trade was a family tradition.[87] Others have looked at how numbers of engagés changed over time and varied from parish to parish, depending on local economic contexts and governmental regulations.[88] Dechêne asserts that "the practice of recording all transactions touching the fur trade (such as partnerships, obligations, and hiring) in notarized contracts had become so entrenched by the beginning of the eighteenth century that notarial records can be used to quantify voyages to the west."[89] Fernand Ouellet, however, argues that the notarial records do not contain all the engagements and that licenses or congés record a significant portion of men entering the trade. Allaire tempers Ouellet's charge by maintaining that the engagements can reflect general patterns of men in the service. He goes on to provide comparisons of notarial records with congés.[90] In the post-conquest period, however, the notarial records of engagements become less useful in illustrating men's entrance and continuing involvement in the fur trade. Much of the engaging took place on an informal basis by bourgeois and clerks at small interior posts.[91] It is difficult to ascertain if contracts were signed in these cases, and if so, whether the contracts survived a journey to Montreal to be filed with other notarial records. Usually individual notaries preserved their own notarial records.[92] Because no notaries were present during the arrangements of contracts made at interior posts, it is unlikely that the engagements survived. For all these reasons quantitative analysis of the engagements found in notarial records for French Canadians after the mid-eighteenth century is unreliable in determining concrete demographic patterns. However, the contracts reveal much about the structures and substance of fur trade labor.

The labor contracts of all partnerships, both within and outside the NWC, were remarkably similar. The contracts required voyageurs to obey the bourgeois, to work responsibly and carefully, to be honest and well behaved, to aid the bourgeois in making a profit, and to remain in the service. For example, a contract form (blank) for the firm McTavish, McGillivrays & Co. and Pierre de Rocheblave, likely used in the years between 1804 and 1821, clearly instructs the engagé

> *to take good and proper care, while on routes, and to have returned to the said places, the Merchandise, Provisions, Furs, Utensils, and all the things necessary for the voyage; to serve, obey and to faithfully carry out all that the said Bourgeois, or all others representing their persons, to whom they may assign the present contract, may lawfully and honestly command, to make their profit, avoid damage, to warn them if he has knowledge [of danger]; and generally all that a good and loyal servant must and is obliged to do, without doing any particular [private] trading; not to leave or quit the said service, under the pain carried by the laws of this Province, and the loss of his wages.*[93]

In addition contractual obligations for the NWC after 1804 often included voyageurs devoting several days to clear land around Fort William.[94] The contracts of summer men and winterers specified their different duties and the length of time they were to serve.[95]

In all contracts bourgeois were bound to pay the voyageurs' wages and provide them with equipment. The substance of the equipment and the provision of food and welfare for the engagé were rarely specified in contracts and thus provided one of the few places for obvious negotiation between the masters and servants.[96] Custom came to dictate that equipment consisted of one blanket, one shirt, and one pair of trousers.[97] Sometimes yearly "equipment" included a supply of tobacco.[98] Rations usually consisted of the food that was available depending on the place and time of year. John McDonell

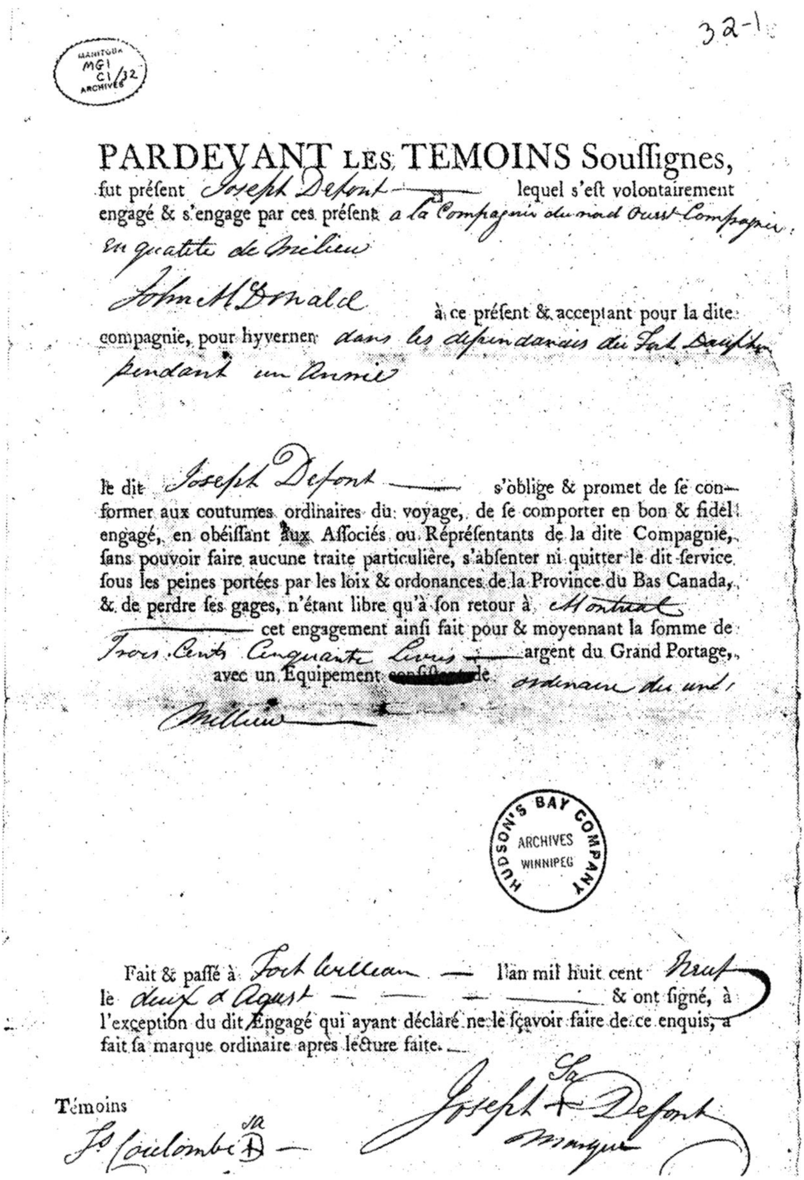

32-1

MANITOBA MG1 C1/32 ARCHIVES

PARDEVANT LES TEMOINS Souſſignes,
fut préſent Joseph Defont —— lequel s'eſt volontairement engagé & s'engage par ces préſent a la Compagnie du nord Ouest Compagnie en qualité de milieu

John McDonald à ce préſent & acceptant pour la dite compagnie, pour hyverner dans les dépendances du Fort Dauphin pendant un Année

le dit Joseph Defont —— s'oblige & promet de ſe conformer aux coutumes ordinaires du voyage, de ſe comporter en bon & fidel engagé, en obéiſſant aux Aſſociés ou Répréſentants de la dite Compagnie, ſans pouvoir faire aucune traite particulière, s'abſenter ni quitter le dit ſervice ſous les peines portées par les loix & ordonances de la Province du Bas Canada, & de perdre ſes gages, n'étant libre qu'à ſon retour à Montreal —— cet engagement ainſi fait pour & moyennant la ſomme de Trois Cents Cinquante Livres —— argent du Grand Portage, avec un Equipement [illegible] de ordinaire du un Millieu ——

HUDSON'S BAY COMPANY ARCHIVES WINNIPEG

Fait & paſſé à Fort William —— l'an mil huit cent Neuf le deux d'Aoust —— & ont ſigné, à l'exception du dit Engagé qui ayant déclaré ne le ſçavoir faire de ce enquis, a fait ſa marque ordinaire après lecture faite. ——

Témoins
Js. Coulombe
Joseph + Defont
Sa marque

Fig. 2. Engagement for Joseph Defont, made at Fort William for the North West Company, 1809. MG1 C1, vol. 32, Fort William Collection, Archives of Manitoba, Winnipeg, Canada.

recorded that a voyageur's full allowance while at Grand Portage in 1793 was "a quart of lyed Indian Corn or maize and one pound of grease a day." That year voyageurs were only provided with half that amount because provisions had not yet come in by ship.[99] When generalizing about French Canadians in a narrative published in the early 1830s, Ross Cox wrote:

> *[Voyageurs'] rations at first view may appear enormous. Each man is allowed eight pounds of solid meat per diem, such as buffalo, deer, horse, &c., and ten pounds if there be bone in it. In the autumnal months, in lieu of meat, each man receives two large geese, or four ducks. They are supplied with fish in the same proportion. It must, however, be recollected that these rations are unaccompanied by bread, biscuit, potatoes, or, in fact, by vegetables of any description. In some of our journeys up the Columbia they were allowed pork and rice; and on particular occasions, such as wet weather, or making a long portage, they received a glass of rum.*[100]

Extra provisions informally promised to voyageurs on special occasions, such as drams and tobacco, were sometimes referred to a *phiol d'engagement*.[101] Alexander Henry the Younger explained that alcohol was customarily provided to men when they reengaged at Grand Portage.[102]

Mentions of engagements made at interior posts sometimes repeated the terms of a specific contract, such as the length of time, salary, and promise of food and clothing.[103] In one example at Fort Alexandria, bourgeois Archibald Norman McLeod recorded in his journal in January 1801, "I engaged La Hanee [Hanche?] for two years &. Cadien [Cadieu?] for three, the ordinary wages of the Fort, but I promised each a Gun &. House, One of them /Cadien/ being free at the Grand Portage."[104] On rare occasions the terms were laid out like a contract. In a letter to McKenzie, Oldham & Co. in 1803, T. Pothier described the terms of engagement:

> *There are the Terms up on which I Shall engage [Joseph Robillard] for One year to Winter at McKinar of Mississippi [&?] Montreal, oblige [illegible] as another Winterer, & obliges to work at his trade*

> *as Cooper when Required.—Wage, 850 [livres] & an Equipt Const of 2 Blankets, 2 Shirts, 2 prs Trousers, 1 pr Shoes, 1 Collier. I shall [illegible] Security to you provided he fullfill his Engt With me for Two Hundred Livres—and if he Continues in my Employ Will Stop the Remainder of the Dept the Ensuing Year Say 254 [livres] 5 [sols]—Should he discontinue With me, You Know I have a right to Send him Back here, which I Shall do if he try not pay the Said Sum, You Will please observe that I [illegible] not become responsible more than What I may have in my power to do for you Should the man Run away, Leave my Employ or Die, my Responsibility becoming Annulle. Should this Suit you please so have him Engt passed and advance him in money One Hundred and Twenty Livres which I Shall Pay you When you Come to Town.*[105]

Even if the terms of the contract were not laid out on paper, masters expected voyageurs to be obedient and loyal in exchange for their wages, provisions, and equipment, which mirrored engagements drawn up by notaries in Montreal. In engagements unique to the interior, voyageurs could be hired for a single season to guide or to hunt and fish for a post, though these positions were usually filled by freemen or uncontracted French Canadian laborers living independently in the Northwest.[106]

It is difficult to determine the real value of wages for voyageurs. Some historians have shown that the money sent back by voyageurs to their habitant families in Lower Canadian parishes made a significant impact on the economy, which indicates that becoming a voyageur was a serious economic strategy that was often successful.[107] Voyageurs usually (though by no means universally) sent their wages home.[108] The bourgeois often made these arrangements by paying men in drafts that were sent to relations or friends in Lower Canada.[109] Men also sent money home to their families through other voyageurs who were returning to Canada, as Joseph Faignant described.[110] There seemed to be somewhat of a traffic in goods between French Canadian families and their men in the pays d'en haut. Voyageurs sent home shoes, presumably moccasins that they procured from Aboriginal people in the interior, as well as other Aboriginal artifacts, such as *plumes*, or feathers.[111] Shoes were popular, as they were also sent from French Canada to voyageurs in the interior in addition to other personal effects, such as *tabliez* (cloth smocks or overalls).[112]

One of the reasons it is difficult to determine the real value of voyageurs' wages is that different kinds of currency were used in the fur trade, and their value fluctuated tremendously. The main units of exchange in British North America were gold, silver, and copper coins. Value depended on their weight and purity. Merchants traded with one another by converting coins to a common currency, such as "sterling pounds" or "Halifax currency," yet exchange rates varied to a bewildering degree. Ordinances issued by the British Crown in 1764, 1777, and 1796 attempted to standardize rates of exchange within the colonies, but merchants did not always follow the ordinances.[113]

Although barter dominated the economy of exchange in the pays d'en haut, voyageurs were paid in currency and sold goods priced in currency. "Moneys of account," or credit notes, (rather than coinage) were issued in a variety of currencies, including Halifax, sterling, and livres.[114] The bourgeois also came to issue their own kind of currency, called "Grand Portage currency" or "north west currency," which was probably confined to their employees because of the high inflation of prices in the interior. John McDonell noted: "The currency of the north west is double that of Canada which currency had its origine, I presume, from the men's wages being formerly paid in peltries and it was supposed that one Liver's worth of furs would be worth 2 livers to the person who took it to Mtl to be paid."[115]

The wages paid to voyageurs varied according to their position. Pork eaters were paid less than northmen. Within the canoe paddlers called middlemen, or *milieux*, were subject to the authority of the foreman and steersmen, or *devant* and *gouvernail*, collectively called *bouts*, who usually acted as canoe and brigade leaders. Bouts could earn from one third to more than six times as much as milieux.[116] Jean Mongle, for example, had managed to work his way up from a milieu to a bout just before he died. At this point Mongle's wages would have been high, and it would have made more urgent

Table 2. Annual Wages of Voyageurs

Year	Middlemen/ milieux	Foremen & steersmen / bouts	Guides	Interpreters	Ratios of wages between positions	Unspecified general wage
1790[b]	P: £15	P: £25	P: £45		P: 1:2:3	
	N: £22	N: £50	N: £103		N: 1:2:5:4	
1795[c]	U: £25–£50	U: £25–£50	U: £42–£125	U: £42– £125	U: 1:1:1.5:1.5	
1798[d]	P:£10–£15	P: £17–£25	U: £33–£42	U: £42– £167	P: 1:1.75:3.25:4+	
	N: £33	N: £50			N: 1:1.5:1:125+	
Ca. 1800[e]	U:£25	U:£42			U: 1:1.75	
1800[f]						£100
1802 wage war[g]	U:£83–125£					
1803[h]	N and cooper: £850 [G.P.Cy.?]					
1804[i]	P:£500 G.P.Cy.	P:£700 G.P.Cy.			P: 1:1.5	
1806[j]	N: £300–£500 [G.P.Cy.?]	N: £350–£700 [G.P.Cy.?]			N: 1:1.25	
1807[k]						£25–£60
1812[l]						£80–£100
1824[m]	U:£20	U:£125			1:6	

Note: P=Pork Eater N=Northmen U=Unspecified £=pounds. All wages have been roughly converted into the Halifax currency, except for those years listed in Grand Portage currency.[a] The ratios are listed, where data is available, as milieux: bouts: guides: interpreters. [a] Conversions from sterling to Halifax currency are based on a .83:1 ratio, and conversions from livres to Halifax currency are based on a 24:1 ratio. McCullough, *Money and Exchange in Canada*, 20, 292. I have been unable to find evidence for conversion rates between Grand Portage currency and Halifax currency. [b]Heriot, *Travels through the Canadas*, 248, 254. [c]OA,MU 2199, box 4, no. 1, photostat of "An Account of the Athabasca Indians by a Partner of the North West Company, 1795. [d]Mackenzie, "General History," 34–35. [e]Cox, *Adventures on the Columbia River*, 305. [f]Henry (the Younger), *New Light*, September 19, 1800, 1:100. [g]NAC, MG19 B1, D. McGillivray to the Gentlemen Proprietors of the NWC, Sault, May 23, 1802, 183. [h]NAC, MG19 B6, Letter of T. Pothier to McKenzie, Oldham & Co. containing terms of engagement of Joseph Robillard, February 3, 1803, Montreal, 2. [i]Henry (the Younger), *New Light*, July 1, 1804, 1:247. [j]Wallace, *Documents*, 213–15. [k]MRB, MC C.27, March 27, 1807, 23. [l]Minutes of the Meetings of the NWC at Grand Portage and Fort William, 1801–7, with Supplementary Agreements, in Wallace, *Documents*, 272. [m]MRB, MC C.27, 1807–24, MacKenzie River, March 1, 1824, 3.

Marie St. Germain's efforts to collect her husband's wages up until the moment of his death. The longer one worked in the trade, and the more experience one gained, the more profitable such work became. The most experienced and skilled of all engagés were interpreters and guides. These men were paid between two and four times as much as other engagés.[117] Table 2 shows the extent to which voyageurs' wages varied year by year.

The ratios between wages for different positions varied tremendously. The huge jump in wages in 1803 probably marks the introduction of "north west currency," which might have been a way to contain wage wars. Despite the fluctuations, it is clear that northmen were paid more than pork eaters, bouts were paid more than milieux, and guides and interpreters were paid more than canoemen.[118]

Some wages also seemed to vary among the interior posts. Minutes from annual meetings of the NWC from 1806 provided lists of wages, organized by where men were posted. Men were paid the least in the departments that were closest to major administrative centers. Wages increased for departments farther west and north. Men were paid the most in the departments of Athabasca, Athabasca River, and Rocky Mountain, at one and a half to two times as great as the lowest wages.[119] In other cases a contract could specify that the wage increase every year, so that a voyageur could earn eighty pounds in the first year, ninety pounds in his second, and one hundred pounds in his final year.[120]

When men first signed their contracts, they sometimes received an advance on their wages, which could be as high as one third.[121] The bulk of wages were paid on an annual basis, usually in a lump sum at a major administrative post, such as Grand Portage, Fort William, or Montreal.[122] Some men chose to have their earnings sent directly to Canada, as Jean Mongle was trying to arrange when he worked for the HBC.[123] Wages were usually paid in cash or credit notes but could also be paid in goods. When the men officially began their term of work, they received their equipment at the site of departure.

In addition to wages, food, and equipment, voyageurs sometimes received a pension if they had been in the service for a long time. The minutes of an 1808 meeting of the partners of the North West Company record:

> *The Agents represented the unfortunate Case of many Old Voyageurs lately discharged from the Companys Service, who have no means of Support—and too Old and Infirm to work in Lower Canada; and recommended some provision to be made for these objects of charity—It was therefore agreed that the Agents of the nwco should have placed at their disposal on the general Account, a Sum not exceeding One hundred pounds Currency per Annum, for the above purpose, to be divided in such manner, as in their Judgment appeared best, but no Individual to receive more than Ten pounds Currency in One Year.*[124]

Evidence for the fund is sketchy, but mention of it can be found as early as 1799 and as late as 1811.[125] Some contracts include a deduction of 1 or 2 percent for the voyageur fund, or "le Fonds des Voyageurs."[126]

Voyageurs could earn additional money by doing odd jobs for bourgeois. Incentives were paid on top of regular wages for hunting and for either guiding or escorting bourgeois to locations outside of their posting.[127] While on canoe journeys, voyageurs were sometimes paid extra for carrying additional baggage on the canoes.[128] Voyageurs could also supplement their earnings by doing odd chores for other fur trade companies.[129] Sometimes they did this without the permission of their masters. When he was a clerk for the NWC, George Nelson suspected that the voyageur Joseph Constant was "deal[ing] with [his] opponent [HBC] underhandedly."[130] On rare occasions voyageurs hired one another to do odd jobs. For example, one voyageur hired two others to cut and haul wood for him, a task that was a part of his duties.[131] Another voyageur hired someone to take his place on a journey because he did not want to leave his Aboriginal wife for an extended period of time.[132]

Flexibility existed in voyageurs' contracts and terms of labor. They could sometimes trade jobs if they desired. For example, at a post in the Qu'Appelle River valley in 1793, then clerk John McDonell recorded that "Antoine Azure exchanged with Ante. Fontaine who went off to the Forks [confluence of Red and Assiniboine Rivers] in his stead."[133] When men were injured or ill, tasks were often shuffled to accommodate them. While stationed north of Lake Athabasca on the "Mackenzies River" in 1807, bourgeois Ferdinand Wentzel was grateful to bourgeois Peter Warren Dease for sending voyageur Jean Rangé "as a substitute in place of Alexis Gibeau who could not return on account of Swelled Ledges [legs] occasioned by the *mall de Racquettes* [injuries from snowshoeing]."[134] Usually the masters controlled these exchanges, and they often lent men to one another if they were in need. On a journey up the Columbia River in 1811, Alexander Ross exchanged with David Thompson an engagé from the Sandwich Islands (Hawaii) named Cox for a French Canadian voyageur named Boulard. Both bourgeois thought they had made a good deal, as Ross recorded that "Boulard had the advantage of being long in the Indian country, and had picked up a few words of the language on his way down. Cox, again, was looked upon by Mr. Thompson as a prodigy of wit and humour, so that those respectively acceptable qualities led to the exchange."[135] The bourgeois and clerks could also trade particular voyageurs with whom they had difficulties or personal conflicts.[136] In one case William McGillivray sent a voyageur named La Tour from Lake Vermilion to winter at Grand Portage because the Aboriginal people "complained much of his conduct last Winter the Queu de Porcupicque came here on purpose to desire *he* should not Winter on his Lands."[137] In another case George Nelson deemed the voyageur Charbonneau too old to travel between posts in the winter and so replaced him with Longuelin.[138] Masters extended their control over the voyageurs as far as they could. They tried to prevent their men from contracting with competing companies or becoming freemen.[139] Particularly unmanageable or obnoxious voyageurs were shipped off to remote corners of the Northwest interior, frequently relocated, and prevented from traveling to the annual summer meetings at Lake Superior.[140]

One significant obstacle faced by voyageurs in their efforts to accumulate wages was their bourgeois. Bourgeois frequently advanced wages and encouraged voyageurs to incur debt as a means of exerting control over them. Voyageurs used advanced wages to purchase goods in Montreal and at the major depots in the interior, such as Fort William and Cumberland House.[141] Voyageurs also purchased alcohol and tobacco regularly from clerks and bourgeois in the interior.[142] Masters brought limited quantities of rum and tobacco into the interior to trade or give to Aboriginal peoples, and they sometimes refused to sell these items to voyageurs in debt.[143] The French Duke de La Rouchefoucauld Liancourt, traveling through North America in the late eighteenth century, charged the NWC with encouraging "vice" among their men by paying them in merchandise, especially luxuries, and rum, so that none of them ever earned a decent wage.[144] Lord Selkirk, certainly no admirer of the NWC, criticized NWC bourgeois for exploiting their men, pointing out that engagés often left their French Canadian families in distress and were unable to provide for them because the cost of goods in the interior was double or triple the price in Canada, and men were usually paid in goods rather than cash. He claimed that the NWC saved further costs on men's wages by encouraging cravings for alcohol and then paying their wages in rum at highly inflated prices. The company also placed no ceiling on their men's credit, so that many of them fell deeply into debt.[145]

Despite Selkirk's obvious hostility to the NWC, he was not alone in his misgivings about Montreal fur trade companies' labor practices. As a new clerk in the XYC, George Nelson was instructed by his immediate superior to sell any trade goods his men might ask for, and to encourage them to spend their wages on any of the trade goods on board the canoe. Nelson was initially uneasy with this mode of dealing: "[F]or thought I what is there more unnatural, than to try to get the wages [of] a poor man for a few quarts of rum, some flour & sugar, a few half fathoms of tobacco, & but very little Goods who comes to pass a few of his best years in this rascally & unnatural Country to try to get a little money so as to settle himself happily among the rest of his friends & relations." Eventually Nelson came to justify his participation in this system of exploitation because he felt that the men would ruin themselves anyway, and that most of them were disobedient "blackguards" for whom slavery was too good.[146] Nelson's sympathy with the voyageurs abated over time, especially after he came to believe that men entered the fur trade for love of freedom and adventure. Yet Nelson was surprised that these men could live such a carefree existence while deeply in debt and with few material possessions.[147]

Nelson's comments about the "carefree" existence of extravagant voyageurs are echoed widely in the writings of the fur trade literate.[148] An unnamed HBC clerk in 1810-11 wrote in the Fort Churchill post journal:

> *[T]he nature of Canadians is as opposite to that of Scotchmen or Orkneymen as black is to white. The former are little removed from Savages indeed the reader may easily conceive what offspring must shoot from the union of a volatile vain shiftless tho' not ruffle-less Frenchman with a toy-loving daughter of our Indian Scalper[.] A Scotch or Orkney servant identifies himself with his Money and conceives a favourable or unfavourable opinion of his Employers or Employment as he finds them subservient to his purpose of amassing wealth[.] a Canadian is ever in debt in advance to his Employers who greedily take advantage of all the propensities of their servants.*[149]

Bourgeois and clerks frequently reported voyageurs "squandering" their money on rum and "baubbles," especially when paid at Fort William during the rendezvous festivities.[150] The bourgeois may have employed these rhetorical devices as a means of justifying unfair labor practices. Their views of the voyageurs were informed by their own values and reflected their own insecurities. Their criticisms of voyageurs' seeming inability to save money were more illustrative of bourgeois values than reflective of voyageurs' values.

Yet voyageurs who remained in the interior did not become wealthy. Did they carelessly squander their money? In his study of eighteenth-century sailors, Marcus Rediker found that seventeenth- and eighteenth-century observers "never tired of pointing out how seamen were 'careless' and 'irresponsible' with their money." Rather than save, seamen engaged in "unruly debauches and sprees of spending that squandered many months of wages in a matter of days," and rather than looking to the future, they immersed themselves in the rich pleasures of the present. Rediker does not attribute this observed behavior to simply another case of the higher orders lamenting about the lower; he asserts that an ethic of nonaccumulation ran deep among sailors. Seamen took seriously their mottos of "a Rowling

Stone never gathers Moss" and "a merry life and a short one." They "sought money but not capital; acquisition but not accumulation; the present, often at the expense of the future; gratification and consumption over deferral and savings."[151] This same ethic of nonaccumulation seems to have characterized the culture of voyageurs who wintered in the pays d'en haut. They had short-term rather than long-term goals. Wages were always important, but their value and meaning could shift.

It is clear that voyageurs entered the fur trade service to earn money for their families in Lower Canada and that these earnings had a substantial economic impact. But some voyageurs were not like Jean Mongle. They stopped sending their money back to Canada and shifted their loyalties to their new lives in the interior. Those voyageurs who decided to stay in the fur trade service for as long as they could manage the strenuous work, who became freemen, and who lived with their Aboriginal families in the interior seemed to have different ideas about money. Amassing capital was not a goal for these men. Perhaps to some voyageurs, "wealth" came to mean living a good life, being well-fed, and enjoying "luxuries" such as finery, alcohol, and tobacco. Voyageurs often demonstrated their wealth through their possessions, consumption, and generosity, and not through their savings. Becoming a voyageur may have been about money, but often being a voyageur was not.

Family Ties

Most voyageurs entered the fur trade service in large part to help out their families, and family determined whether a voyageur maintained ties to his home parish. Those who continued to send money home to the St. Lawrence valley usually maintained close ties with their families and friends there. The question arises, however, as to how wintering voyageurs, away for years at a time, could have communicated with their loved ones thousands of miles away. Messages were sent via word of mouth, as voyageurs returning to Montreal carried tidings between voyageurs and their families.[152] But, surprisingly, voyageurs and their families sometimes sent written messages to each other as well, as we have seen with the case of Jean Mongle. An exceptional collection of sixteen letters, contained in the Hudson's Bay Company Archives, allows us a rare glimpse into voyageurs' psyches and the emotional impact of the fur trade on the lives of habitants in the St. Lawrence valley. These letters were composed by the families and friends of voyageurs working in the service of the HBC in the 1830s and sent through official HBC channels. The letters have survived in the documentary record because they were never delivered. The voyageurs to whom they were addressed had died in the service.

Literacy rates in the French Canadian countryside were extremely low.[153] Yet some habitants used letters as a tool of communication even though they lacked the ability to read and write for themselves. They relied on their curé (priest) or other literate of the community to read and write letters for them. Similarly in the pays d'en haut, voyageurs relied on the literate of the fur trade to read and write their letters. Bourgeois Gabriel Franchère recalls an incident at Lac la Biche concerning a freeman who guided for fur trade companies: "He begged me to read for him two letters which he had had in his possession for two years, and of which he did not yet know the contents. They were from one of his sisters, and dated at Varennes, in Canada. I even thought that I recognized the handwriting of Mr. L. G. Labadie, teacher of that parish."[154]

The frequency of letter writing among habitants and voyageurs was probably very low, especially compared to the high rates at which the literate of French Canada corresponded on a yearly basis.[155] The scant evidence prevents any kind of systematic assessment, but probably those who did communicate through letters did so once a year, given the length of time it would take for a letter to arrive at its destination. In one letter a father reported that he had received a letter from his son, a voyageur, five years ago and had since sent him three letters, though he had not received a response to these.[156] Another voyageur sent his wife two letters in one summer.[157] At the opposite extreme, a mother had not heard from her son in eight or nine years.[158] These letters probably portray situations of little communication because they were recovered from undelivered HBC mail. In a letter to his voyageur brother Isidore, Charles Boimier wrote with impatience: "Finally I break The Silence and Cry out for news of you."[159] Perhaps Charles was frustrated because he had expected messages from Isidore and had received none. This leads us to question whether writing letters was the exception or whether it was a usual practice.

If letters were frequent, a reliable system to transport the messages must have been developed by voyageurs. Habitants and voyageurs could send their letters with the brigades traveling between Montreal and Lake Superior. One mother wrote to her son: "I beg you, Dear child, if you really Can Not come down this year I hope that at least you will be good enough to Write us this autumn by way of the voyageurs who will come down [to Montreal]."[160] Correspondence was sent through people identified in the letters.[161] Sometimes two letters were sent at once, either by two different people to the same voyageur or with the intention of sending letters through different routes to increase the chances of the letter arriving at its destination.[162] Letters could be sent "au azard" (by hazard), or without an address, with the hopes that the letter would find its way to the voyageur regardless.[163]

The content of letters from habitants to voyageurs in the interior underscores the emotional ties between voyageurs and friends and families in Canada. Voyageurs appear to have been regarded as important members of the parish communities. Friends and relatives reported on births, deaths, and marriages in the family and parish as well as on new houses built and roads improved.[164] One letter reminded a voyageur of a potential wife waiting for him in the parish, while another informed a voyageur of the state of his land.[165] All the letters sent greetings from friends and family and wished the voyageur well, and most inquired as to when the voyageur would be returning. One habitant chided his voyageur brother to save his money and behave well.[166] Messages from voyageurs are sometimes recorded in these letters addressed to them. Generally the messages reported on good health and success in travel.[167] One voyageur complained of "La Cruel misere [the cruel misery]" in "ces miserables endroits [these terrible places]."[168] Presumably he was homesick. Other voyageurs made arrangements through their families to buy and sell land in Canada, which was a clear indication that they continued to act as part of their parish community.[169]

Many of the letters express the pain of separation felt by those left behind, as did those between Marie St. Germaine and Jean Mongle. Joseph Grenier of "Ruisseau des chenes" begged his son in the Columbia District to return:

> *I assure you, dear child, that you cause us a great deal of worry and concern in our old age to see our dear child that we took so much trouble to raise and believing that he would give us care and consolation and now to see him so far away. Dear child, have you forgotten us and have you completely lost the memory of our tenderness to you in your youth? Believe me, dear Joseph [his son], I and your poor mother want very much to see you once again before we die because if you do not come home quickly, you could well not see us alive because we assure you that our hair has gone quite white since you left us. So take courage, come home and see us again. We will receive you with open arms and your arrival could well help us to live a few years longer because of the joy that you would give us and your poor grandmother Sicard who is now eighty-nine years old. She always says that she asks God to see you before she dies and she embraces you and prays God for you that God will help you to recognize the duty that you owe to your dear mother and father.*[170]

This letter reveals deep emotional ties between parents and children. Spouses also begged husbands to return, as did Nellie St. Pierre in Trois-Rivières, writing to her husband Olivier "au font de la maire [at the end of the sea]":

> *"I do not believe that you doubt my own pain and anxiety and uneasiness. If I hadn't feared reproach I would never have consented to your departure. I have no consolation and am always in pain and anxiety. The longer I live, the more I worry and the greater is my pain. When I think that I must pass two more years without*

> *having the pleasure of seeing you, I despair that time will be long, but in the end I must bend to the will of God and live in hope that you will come home as soon as your time is up."*[171]

One future sister-in-law said she was waiting for the voyageur to return before she married his brother.[172]

The letters, on the other hand, also recognize that voyageurs had established a life in the interior separate from that in French Canada. Asking to see the voyageur once more before death may have been a figurative expression, or it may have been a pragmatic request. One letter, addressed to a voyageur "ausos du pay nord," passes along greetings to the voyageur's wife and family, which must be an acknowledgment of his Aboriginal or métis family in the interior.[173] Sometimes voyageurs brought their Aboriginal or métis families back with them when they returned to Lower Canada.[174]

This chapter began with a close look at the only known surviving correspondence written by a voyageur. Jean Mongle's touching letter to his wife, Marie St. Germain, reveals that although French Canadian habitants entered the fur trade service and traveled thousands of miles away from their homes, they could maintain close emotional and economic ties with their families in the St. Lawrence valley. Most voyageurs entered the trade to earn money for the family farm, many voyageurs sent part or all of their wages to their families immediately, and some rare voyageurs wrote letters home. Yet in this chapter we have also seen glimpses of voyageurs shifting their attention away from French Canada and toward life in the pays d'en haut. Voyageurs could be drawn into the trade by the promise and freedom and adventure, many voyageurs did not send their money home or even save any of their wages, and some voyageurs did not return home at all. In the following chapters we will examine what distracted voyageurs from their habitant families, such as voyageurs' rites of passage, festivities, friendships, and new romantic relationships with Aboriginal and métis women.

3. Rites of Passage and Ritual Moments

Voyageur Cosmology

> *As you Pass the End of the Island of Montreall to Go in a Small Lake Cald the Lake of the Two Mountains[,] thare Stans a Small Roman Church Aganst a Small Rapead[.] this Church is Dedacateed to St Ann who Protescts all Voigeers[.] heare is a Small Box with a Hole in the top for ye Reseption of a Lettle Muney for the Hole father to Say a Small Mass for those who Put a small Sum in the Box[.] Scars a Voigeer but Stops Hear and Puts in his mite and By that Meanes thay Suppose thay are Protacted while absant[. . . .] after the Saremoney of Crossing them Selves and Rapeting [?] a Short Prayer we Crost the Lake and Entard the Grand [Ottawa] River.*[1]

Trader Peter Pond's observations written in the early nineteenth century on voyageurs departing from Montreal to begin their journey in the pays d'en haut provide an intriguing glimpse of how voyageurs perceived their world and positioned themselves in it. The small church in the parish of St. Anne was the last Roman Catholic church that voyageurs could easily visit along the fur trade routes. Here they had their final opportunity to visit a church and on consecrated ground pray to St. Anne, the mother of the Virgin Mary, for protection during their voyages in the pagan upcountry. The ritual of visiting this church and giving money before embarking across Lac de Deux Montagnes (Lake of Two Mountains, immediately west of the island of Montreal) can be interpreted as a sign that Catholic beliefs and practices were important to voyageurs and that they intended to maintain their faith during their travels. The ritual prayer and donation might have been seen by some voyageurs as a marker of the edge of the Catholic world and their entrance into new worlds governed by other spiritual forces. Here voyageurs would need both special assistance from their patron saints and good will from these foreign spiritual powers to survive. The passage also demonstrates that voyageurs engaged in rituals to mark important moments along canoe voyages, within their occupation, and during their lives.

Rituals are exceptionally expressive forms of action because they create and dramatize meaningful symbols and convey something of how humans think about their position in time and place in the cosmos. Voyageurs relied on their Roman Catholic backgrounds to help them understand their cosmological location, but as they traveled farther from the institutional reach of the church, they turned to beliefs that they learned while working in the trade. The rituals voyageurs performed while working in the fur trade reflected their changing identities from feudal peasants in the St. Lawrence valley to widely traveled indentured servants performing dangerous and backbreaking labor. The rituals also reflected their changing views of the cosmos as they traveled farther into the pays d'en haut and encountered increasing numbers of Aboriginal societies that differed dramatically from French Canada. Voyageurs' rituals were both self-reflexive and didactic, functioning as a means to help voyageurs shape their changing values and teach these new values to one another.

This chapter will explore the rituals performed by voyageurs as they traveled across many new worlds and created an occupational identity. Along the canoe journey out of Montreal and into the pays d'en haut, there were points of transition into the voyageur occupation, and the journey itself was a social space for the teaching of new values. Mock baptisms along canoe journeys, marking distances by landscape features, and infusing the workplace with French terms all constituted means by which voyageurs shaped their world, reflected their changing views of their cosmos, and reconfigured their religious practices.

Rituals

Ritual, or ceremony, is an imprecise concept that has been subject to many different interpretations and usages. Scholars of classical Europe have contended that rituals conveyed "truths" in myth and art, while social scientists have considered ritual an important component of community and an expression of communal beliefs.[2] Cultural anthropologist Victor Turner defined rituals as "*performances*, as *enactments*, and not primarily as rules or rubrics. The rules are from the ritual process, but the ritual process transcends its form."[3] For Turner the ritual process created community, or "communitas," which he specifies as a modality of social relationships.[4]

Historian Edward Muir proposed a means for using rituals to understand history by explaining that a ritual is simultaneously a model and a mirror. Rituals reflect what people think and believe and teach ideals to strive for. He outlined at least three related ways in which ritual is understood. Some scholars think of ritual as primarily an enactment that creates social solidarity or forms of social identities. Others focus on ritual as a form of communication that allows people to tell stories about themselves. And yet others primarily see ritual as a collectively created performance that constructs, maintains, and modifies society.[5] Muir argued that rituals present both unified visions of society and discordant voices to challenge these visions. Hence he sees rituals as "inherently ambiguous in their function and meaning. They speak with many voices."[6] This chapter will follow Muir's lead in considering rituals in all their broad and versatile forms. Rituals can create, express, teach, and remind participants of the meanings and values of their community and of their identity. Rituals can form communitas, bolster communal bonding, and at the same time provide a forum for the expressions of individual selfhood that challenge communal bonds. The instability and fluidity of the voyageur occupation made rituals of vital importance to the development of common values and working patterns among voyageurs, but they also provided a site for contrary discourse. For example, races along lakes lead to both fraternal bonding among men in one crew and feeling of competition and social divisiveness between different crews.

Voyageurs' first ritual acts when they entered the trade and journeyed out of Montreal were closely tied to rituals in the Catholic Church. Other rituals performed along canoe journeys did not mirror Catholic acts of sacrament to the same degree, but they served a similar function by integrating people into a community. The rituals taught voyageurs how to work successfully in the pays d'en haut, become full members of the occupation, and shape a community. The many rituals along canoe journeys, in addition to mock baptisms, marked entrances to new cultural landscapes and marked the passages entailed in a neophyte's initiation into new stages of occupation and manhood. For example, celebrations and pageantry honored the arrivals and departures from Montreal and interior fur trading posts (as discussed in chapter 6). The men sang while they worked to set the pace of paddling and to distract themselves from the tedium (see chapter 4). These rituals facilitated communal bonding as well as expressions of individual selfhood.

Leaving Montreal

The Catholic customs practiced by voyageurs that infused their working rhythms began as soon as voyageurs embarked on their voyages. As Pond described in the quotation at the beginning of this chapter, departures from French Canada were marked with the solemn ritual of stopping at St. Anne's Church at the western extremity of the island of Montreal. St. Anne, mother of the Virgin Mary, was the patron saint of Brittany and of New France. For centuries sailors and fishers had prayed to St. Anne before they set out on each journey.[7] St. Anne became the patron saint of voyageurs as well. As men portaged around the rapids by the church, they stopped to pay homage to St. Anne, asking for protection during their voyage.[8] The crews contributed donations to have prayers said for the prosperity of the voyage and a safe return as well as prayers for their friends and families.[9] The priests at St. Anne's sometimes held an outdoor mass where voyageurs would lie on the ground while receiving the priest's benediction.[10] The ceremony became a site for the expression of the seriousness of leaving for the interior and an acknowledgment of the risk of travel in the pays d'en haut.

Fig. 3. *Ex voto of the Three Castaways*, anonymous artist, 1754, oil on panel, 32.4 x 52.1 cm. St. Anne was venerated in other parishes in the St. Lawrence valley, such as Ste. Anne de Beaupré, just east of Quebec City. This image shows St. Anne assisting people whose canoe had capsized. Courtesy of Sanctuaire de Ste. Anne de Beaupré, Quebec City.

French Canadian voyageurs grew up in a community dominated by the Roman Catholic Church. Like many peasants, their understandings of the cosmos were influenced by non-Catholic notions and old ideas and practices (often labeled as magical, superstitious, or pagan by the church or cultural outsiders) passed down through families. The Roman Catholic Church was a central institution in eighteenth-century Canada. The church was considered one of the estates of colonial power, priests acted as community leaders, and parishes were the social centers for habitants living in the St. Lawrence valley.[11] Roman Catholicism influenced French Canadian cosmology and regulated the lives of the colonists by explaining the origin of humans and their place in the world and providing a clear moral code. Yet like many people in early modern Europe, Canadian colonists sometimes understood the sacred or supernatural in ways that fell outside the institutional regulation of the church. Often called magic, sorcery, or superstition in French Canada, these beliefs and practices thrived where definitional boundaries between sacred and magical were fluid.[12] In his study of the cosmology of a sixteenth-century miller in Friuli, Carlo Ginzburg uncovered traces of pre-Christian beliefs that blended with dogma of the Catholic Church in surprising ways.[13] Likewise, Keith Thomas demonstrated that European notions of both religion and magic helped sixteenth- and seventeenth-century English people make sense of their world.[14] Rituals practiced by French Canadian Catholics easily intertwined beliefs and practices from everyday activities and from metaphysical questions concerning the nature of the cosmos.[15]

The priest at St. Anne's probably tried to instill voyageurs with a strong sense of devotion before they headed out into the pays d'en haut. Here voyageurs would have been reminded of the seven sacraments in which they could encounter God: baptism, confirmation, confession, communion (taking the Eucharist), marriage, ordination, reconciliation or penance (usually at death), and anointing the sick.[16] Voyageurs managed to incorporate into their occupational life aspects of some of these rites in myriad and imaginative ways. What remains to be explored is how much voyageurs' renditions of these rites digressed from Catholic meaning and what the rites conveyed about voyageurs' changing identities.

Baptism

In the summer of 1793, a crew of French Canadian voyageurs left the NWC's fur trade post of Grand Portage on Lake Superior and headed west toward Rainy Lake. John McDonell, a newly hired clerk traveling with the party, recorded in his journal:

> *Passed the Martes, les Perches and Slept at the height of Land, where I was instituted a North man by Batême performed by sprinkling water in my face with a small cedar Bow [bough] dipped in a ditch of water and accepting certain conditions such as not to let any new hand pass by that road without experiencing the same ceremony which stipulates particularly never to kiss a voyageur's wife against her own free will the whole being accompanied by a dozen of Gun shots fired one after another in an Indian manner. The intention of this Bâtême being only to claim a glass. I complied with the custom and gave the men . . . a two gallon keg as my worthy Bourgeois Mr Cuthburt Grant directed me.*[17]

McDonell's fascinating passage describes a common rite of initiation that was modeled on a Catholic sacrament. At several points of geographical significance along the transport routes in the pays d'en haut, novices who had never before passed that point were obliged to participate in a ceremony of mock baptism. The ceremony of baptism, representing the purification from original sin, is usually performed on infants and involves putting water on the individual's head through immersion or sprinkling. In the case of voyageurs in the fur trade, it represented primarily the initiation of neophytes into the occupation.[18] As the first of Catholic sacraments, it was recognized as the door to church membership and to spiritual life, but ironically the ritual baptism marked voyageurs' departure and increasing separation from the settled Christian world.[19] At the same time the ceremony marked voyageurs' entrance or initiation into the occupation, and it represented the continuing practice of Catholicism, albeit in modified form, in the interior. The writings of fur trade masters and explorers reveal at least three of these sites, each located at the beginning of a segment of the fur trade route from Montreal to the far Northwest.

The point of baptism along the Grand, or Ottawa, River was the first place on the route out of Montreal where the bedrock or Precambrian shield could be seen. It was located about two hundred miles northwest of the modern city of Ottawa, where the Deep River, or the Rivière Creuse, entered the Ottawa River, at the upper end of Lac des Allumettes.[20] Here canoe brigades passed through a narrow, deep, and swift part of the river, where towering cliffs of granite provided a significant visual marker for the entrance into a new land. Immediately after this difficult passage, brigades stopped at a sandy point, where canoes could be easily grounded and the crew could pause for a rest. Known as "pointe au baptême," it was the oldest and most well established site of ritual baptism along fur trade routes. As early as 1686, the Chevalier de Troyes mentioned the practice as an established custom: "Our French have the custom of baptizing at this place those who have not passed before."[21] The "Pointe aux Baptêmes" is today marked on maps.[22]

About fifty miles west of Lake Superior, voyageurs ritually marked the crossing of the height of land that separated the waters draining into the Great Lakes from those draining into Lake Winnipeg and Hudson Bay.[23] There were at least two parallel paths along the route from Lake Superior to Rainy Lake, and so there were two points of baptism: the first (and earlier) along the route west from Grand Portage and the second along the route west from Fort William. "Heights of land" demarcated the boundaries of watersheds, and their crossing often entailed a major portage to enter the new river system. Because traders depended on the water systems for transport, they were keenly attuned to shifts in drainage patterns. The move from one river to another meant that the journey became either easier or harder, depending on a crew's direction.

Less commonly mentioned was a third site of ritual baptism at Portage La Loche, also called Methy Portage, north of Ile à la Crosse, at Clearwater River, which flows into the Athabasca River. The portage of twelve and a half miles was located on the height of land separating the waters flowing into the Churchill River and Hudson Bay, from waters draining into the Mackenzie River and the Arctic Ocean.[24] Although mention of the ceremony occurring here was rare, the site was long recognized as one of the most difficult and beautiful portages in the north. Most of it stretched over level ground, and the last mile of the portage comprised a succession of eight hills. The trail followed the edge of a steep precipice that fell about one thousand feet to the plains below. NWC bourgeois Alexander Mackenzie commented on the precipice's "most extensive, romantic, and ravishing prospect."[25] The explorer John Franklin also waxed poetic about the beauty and sublimity of the view from the edge of the portage, which contrasted with the "wild scenery" of the deep ravines and narrow and dangerous pathways of the portage itself. After he completed its traverse, Franklin wrote, "I could not but feel astonished at the labourious task which the voyageurs have twice in the year to encounter at this place in conveying their stores backwards and forwards."[26] This site represented the entrance to a new state of "northness," as the change in drainage system toward the Arctic Ocean took voyageurs more quickly and easily into new northern frontiers.

Each of these sites of ritual baptism marked a striking transition, the entrance to a socially recognized "new land" or region within fur trade country, and the beginning of a new discernable segment of the vast canoe route of the Montreal fur trade.[27] The sites represented points of no return. Once they were reached, the brigades were too far along in their journeys for men to desert and easily return to the safety of Montreal, Grand Portage, or Ile à la Crosse. The oldest of the sites was the closest to Montreal, and the most recent of the sites was in the farthest reaches of the pays d'en haut. The sites followed the extension of the fur trade north and west and came to represent the expanding boundaries of the pays d'en haut.

The mock baptism combined Roman Catholic rites with Aboriginal customs, such as an "Indian" gun salute, and stipulated rules about the treatment of women as well as the regulation of novices in the trade. Like many early modern rituals, the mock baptism reversed the customary ordering of power.[28] Servants issued orders to masters and clerks and demanded payment in the form of alcohol, money, or goods. This ceremony, however, had a unique dimension. Experienced voyageurs imposed power in symbolic terms over novices by regulating their transition to new states of occupation and manhood. Rituals such as the mock baptism helped voyageurs order their working world. In particular the ritual baptisms revealed how voyageurs "mapped" the pays d'en haut and gave expression to their cultural perceptions of land and the regional variations in voyageurs' occupation.

The ritual mock baptism closely mimicked the Catholic ceremony. John McDonell's description noted that the baptism was "performed by sprinkling water in [his] face with a small cedar Bow dipped in a ditch of water." McDonell, a devout Catholic who eventually became known as Le Prêtre because of his piety and his insistence that his men observe Roman Catholic feasts, can be trusted as a keen observer.[29] Sprinkling of water on the head was a widely accepted means of performing baptisms. Receiving a drizzling in the face was probably a form of satire. In this case the asperges or aspergillum (instrument used to sprinkle water) was a cedar bough. This is an appropriate choice because cedar was used in some Christian ceremonies of purification.[30] Other descriptions mention dunking individuals in water. Traveler George Heriot recorded in 1813 that the "rude ceremony [was there] performed of plunging into the waters of the Outaouais [River]."[31] Daniel Harmon also referred to the baptism as a "Ducking" in the river.[32] Either partial or full immersion in water was certainly an acceptable way of performing a baptism, but the method of full immersion was probably heartily embraced by high-spirited voyageurs who wished to cause the initiate as much discomfort as possible.

Aspects of the ceremony in the ritual baptism were equivocal. McDonell wrote that the sprinkling of water and pledges were "accompanied by a dozen of Gun shots fired one after another in an Indian manner." Shots were fired in succession rather than as a volley, and at least two men were engaged in this practice, because of the time required to reload a gun after each shot. Was this an Aboriginal custom, or Europeans' idea of one?[33] The ceremonial inclusion of a supposedly "Indian custom" symbolically represented the central importance of Aboriginal peoples in the lives of the voyageurs, but in a highly ambivalent fashion. Not only did Aboriginal peoples make the fur trade possible, they also culturally influenced European Americans living in the North American interior. Traders borrowed many cultural materials to help them survive and prosper, such as canoes, snowshoes, moccasins, and pemmican. Borrowings and exchanges of values and beliefs occurred among those voyageurs who spent a lot of time in the pays d'en haut and came into close contact with Aboriginal peoples.[34] Mangeurs de lard had very little contact with Aboriginal peoples. Hommes du nord and Athabasca men, however, were regularly sent out individually or in pairs with a small complement of goods to trade directly with Aboriginal peoples in their encampments (called trading *en dérouine*, see chapter 7).[35] Voyageurs sometimes lived at Aboriginal lodges for months at a time, forming close friendships and kin ties with Aboriginal families.

John McDonell's description of an Indian-style firing of guns occurred at the Lake Superior height of land. Who fired the guns? Was this part of the ceremony at all the points of baptism? Did the practice have the same meaning at all sites? Unfortunately, the documentary record is too thin to answer these questions. However, similar practices in the fur trade world help illuminate the significance of this custom. Firing shots into the air during holiday celebrations and at arrival and departure parties for brigades was common at the interior posts (see chapter 6).[36] "Indian war whoops" were often shouted at fur trade parties, such as those held when brigades left Montreal, and at Beaver Club dinners, meetings of elite fur trade masters in Montreal who had spent at least one winter beyond Lake Superior.[37] Incorporating elements of "Indianness" into carnival and misrule in North America was widespread, the most famous examples being Americans dressing up as Aboriginal people and bellowing Indian war whoops during the Boston Tea Party and New York's Tammany dinners. Historian Philip Deloria has argued that Americans came to associate Indianness with political resistance and revolution, and the association allowed rioters to invent American customs that they sorely lacked. Later Americans, especially fraternalists, "played Indian" to define themselves as exotic and separate from mainstream society and as possessing special secret knowledge.[38] Similarly, in fur trade ceremonies the firing of guns "in an Indian manner" may be an instance of appropriating what were thought to be Aboriginal practices in an attempt to fit into "Indian Country." If voyageurs were firing the guns, then perhaps they tried to indigenize themselves and their ceremonies to help them assume a new sense of belonging in the foreign land.

A single intriguing passage links the site of ritual baptism on the Ottawa River to a sacred Aboriginal site. In 1686 Chevalier de Troyes wrote:

> *One sees on the north side, following the route, a high mountain [hill] whose rock wall appears straight and very steep, the middle appears black. Perhaps this comes from the fact that it is where the Indians make their sacrifices, shooting their arrows over it, which have small bits of tobacco tied to the ends. Our French have the custom of baptizing at this place those who have yet never before passed. This rock is named the bird by the savages and some of our people wishing not to lose the ancient custom throw water on themselves, we have camped at the bottom of the portage.*[39]

Sacrificing arrows and tobacco was a common practice among many Aboriginal groups.[40] Voyageurs traversed the Ottawa River frequently and came to know the Algonquian peoples who also used the river and the locations of their spiritual ceremonies. Is it an accident that the point of baptism was situated on an existing site of Aboriginal spiritual significance? Were the other points of baptism also on Aboriginal sacred sites? Scholars David Meyer and Paul Thistle argue that along the Saskatchewan River fur traders built their posts in the vicinity of annual religious gatherings of Cree people.[41] On a practical level voyageurs may have chosen points of baptism close to Aboriginal spiritual sites so that they would be likely to meet Aboriginal people along their canoe routes and trade for supplies, such as meat or moccasins. On a symbolic level mimicking the location of an Aboriginal spiritual site may have been another attempt at indigenizing themselves or perhaps even garnering spiritual power and protection from Aboriginal forces to bolster the protection of their Catholic saints.

McDonell's description of the ritual baptism included a stipulation "never to kiss a voyageur's wife against her own free will." Yet frequently at Christmas and New Year's celebrations, the women at a post, usually wives of voyageurs and bourgeois, lined up to be kissed by the men (see chapter 6). What did these rituals mean? Most obviously they were a clear acknowledgment of the presence of Aboriginal women at fur trade posts.[42] Voyageurs encountered Aboriginal women primarily during trading ceremonies and while spending the winters in the pays d'en haut (see chapter 8). Their relationships ranged from casual sexual contact to stable and permanent marriages, but voyageurs most often established temporary and seasonal relationships with Aboriginal women at interior posts. The stipulation in the ritual baptism might have served as a sign that social and sexual rules were different in the pays d'en haut, and Aboriginal and métis wives should be treated with respect and dignity, especially since the women were vitally important to fur trade operations. Women often acted as key negotiators in establishing trading relationships and also aided their trading husbands by teaching them to survive in the Northwest.

Fraternity

The fraternal initiation at the points of baptism had a different meaning at each site, as voyageurs passed through different stages of their occupation. Although voyageurs did not leave a record of their reflections on the ritual baptisms, their actions are revealing. The baptism along the Ottawa River encouraged a feeling of distinction in men who had just left their families for the first time in Montreal and surrounding parishes. This would help define the voyageurs as a group and focus their attention and loyalty on their brigade. Voyageurs' ritual baptism gave the young men a sense of belonging and helped unite the crews, which was crucially important to the effectiveness and safety of the job.[43] Socializing as a group during the ceremony reinforced the fraternity and fellow feeling of the crews and brigades. It helped voyageurs to overcome whatever social divisions may have arisen between men of different parishes of origin or of different ages. The celebrations and drinking that accompanied the ceremonies also relieved, in the words of Daniel Harmon, their "heavy hearts and eyes drowned in tears" caused by leaving their families in Montreal and the anxiety of entering a new world.[44]

The ritual baptism helped to induct men into a new fraternity of fellow laborers and in this sense it is reminiscent of the very old tradition among sailors to baptize and haze men the first time they crossed the equator. Marcus Rediker sums up the practice neatly: "The 'sailor's baptism,' a classic rite of passage, was enacted when novices first 'crossed the line,' that is, the equator. Practiced by all seafaring nationalities and therefore part of an international maritime culture, the seaman's baptism was essentially an initiation ceremony that marked the passage into the social and cultural world of the deep-sea sailor."[45] The custom of baptizing men along the Ottawa River during the French regime was probably first inspired by the knowledge of sailors' customs. Some bourgeois linked the ritual baptism directly to the sailors' custom. While still a new clerk in the NWC, Harmon wrote: "Those voyagers I am told have many of the Sailors customs, and the following is one of them:—from all who have not passed certain places they expect a *treat* or something to drink, and should you not comply with their whims, you might be sure of getting a Ducking which they call *baptizing*."[46] The habitants, however, had other reminders of the practice, as it became common among French Canadian soldiers in the mid-eighteenth century to mark pointes aux baptêmes on the St. Lawrence River between Montreal and Quebec. The soldiers would "baptize" those who came into sight of either settlement for the first time or would accept a *pourboire* in place of the ceremony.[47]

Social Distinctions

At the same time as they created a feeling of fraternity, the ritual baptisms also instilled a sense of hierarchy among the voyageurs. The positions within a canoe were subject to a rigid ranking: milieux, or middle paddlers, were at the bottom of the labor hierarchy; bouts, or ends, (foresmen and steersmen) were one step above; guides the next step up; then *commis* (clerks), and finally the bourgeois (see chapter 4). A hierarchy was also applied to the regionally based variations in voyageur status. Hommes du nord were better than mangeurs de lard, while Athabasca men were the best of all. The ritual baptism at the height of land west of Lake Superior thus symbolized rebirth as a professional voyageur. Hommes du nord were more committed to constructing a stable and workable occupational culture than were men who paddled only during the summers. They signed contracts not simply for a summer job but usually for at least a three-year period and entered the pays d'en haut to make a life for themselves.[48] Likewise, the ritual baptism at Methy Portage symbolized yet another occupational rebirth, this time as an Athabasca man. These men were usually committed for life to working in the fur trade. The occupational distinction between mangeurs de lard, hommes du nord, and Athabasca men reflected recognized rankings of toughness and manliness among voyageurs.

Although the duties performed by pork eaters and northmen were similar, voyageurs exaggerated their differences in their language and deeds. Many northmen were pork eaters at one point during their careers, but they did their best to divide the occupational categories. Northmen treated the pork eaters with disdain and sometimes sided with bourgeois to discriminate against them. The discrimination was often so bad that in 1800 many pork eaters refused to make the journey from Grand Portage to Lac la Pluie, which had become the eastern depot for the Athabasca brigades in 1787.[49] For northmen the term *pork eater* came to symbolize weakness, ineptitude, and laziness. Northmen teased and insulted men who were less skilled and weaker than themselves by referring to them as pork eaters.[50] Sometimes men earned the permanent nickname of pork eater during their careers. At Slave Lake in 1800 a voyageur named Lanche was regularly referred to as such. In July the clerk for the post, W. F. Wentzel, first mentioned "the Porkeater."[51] Two months later bourgeois James Porter wrote in his journal that the voyageur Bastone "would not venture himself in a Canoe with the Porkeater [Lanche]." Porter suspected Bastone simply wanted to stay near his Aboriginal wife, but a couple of months later Lanche reported to Porter that no Chipewyans would let him winter at their lodge "because he was a porkeater."[52] Lanche's reputation seemed hard to shake and affected his relationship not only with his bourgeois, clerk, and fellow voyageurs, but also with neighboring Aboriginal people. Four years later, in the same district but at a different post (Fort of the Forks at the Grand [Mackenzie] River's confluence with the Laird River), the clerk Wentzel described the voyageur Boyé as a pork eater and hence not experienced enough to accompany the winter express to Slave Lake. Unlike Lanche, Boyé was able to overcome his nickname and was soon entrusted with trading en dérouine, hunting for the post, and eventually accompanying the winter express.[53]

Northmen worked hard to cultivate an image of success at their jobs. They frequently stopped just before they reached a post to spend time grooming and changing into their best clothes.[54] Voyageurs may have hoped to impress Aboriginal women at the posts in their efforts to search for sexual partners or mates. Crews made a great show of arriving by singing upon their approach, which would add to the image of completing a journey looking strong and fresh rather than tired.[55] HBC officer Robert Ballantyne commented that when crews arrived at posts, "it is then that they appear[ed] in wild perfection. The voyageurs upon such occasions [were] dressed in their best clothes; and gaudy feathers, ribbons, and tassels stream[ed] in abundance from their caps and gaiters."[56] The rituals of cleanliness and adornment were developed by northmen working in the interior, who had much more invested in their jobs than those who only worked in the summers between Montreal and Lake Superior. Even while in danger from threatening Aboriginal people, northmen took the time to clean up before arriving at a post. Ross Cox describes his crew's approach to Ile à la Crosse in late June 1817: "Stopped here for half an hour *pour se faire la barbe*, and make other little arrangements connected with the toilet. These being completed, we embarked, but having the fear of Crees before our eyes, our progress was slow and cautious across the lake, until our avant-couriers announced to us that the flag of the North-West floated from the bastions, and that all was safe."[57] *Se faire la barbe*, or shaving, suggests that northmen valued dignity, courtesy, and comfort, rather than behaving like uncaring and slovenly brutes. But their motives for cleaning themselves before they entered a post may also have been to create the impression that the journey required little exertion and was executed with ease, which underscored the northmen's strength, skill, and endurance. Northmen set high standards and mocked the manhood of those who could not meet them. Regarding voyageurs' behavior, Landmann speculated:

> *[They] are ambitious of being styled, homme-du-nord, a Northman, one who voluntarily leaves his family, and the comforts of a tranquil life, to voyage in Indian country, and pass at least one winter in the North, usually understood to be beyond the western banks of Lake Superior. These men, hommes-du-nord, regard themselves, and are regarded by their friends, as very superior beings—men of a high courage, who have proved that they hold the effeminacies of civilised life in contempt, and that they can cheerfully submit to every kind of hardship; as they live upon Indian-corn and grease without any salted or other meat but that procured by the gun—they apply the epithet of mangeurs-de-lard, or pork-eaters to all those who have never passed a winter in the north.*[58]

This passage suggests that leaving loved ones behind, disdaining sentimental attachments, and depriving oneself of comfort and good food was necessary to be a true homme du nord. Living without the "effeminacies of civilised life," which in the fur trade meant living like Aboriginal peoples, was the ideal of masculinity. Georges Dugas's biography of the voyageur Jean-Baptiste Charbonneau suggests that all voyageurs wished to live like Aboriginal peoples, wearing Aboriginal clothes, sleeping in tents, and hunting to eat.[59]

Voyageurs focused on food as an element of masculinity. Inexperienced summer men were signified by the food that they ate. Voyageurs seemed to genuinely prefer wild meat to salted or domesticated meat and also preferred any kind of meat to fish.[60] Perhaps they believed that food made the man and that the softness or weakness of men came from the food itself. Fur trade scholar Elizabeth Vibert has found that traders generally disdained "weak" fish and preferred "strong" red meat, believing they could incorporate "some measure of the special powers of the animal consumed—the strength, aggression, sexuality, and other elements seen as the 'animal nature' of humans."[61] It is thus not surprising that the weak, domesticated meat of pigs was viewed as weakening the men who consumed it. Yet northmen usually ate whatever food they could find in the interior, including oats and wheat, and did not pass up pork during the summer rendezvous at Grand Portage and Fort William.[62] Access to food, rather than what men actually ate, seemed to be of greater importance. Northmen emphasized that by placing themselves in situations where food supplies were precarious, they were being tough and brave. The emphasis on food reflects its centrality in the lives of voyageurs. Voyageurs took great pleasure in their food and in feasting, especially since survival could be so precarious in the interior, and their victuals were often mundane and limited. Bourgeois and clerks often commented on the voracious appetites of the voyageurs and their love of eating. NWC bourgeois David Thompson wrote, "[A] French canadian has the appetite of a Wolf, and glories in it; each man requires eight pounds of meat p^r day, or more; upon my reproaching some of them with their gluttony, the reply I got was, 'What pleasure have we in Life but eating.'[63]

While the baptism along the Ottawa River separated habitants from voyageurs, the baptism west of Lake Superior separated pork eaters from northmen and symbolized the start of a new life, a rebirth as a professional voyageur. The site of the baptism at Methy Portage marked yet another stage or distinction within the voyageur occupation. Men who had made the portage and especially those who had wintered north of it were thought to be the crème de la crème of all voyageurs. The British scientist and surveyor John Henry Lefroy remarked in 1844, "After passing the Portage de la Loche (the great Portage) a man is no longer a 'mangeur de Lard,' he calls himself 'voyageur du Nord, Baptème!' and the very musquitoes do or ought to respect him."[64] By the 1840s the terms used to distinguish different categories of voyageurs may have shifted so that only those working in the Athabasca were called northmen. Or Lefroy may have been confused on the terms voyageurs used to refer to one another. Yet he understood that men who made that portage entered a more revered state of occupation and manhood. Athabasca men were thought to be the toughest of all voyageurs in the Northwest. While traveling on Lake Winnipeg, a brigade destined for the Athabasca District challenged another heading to the Fort des Prairies along the Saskatchewan River to race through Lake Winnipeg. The young clerk Duncan McGillivray wrote, "The Athabasca Men piqued themselves on a Superiority they were supposed to have over the other bands of the North for expeditions marching [canoeing], and ridiculed our men *a la facon du Nord* for pretending to dispute a point that universally decided in *their* favor." Despite the confidence of the Athabasca men, both brigades reached the northern end of the lake after forty-eight hours of continuous canoeing and declared a tie.[65] Brigades that set out to explore new fur trading areas under the direction of Alexander Mackenzie and Simon Fraser were regarded as especially tough and brave. On their quests for an overland route to the Pacific, the bourgeois often relied on the men's concern for their reputations and ambition for fame to carry them farther north and west than any voyageurs had ventured before. Mackenzie pushed his brigades very hard in his attempts to find a passage from Fort Chipewyan over the Rocky Mountains to the Pacific Ocean. After many mishaps with broken canoes and lost ammunition on a journey in 1793, his men began to threaten to desert. Mackenzie managed to dissuade them by reminding them of "the honour of conquering disasters, and the disgrace that would attend them on their return home, without having attained the object of the expedition. Nor did [he] fail to mention the courage and resolution which was the peculiar boast of the North men; and that [he] depended on them, at that moment, for the maintenance of their character."[66] Being the first white men to cross the Rocky Mountains was considered to be an especially awesome feat.[67] The bourgeois understandably encouraged the rugged ethos of the voyageurs, who competed with one another to perform feats of strength and endurance, which conveniently suited the bourgeois agenda for quick, efficient, and profitable fur trade operations. Yet it is clear that both the bourgeois and the voyageurs privileged men who had been farther north than any other traders and attributed particular strength and courage to them. The Athabasca men thus embodied an idealized masculinity for all voyageurs in the Northwest fur trade. Not only were men's reputations significantly bolstered by working in the Athabasca, but men also stood to lose "masculine capital" if they did not complete expeditions there.

Likewise the bourgeois also measured masculine prowess by geography. They valued the distinction between men who had wintered in the pays d'en haut and those who had not. Only those bourgeois who had spent at least one winter beyond Lake Superior could join the elite Montreal Beaver Club, which excluded the "lower orders" of clerks, voyageurs, women, and Aboriginal people. This dining club met once a fortnight during the winter months in a prestigious Montreal tavern between 1785 and 1824. Under the guise of urbane civility, club members indulged in an idealization of the rough and ready fur trade world. Club dinners started off with formal meals but quickly degenerated into drunken revelry, with bourgeois singing voyageur songs, reenacting the shooting of rapids, and reminiscing about their rugged fur trade days. The dinner fare reflected the mingling ideals of "wild" men and gentlemen. Country food, such as wild rice and venison, was served in crested glass and silverware in stately settings. Like voyageurs the bourgeois also tried to indigenize themselves in the Northwest, but they imitated *voyageurs* in addition to Aboriginal people.[68]

Landscape

The sites of the ritual baptism became more geomorphologically significant and dangerous as voyageurs moved farther into the interior. The point along the Ottawa River did not mark a change in water flow or a portage; rather it marked the first glimpse of bedrock on the journey out of Montreal. The second site west of Lake Superior entailed a height of land, separating two major water systems, and several portages of over one thousand feet.[69] The site farthest northwest entailed a laborious portage of twelve and a half miles, including a stretch over slippery rock and narrow defiles. Crossing the Rocky Mountains was also considered to be a major feat of manhood.

The voyageurs' sense of social geography intertwined distances traveled with levels of masculine prowess. The voyageurs also marked the landscape over which they traveled in other ways. The priests would have been pleased that Catholic rites marked many points of the voyage into the interior. Daniel Harmon noted, "The Canadian Voyagers when they leave one stream to follow another have a custom of pulling off their Hats and making the sign of the Cross, and one in each Brigade if not in every Canoe repeats a short Prayer."[70] Voyageurs probably organized their appeals to the saints and their prayers around discrete distances along canoe routes, such as a single stream or parts of landscape divided by forks in a river, islands, portages, and large topographical features, such as rocks, hills, and cliffs. Every time they entered a new part of the journey, they would appeal to God and the saints for protection. The regular religious appeals meant that voyageurs both actively divided their journeys into sections marked by landscape features (which helped them keep to their course and estimate the time of their travels) and constantly invoked spiritual forces for protection. Voyageurs measured distances along canoe routes by the number of times they stopped to fill their pipes.[71] Some voyageurs may have seen smoking as an act of prayer, mimicking the common Aboriginal custom of offering tobacco to spirits.

Although there were very few churches in the Northwest before the 1820s, voyageurs regularly engaged with the cosmos through rituals and prayers.[72] They treated abandoned Jesuit missions in the interior with "pious reverence."[73] They attributed awesome features in the land to the work of supernatural forces. Ross Cox reported that in May 1817, at junction of Rocky Mountain River and Peace River, his crew saw an enormous glacier, made even more spectacular by the reflection of the sun and the rumbling and explosion of an avalanche. After gazing in silent wonder at the glacier, one of the voyageurs exclaimed with much vehemence, "I'll take my oath, my dear friends, that God Almighty never made such a place!"[74] Although the voyageur did not attribute this particular work to God, he recognized the sacred or magic at work in nature.

Many Aboriginal beliefs and practices concerning landscape were incorporated into voyageurs' work rituals. Clerk George Nelson recorded an incident involving one of his voyageurs, Joseph Labrie, who prayed to the "mère des vents," or Mother of the Winds, while the crew was in Lake Superior in June 1802. He dropped a penny piece, a bit of tobacco, and flint steel into the lake as sacrifices for a good wind. Labrie was successful, as a good wind filled the sail. Laura Peers and Theresa Schenck suggest that "Labrie's sacrifice seems to be a combination of Ojibwa sacrifices of goods, especially tobacco, to powerful spirits who controlled the waters (often made as they were crossing large lakes) and non-Native Catholic gifts of flowers and votive offerings in thanks to saints for answered prayers."[75] Some voyageurs came to believe in the spirits called forth by Algonquians in shaking tent ceremonies.[76] In this ceremony an Algonquian medicine man (sometimes woman) would enter a designated tent to call forth spirits and communicate with them. The tent would shake, and voices of the spirit could be heard by those outside the tent.

Language

Clearly voyageurs who learned Aboriginal languages to some degree became the most influenced by Aboriginal peoples. The records of bourgeois and clerks show that voyageurs spoke primarily French, without revealing the degree to which voyageurs may have learned Aboriginal languages. Most Anglophone masters learned French to communicate with their workers. Specific French terminology arose in the trade, and some terms were carry-overs from the days of the trade before the conquest, such as *voyageur*, *bourgeois*, *commis* (clerk), *pays d'en haut*, *portage*, and *courir en dérouine*. By virtue of their numerical dominance and importance to trade operations, voyageurs often determined which general terms continued to be spoken in French. Alexander Ross attributed the term *bourgeois* to voyageurs, commenting that "the Canadians, or voyageurs, dignify their master by the name of Bourgeois,—a term handed down from the days of the French in the province of Canada."[77] Other terms in the trade came from the French Canadian voyageurs, both before and after the conquest. The pamphleteer Samuel Hull Wilcocke, quoting from Benjamin Frobisher's damaged journal, noted that "to *march* is the Canadian term for traveling, and is as frequently, if not oftener, applied to express the progress of a canoe or boat, as of a pedestrian."[78]

Many canoeing terms specifically related to voyageurs were of French origin, such as *milieux* (paddlers in the middle of the canoe), *devant* (foresman), *gouvernail* (steersman), *bouts* (ends or foresman and steersman), *demicharge* (unloading half a canoe to shoot rapids), and *décharge* (unloading the entire canoe to shoot rapids). Traveling around Lake Superior in the 1850s, Johann Georg Kohl remarked, "[T]here is not a single part of the canoe to which the Canadians do not give a distinct name." They referred to the ribs of a canoe as *varangues*, canoes without cargoes as *canots à lège*, and fully loaded canoes as *canots de charge*. Traveling by canoe was called *aller à l'aviron*, or to go by the paddle.[79] The French term *dégradé* in the writings of Anglophone bourgeois meant a crew was forced ashore by bad weather.[80] Sunken trees in rivers and streams were called *chicots* by voyageurs.[81] The widely used French term *pause* (usually spelled phonetically as *pose*) referred to the stopping places found at intervals on every long portage (see chapter 4).[82]

Other terms that seemed to be picked up by everyone who worked in the trade regardless of his mother tongue varied widely from actions to material objects. In the trade *faire la chaudière* meant cooking.[83] Voyageurs called one type of snowshoes *racquette pattes d'ours* (bear's paws), which may have been an adaptation of an Aboriginal term, as snowshoes were named after the animal tracks that they resembled, and usually these styles corresponded to clans, totemic identities, or to individual spirit helpers of the snowshoe makers.[84] *Mal de raquette* referred to the acute pain in feet and legs suffered by those unaccustomed to snowshoeing.[85] These terms reflected areas of both particular interest and expertise of voyageurs: traveling and provisioning. However, English bourgeois adopted other French Canadian expressions. One expression widely used by the NWC bourgeois, clerks, and voyageurs was *potties* to refer to the XY Company. The term *petite potée* meant a collection of things or people of small value. NWC masters applied it to the XYC to underscore the small size and limited success of their enterprise.[86]

French terms were employed widely in the trade, even by bourgeois and clerks who could not speak French. Most of the literate kept journals and wrote letters in English, which was the official language of the postconquest companies, but French terms were scattered throughout their writings, reflecting the everyday parlance of the trade. Most English bourgeois and clerks learned to speak French quite well, which was a necessity in managing their French-speaking crews. In his first couple of years of service, the American Daniel Harmon complained about not being able to speak French and commented on other new clerks, recently arrived from Scotland, who could speak as little French as he. Harmon was relieved when other Anglophone bourgeois and clerks were around so he could talk to someone, though he found consolation and company in his books (especially the Bible).[87] He comments that he was usually not left alone in charge of voyageurs before he could speak proficient French, and he started to study the language as soon as he arrived in the interior. After two years, when he had mastered elementary French, he complained that even if he could speak fluently in French, "what conversation would an illiterate ignorant Canadian be able to keep up. All of their chat [was] about Horses, Dogs, Canoes and Women, and strong Men who [could] fight a good battle."[88] Yet his experience shows the necessity of learning French.

The influence of voyageurs' language extended not only to their masters. It is likely that when voyageurs traded with Aboriginal peoples at their lodges and especially when they formed close relations with Aboriginal women, French terms infused their repertoire. Some descendants of European fur traders and Aboriginal women, known as métis, created the unique language of Michif. Michif is a mixed language drawing its nouns from French and verbs from Cree, but speakers rarely know both Cree and French. Linguist Peter Bakker comments that "no such mixture of two languages has been reported from any other part of the world."[89] He explains that this highly unusual language came about because bilingual métis "were no longer accepted as Indians or as French, and they formulated their own ethnic identity, which was mixed and in which a mixed 'language of our own' was considered part of their ethnicity."[90]

In addition to infusing their relationships with Aboriginal peoples and their masters, voyageurs' language also infused the vocabulary of the landscape over which they traveled. Voyageurs named geomorphologic features, such as rivers and portages. Ross Cox commented, "The Canadians, who are very fertile in baptizing remarkable places, called an island near our encampment of the 6th *Gibraltar*, from the rocky steepness of its shore."

While traveling along the Winnipeg River, he complained that "[i]t would be tiresome and useless to give the various names by which the Canadians distinguish[ed] those places" because there were so many of them.[91] The voyageurs seemed to have had a very intense relationship with space. On a trip from Pais (Pays) Plat (translated as Flat Country) near Lake Superior to Portage de L'Isle in the Winnipeg River during the summer of July 1784, the crew of Edward Umfreville recorded the French names of many portages, including Portage de detour, Portage de deux Rapids, Portage des Grosse Roches, Portage des Trembles, and Portage de Petite Rivière, which described the physical features of the portages.[92] Other place names that reflected the physical surroundings included Portage du Thé, named after a species of mint that grew there; Les Terres Jaunes, which referred to the yellow banks in the Rocky Mountains; La prairie de la Vache, which meant cow country or buffalo country; Le Rocher de Miette, which meant small rocks.[93] It is impossible to say whether voyageurs named these places or translated them from Aboriginal names. Other placenames are obviously the French translations or renditions of Aboriginal names, such as Lac Ouinipique (Lake Winnipeg).

Naming, or translating the name from an Aboriginal language, of points along fur trade routes reflects the history and experiences of fur trade laborers, and these names usually persisted for years. Clerk George Nelson provides a very detailed description of a trip between Fort William and Cumberland House in the summer of 1822, mentioning the prevailing names of many of the portages and the stories that went with them. Portage Ecarté (remote or isolated) was so named because a man had been lost in it for nearly two days, and because the path through the portage was obscured by large stones. Another named Racoursi (shortcut) was so difficult that according to Nelson only maniacs tried to run it, such as the Iroquois and a few French Canadians. He described Petit-Portage des Chiens as slippery and smooth, commenting that the men frequently slid on their backsides or fell on their faces while racing with their heavy packs. Portage à Jourdain was named after a guide who had broken his canoe there. Another portage where a couple of men had died was called Portage des Morts. Voyageurs called Portage du Lac la Pluie *le bout des Terres* (end of the land), which was an old name that Nelson thought might have originated prior to the conquest, when the French traders only traveled to that point in the interior and thought that the Great Lakes were simply branches of the western sea. Portage Des. Rocher à Chaurette was named for a guide who broke his canoe and lost his cargo there. At Chute à Jacqeau (Jack Falls) Canadians customarily raced with their loads and frequently fell with them. Some "fools" also raced across Portage Barrière but were often killed. One portage on an island was named Beau-bien, after a voyageur who was ordered by his bourgeois to run the rapid against his will. The canoe was swamped, sucked into an eddy, and several people drowned and much property was lost. Nelson commented that voyageurs "perverted" many Aboriginal placenames.[94] Most of the names he listed, however, seemed to have arisen from voyageurs' experiences, such as naming portages after particular voyageurs who had died or been injured there.[95] The names of the portages might have served as markers for difficult portages as well as reminders of those men lost in the service. For example, Portage des Noyés (the drowned) marked the location where five men had drowned.[96]

Power

The imprinting of voyageurs' names onto features of landscape represented voyageurs' importance in the trade and their control over canoe journeys and routes. Language and naming provided voyageurs with means to garner some power and control over their working lives. In some instances voyageurs diminished the authority of the bourgeois and clerks by giving them nicknames. Although nicknaming was common practice among both French Canadians and Scots, servants assigning nicknames to masters could be a subtle way of curtailing their masters' power. Unfortunately most clerks and bourgeois probably did not record nicknames, especially if they were unflattering. Ross Cox recalled: "It is laughable to hear the nominal distinctions [voyageurs] are obliged to adopt in reference to many of the partners and clerks, who have the same surname. They are Mr. Mackenzie, *le rouge*; Mr. Mackenzie, *le blanc*; Mr. Mackenzie, *le borgne*; Mr. Mackenzie, *le picoté*; Mr. McDonald, *le grand*; Mr. McDonald, *le prêtre*; Mr. McDonald, *le bras croche*; and so on, according to the colour of the hair, the size, or other personal peculiarity of each individual."[97] He reported that voyageurs called one of the agents, Mr. Shaw, Monsieur Le Chat (Mr. Cat), and one voyageur who met Shaw in Montreal referred to his children as *les petits Chatons* (the little kittens).[98] In the 1850s Johann Georg Kohl noted that old French Canadians living around Lake Superior referred to bears as shaggy bourgeois.[99] In this case it is difficult to tell if this designation was meant to note the human qualities of bears, insult bears, or acknowledge the power of bourgeois. These clues probably only reflect the tip of the iceberg of voyageurs' nicknames for the bourgeois and clerks. Through nicknaming voyageurs could symbolically undermine master authority while asserting their own values of levity and mirth.

Although the power relations between voyageurs and their masters are discussed at length in chapter 5, and carnival is discussed in chapter 6, it is worth noting here how exceptionally useful rituals were for voyageurs to reverse the normal ordering of power.[100] One of the most obvious of these was the mock baptism. The bourgeois and clerks seemed to view the ceremonies primarily as occasions for voyageurs to demand drams of alcohol. Harmon noted that during the ritual baptism "from all who ha[d] not passed certain places they expect[ed] a *treat* or something to drink."[101] At this early point in his career, Harmon tended to portray voyageurs as opportunistic bullies, looking for alcohol, money, or a brawl, probably because he felt intimidated by and superior to them. But this observance of the ritual baptism cannot be dismissed simply as the reaction of an inexperienced young clerk. In 1791 traveler George Heriot reported that he was able to avoid a dunking in the Ottawa River by paying a fine.[102] Voyageurs certainly enjoyed the *regales*, or treats, accompanying rituals and ceremonies during canoe journeys, but the ritual baptism was much more significant. By forcefully including clerks, bourgeois, and travelers, voyageurs were symbolically and practically demonstrating their power on the journeys and encouraging the bourgeois and clerks to be fair masters. Master Edward Umfreville recorded "paying [his] Baptême," which may have been both a symbolic and a real price masters paid to ensure servant obedience.[103] Marcus Rediker found that among eighteenth-century sailors, the ritual of "crossing the line" relaxed the barriers between captain and crew and sometimes temporarily reversed the ship's official hierarchy. Greg Dening warns, however, that the ceremony had a more ambiguous meaning and that "crossing the line" on board sailing ships was a satire more than a challenge of the institutions and roles of power. The ceremonies bordered uncomfortably on "reverse world" rituals, where sailors proudly asserted their independence and quaint customs and yet humbly acknowledged how they were governed.[104] However, the dearth of extensive descriptions of mock baptisms may suggest that the ritual had more to do with relations among voyageurs than with master and servant dealings.

Struggles for power and respect between voyageurs and the masters could enter the religious arena. Roman Catholic rites became a way for voyageurs to identify themselves as distinct from their Protestant masters. One contested site was the observance of Sabbath.[105] Although flags were customarily flown at forts on the Sabbath, time and resource constraints meant that men usually worked on Sundays, especially during the canoe journeys when they were in a great rush to beat the freezing of canoe routes, and when they first arrived at their wintering site and were busy constructing a post.[106] HBC officer Robert Ballantyne explained: "The Sabbath day in such a voyage as this cannot be a day of rest, as, from the lateness of the season, every hour is of the utmost importance. Delay may cause our being arrested by ice when we reach the heights of land; and even now we fear that, unless the season is a late one, we shall experience great difficulty in reaching Canada."[107] Voyageurs could demand the right to observe the Sabbath, thereby enforcing a day of rest. Some bourgeois decided that antagonizing the voyageurs was not a good idea and agreed to provide the men a later holiday when they were forced to work on the Sabbath.[108]

Religious observance during major customary holidays became another site of contested terrain between masters and servants. Voyageurs and bourgeois agreed that refraining from work during the holiday was thought of as a means of sacrifice and deference to God to sanctify the day.[109] But evangelical Protestant Daniel Harmon complained at great length about the heathen ways of the Roman Catholic voyageurs, especially at Christmas: "This being Christmas Day our people pay no further attention to Worldly affairs *than to Drink all Day*," and he fretted that their excessive drinking and fighting defiled the day's importance. He was delighted in 1806 when most of the voyageurs were absent from the post, and he felt free to honor Christmas with reading the Bible and meditating on the birth of Jesus rather than being distracted by unruly partying.[110] Protestant bourgeois were often hostile or oblivious to the religious rites of voyageurs, whose habitant Catholic backgrounds may have taught them practices of worship unrecognizable to the bourgeois. Voyageurs did not consider indulging in alcohol and revelry antithetical to religious observance.

Rites of Danger and Death

To imprint themselves on the landscape by naming portages, geographic features, and places where their mates had perished not only demonstrated voyageurs' agency in their workplace but also illustrated the sinister side of their work. Naming sites along the journey became a way for voyageurs to manage and minimize the fear of swift flowing waters, difficult rapids, impassable portages, rough weather, wild animals, and hostile Aboriginal peoples. Yet bestowing intimidating names on certain locations may also have helped voyageurs remember what to expect along routes and warned new voyageurs when tough times were ahead. For instance, bourgeois Angus Mackintosh noted that a very large opening in a rock on the north side of the French River was referred to as "the entrance to Hell" by his voyageurs.[111] Voyageurs could preserve their strength and prepare for a difficult portage if they were reminded of its location on a fur trade route. These names reflect work experiences that voyageurs deemed important.

The circumstances of the fur trade came to shape voyageurs' religious customs. Catholic rites were most often practiced by voyageurs in harrowing or tragic circumstances. One group caught in a storm on Lake Winnipeg became frightened when they lost their sail and began to count their rosary beads and cross themselves.[112] In another instance when voyageurs were caught in a storm on Lake Winnipeg, while traveling from Fort Alexander to Jack River, all the voyageurs knelt, took out their rosaries, began to pray to various saints, and vowed that if they lived to see a priest they would have a mass offered up as a thanksgiving to the Virgin Mary for their "miraculous deliverance." Bourgeois Alexander Ross commented that "vows of this kind [were] always religiously observed by old voyageurs."[113] The seriousness of their prayers underscored the danger of fur trade work.

In the absence of the guidance of priests and Catholic liturgy while traveling in the pays d'en haut, voyageurs often infused Catholic practices with their own notions of how best to commune with the cosmos and its deities, and these notions were informed both by old peasant traditions and by Aboriginal customs that voyageurs observed on their travels. The blurred boundaries between Catholicism and "magic" among peasants and the liminal status of voyageurs during their travels created an atmosphere particularly conducive to incorporating extra-institutional sources of spiritual power and protection into religious observances. In one example of a popular voyageur story, around the time of the conquest, a canoe of voyageurs returning to Montreal from the pays d'en haut met a large group of Iroquois at Grand Calumet portage on the Ottawa River. The Iroquois began to chase the Canadians, who managed to shoot through dangerous rapids to escape them. After their miraculous feat, all the voyageurs prayed and vowed to hold masses for their deliverance. The Iroquois stopped chasing the crew when, according to the story, they saw a tall woman in white robes standing in the bow of the canoe. The voyageurs believed this woman was the Virgin Mary conducting the canoe and frightening away the Iroquois.[114] In another incident, during one of the frequent storms on Lake Winnipeg a voyageur recounted to bourgeois Alexander Ross that three strange lights appeared to guide the boat to shore through treacherous narrows. Some of the voyageurs thought the three lights represented the apostles Peter and Paul guarding the Virgin Mary, while others considered the appearance ominous and predicted that three men would drown or that only three out of the nine would be saved in a future storm.[115]

The supernatural appeared not only to help troubled canoes, but to portend danger. While on the Columbia River in 1814, a brigade of voyageurs was attacked by a group of Aboriginal people, probably Chinooks. They took refuge on an island and attempted to establish a truce. The voyageurs feared they would die because during the night ravens flew overhead, which they believed signified approaching death.[116] Premonitions of death could also come in the form of visions or ghosts. John McDonald of Garth reported the story of one voyageur working at Ile à la Crosse in 1792 who saw a vision of white horses pulling a coach with two men in it. The following season he and another voyageur went duck hunting on the same river and were never seen again. When their canoe was found on that river, McDonald admitted that "there [was] surely some more in this than superstition."[117] Regardless of whether such incidents occurred, the telling of these types of stories reinforced the belief in magical powers in the universe that operated outside the boundaries of the church.

Many extra-institutional magico-religious rites of the French Canadians were similar to Aboriginal and particularly Algonquian beliefs. It was at these cultural junctions that voyageurs and Algonquians most often borrowed from one another and found common sites of understanding. One point of cultural intersection was the belief in possession by evil spirits. Clerk George Nelson recorded several "legends of the Voyageurs" while traveling from Montreal to Sault Ste. Marie. In one story a Mackinac trader named Mr. Lafremboise was returning to Montreal with a crew when he suddenly fled into the woods. When his fellows pursued him to see what was wrong, Lafremboise would not allow them to come near and fled further into the woods. After a long and fruitless search, the crew decided to leave him and continue on their journey. They hoped that another canoe passing might pick him up and tied a letter to a long pole giving an account of the affair and pleading for the mercy of God and the saints. But the next day, to the crew's astonishment, they saw him further along their route. He seemed wild and alarmed, and they again unsuccessfully chased him into the woods. Again in the afternoon the crew spotted him in another distant place on their journey. They thought that an evil spirit must have transported him because it was impossible for humans to travel such immense distances so rapidly without aid. The next day the crew discovered him again in a bend of the river. They cautiously surrounded him on the shore and managed to bring him aboard the canoe. Clerk George Nelson commented, "He showed all the signs of horror & anxiety upon being *seized*; they secured & carried him *on board*. he looked quite wild & dejected, & his clothes were all in rags!" Nelson dismissed the incident, considering it evidence of the man's insanity or his trickery.[118] The incident is similar to European stories of possession and Algonquian stories of windigos and may have served as a cultural conjunction.[119]

Voyageurs learned about many Aboriginal spiritual beliefs and practices, and their responses to them ranged dramatically. In 1803 some starving voyageurs tried to imitate Aboriginal chanting, singing, dancing, and smoking while asking for food from a group of Ojibwes, who were amused, took pity on the voyageurs, and gave them food.[120] In this case the voyageurs were driven to desperate measures to find food. Were imitations of Aboriginal peoples a genuine strategy to appeal to Aboriginal spirits, an attempt to communicate with the Ojibwes, or meant as a mockery of Ojibwe culture? Teasing and joking were common among Aboriginal peoples. The trickster, or Nanabozo among the Ojibwes and Wisahkecahk among the Crees, was a major spirit who had the power both to create and to destroy using laughter, humor, and irony.[121] The voyageurs may have learned about the trickster and thus engaged in an imitation of Aboriginal rites as a serious means of connecting with the Ojibwes to find food. But the joke might also have accidentally revealed a place where the two cultures converged.

Voyageurs' lives were filled with hardships, which included starvation, canoeing accidents, injuries, and illnesses. As was the case with the undelivered letters discussed in chapter 2, many voyageurs perished while in the service. Voyageurs who died in the pays d'en haut were generally buried in a Roman Catholic manner. The regular canoe routes were scattered with wooden crosses marking the spots where voyageurs had drowned or met their death by some other accident.[122] When a brigade passed by crosses on the shore, voyageurs pulled off their hats, made the sign of the cross, and paused to say a prayer. Daniel Harmon complained, "[A]t almost every Rapid that we have passed since we left Montreal, we have seen a number of Crosses erected, and at one I counted no less than thirty!"[123] The crosses often marked the name of the voyageur and the date of his death. On occasion the site was named after him, such as Lapensie's Island close to Jasper House.[124] Pointe aux Croix (Crosses), or Pointe des Noyés (of the Drowned), on Lake Nipissing was named after an accident in the mid-1780s in which eleven men drowned, and crosses were erected for each of them.[125] The crosses often served as warnings to travelers of the dangers of a particular set of rapids or a portage.[126]

Deceased voyageurs were also buried at impromptu graveyards near posts.[127] Voyageurs could be very particular about the location of these graveyards, wanting to ensure that the graves were protected. After one of his men died, bourgeois James McKenzie complained: "[T]hree Men were this day employed but to no purpose to Dig a Grave among the Rocks behind the Fort- I told them before they began that the prettiest as well as the easiest place to Dig a Grave would be on Pointe au Sable but with that Spirit of Contradiction which is peculiar to all Frenchmen they every one of them denied it at the same time ridiculing me for proposing to inter a *Français* who by being so is sacred on a piece of land where the Indians always encamped & might profane his Tomb by scraping skins on it, &c., &c."[128] On some occasions remains were transported back to Canada to be buried in consecrated ground.[129]

Sometimes voyageurs who had left the service but continued to work in the pays d'en haut as independent traders (called freemen, see chapter 9) were also buried according to the rites of the Roman Catholic Church. One aged freemen, Jean Baptiste Bouché, died at sixty-nine. Alexander Ross and his crew "buried him in [their] camp, and burned the grave over, so that no enemy might disturb his remains; and near to the spot [stood] a friendly tree, bearing the inscription of his name, age, and the date of his death."[130] Because the man was sick for a long time before his death and was immobilized for his last ten days, we may assume that the voyageurs followed his wishes for a Catholic burial. Sometimes voyageurs had their Aboriginal wives buried according to Roman Catholic tradition.[131] In an exceptional case a voyageur performed an emergency baptism of another voyageur's Aboriginal wife on the verge of her death.[132] Voyageurs could have their children in the Northwest baptized and buried according to rites of the Roman Catholic Church.[133] Catholic rites were primarily observed in times of danger or death and served as vivid signs of voyageurs' roots.

Voyageurs' "magico-religious" beliefs and practices both shaped and were shaped by their workplace in the pays d'en haut in numerous ways. After they left the parish churches of Montreal, voyageurs were obliged to remember as best they could supplications to God and the saints and repudiations of Satan without the guidance of a priest. Improvisations of these rites became the order of the day as voyageurs moved farther away from the St. Lawrence valley and stayed in the pays d'en haut for lengthening periods of time. They became more open to nonchurch influences that included their journeys, the environment, their masters, and Aboriginal peoples. Rituals performed both on canoe journeys and at interior posts served as both models and mirrors of voyageurs' identity, reflecting changes in preoccupations and visibly displaying new values. The ritual prayer at St. Anne's, described in the quotation at the beginning of this chapter, mock baptisms, and burial practices show voyageurs' continuing adherence to Roman Catholicism, while prayers or appeals to deities reveals that many voyageurs embraced aspects of Aboriginal cosmologies. Voyageurs' practice of naming is most illustrative of voyageurs integrating themselves with the spaces over which they traveled, constructing a place for themselves in the pays d'en haut. By participating in rituals of identity, voyageurs made their cultural values distinct and clear and defined and asserted their power. In the next chapter we shall see how voyageurs asserted their power through their labor and expressed cultural values through song.

4. It Is the Paddle That Brings Us

Voyageurs Working in Canoes

C'est l'aviron qui nous mène

M'en revenant de la joli' Rochelle,
J'ai recontré trois jolies demoiselles.
C'est l'aviron qui nous mèn', qui nous mont',
C'est l'aviron qui nous monte en haut.

It is the Paddle That Brings Us

Riding along the road from Rochelle city,
I met three girls and all of them were pretty.
It is the paddle that brings us, that brings us,
It is the paddle that brings us up there.[1]

Imagine voyageurs paddling up the Ottawa River, fourteen men in a large canoe, coordinating their strokes with the song "It Is the Paddle That Brings Us," repetitive and melodic, creating ambiguous images of frustrated lovers and romantic foils. The song describes how a young man accompanied a woman to her home, where she toasted her father, mother, brother, and sisters, and her lover! This song was one of many that voyageurs sang while they paddled canoes, transporting furs and trade goods vast distances among the far-flung posts. Canoe crews ranged from four people to as many as eighteen per canoe, and coordinating strokes required some kind of verbal direction. Instead of relying on counting, coxswaining, or chanting, voyageurs sang repetitive songs.

Although voyageurs' voices are difficult to find in the documentary record, echoes of them can be found in their songs. German explorer Johann

Georg Kohl, who traveled around Lake Superior in the 1850s, observed: "The Voyageurs accompany and embroider with song nearly everything they do—their fishery, their heavy tugging at the oar, their social meetings at the camp fire; and many a jest, many a comic incident, many a moving strain, which, if regarded closely, will not endure criticism, *there* serves to dispel ennui. If even at times no more than a 'tra-la-la-la!' it rejoices the human heart that is longing for song and melody."[2] Voyageurs' elaborate repertoire of songs constituted an expressive literary genre. Some song lyrics portrayed the material details of voyageurs' working lives, such as the line "My canoe's of bark, light as a feather" from the song "My Birch-Bark Canoe."[3] Other songs were long lamentations, called *complaintes*, which told stories of particularly tragic events in the fur trade, commemorating the victims. The most famous of these, "The Little Rock," records the story of Jean Cadieux (or Cayeux), who sacrificed himself to help his crew escape from some enemy Iroquois.[4] Many of the songs were old French ballads such as "At the Clear Running Fountain," "In the Gay Spring Time," and "It Is the Paddle That Brings Us," predating voyageurs' work in the fur trade and even predating the establishment of New France's colony in the St. Lawrence valley.[5] The range of songs reveals both voyageurs' deep ties to their homes in French Canada and their efforts to create a place for themselves in the pays d'en haut.

Voyageurs' singing accompanied many of their activities while working on the canoes, such as loading cargo, paddling, running rapids, portaging, tracking, and unloading the lading when they arrived at their destinations. Voyageurs were stereotyped by their masters as loyal "beasts of burden," unthinkingly performing feats of brute strength and endurance. Their actual working routines, however, showed that voyageurs were competent, highly skilled laborers, who performed tasks that required organization, skill, resourcefulness, and dexterity. Labor historians studying the social construction of skill among presumably unskilled workers, such as loggers, shantymen, or sailors, have shown a pattern where certain jobs were labeled as unskilled simply because a large pool of men had learned the required manual skills in boyhood.[6] This was true of voyageurs. They developed the strength and expertise to pack and carry goods while growing up on farms and could quickly learn paddling techniques while on-board the canoes. The postconquest British bourgeois may have viewed voyageurs as somehow "innately" suited to this difficult job because of the long tradition of fur trading in New France. Since the beginning of the French colony, settlers in the St. Lawrence valley had been coureurs de bois and voyageurs. The British bourgeois probably thought that long tradition was ingrained in all French Canadian men.

As farmers in the St. Lawrence valley, voyageurs were accustomed to grinding toil and dealing with the tribulations of weather and rough terrain. Although setting out to work in the unknown Northwest was more challenging than farming on a physical and psychological level, their experiences in the St. Lawrence valley provided some preparation. As on their farms, the working lives of voyageurs followed seasonal patterns.[7] In the summer months, when waterways were free of ice, voyageurs worked at a frenetic pace, transporting goods and furs to and from Montreal, interior depots, and far-flung posts. In the winter months, at a slightly more relaxed pace, voyageurs built and maintained posts, established trading and social ties with Aboriginal peoples, and built up food stocks of pemmican and dried meat and fish. There is no question that the job of voyageurs was difficult. They were hired to perform near-miraculous feats of transporting goods and furs over immense distances and challenging canoe routes. Colonel George Landmann described the work of voyageurs in the late eighteenth century: "No men in the world are more severely worked than are these Canadian voyageurs. I have known them to work in a canoe twenty hours out of twenty-four, and go on at that rate during a fortnight or three weeks without a day of rest or any dimminution of labour; but it is not with impunity they so exert themselves; they lose much flesh in the performance of such journies, though the quantity of food they consume is incredible."[8] Although this is probably an exaggeration, it reflects the extent to which voyageurs' jobs were considered difficult. They paddled for long days through all sorts of challenging rivers and lakes and carried the ladings over numerous and difficult portages. Voyageurs took pride in difficult feats of strength, endurance, and daring, which helped create a space for accommodation between them and their employers. Yet they exerted some control over the work. They organized time in a particular way, in terms of both hours and days. Weather, tasks, daily needs, and leisure, such as pipe smoking, determined the pace of the work. Singing became especially important as a means to humanize the work place. Singing had two primary functions: setting the pace of work, and providing a forum for pleasure and creativity. This chapter will explore voyageurs' work in the canoe, paying particular attention to how songs were woven into these daily tasks.

Songs and Their Sources

Certainly many groups of all male sojourners, such as sailors and lumberjacks, sang while they worked. But what made singing central to voyageurs' working lives was its important function of coordinating paddling. Voyageurs learned many songs while growing up on farms in the St. Lawrence valley, but they refashioned these songs in distinct ways when working in the fur trade. Bourgeois, clerks, explorers, and travelers in the pays d'en haut virtually always mentioned voyageurs' singing. The French Duke de la Rouchefoucauld Liancourt, visiting Upper Canada from France in the 1790s, commented that French Canadian voyageurs "according to their custom ceased not a moment to sing. . . . they [were] only interrupted by the laugh they occasion[ed]."[9] Fur trader Ross Cox commented in 1816 that "the light-hearted Canadians under [springtime] influence . . . chanted forth their wild and pleasing *chansons à l'aviron* [songs of the paddle]."[10] In 1832 Captain George Back, former member of Sir John Franklin's 1821 Arctic exploration, was exploring in the barren lands north of Lake Athabasca when he wrote that voyageurs in his canoe "roared out to [the voyageurs on shore] to 's'embarquer [to embark],' and they paddled away to the merry tune of a lively canoe song."[11]

Some of these commentators recorded the titles of songs sung by the voyageurs. Thomas L. McKenny, the American superintendent of Indian affairs, who traveled around the Great Lakes in the 1820s, and R. M Ballantyne, who worked for the HBC in the 1840s, both noted the song "Rose Blanche" (White rose) as a favorite of voyageurs.[12] American naturalist and explorer Robert Kennicott, who traveled extensively in the northwest of North America, cited the song "À la Claire Fontaine" (The clear-running fountain) as a quintessential voyageur song.[13] The prominent Irish writer Anna Jameson, visiting Canada in the 1830s, noted several titles in the following passage: "They all sing in unison, raising their voices and marking the time with their paddles. One always led, but in these there was a diversity of taste and skill. If I wished to hear 'En roulant ma boule, roulette,' [My ball is rolling along] I applied to Le Duc. Jacques excelled in 'La belle rose blanche' [The beautiful white rose], and Louis was great in 'Trois canards s'en vont baignant' [Three ducks bathing]."[14] One wonders about the extent to which these voyageurs were performing for Jameson, but nonetheless their apparent glee in singing reveals their enjoyment. Better singers were usually selected to lead the crew in song, which signified that the voyageurs made efforts to improve the quality of their singing and took pride in their performances. Duke de la Rochefoucauld Liancourt observed, "[O]ne of them sings a song, which the rest repeat, and all row to the tune."[15]

Unfortunately few of these observers recorded the lyrics to these songs. The sparse evidence is exciting because it reveals both lyrics that voyageurs created as well as instances where voyageurs changed or customized lyrics to French ballads. An exhaustive study of the development of these songs is beyond the scope of this book, but a few examples are illuminating. Folklorist Marius Barbeau asserts that voyageurs sang well-known French Canadian folksongs, but "alive and variable, [the songs] constantly yielded a trifle to the mannerisms of individual singers and the utilities they served either in the settlements or in their peregrinations. Canoemen, more than others, were apt to fashion refrains that reflected new surroundings and features, like canoe and paddle."[16] The well-known Irish poet Thomas Moore visited Canada in 1804 and was delighted by the voyageurs that transported him from Montreal to Kingston. He recorded:

> *Our Voyageurs had good voices, and sung perfectly in tune together. The original words . . . appeared to be a long, incoherent story, of which I could understand but little, from the barbarous pronunciation of the Canadians. It begins Dans mon chemin j'ai recontré / Deux cavaliers très-bien montés; [In my street I met / Two soldiers on horse] . . . and the refrain of the verse was, A l'ombre d'un bois je m'en vais jouer, / A l'ombre d'un bois je m'en vais danser. [In the shade of a tree I'm going to play; / In the shade of a tree I'm going to dance]. I ventured to harmonize this air, and have published it. Without that charm, which association gives to every little memorial of scenes or feelings that are past, the melody may perhaps be thought common or trifling; but I remember when we have entered, at sunset, upon one of those beautiful lakes, into which the St. Lawrence so grandly and unexpectedly opens, I have heard this simple air with a pleasure which the finest compositions of the first masters have never given me; and now, there is not a note of it which does not recal to my memory the dip of our oars in the St. Lawrence, the flight of our boat down the Rapids, and all those new and fanciful impressions to which my heart was alive during the whole of this very interesting voyage.*[17]

Although Moore published his famous "Canadian Boat Song" in 1806, he was apparently not inspired enough to extensively record these songs.[18] The Baltimore artist Frank Blackwell Mayer regretted not recording songs he had heard in the 1850s around the Great Lakes. He wrote: "I was unsuccessful in procuring any comple[te] records of these musical rarities, the politeness of many of my French friends consisting rather in smiling promises than a conscientious fulfillment."[19] He did record a few bars of music of a "Canadian Voyageur song" that he also titled "Chanson du Nord."[20]

Fortunately, one fur trader recorded the lyrics of a handful of voyageur songs. Edward Ermatinger, an apprentice and clerk for the HBC from 1818 to 1828, traveled extensively between York Factory, Red River, and the Columbia

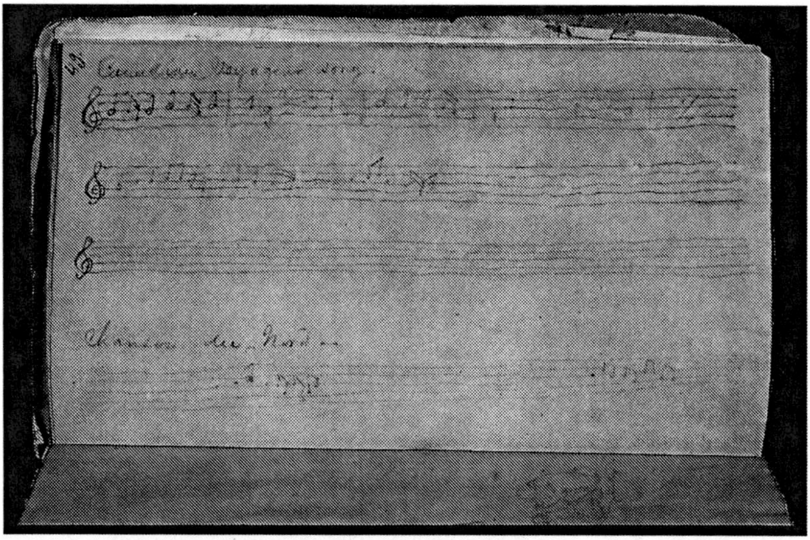

Fig. 4. "Chanson du Nord," by Frank Blackwell Mayer. Sketchbook no. 43, Minnesota 49, Oversize Ayer Art. Courtesy Edward E. Ayer Collection, The Newberry Library, Chicago.

River and had ample opportunity to learn voyageur songs. He transcribed eleven voyageur songs, which remained hidden in the Ermatinger family archives in Portland, Oregon, until 1943, when they were lent for copying to the Public Archives of Canada.[21] Marius Barbeau published Ermatinger's collection of eleven voyageur songs in 1954 in the *Journal of American Folklore*.[22] These songs are all old French ballads, including "J'ai Trop Grand Peur des Loups" (I am very scared of the wolves), "Mes Blancs Moutons Garder" (Minding my white sheep), "C'est L'Oiseau et L'Alouette" (Here is the bird and the lark), and "Un Oranger Il y a" (There was an orange tree).

The traveler who paid the most attention to voyageurs' songs was Kohl. After questioning many of the old and retired voyageurs in the Lake Superior area, he speculated that in addition to old French ballads, voyageurs sang many songs that were informally composed and constantly changing but never written down: "I here allude especially to the songs composed on the spot which are characteristic of the land and its inhabitants, as the people paint in them their daily adventures themselves, and the surrounding nature. . . . Generally they designate their own most peculiar songs as 'chansons de Voyageur,' and exclude from them songs they have derived from France and elsewhere."[23] Kohl goes on to emphasize that the voyageurs' own songs (rather than French ballads) were very long and repetitive, which were particularly suitable to long canoe journeys: "They pause upon every idea, repeat it with a certain degree of admiration, and break off into musical refrains and repetitions."[24] Voyageurs were often more interested in the sound of a word and its capacity for rhyme and repetition than in its meaning. In her cataloging of voyageurs' songs, however, scholar Madeleine Béland has demonstrated that many aspects of voyageurs' lives were expressed in their songs, such as their engagements, departures, food, and loneliness.[25] Expressing significant experiences and recording them in work songs was part of a unique voyageur oral tradition. For example, the song "Quand un Chretien se determine a voyager" (When a Christian decides to travel) is about a priest who counsels novices on the difficulties that the job entails, clearly outlining dangers such as the weather, waves, exhaustion, mosquitoes, fatal accidents, and hostile Aboriginal peoples.[26]

These scattered references show that voyageurs sang three kinds of songs: romantic and melodic French ballads, lamentations for tragedies that occurred to fellow voyageurs, and everyday work songs, composed on the spot and constantly changing. The French ballads reflect the deep-rooted tradition, carried over from France by their ancestors, of honoring romantic love and family. Later lamentations retained the form of the French ballad, but the words reflected voyageurs' own growing development of a tradition and the history of working in the fur trade. Everyday work songs allowed voyageurs to turn their work into lively and repetitive songs, which helped them maintain a pace, pass the time, and complain about their lot.

Routes

How did conditions of working in a canoe shape voyageurs' singing? After voyageurs signed a contract, they met their new masters in Lachine, a community a few miles west of Montreal, where the Ottawa River flows into the St. Lawrence River at Lac de Deux-Montagnes (Lake of Two Mountains). Here men were divided into groups by their destinations, and crews were formed and assigned to canoes. Pork eaters, or the men hired to work in the first leg of the journey, between Montreal and Grand Portage or Fort William at the western tip of Lake Superior, were separated from the northmen, those hired to go on to the Northwest interior posts. Pork eaters and northmen probably did not paddle in the same canoes, even though they would all be headed toward Lake Superior. Pork eaters worked for only the summer months, during the ice-free season, while northmen had engaged to work year-round for their masters. The bourgeois probably tried to keep these two groups separate and encouraged competition between them. The Athabasca men wintered north of Lake Athabasca, had to traverse the most difficult portages and travel the longest distances. In the limited ice-free season they could not make it to Lake Superior and transported their cargo as far as they could, usually to Rainy Lake, missing the summer rendezvous at Lake Superior (see chapter 6). Thus they did not interact at all with pork eaters and interacted very little with northmen.

Despite the differences between these workforces, absolute boundaries should not be drawn between them. Usually northmen and Athabasca men started their voyageur careers as pork eaters, and men often moved back and forth among the three groups. These occupational categories were distinct, but they were closely connected to one another. Not only did many northmen become trained in the service while they were pork eaters, but their tough reputations depended on comparing them to the less-experienced pork eaters. Likewise, all voyageurs were measured against Athabasca men.

Another formative element of voyageurs' working lives was geography and their specific canoe routes. The trade extended vast distances in North America, and bourgeois constantly explored new ground further west and north, especially during the period of increasing competition between the Montreal-based companies and the Hudson's Bay Company. The immense transportation route was divided into two parts. The first comprised the routes between Montreal and the major provisioning center on Lake Superior, which was Grand Portage until 1804, when it moved fifty miles north to Fort Kaministiquia, which was renamed Fort William.[27] This part of the transportation system had two major routes. The first was up the St. Lawrence River and through the Great Lakes, passing by centers such as York (present-day Toronto), on the north shore of Lake Ontario; Niagara, between Lake Ontario and Lake Erie; Detroit, between Lake Erie and Lake Huron; Michilimackinac, between Lake Huron and Lake Michigan; and Sault Ste. Marie, between Lake Huron and Lake Superior (see map 2). Most of the route was upriver, against the current. Lake schooners and sloops came to be used on the Great Lakes by the early eighteenth century to help transport goods and provisions.[28] The second route was up the Ottawa, or Grand, River, then west along the Mattawa River, across Lake Nipissing and along the French River, to Georgian Bay and Lake Huron and finally through to Lake Superior (see map 2).[29] Most of this route was upstream when traveling west (although the section between Lake Nipissing and Georgian Bay was downstream). It was thus much faster to travel east to Montreal than it was to travel west to the interior. For both routes crews canoed along the north shore of Lake Superior, which involved a set of challenges and skills distinct from river travel. Rather than dealing with currents and portages, crews had to monitor wind, waves, and tides.

The second major part of the Montreal fur trade transportation system operated out of Grand Portage and Fort William and spread out thousands of miles west, north, and south to the interior fur trade posts (see map 3). The portage at the western point of Lake Superior was between eight and ten miles (depending on the location) and took about fifteen days to cross. The height of land was passed just west of Lake Superior, after which travel westward was with the current. Travel to the interior thus was faster than the return to Lake Superior because it was mainly downstream. The drainage systems into Hudson Bay and the Arctic and Pacific Oceans complicated routes even further.[30]

Routes to different departments varied. The easiest posts to reach were those around the Great Lakes, Lake Nipigon, and the region north of Lake Superior, but most brigades were sent out far to the north and west, especially as regions closer to the Great Lakes became overtrapped after 1805.[31] These brigades traveled to Bas de la Rivière, renamed Fort Alexander in 1807, where the Winnipeg River flows into Lake Winnipeg. Various routes

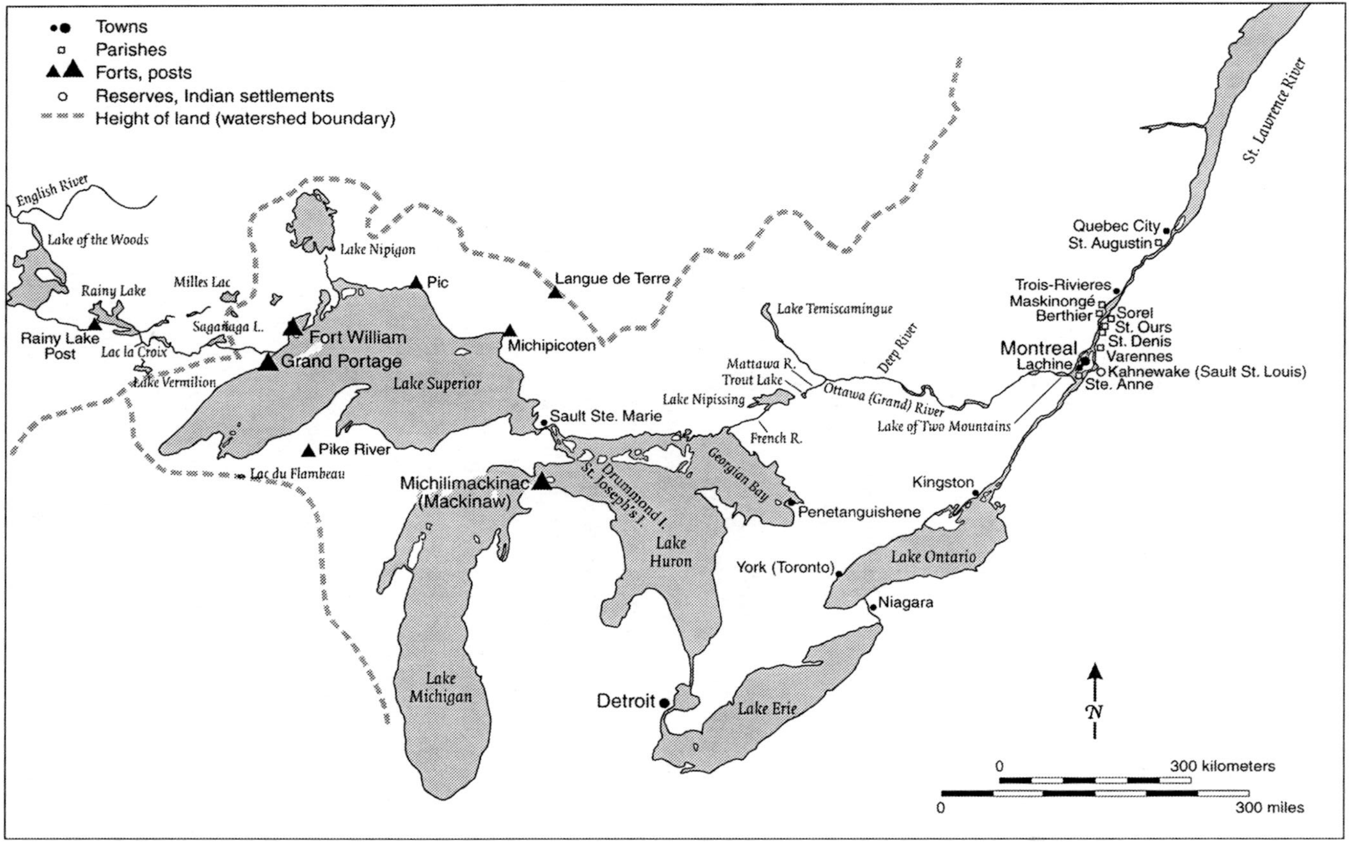

Map 2. Routes of the pork eaters

led through the Rainy Lake and Lake of the Woods river systems before entering the Winnipeg River.[32] Fort Alexander acted as an interior depot and as a hub for interior travel. The main routes that set out from Fort Alexander included southward up the Red River to Pembina and the Missouri Country and west along the Assiniboine River; to the northern tip of Lake Winnipeg, west along the Saskatchewan River, following both the south and north branches; and further north from Cumberland House along the Churchill or the English River to the Athabasca District (see map 3).

Rates of Travel

Waterways in the Northwest were free of ice for about five months of the year, but of course the ice-free season shortened as one traveled north. Canoe brigades had to complete their return trips to Lake Superior from either Montreal or the interior post in that time. Transporting lading the three thousand miles between Athabasca and Montreal was taxing.[33] The longer the trip, the faster the men were obliged to travel to beat the ice. Rates of travel could be controlled by the pace of the song, but the size of the canoe as well as travel conditions determined progress.

The small and light express canoes, which carried mail and news as their only lading, traveled the fastest. Canoe speed was also affected by the size of the lading: the more heavily packed the canoe, the slower its speed. For this reason smaller north canoes, or *canots du nord*, generally tended to travel more quickly than the larger master canoes, or *canots du maître*, used on the Great Lakes run, but the master canoes could better withstand the waves and strong currents of large rivers and lakes. The canots du maître were usually thirty feet in length but could be up to thirty-six feet long and were from four to six feet wide in the middle. The canots du nord were smaller, usually twenty to twenty-seven feet in length, and could carry a little more than half the cargo of a canot du maître. Sometimes voyageurs traveled in a *canot bâtard*, or bastard canoe, which were larger than north canoes but smaller than master canoes.[34] One type of bastard canoe was between twenty-nine and thirty-three feet long, with crews between six and eight.

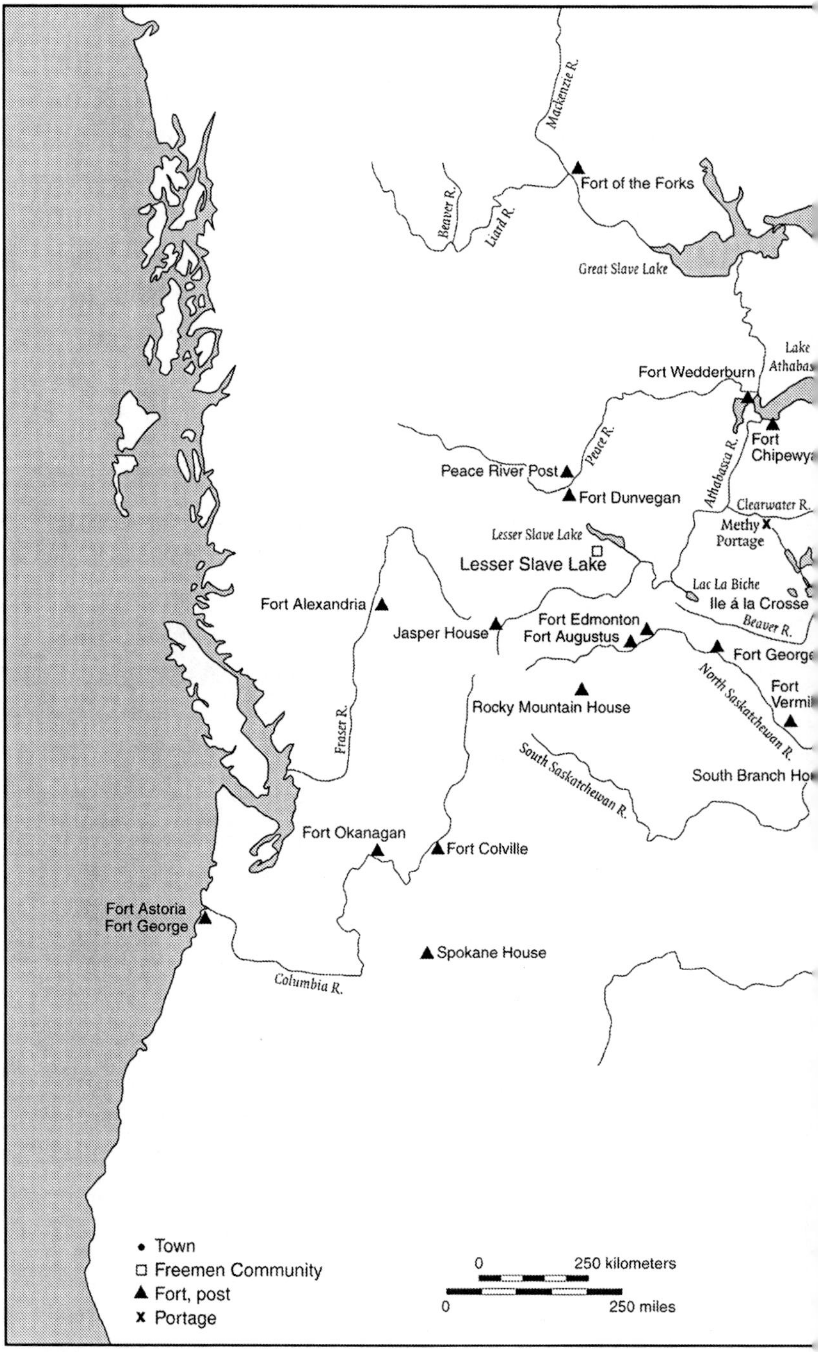

Mackenzie R.
Fort of the Forks
Beaver R.
Liard R.
Great Slave Lake
Lake Athabas
Fort Wedderburn
Fort Chipewy
Peace R.
Peace River Post
Fort Dunvegan
Athabasca R.
Clearwater R.
Methy Portage
Lesser Slave Lake
Lesser Slave Lake
Lac La Biche
Ile á la Crosse
Fort Alexandria
Jasper House
Fort Edmonton
Fort Augustus
Beaver R.
Fort George
North Saskatchewan R.
Fort Vermi
Rocky Mountain House
Fraser R.
South Saskatchewan R.
South Branch Ho
Fort Okanagan
Fort Colville
Fort Astoria
Fort George
Spokane House
Columbia R.
Town
Freemen Community
Fort, post
Portage
0
250 kilometers
0
250 miles

Map 3. Routes of the northmen

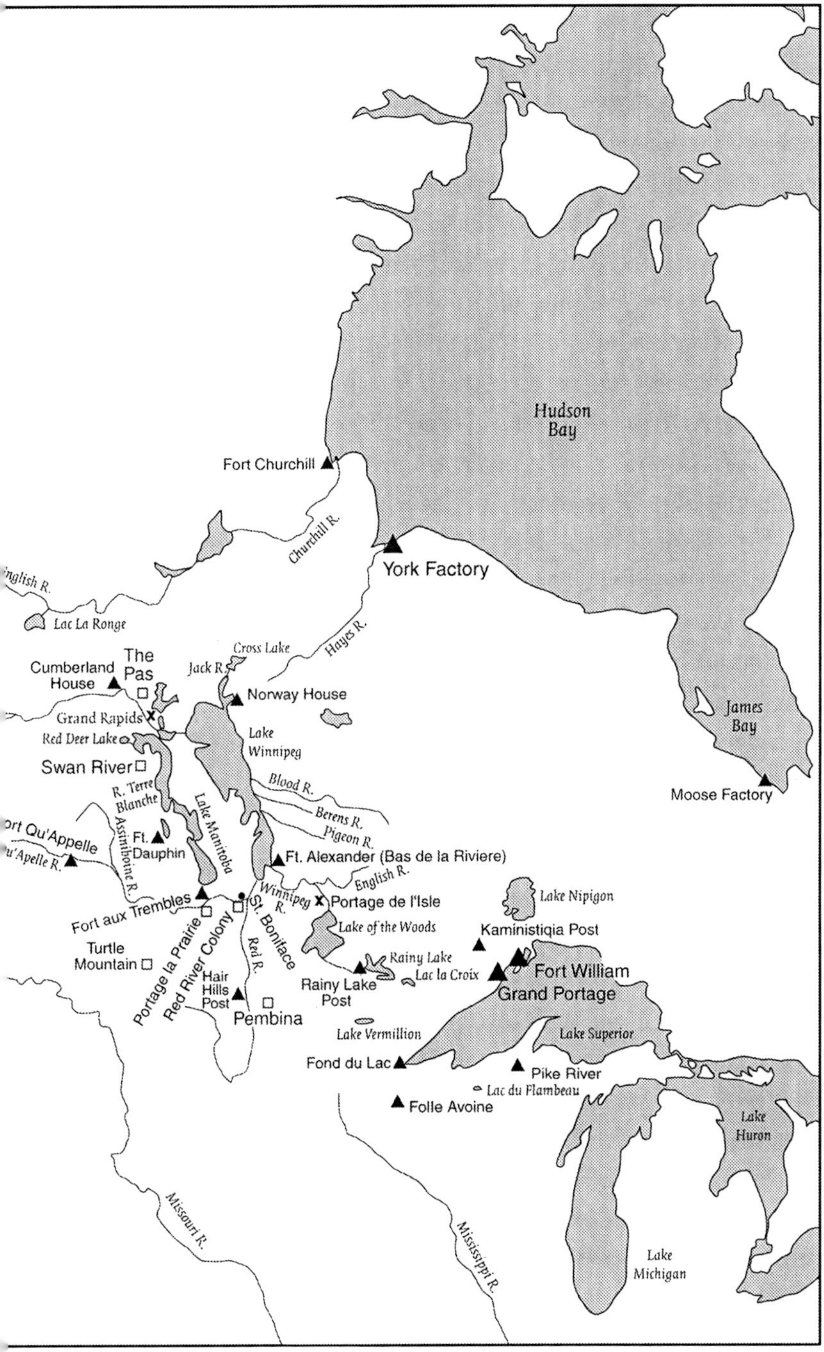
Hudson Bay
Fort Churchill
Churchill R.
York Factory
nglish R.
Lac La Ronge
Hayes R.
Cross Lake
Jack R.
The Pas
Cumberland House
Norway House
Grand Rapids
Red Deer Lake
Lake Winnipeg
Swan River
Blood R.
R. Terre Blanche
Lake Manitoba
Berens R.
Pigeon R.
ort Qu'Appelle
u'Apelle R.
Assiniboine R.
Ft. Dauphin
Ft. Alexander (Bas de la Riviere)
English R.
Fort aux Trembles
Winnipeg R.
Portage de l'Isle
St. Boniface
Red R.
Portage la Prairie
Red River Colony
Turtle Mountain
Hair Hills Post
Pembina
Lake of the Woods
Rainy Lake
Lac la Croix
Rainy Lake Post
Lake Vermillion
Lake Nipigon
Kaministiqia Post
Fort William
Grand Portage
Lake Superior
Fond du Lac
Pike River
Lac du Flambeau
Folle Avoine
James Bay
Moose Factory
Lake Huron
Lake Michigan
Missouri R.
Mississippi R.

A second type of bastard canoe was between eighteen and twenty-four feet long with crews between two and four.[35] Canoe speed was also affected by the direction of the current and the number of rapids and portages along the route. Weather was the most unpredictable variable, as strong winds and rain could slow and often halt brigades during their journeys.[36] Low water levels in dry years slowed travel and increased the number of portages. If crew members were ill or injured, crews were slowed by the decrease in manpower and were sometimes grounded until wounds healed and illnesses passed or replacement paddlers could be found. Finally, canoes generally traveled faster at the beginning of the transport season, when crews were still fresh from a winter of relative rest. It was thus fortunate for the men working the Great Lakes routes, as their journey to Lake Superior was against the current, while their journey back to Montreal at the end of the season was with the current. The interior brigades were not so fortunate, as most of their journeys to Lake Superior were with the current, while their journey back to the interior was against the current.

Bourgeois Peter Grant estimated that canots du nord traveled an average of six miles an hour but could increase their speed to eight or nine miles an hour when the men put up a sail in a good wind.[37] At these rates voyageurs could travel between about 75 and 125 miles a day, but portaging would likely have reduced this to an average maximum of 50 miles a day, provided weather was optimal for travel. Fur trade historian Clairborne Skinner speculates that seventeenth-century fur trading canoes could at best travel 20 miles a day and often as little as 12 miles a day.[38] However, in 1793 John McDonell recorded traveling as far as 24 leagues in a day in a canot du maître, with fourteen paddlers and little cargo. Charles Gates asserts that canoemen used the term league to refer to 2 miles; McDonell's estimate would thus be close to 50 miles in a day.[39] Skinner's dramatically lower estimates may be confined to the routes between Lake Superior and Lake Winnipeg, which had more (and more onerous) portages than most other routes. At the generous estimate of 50 miles a day, canoes could travel about fifteen hundred miles in a month, provided every day had ideal weather, which was unlikely. Eric Morse asserts that a freight or master canoe could only do one thousand miles per month at best.[40] Crews traveling to the farthest outposts in the Athabasca and Rocky Mountain districts had to travel more than four thousand miles in the months when the waterways were free.[41] Every day counted in the race to beat the winter freeze.

Men employed in the Great Lakes run were usually away from Montreal for five months, the length of time in which waterways were ice free.[42] The trip from Montreal to Grand Portage and Fort William averaged a month and a half to two months. The return trip to Montreal was much faster, traveling with the current, and averaged three weeks to a month. In June 1800 George Landmann set out to break the record for the journey from St. Joseph's Island near Detroit to Montreal, which had been set by Simon McTavish at seven and three-quarters days. After purchasing a new canoe, hiring the best men available, including a famous guide for the Ottawa River, and taking a full load himself at portages, Landmann was able to perform the journey in seven and one-quarter days.[43] Those men whose yearly trips were shorter spent the extra time during the summer sorting and packing the goods and furs at Grand Portage and Fort William.

Interior canoes left Lake Superior in mid-July, and the longest distance to travel was to the Athabasca District; these brigades usually shortened their journey by using the Rainy Lake post as the terminus, rather than Lake Superior, which shortened the journey by about ten days. The trip from Rainy Lake to the next inland administrative center at Fort Alexander, or Bas de la Rivière, at the mouth of Lake Winnipeg averaged about a week.[44] The eastward journey from Fort Vermilion on the North Saskatchewan River to Fort William could take a month.[45] The journey from Cumberland, at the north end of Lake Winnipeg, eastward to Rainy Lake averaged about ten days.[46]

Canoes

Securing canoes for transport was a vital part of the trade, and canoes assumed a central place in voyageurs' lives. At least one song was specifically devoted to this important means of transportation. The song "My Birch-Bark Canoe," recorded by a French-Canadian ballad writer and originating among voyageurs in the Northwest, goes:

In my birch-bark, canoeing, in the cool of evening I ride
Where I have braved every tempest in St. Lawrence's rolling tide.
My canoe's of bark, light as a feather
That is stripped from silvery birch;
And the seams with roots sewn together,
The paddles white made of birch.
I take my canoe, send it chasing
All the rapids and billows acrost;
There so swiftly see it go racing,
And it never the current has lost.
It's when I come on the portage, I take my canoe on my back.
Set it on my head topsy-turvy; it's my cabin too for the night.
Along the river banks I've wandered, all along the St. Lawrence's tide
I have known the savage races and the tongues that them divide.
You are my voyageur companion!
I'll gladly die within my canoe.
And on my grave beside the canyon
You'll overturn my canoe.
His cart is beloved of the ploughman, the hunter loves his gun, his hound;
The musician is a music lover—to my canoe I'm bound.[47]

The song suggests to novice voyageurs how canoes are made and how to carry the canoe across a portage, as well as cautioning new voyageurs about the many Aboriginal societies they will encounter along the canoe routes.

Despite the canoe's ubiquity, very few voyageurs, clerks, or bourgeois became expert canoe makers. Constructing canoes well took more time and skill than most voyageurs could afford on their rushed journeys as porters. Most of the canoes were purchased either from canoe "shops" in Canada or more regularly from Aboriginal peoples in the Northwest. Brigades setting out from Montreal purchased canoes from manufacturers in Montreal and Trois-Rivières.[48] Bourgeois sometimes built up a store of canoes and other boats at the point of departure in Lachine.[49] Other canoes were built at posts in the pays d'en haut, such as at the island of St. Joseph near Michilimackinac, Sault Ste. Marie, Grand Portage, and Fort William.[50] In the interior canoes were procured from Aboriginal people, who were often hired specifically to build them.[51] Foremen or steersmen were sometimes allowed to choose a canoe when a brigade came upon many canoes for sale en route. For example, Duncan McGillivray records that when his crew found nine canoes, "after [their] foreman had chosen one for himself, the Men cast lots for the rest to avoid jealousy and confusion."[52]

The voyageurs who learned the skill of building canoes were held in high regard by everyone in the pays d'en haut. Because canoes were damaged frequently, most men became proficient at repairing them. Through constant repair, a few able men learned the next step of building a canoe from scratch. Bourgeois and clerks frequently wrote about being in need of more or stronger canoes.[53] In May 1806, after spending a day taking apart a canoe, regumming and resetting it, only to find it still leaked, Simon Fraser complained: "This is the new canoe that La Malice made at Trout Lake. it is not only ill made but the bark is very bad. I have the canoe I came off with from Lac la Pluie last summer which is not much better than the other. It was a good canoe but got much spoiled last Fall in the ice at Trout Lake and afterwards going down the Portage and I could not get it renewed this spring for the want of a canoe maker."[54] Canoes were occasionally stashed along a route when they were no longer needed or stored for the winter. For example, on Rivière des Saulteaux in the fall of 1803, George Nelson had his men hide their canoes in a swamp until the following spring, when they would be used again.[55] Unfortunately canoes sometimes did not last through the winter, as they became damaged by animals or the elements.[56]

Canoes were generally made from birch bark, sewn together in large pieces with *wattape*, or spruce roots, and stretched over a wooden frame, which could be made from birch, spruce, or cedar, or whatever was available. The seams were sealed with gum from spruce or pine.[57] Although canoes were light and seemingly flimsy, they could carry a tremendous weight, canots du maître up to five tonnes and canots du nord up to a tonne and a half.[58] Long poles called *grands-perches*, three to four inches in diameter, were laid along the bottom of the canoes, across the ribs, to help distribute the weight of the cargo and crew evenly. Men sat on rolled-up blankets while they paddled.[59] Although the design and construction of canoes were copied from Aboriginal technology, fur traders' canoes were generally larger than Aboriginal peoples' canoes and designed to carry far more lading.[60]

Traders piled their canoes high with cargo.[61] Aside from the men and ladings of trade goods and furs, the canoes also carried provisions and maintenance equipment. The usual load for a canot du maître was about sixty to sixty-five packs, each weighing ninety pounds.[62] Canots du nord heading from Grand Portage into the interior carried about thirty-five packs, about 70 percent of which were trade goods, the other 30 percent being provisions, stores, and baggage. In the late eighteenth century, Alexander Mackenzie described the lading of a brigade leaving Lachine, headed for the interior. Each canoe contained the men's baggage and sixty-five packages of goods. In addition, each had six hundredweight of biscuit, two hundredweight of pork, and three bushels of peas for the men's provisions.[63]

The complement of goods was completed with two oilcloths to cover the goods, a sail, an axe, a towing line, a kettle, and a sponge to bail water, with a quantity of gum, bark, and wattape to repair the vessel. Passenger Colonel George Landmann remarked on how carefully equipment was stowed in the canoes during his 1798 voyage from Montreal to the interior. Packs were placed on the poles laid along the bottom of the boat so that none touched the fragile bottom or sides of the canoe. In addition to the equipment mentioned by Mackenzie, Landmann noted that voyageurs brought their own ten-foot setting poles and paddles.[64]

Brigades traveling on the Great Lakes route were made up of from three to six canoes.[65] In each brigade a captain was responsible for steering and guiding, tending the canoes and property on board, and commanding the men.[66] Crews manning the larger canots du maître, used on the Great Lakes run, usually consisted of a guide, steersman, and eight middlemen or paddlers.[67] Cargoes in a canoe depended on the number of men on board. George Heriot asserted: "The [North West] company trading to the north-west sends every year, to the posts on Lake Superior, about fifty canoes loaded with merchandise. . . . Sixty-five pieces of merchandize of ninety pounds each; eight men,

Fig. 5. Canot du maître. *Shooting the Rapids*, by Frances Anne Hopkins, 1879, oil on canvas. Accession 1989-401-2, reproduction C-002774. Courtesy of the Library and Archives Canada, Ottawa.

each weighing at least one hundred and sixty pounds; baggage allowed to these men, at forty pounds each, together with the weight of their provisions. The whole cargo of a canoe is, therefore, not less than eight thousand three hundred and ninety pounds."[68] A canot du maître could carry up to fourteen men but could be paddled with as few as five paddlers, one clerk, and one interpreter when the cargo was particularly bulky or when labor was in short supply.[69] Canots du maître were not built to a standard size, so instances of larger canoes carrying more men and goods occasionally appear in the sources. For example, on May 24, 1810, Gabriel Franchère recorded nineteen men—four bourgeois, one clerk, and fourteen voyageurs—traveling in one lightly equipped canot du maître from Montreal to Michilimackinac.[70] On a journey from Fort William to Montreal in the summer of 1814, Franchère reported "fourteen stout voyageurs to man [their] large canoe."[71]

At Grand Portage or Fort William, ladings were exchanged between the canots du maître and smaller canots du nord traveling into the interior on smaller waterways. Large brigades of between five and thirteen canots du nord left Grand Portage together every fall and gradually split up as each went its separate way to different departments.[72] Crews usually comprised five to six men.[73] Table 3 shows that in the early fall of 1808 and 1809, crews traveling from Fort William to various inland posts ranged from four to seven men, including some with their families.

Aboriginal wives of voyageurs and bourgeois, and their children, could accompany canoes traveling between interior posts and on trips to and from Grand Portage or Fort William. They usually traveled in their own canoes alongside the traders and sometimes helped in gathering provisions for the brigades.

Canoes setting out from Lake Superior heading to the interior traveled in brigades and carried the annual complement of trade goods for their post of destination. Likewise, on return trips from the interior posts to the large administrative centers, canoes also traveled in brigades and carried large cargoes of furs.[74] Large brigades set out from Fort Astoria or Fort George on the Pacific coast, traveling inland on trading missions. Part of the reason traders traveled in larger groups on the Pacific coast was that Aborigi-

Table 3. Crews Traveling Inland from Fort William

Year	Inland post	No. of bourgeois	No. of clerks	No. of guides	No. of interpreters	No. of voyageurs	No. of women	No. of children	Total
1808	Broken River		1			4			5
1808	Pigeon River	1		1	1	4	4	2	13
1808	Grand River	1			1	5	2	4	13
1808	Dauphin River		1			4	1		6
1809	Rivière aux Morts		1			5			6
1809	Broken River		1			5			6
1809	Dauphin River		1			6			7
Average		0	1	0	0	5	1	1	8

Note: Data from TBR, S13, George Nelson's journal, September 1, 1808–March 31, 1810, September 2 , 1808, and September 14, 1809, 2, 37 (my pagination).

nal peoples tended to be a greater threat there than in the continental interior. After the Pacific Fur Company first arrived on the Pacific coast in 1811 and set up Fort Astoria, 102 people in twelve boats headed into the interior to trade.[75] In 1812 a party traveling further inland from Fort Astoria to trade consisted of three proprietors, nine clerks, fifty-five Canadians, and twenty Sandwich Islanders (Hawaiians).[76] A spring brigade in 1814, heading overland from Fort George to Montreal, was made up of ten canoes, each carrying seven men as crew and two passengers, in all 90 people.[77] In the spring of 1817, a North West Company brigade was made up of 86 people, in two barges and nine canoes, each containing an average of twenty-two ninety-pound packages.[78]

Once brigades were in the interior, traveling between posts, crew and cargo complements varied considerably. In one brigade of four canoes, traveling from Red River to Pembina in late August 1800, under the charge of Alexander Henry the Younger, crews were made up of two or three paddlers, a bowman, a steersman, and up to three passengers per canoe, including Henry, a clerk, a guide, three wives, and three children.[79] On a trip from Dauphin River to Cumberland in May 1821, one "large" canoe held five men, twenty-five packs, a trunk, and twenty-five small kegs. A second canoe following a week later carried seven men, three women, and three children.[80] Despite this kind of variation, canots du nord were staffed on average by four to five men.[81]

Crews conveying explorers on their journeys tended to be smaller and more difficult to procure, as the risks were very high, and the work more difficult. Men deserted more frequently than when they worked on regular brigades, especially if the party became short of provisions or was threatened by Aboriginal people, as often happened. Sometimes men were engaged for easy missions, traveling through known areas, and aiding the bourgeois in finding a better route or new trading areas.[82] However, men could choose to desert even if the mission was not particularly threatening. In 1806 the NWC sponsored an expedition up the Missouri to establish trade with the Mandans and the Hidatsas. Alexander Henry the Younger and Charles Chaboillez traveled with eight other men and twenty-five horses. On their return

Fig. 6. Canot du nord. *Simon Fraser Descending the Fraser River*, by Charles William Jefferys, 1808, British Columbia, graphic. Accession 1972-26-6, reproduction C-070270. Courtesy of the Library and Archives Canada, Ottawa.

the party lost their horses, and the men became annoyed when they had to carry the cargoes on their backs. Three deserted at Turtle Mountain.[83]

The brigades of Alexander Mackenzie and Simon Fraser exploring the far north and west faced particularly dangerous ordeals. Mackenzie made several attempts in the 1790s to find an overland route to the Pacific Ocean and during his efforts mapped the Mackenzie River to the Arctic Ocean and the Peace River into the interior of the Rocky Mountains. He had endless difficulties trying to retain his men because his expeditions were so arduous, and because his voyageurs gained a particular independence and pride from their difficult experiences with him.[84] Often explorers could find suitable and experienced crews only at the interior posts. Simon Fraser set out twelve years later, in 1806, to find the route overland to the Pacific and recruited his crew from Rocky Mountain House and Dunvegan. Families sometimes accompanied exploration brigades, and Aboriginal wives especially could provide valuable assistance to the explorers.[85]

When canoes traveled together in brigades, a conductor or pilot was appointed to manage the whole brigade. Every person in the brigade was obliged to obey him, and he received a higher salary than the others.[86] The bustle and confusion of many brigades traveling together, especially as they headed out from Grand Portage or Fort William, called for firm control by the conductors.[87] Sometimes brigades held back to allow others to pass them to minimize the confusion and traffic jams.[88] Canoes in a brigade generally tried to stay as close together as possible. However, if a brigade was in a hurry, it sometimes chose to leave some canoes behind, especially if a canoe was damaged.[89] Brigades must have coordinated their singing among canoes and by doing so coordinated their pace. Presumably the pilot of the brigade either led the singing or appointed someone to do so. In a romantic flourish Robert Ballantyne recalled:

> *I have seen four canoes sweep round a promontory suddenly, and burst upon my view; while at the same moment, the wild, romantic song of the voyageurs, as they plied their brisk paddles, struck upon my ear, and I have felt the thrilling enthusiasm caused by*

> *such a scene: what, then, must have been the feelings of those who had spent a long, dreary winter in the wild North-West, far removed from the bustle and excitement of the civilised world, when thirty or forty of these picturesque canoes burst unexpectedly upon them, half inshrouded in the spray that flew from the bright, vermilion paddles, while the men, who had overcome difficulties and dangers innumerable during a long voyage through the wilderness . . . with joyful hearts at the happy termination of their trials and privations, sang, with all the force of three hundred manly voices, one of their lively airs.*[90]

Traffic in the interior could be surprisingly heavy. On the main travel routes, such as the Great Lakes run and from Lake Superior to Lake Winnipeg, canoes usually traveled in large groups fairly close to one another. For example, at Fort Alexander in late June and early July of 1808, within nine days at least seven brigades passed through or set off from the fort.[91] Minor posts could also become quite busy during peak travel seasons. At Fort Dauphin on the southwestern shore of Lake Manitoba in September 1808, eight canoes arrived in two separate brigades and stayed to repack their goods and make acquaintances with Aboriginal people in the area.[92]

Canoes frequently passed one another along the busy routes during the seasons of high travel in spring and fall. In one day on a journey from Grand Portage to Fort Alexander, Daniel Harmon's brigade was overtaken by the brigade of Charles Chaboillez and passed three canoes of Iroquois engaged to hunt beaver in the upper Red River area. Three days later his brigade passed by the Athabasca canoes.[93] On a trip from Fort Alexander to Fort Dauphin in late June 1809, George Nelson passed a freeman (former voyageur) named Dubois, seven canoes from Slave Lake, and Simon Fraser with thirty canoes.[94] Loud singing served to notify surrounding people that a canoe of voyageurs was approaching.

The task of organizing the transport of trade goods and furs could be quite complicated, and elaborate plans formed by bourgeois had to be carefully followed by crew pilots. For example, in a letter to Duncan Clark at the

Pic in June 1825, Roderick McKenzie at Fort William instructed the bourgeois Clark on the coming season's trade and transport plans. Two boats headed for Michipicoten would stop by Pic and drop off potatoes and articles and would take the Pic packs on board. If the boats were too full to take all the Pic packs, the rest should be sent in the Long Lake canoe. Mackenzie directed that Old Mallette, Belle Heneure, and Antoine Sanregret were to embark in the Long Lake canoe and the "Widow" and the "old woman" to take Mallette's canoe as far as Michipicoten. Mr. Haldane would be passing the Pic some time about the twentieth and would take any remaining furs in his canoe to Michipicoten. Mackenzie warned Clark not to neglect to send down the goods and men to go to Moose Factory. If the two boats could hold all the packs, Antoine Sanregret should remain at the Pic until Haldane passed. The men must not be allowed to remain at the Pic more than a day and a night, and they should sleep in the boat during that period. The packs should be safely stored to protect them from rain.[95] The exceptional detail of the instructions and Mackenzie's minute attention to every particular of transport and travel plans conveyed the complexity of the arrangements, especially in trying to account for uncontrollable variables such as weather and travel time.

Not only was it difficult to plan for transporting the goods, but maintaining sufficient labor could also become complicated. Men were hired along the Great Lakes route both to replace deserters and to supplement crews. In 1793 bourgeois John McDonell tried to hire a man along the Ottawa River to replace another man who had become ill.[96] Gabriel Franchère, partner in the Pacific Fur Company, tried to engage the majority of his crew at Michilimackinac in spring 1810 to convey him to the source of the Missouri and, following the route of Lewis and Clark, to the mouth of the Columbia.[97] Voyageurs were hired at Detroit for both traveling into the interior and to Montreal.[98] Men were also frequently hired at the interior posts (see chapter 2). The bourgeois and clerks often shared their servants with one another in order to best distribute the labor. In one case, on the way from Montreal to Grand Portage, John McDonell reported that one paddler was taken out of each canoe in the brigade to create a crew for a new canoe.[99] In the summer of 1803 on Rivière des Saulteaux, George Nelson "lent" some of his men to another clerk, Chaurette, for eight to nine days to assist him in a long portage.[100]

The interior was culturally and occupationally diverse and brigades passed through the territories of complex Aboriginal societies all the way from Montreal to the Pacific and the Arctic coasts. Voyageurs would have been familiar with Aboriginal peoples living close to the St. Lawrence valley, such as the Algonquian-speaking Montagnais (Innus) and the Iroquoian-speaking peoples living on Christian Indian reserves, including Hurons (Wendakes) at Lorette and primarily Mohawks at Kahnewake.[101] Trading fairs brought many different Aboriginal peoples to Montreal in the second half of the seventeenth century, such as the Odawas, the Ojibwas, and the Illinois.[102] Habitants who became voyageurs and coureurs de bois had the most contact with Aboriginal peoples from the pays d'en haut.[103]

Many people encountered along the route were integrated into the fur trade operations. For example, at the village of Hull at La Chaudière Falls, Aboriginal people (probably Ojibwes, Odawas, or Algonquins) working as raftsmen contracted out their labor to assist the voyageurs in the portage.[104] Farther along the Odawa River at the Longue Sault and Carrillon Rapids, men living alongside contracted out their labor to conduct canoes down the rapids.[105] Freemen also regularly sold provisions to voyageurs in the interior.[106] Robert Seaborne Miles, working for the HBC, met a freeman at the entrance to Lake Nipissing in June 1819 while on his way to Fort Wedderburn in the Athabasca District. He traded biscuits for fish with the freeman, and the freeman informed him that the rest of his brigade had passed by in the morning with their sails set.[107] On a trip from the mouth of the Red River to Cumberland House in early September 1819, George Nelson and his crew encountered several freemen—Lemire, Turner, Montrueil, and Martin—along Rivière du Pas and Lac Bourbon. The men sold provisions to Nelson's brigade and shared information on the comings and goings of other NWC brigades.[108]

Voyageur songs were probably influenced by Aboriginal songs to some degree. Frank Blackwell Mayer describes one journey with voyageurs that lasted late into the night. The voyageurs, he wrote,

> *were determined to be awake themselves, and permitted no one be otherwise, for, at the end of every song, they varied the monotony of the chorus with an Indian yell which fully succeeded in destroying the slumber which we were seeking on the deck, wrapped in our buffalo robes. Three canoes, filled with Indians, accompanied us until late in the night, their presence enlivened by their wild war songs and the dipping of their paddles, while, in the intervals of song, the glimmer of the flint and steel, as they lighted their pipes, now and then revealed them through the starlight.*[109]

Unending Toil

Mayer's description of singing reveals an important clue about voyageurs' work: voyageurs sang to keep themselves awake. Not only was the work of loading and unloading canoes, paddling, tracking, and portaging exhausting, but voyageurs also worked very long hours for weeks and even months at a time, as they raced against the fall freezing of waterways. The endless toil began even before the voyage started. Preparation for setting out on a voyage involved making packs and loading canoes. The voyageurs often took an active part in ensuring that the goods were equally divided among canoes within a brigade and that packs were equally weighted, to prevent any unnecessary work or unfair distribution. Setting out from Fort William in 1833, George Back described the scene:

> *[T]he Canadian voyageur is . . . on no point . . . more sensitive . . . than in the just distribution of "pieces" among the several canoes forming a party. . . . . he has very substantial reasons for being particular in this matter, for he well knows that, supposing the canoes to be in other respects equally matched, a very small inequality of weight will make a considerable difference in their relative speed, and will occasion, moreover, a longer detention at the portages. The usual mode is for the guide to separate the pieces, and then to distribute or portion them out by lots, holding in his hand little sticks of different lengths, which the leading men draw. From*

> *the decision so made there is no appeal, and the parties go away laughing or grumbling at their different fortunes.*[110]

Assembling packs took place on a very large scale at the major administrative posts. Fur presses packaged bundles of furs tightly together, which protected them and saved space.[111] Smaller fur presses (with levers rather than screws) were used at most interior posts.[112] Before departures voyageurs repaired, gummed, and loaded canoes.[113] When canoes arrived at a post, voyageurs immediately began repairing the boats, canoes, and equipment and examining the packages for damages or leaks.[114] Canoes were secured, and packs of furs and goods were often untied and spread out to dry.[115]

A usual day of canoeing started very early in the morning. Brigades usually set off between 3 a.m. and 6 a.m.[116] They paddled for several hours before stopping for breakfast.[117] The working days on a canoe journey were very long and demanding and often tedious. A typical voyage is that made by Robert Seaborne Miles from Lachine to Fort Wedderburn on Lake Athabasca in the fall of 1818. His travel journal is unusual in its daily detail, which allows us a close look at the daily rhythms. While on the Grand (Ottawa) River in early June, Miles recorded the following schedule in his travel journal:[118]

2:30 a.m.	The crew left their encampment
7:30 a.m.	Went ashore to breakfast for an hour
mid-morning	At Portage du Canard, the men hauled the canoe and cargo up with the line and walked over
1:40 p.m.	Went ashore to eat
2:30 p.m.	Resumed paddling

Next day

5:00 a.m.	Set out
7:00 a.m.	Portaged and breakfasted
8:00 a.m.	Set out again
1:15 p.m.	Reached Portage de Roche Capitaine, crossed it, ate
3:00 p.m.	Resumed journey
8:40 p.m.	Stopped and set up camp at Little River

Next day

4:30 a.m.	Set out for day, poled up a number of strong rapids. One of the voyageurs became "very much indisposed."
7:30 a.m.	Put ashore to breakfast
9:00 a.m.	Resumed voyage
1:15 a.m.	Arrived at Portage aux Plain Chan[t], carried the cargo, and ate
3:10 p.m.	Resumed voyage

Next day

4:00 a.m.	On Lake Nipissing, broke up camp and set out
Later in morning	Caught up with Ermatinger's brigade and exchanged a man with him; breakfasted
7:00 a.m.	Re-embarked, crossed Lake Nipissing, during the day met Aboriginal people, a freeman, and an encampment of six North West canoes
9:30 p.m.	Set up camp for night

Next day

2:30 a.m.	Embarked and traveled towards the French River
7:15 a.m.	Entered the French River and then put to shore to breakfast
8:30 a.m.	Re-embarked
1:45 p.m.	Put ashore to eat; one ill man detained the group
3:00 p.m.	Re-embarked
7:00 p.m.	Set up camp for night

Next day

4:30 a.m.	Left camp and entered Lake Huron, meeting Aboriginal people along the way
7:00 a.m.	Put ashore to breakfast
8:00 a.m.	Re-embarked

Next day

3:00 a.m.	Left camp
7:30 a.m.	Met a brigade of four north west canoes

During another typical week of canoeing, in an exploring party lead by Simon Fraser on his first journey along the Fraser River in the late spring and early summer of 1806, much of the same patterns emerge. Although Fraser's writings lack the detail of Miles, he includes notations on how frequently his crew stopped for rests, or "pipes." Fraser's journey was hindered by damaged canoes and a difficult route. On Friday, May 30, 1806, he wrote, "[F]ine weather we set of at half past 4 a.m. but at the second Pipe a stumpt seen through my Canoe which obliged us to put ashore and we lost two hours to repair and gum it." The party lost two hours on shore gumming another damaged canoe. Fraser wrote, "[W]e encountered more misery to day than any day yet and were obliged to cut several logs and embarass to open a Passage. my canoe through the awkwardness of the Bouttes was very much endangered and every soul on board near perishing." Although all hands worked very hard, they traveled only eight and a half miles. The next morning at the second pipe, Fraser's canoe broke on a stump, and it required two hours to mend and gum it. In the afternoon another canoe did the same and required three hours to repair. The next day in the forenoon a voyageur named La Malice broke his canoe, and they put ashore with the intention of mending it quickly. Once the crew was on shore, one of the men named St. Pierre fainted and remained speechless for more than an hour. La Malice decided to take the opportunity of the delay to band his canoe, but this took three hours. Fraser did not mind because his own canoe needed gumming at the time. The next day the group left one of the canoes and separated its load between the other two because all the men were nearly exhausted, especially a voyageur named La Garde who had been steering Fraser's canoe for over a week and had such a sore wrist that he was unable to continue. La Malice took over steering, and Fraser hoped that the trip would be easier with all hands on board the two canoes. The next morning rain detained the brigade until 7:30 a.m. Fraser was glad to have a pretext for allowing the exhausted crew to rest. Both canoes broke again that day and had to be gummed. The canoes were so heavy and shattered that they had to be taken out of the water by four men. Two days later, still struggling along, Fraser complained that the difficult navigation was exacerbated because the canoes were faulty and the bouts, particularly the steersmen, were awkward.[119]

These two examples of journeys reveal that crews worked between fifteen and eighteen hours a day, pausing for two to three hours for meals and breaks and resting at night for six to eight hours to repair equipment, eat, and sleep. The frequency and duration of rests and meals would depend on how much the brigade was pressed for time to reach its destination before waterways froze.[120] On occasion voyageurs paddled throughout the night, especially if a bright moon and clear night allowed enough light to travel.[121]

Provisioning

During the rushed summer travel between Montreal and Lake Superior, and Lake Superior and the interior posts, canoes were provided with as much provisions as possible, because the brigades did not have the time to hunt and fish along the way. Those leaving Montreal were outfitted with flour, corn, pork, and fat. At Lake Superior brigades stocked up with dried meat and fish, flour, corn, and sometimes wild rice. As distances in the trade increased, traders came to rely more on the local economies of Aboriginal people they passed on their routes, purchasing pemmican, fish, and meat from them. According to bourgeois Benjamin and Joseph Frobisher, "[A canoe's] general loading is two-thirds Goods and one-third Provisions, which not being sufficient for their subsistence until they reach winter Quarters, they must and always do, depend on the Natives they occasionally meet on the Road for an Additional Supply; and when this fails which is sometimes the case they are exposed to every misery that it is possible to survive, and equally so in returning from the Interior Country, as in the Spring provisions are generally more Scanty."[122] It was difficult to coordinate the purchase of fresh food, so dried foods, which kept longer, were preferred. The increasing competition among the fur trade companies and thus the greater demand for food to feed the expanding labor force led to the establishment of posts specifically devoted to provisioning the trade. The NWC established posts at Rainy Lake, Fort Alexander, and Cumberland House; the latter two drew especially on the buffalo resources of the plains for pemmican. Crees and Assiniboines who had lost their role as middlemen in the fur trade turned to provisioning as a new economic activity.[123] The Métis along the Assiniboine River turned the pemmican trade into a large-scale organized industry after about 1810, when it became the major provision for the traders.[124]

When traveling in the interior between posts, men sometimes hunted and fished for their own provisions when they were not too rushed.[125] Aboriginal wives were important sources of information and aid, as they often taught their husbands what could be gathered from different areas and often did the gathering themselves.[126] Food gathered along the way included wild onions, plums, panbines (a kind of fruit, origin of placename Pembina), and grapes.[127] A last resort when food was scarce was moss gathered from rocks. Rock moss, or *tripe de roche*, boiled in water to make a *boullion*, often prevented starvation.[128]

Fishing along the route was common. Fishing with a hook and line in eddies was frequently relaxing, particularly after a difficult stretch of the journey.[129] Fish were also caught by setting out nets.[130] More skill was required to catch fish by spearing.[131] In times of scarcity men were often sent ahead to scout for good fishing areas or to catch and dry fish for the whole brigade.[132]

Meat comprised the major part of men's diets, especially in the interior, and they preferred meat to fish.[133] Large game, such as deer, bear, and buffalo, seemed to be the favorites. When in need men ate smaller game, such as beaver, otter, and hare, and sought wildfowl, including pigeons and ducks.[134] On some occasions when they were not in a great rush, men hunted during portages or when their crew members were repairing and gumming the canoes.[135] They were sometimes able to kill small game from the canoe, and on rare occasions they shot large game. Ross Cox described the unexpected treat when one of the bourgeois killed a large black bear that was swimming across the river ahead of the brigades.[136] Sometimes brigades would stop to devote the day to hunting, as did the brigade of Duncan McGillivray in mid-September 1794.[137] If the crew had time, they would pause to dry the meat over a spit so that it would last a long time.[138]

Nevertheless, because they were usually so pressed for time, unfamiliar with the environments in the Northwest, and lacked the skills to hunt and fish efficiently, fur traders procured most of their food from Aboriginal people or freemen.[139] Most often they purchased provisions with trade goods.[140] On occasion they traded for fish and meat with European provisions, such as biscuits.[141] Aboriginal people were sometimes hired to travel with the brigades and hunt for them during the journey.[142] Ironically, voyageur brigades frequently impeded their own hunting and Aboriginal hunting endeavors by the great noise and commotion created by their travel. On their way to establish Park River post near Pembina in September 1800, Alexander Henry the Younger's crew saw many deer and bear along the river, but their Aboriginal companions complained that the men made so much noise all day that it was impossible to kill them.[143] On a journey from Cumberland House to Fort William, the Aboriginal people near Rivière la Savanne could not catch whitefish until the trading brigades had passed by because their noise frightened the fish away.[144]

Traders adopted the Aboriginal practice of caching, storing preserved food in hiding places along well-traveled routes. Pemmican and extra meat and fish that had been dried and pounded were most often cached.[145] Less frequently alcohol and equipment were cached.[146] Retrieving food from caches often constituted important resources to travelers.[147] Specific men, often guides, were designated to remember the location of the caches and to guide men back to the site at a later date, but often the men had difficulty in locating all the cached food.[148] Traders sometimes helped themselves to Aboriginal caches when they stumbled across them while on a journey.[149]

To save time crews frequently took their meals in the canoe or combined meals with other shore activities, such as repairing damaged equipment, gumming canoes, or portaging.[150] Large meals were often prepared at the end of a day, when the crew set up camp for the night.[151] Less frequently crews put ashore for the sole purpose of cooking a meal, which they called *pour faire la chaudière*.[152] Depending on the pace of the journey, crews would eat either two or three meals a day, although men sometimes snacked when they stopped to smoke. In the spring of 1806 Simon Fraser recorded in his journal: "[A]s the men force much in this River we allow then to make three meals a day and as they eat all together out of the same bag of Pemecan we put ashore for that purpose and afterward it is laid aside and not touched until next meal. this we find to be the best way and the men are better off and better pleased than if they ate a little at every Pipe."[153]

Meals times could range from twenty minutes to two hours, depending on the number in the crew and whether the food had to be cooked.[154] Men drank water from rivers or melted snow.[155] Alexander Henry the Younger commented that his men were usually perspiring and hot from their tough physical exertions and would often lean into a river to take long draughts of icy water.[156]

Positions in a Canoe

Not all voyageurs working in canoes had to endure the monotony of paddling; higher ranks of voyageurs did less physically challenging jobs. There were three positions in a canoe. The first was the *devant*, or foreman, also called *ducent*, conductor or bowsman, who helped to guide the canoe through waterways and acted as a lookout. The second was the *gouvernail*, or steersman, positioned in the back of the canoe.[157] The devants and gouvernails, collectively called bouts, directed the paddling, called out the command to begin or to end, set the rhythm, and were responsible for carrying the canoe over portages.[158] One of these men usually acted as the captain of the canoe, directing the men and making decisions about the division and organization of the labor. Either of these two men was often left in charge of individual canoes or brigades when the clerk or the bourgeois had to attend to other business.[159] The bouts probably guided the singing in the canoe most of the time.

Guiding required the most skill and expertise. Either the devant or the gouvernail could be guides, who helped choose routes and navigate through rivers, lakes, and portages. Guides decided whether canoes should attempt to shoot rapids, be tracked from shore, or be portaged. Navigating the canoes through rivers and streams was a difficult job that required experience and knowledge of waterways and canoe travel. In 1822 when arriving at Fort William, George Nelson wrote:

> *I could not sufficiently admire the adroisse [adroitness] of our bowsmen in avoiding the numerous stones; how quick and exactly they made the most acute angles in spite of the mist, strength of the current and the velocity which we went, for sometimes all the crew paddled. One time in particular they had 3 very acute angles to make to avoid several Large and sharp stones and so near each other that it seemed impossible to avoid being dashed to atoms even on the first. But they ran perfectly light, only a few men in each canoe—We were looking on with the greatest anxiety and wonder—they shipped some water in the terrible swells, but did not even touch one stone.*[160]

Before starting out, the devant or the gouvernail would ensure that the canoes were in good repair and well packed and would check the state of the water.[161] As fur brigades traveled further north and west into unknown lands, they frequently hired freemen and Aboriginal people to help choose routes and guide the canoes.[162]

The third position was that of the milieu, or middleman. These voyageurs were responsible for paddling and carrying the cargo over portages. Middlemen were paid less than foremen or steersmen, and their jobs were less skilled and less prestigious.[163] The job was also much more monotonous than other positions, as middlemen were expected to paddle all day.[164] Only on rare occasions did clerks or bourgeois join the middlemen to help paddle, such as when labor was in short supply, the route was particularly grueling, or the brigade particularly rushed.[165] Milieux were responsible for bailing and were stationed at the *bar d'éponge*, the position in the canoe designated specifically for bailing; they used a sponge to keep the water level in the canoe as low as possible.[166] Bad weather, such as rain and high waves, and a leaky canoe determined the frequency of bailing, which could be a full-time duty.[167]

Breaking the Monotony

How did singing fit into this unrelenting toil? The utility of singing for creating a pace and synchronization was undisputed.[168] The observant traveler Johann Georg Kohl noticed that voyageurs' songs were classified according to the kind of canoe they used for the journey. Slow *chansons à la rame* were sung in canoes where large paddles were used and the paddling was heavier and slower, which provided more power and control in rapids than did lighter paddles. Quicker chansons à l'aviron were sung in small canots du nord, where paddling was swift and light. Finally, *chansons de canot à lège* were sung in the express canoes, which carried no lading, only news and passengers, and traveled very fast; thus these songs had a fast tempo. Singing provided rhythm and the mental energy necessary for the intense physical exertion of paddling.[169] If voyageurs were tired, they sang slow songs to ease the pace of the journey. Margaret Creighton found that nineteenth-century whalers also used singing to slow the pace of work, especially when they were engaged in particularly heavy labor.[170] If voyageurs were anxious to arrive at their destination, fast songs helped them maintain a fast pace. Singing all day to set the pace seems like a burden on vocal chords, imagination, and enthusiasm. Presumably the milieux could take turns singing under the guidance of the bouts.

Commentators almost uniformly agreed that voyageurs needed little encouragement to sing and took great pleasure in it.[171] Singing dispelled the monotony of paddling and distracted voyageurs from their fatigue, boredom, hunger, and the hardships of the journey. Ross Cox commented in the fall of 1817 along the Ottawa River: "The poor *voyageurs*, who were in a starving condition, kept up *les chansons à l'aviron* until daybreak, to divert their hunger."[172]

Another facility that eased the monotony of paddling all day was to put up sails in canoes. These could be improvised from blankets or oilcloths. The makeshift sail would be raised on a pole secured to the side of the canoe, with the ends of the cloth tied to either end of the canoe, and voyageurs could then enjoy a brief respite.[173] With a good wind, canoes could travel at an average speed of eight or nine miles an hour.[174] When the wind became too strong, however, sailing was too great a risk, and canoes sought shelter along the shore.[175] As the NWC gained more experience in outfitting brigades, canots du maître, especially those on Lake Superior, were equipped with sailing sheets.[176]

The long days of tedious labor were also broken up by various stops along the journey. They stopped most frequently to smoke a pipe of tobacco, on average every two hours.[177] Stopping for a pipe became so entrenched in the work of voyageurs that distances came to be measured in "pipes."[178] Small rest stops during canoe journeys and portages were often referred to as *pauses* (often spelled phonetically as *poses*), which was a French Canadian term for "laying down" their packs.[179] On a portage a pause was not only a resting place; it was also a used as a temporary depot. All packs were brought to the first pause before any were carried to the second, to increase security during the portage. The same places were generally used as pauses by all who passed, and it came to be common to measure the length of a portage by the number of pauses along the trail. The distance between two pauses varied from six hundred to eight hundred yards, depending on the conditions of the trail.[180]

Dealing with Obstacles

Yet not all stops along the way were welcome. When voyageurs encountered impassable rapids or waterfalls, they had to land on shore and carry their canoes and ladings around the obstacles. Portaging was the most onerous task in canoe travel. When they arrived at a portage, the bowsman usually jumped into the water to prevent the canoe from touching the bottom and guided it to shore. The middlemen unloaded the canoe and prepared the packs to carry over the portage. They tied their slings, referred to as portage collars, *colliers à porter*, carrying straps, or tumplines, to the packs and slung them over their backs to carry them over the portage.[181] The slings were usu-

Fig. 7. Portaging. *Burial Place of the Voyageurs (Ontario)*, by William Henry Bartlett, 1841, hand-colored engraving. Accession 1972-188-885, reproduction C-040707. Courtesy of the Library and Archives Canada, Ottawa.

ally straps of leather about three to four inches wide, with smaller straps attached to the packs.[182] The first pack rested near the lower part of the back, while the collar was placed across the forehead. Men leaned forward so that the packs were supported by their backs and stabilized by the straps around their heads. One or two additional packs were placed on top of the first, and the load sometimes reached as high as their heads.[183] This method of carrying may have been modeled on the Aboriginal use of tumplines. The Jesuit missionary Paul Le Jeune described Innu travelers using tumplines as early as 1634.[184] Another aid in carrying that became identified with voyageurs was the *ceintures flechées*. These wide multicolored sashes tied around voyageurs' waists eased the strain on their backs and served as belts from which to hang their equipment.[185] Most men carried two packs at ninety pounds each, though sometimes men carried three packs at one time, as a show of strength. John Johnston commented, "[H]e is not looked upon as a man Who cannot carry two [packages]. there are many Who even take three and out Run their fellows."[186] Carrying more than two packs was a show of strength and a mark of distinction among voyageurs.

Portaging experiences varied greatly. Canoes carrying only passengers and no cargo were easy to carry over, because the entire crew could help carry the canoe. Portages tended to be most onerous on the route between Montreal and Lake Superior because larger canoes were used in travel. Approximately six men were required to carry the canot du maître, which could weigh between 650 and 1,500 pounds. A canoe could be especially difficult to carry when the ground was uneven because the weight of the canoe would be distributed unequally. It took great skill for men to shoulder the canoe and carry it with no accident.[187] In the interior the task of carrying the smaller canot du nord was considerably easier and was reserved for the bowman and the steersman.[188]

Long and treacherous portages were difficult, time-consuming, and required great skill. British surveyor and scientist John Henry Lefroy recorded one portage on the Savanne River that was two and a half miles long with a steep hill. The crew started the portage and completed only half of it by nightfall, and they slept without their blankets because they were too tired to return across the portage to retrieve them.[189] Canoe brigades could be detained by difficult portages for as long as twenty-two days.[190] In describing the portage at Grand Portage, bourgeois Peter Grant marveled that "the whole [was] conducted with astonishing expedition, a necessary consequence of the enthusiasm which always attend[ed] their long and perilous voyages."[191] Grand Portage west of Lake Superior spanned nine miles; voyageurs usually had to carry eight packs each during the portage and were paid a Spanish dollar for every extra pack they could manage. Alexander Mackenzie noted: "[S]o inured are they to this kind of labour, that I have known some of them set off with two packages of ninety pounds each, and return with two others of the same weight, in the course of six hours, being a distance of eighteen miles over hills and mountains."[192]

Sometimes canoes waiting for the rest of a brigade to cross the portage made effective use of their time by gathering wood for paddles and bark for canoe repairs. Other men could be sent to help the other canoes cross the portage more quickly.[193] Bourgeois frequently used the portages as occasions to write letters and journal entries.[194] In other cases the men simply waited with impatience for the rest of the brigade to finish or "made merry" if they had wine or rum on hand.[195]

The frequent accidents slowed the progress of brigades. Wet ground and rocks made portages slippery, and men could easily fall while carrying the canoe or their packs, especially if they were inexperienced. On these occasions they usually carried only one pack as a measure of safety.[196]

Not all rapids required a full portage. When the rapids were not too onerous, the bouts would shoot the rapids with an empty canoe, called a *décharge*, or with half of the cargo, called a *demicharge*.[197] The middlemen would wait on the shore, leaving one or two men, usually the foreman and the steersman, to guide the canoe through the rapids. These men would have to jump out of the canoe if they had difficulty.[198] Voyageurs were keen to avoid portages whenever possible and thus chose to run through many dangerous rapids with a full canoe. Bourgeois Peter Grant explained:

> *When they arrive at a rapid, the guide or foreman's business is to explore the waters previous to their running down with their ca-*

> *noes, and, according to the height of the water, they either lighten the canoe by taking out part of the cargo and carry it over land, or run down the whole load. It would be astonishing to an European observer to witness the dexterity with which they manage their canoes in those dangerous rapids, carrying them down like lightening on the surface of the water. The bowman, supported by the steersman, dexterously avoids the stones and shoals which might touch the canoe and dash it to pieces, to the almost certain destruction of all on board. It often baffles their skill, when the water is very high, to avoid plunging in foaming swells on the very brink of the most tremendous precipes, yet, those bold adventurers rather run this risk, for the sake of expedition, than lose a few hours by transporting cargo over land.*[199]

Many masters and travelers echoed these praises of the voyageurs' skill and dexterity at running rapids.[200]

Another means of navigating through rapids was to pull a canoe through water with a rope, called tracking or lining. This method of transport was used when shooting the rapids proved too dangerous or unfeasible, when a canoe could not be carried around a rapid or a fall because the shoreline was too rocky or the vegetation too dense, when traversing a minor rapid upstream, or when in very shallow water.[201] Tracking lines were usually stored as part of a regular canoe's equipment.[202] Voyageurs tied this line to the canoe and dragged it either from within the water or from shore. Sometimes a couple of men stayed in the canoe to pole while they were tracking the canoe, which entailed pushing or anchoring the canoe from the bottom of the riverbed with long poles.[203] Other times one man stayed in the stern of the canoe to help keep the canoe in the proper channel while it was being pulled.[204]

Other techniques were used to help the canoes through difficult parts of a river passage. Poles constituted part of the regular equipment of a canoe. They were used to help ascend small rapids when the water was not too deep.[205] Poles were also used to help push canoes through water too shallow to support a normal load. Men would sometimes leave the canoes to lighten them and push them to deeper water or walk alongside them until they reached a deeper part of the river.[206] They were also forced to walk when the river was clogged with vegetation, and they had to lighten the load to try to float the canoe over it or to try to cut a passage through it.[207]

Bad weather could force brigades to stop, and waiting out a storm could be an unexpected bonus if a crew was fatigued.[208] Breaks were also incorporated into stops for canoe maintenance. In especially harsh and cold waterways, men had to frequently gum and mend canoes that were prone to cracking.[209] Gumming involved smearing melted spruce gum along the seams and in cracks and holes of the birch bark to prevent leaks and repair damage. Fibers of bruised bark were moistened with liquid gum and applied to large breaches in the canoe; rags then covered the hole, and the edges were cemented with gum.[210] Gum was gathered from trees along routes but sometimes had to be purchased when it was in short supply.[211] Voyageurs often gummed the canoes when other stops were made for portages, meals, or seeking information from people along the route.[212] To save time canoes were often gummed at night by torchlight, after the party had stopped for the night.[213] Canoes were also gummed and repaired whenever they arrived at a post.[214]

As part of long-term maintenance, canoes were regummed when they were repaired, which was often. Most traders' journals are filled with references to damaging canoes on rocks and in rapids. For example, on a voyage in the summer of 1800, Alexander Henry the Younger reported that his brigades stopped to repair a damaged canoe at least seven times between Grand Portage and Fort Alexander over the course of a month, and at least three more times in a little over a week when they continued on their journey south to the Park River post at Pembina.[215] Canoes were constantly being repaired and refashioned while en route. On a journey from Pays Plat in Lake Superior to Portage de L'Isle in the Winnipeg River in the summer of 1784, Edward Umfreville's men improved their canoe for the interior waterways by removing, washing, and shortening the canoe's ribs of timber to make it lighter.[216] Taking care of canoes could take up an extraordinary amount of time if the canoes were in a bad state. As we have seen, while Simon Fraser was attempting his first exploration of the Fraser River in the spring of 1806, he was plagued by poor canoes, and his crew spent hours each day on shore gumming them.[217] Entire days during a journey could be devoted solely to repairing canoes.[218] Traders were sometimes able to hire Aboriginal people to fix their canoes or to purchase new ones from them en route, which could save a lot of time. However, as Henry complained in the summer of 1800, Aboriginal people did not always oblige as quickly as the traders desired. Henry became so frustrated with the Ojibwes he had hired to build him a new canoe at Lake des Perches near the height of land on his way from Grand Portage to Lake Winnipeg that he had his own men finish the job.[219] During the voyage men were sent out to gather cedar and bark for the canoe repairs and wood to fashion paddles and poles that were lost or damaged.[220] They often gathered the supplies in advance if they knew that the country further along their journey could not provide the needed materials.[221]

Accidents

Voyageurs' work in canoes was made up of both monotonous toil and potential dangers. The song "When a Christian Decides to Travel," about a priest who warns voyageurs of what the occupation holds in store for them, describes some of the hazards. The opening verse sets a grave tone: "When a Christian decides to travel / He must think carefully / About the dangers of his destination. / Millions of times death passes / Before his eyes, / Millions of times he damns his departure / During the course of his trip." Later stanzas refer to "winds and gales rumbling cruelly," overturned canoes, swarms of flies, the sting of mosquitoes, rough rapids, difficult portages, and warlike Indians.[222]

Running rapids was probably the most dangerous task connected with canoeing. Canoes broke, cargoes were lost, and men drowned.[223] Men sometimes attempted to run rapids when it was impossible to portage around them. In an extreme case on June 1, 1808, while exploring the Fraser River,

Simon Fraser and his partner, Stuart, chose to run some rapids because the riverbanks were too high and steep to climb. In the river their canoe faced ceaseless danger as it was tossed from one eddy to another. The men running the first canoe through the rapids were able to jump out and drag it onto a rock platform on the bank. The rest of the crew had to save them by scaling down the sheer rocky walls of the bank and dragging the men and canoes up to safety, which took a whole day. The crew then faced the treacherous hills of the portage with heavy loads on their backs.[224] Only three days after this incident, Fraser recorded in his journal: "visited the lower part [of the rapid]; having found it strong and full of tremendous Whirlpools we were greatly at a loss how to act—: However, the nature of our situation left us no choice; for we were under the necessity either to run down the Canoes or to abandon them" because the shore was too dangerous. This "desperate undertaking" exhausted the men. They decided to try to pass the rapid by land after several near fatalities. Even on this safer course one of the men nearly slipped and fell into the turbulent river.[225] Only five days later Fraser's crew faced an equally perilous situation:

> *[I]t being absolutely impossible to carry the canoes by land, all hands without hesitation embarked, as it were a corp perdu, upon the mercy of this awful tide.—Once engaged the die was cast, and the great difficulty consisted in keeping the canoes within the medium, or fil d'eau, that is clear of the precipice on one side, and of the gulphs formed by the waves on the other.—then skimming along as fast as lightening the crews notwithstanding cool and determined, followed each other in awful silence. And when we arrived at the end we stood as it were, gazing congratulation at each other upon our narrow escape.*[226]

Tracking could be as arduous, tedious, and dangerous as portaging or running rapids. Along the Saskatchewan River, Duncan McGillivray wrote in September 1794: "arrived at the end of the tracking ground to the great satisfaction of the men many of whom are estrepied [*estropié*, or exhausted] by the hard duty they have performed for some days Past."[227] Again along the Saskatchewan River, this time in September 1808, after a long day of using towing lines, Alexander Henry the Younger reported that his men were pleased to have reached smoother water "because they were heartily tired of the tedious business" of tracking. The previous day one of his men had a narrow escape from drowning while untangling the towing line from vegetation along the shore. When the rope jerked free, he was tossed headlong into the water and was rescued after he had been swept downstream and swallowed a lot of water.[228]

Those who were not lucky enough to escape from accidents were often immortalized in one type of voyageur song, called complaintes, which were similar in form to the old French ballads but were composed by the voyageurs. The songs could be eulogies to the deceased or lamentations for their lives of hardship and toil. Complaintes also commemorated tragic events, such as deadly accidents, and sometimes assumed the status of folktales, warning against dangers and teaching lessons of survival in the pays d'en haut.[229] The complaintes were much like the "sailors' lament," an "early form of the blues" that wistfully commemorated home.[230] Similarly, Ian Radforth has found that lumberers working in nineteenth-century Ontario created songs about the dangers of the job and the bravery of the men. He suggests that their "vibrant, sometimes haunting songs were an important way in which the woodsmen dealt with the extraordinary dangers of the work" by boosting their courage and commemorating the deceased.[231] The most famous of the voyageur complaintes was the song about Jean Cadieux (or Cayeux). While traveling along the Ottawa River, his crew was chased by Iroquois. Cadieux jumped out of the canoe to help guide the crew through some dangerous rapids. The Virgin Mary appeared to help the canoe safely negotiate the rapids, and the Iroquois did not dare follow. Unfortunately the Iroquois chased Cadieux into the woods, where he eventually died of hunger while hiding from them. The song devoted to him, titled "Petit Rocher," or "Little Rock," is about Cadieux saying his last farewell to the world and preparing himself for death.[232]

The voyageurs' occupation of transporting goods via canoes required strength, endurance, skill, and courage. Although the occupation became specialized into positions within a canoe, and regional groups needed for remote locations, harsh environments, and conveying explorers into parts unknown, all voyageurs were at the mercy of low water, high winds, storms, rapids, falls, and difficult portages, and all needed to know how to paddle, steer, pole, sail, track, trade, hunt, and fish. Voyageurs distracted themselves from their demanding and precarious occupations with song. They made up songs that reflected their workplace or eulogized those who had been victims of tragic accidents and sang French love ballads. Voyageurs' singing could be very beautiful and was romanticized by many travelers. In November 1818, while traveling along the upper St. Lawrence, John M. Duncan commented:

> *I could have endured the rain for an hour or two, to listen to the boat songs of the Canadian voyageurs, which in the stillness of the night had a peculiarly pleasing effect. They kept time to these songs as they rowed; and the [s]plashing of the oars in the water, combined with the wildness of their cadences, gave a romantic character to our darksome voyage. In most of the songs two of the boatmen began the air, the other two sang a response, and then all united in the chorus. Their music might not have been esteemed fine, but those whose skill in concords and chromatics, forbids them to be gratified but on scientific principles; my convenient ignorance of these rules allowed me to reap undisturbed enjoyment from the voyageurs' melodies, which like many of our Scottish airs were singularly plaintive and pleasing.*[233]

Voyageurs generally worked in an all-male atmosphere, and their culture was strongly influenced by a rugged, risk-taking masculine ideal. Yet their surviving songs have a feminine quality, with pretty and delicate lyrics about romantic love and longing. The songs reminded voyageurs of their families and friends back at home in the St. Lawrence valley, but they also helped voyageurs make sense of their demanding jobs and provided advice for labor relations, a topic that is explored in considerable detail in the following chapter.

5. The Theater of Hegemony

Masters, Clerks, and Servants

> *At sunset we put ashore for the night, on a point covered with a great number of lopsticks. These are tall pine-trees, denuded of their lower branches, a small tuft being left at the top. They are generally made to serve as landmarks, and sometimes the voyageurs make them in honour of gentlemen who happen to be travelling for the first time along the route, and those trees are chosen which, from their being on elevated ground, are conspicuous objects. The traveller for whom they are made is always expected to acknowledge his sense of the honour conferred upon him, by presenting the boat's crew with a pint of grog, either on the spot or at the first establishment they meet with. He is then considered as having paid for his footing, and may ever afterwards pass scot-free.*[1]

The "conspicuous objects" that HBC officer Robert Ballantyne described in the mid-nineteenth century while traveling to Norway House, variously called *lopsticks*, *lobsticks*, *mais*, and *maypoles* in the documentary record, could be found along the most traveled fur trade routes. These stripped trees, which in the subarctic were probably most often spruces, not pines, were reminiscent of poles erected to honor captains of militia in Lower Canada and of maypoles in Europe. They perhaps resonated with sacred poles or trees in some Aboriginal communities, such as those of the Iroquois, Mahican-Munsees, and Omahas.[2] During canoe journeys voyageurs created maypoles for some bourgeois and passengers in their company, usually those perceived to be wealthy or of high social rank. In return the person honored was required to treat voyageurs to a drink of rum, wine, or whatever alcoholic beverage was available. The bourgeois and passengers were usually pleased to receive such a striking honor from voyageurs, and in turn voyageurs were glad to acquire a treat. The ceremony of constructing maypoles and the lasting symbol of the maypole itself reflected the delicate negotiation of power that characterized relationships between masters and servants. In the fur trade the maypole ritual allowed masters to claim authority and permitted servants to demand material rewards, as well as providing markers along routes.

This chapter turns to voyageurs' relationships with their masters, both clerks and bourgeois. Once they signed engagements, or contracts, they entered into a master-servant relationship that was typical of indentured servitude in New France and other colonial settings. This system was based on masters asserting authority over their servants and servants obeying masters' orders. However, the organization of the labor system and the particulars of the fur trade workplace made the master-servant relationship more flexible than did many other early modern settings. In the fur trade voyageurs were able in limited ways to shape their workplace and control the pace of their work through forms of resistance that ranged from acts of minor disobedience to large-scale strikes. Although the master-servant relationship was based on inequality, its flexibility provided voyageurs with agency, or the ability to shape their working lives.

Fur trade servants vastly outnumbered their masters and worked far away from colonial structures of rule and policing. Masters depended heavily on their servants not only for the successful functioning of the trade but also for their very survival. How did this system of inequality and hierarchy sustain itself? How did the bourgeois rule over voyageurs without physical might? The Italian Marxist philosopher Antonio Gramsci argued that the ruling classes were able to maintain their domination over lower classes without the use of physical coercion through the dominant ideologies of inequality that were promoted by cultural institutions, such as schools, the media, and religions, and thus became normative.[3] Although Gramsci was building on Marxist theories to explain the consent of proletariats to subordination by the bourgeoisie in capitalist settings, the theory has become widely applicable to explaining many contexts of hierarchical rule.

Masters and servants accepted their positions as rulers and ruled. Voyageurs could challenge the substance and boundaries of their jobs to improve their working conditions without contesting the fundamental power dynamics. Voyageurs' acceptance of bourgeois (and sometimes clerk) domination was based on a deeply held belief in the legitimacy of paternalism. Voyageurs certainly became discontented, resisted the authority of bourgeois and clerks, and sometimes revolted, but it was outside their conception of the world to challenge the system of paternalism.[4] Thus cultural hegemony was not inconsistent with the presence of labor strife. Although voyageurs challenged the terms of their employment and contracts, they did not fundamentally challenge their position in the power relationship because they participated in constructing the system. Voyageurs, bourgeois, and clerks engaged in a dialogue of accommodation and confrontation as a means of constructing a workable relationship.[5] Hegemony did not prevent voyageurs from creating their own modes of work and leisure or from forming their own rituals. Hegemony offered, in the words of E. P. Thompson, writing of the eighteenth-century English plebeians, a "bare architecture of a structure of relations of domination and subordination, but within that architectural tracery many different scenes could be set and different dramas enacted."[6]

E. P. Thompson's emphasis on theater is also instructive for understanding master-servant relations in the fur trade. Thompson asserted that plebian culture was "located within a particular equilibrium of social relations, a working environment of exploitation and resistance to exploitation, of relations of power which are masked by the rituals of paternalism and deference."[7] Both rulers and ruled expressed paternalism and resistance to it "in ritualized or stylized performances."[8] Rulers performed exercises of authority, and the ruled performed both subordination and resistance in recreation and protest. This was the case in the fur trade. The bourgeois and the clerks strove to assert their authority in performances of domination, while voyageurs both enacted their subordinate status and played out "scenes of misrule" in efforts to better their lot. Maypole rituals included the theaters of both rule and resistance by providing a space for the expression of bourgeois superiority and an opportunity for voyageurs to improve their material welfare. Voyageur rituals provide a unique window into understanding the relationships between masters and servants and the ways that voyageurs created a unique workplace.

Theater and Maypoles

The quotation that begins this chapter illustrates a striking performance of the master and servant relationship in the fur trade. Unfortunately the documentary record does not provide a view of the ceremony through voyageurs' eyes nor reveal how voyageurs chose those they wished to honor. Clues to voyageurs' ideas about their masters and ceremonies of tribute can be discerned only in their actions. Voyageurs selected a tall tree standing out on a lake, "lobbed" off all its branches except for those at the very top, carved into the trunk's base the name of the bourgeois, clerk, or passenger to be honored, and gathered around the maypole to cheer and fire muskets. The honoree then provided *regales*, or treats, to all in the brigade. The ceremony became associated with creating occasions for a party.[9] While traveling up the Columbia River in the spring of 1811, fur trader Alexander Ross noted:

> *It is a habit among the grandees [bourgeois] of the Indian trade to have May-poles with their names inscribed thereon on conspicuous places, not to dance round, but merely to denote that such a person passed there on such a day, or to commemorate some event. For this purpose, the tallest tree on the highest ground is generally selected, and all the branches are stripped off excepting a small tuft at the top. On Mr. [Alexander] McKay's return from his reconnoitring expedition up the river, he ordered one of his men to climb a lofty tree and dress it for a May-pole. The man very willingly undertook the job, expecting, as usual on these occasions, to get a dram.*[10]

This dramatic performance of authority had different meanings for participants. The bourgeois demonstrated their superiority over their servants, in part by rewarding voyageurs who performed a difficult and dangerous task for no apparent benefit other than to assert the masters' own eminence. Voyageurs, on the other hand, probably welcomed the occasion to rest from paddling and enjoyed the treats and revelry that accompanied the ceremony.

Maypoles honoring important people were common in Lower Canada and had deep roots in feudal Europe. Bushes, trees, or poles were arranged in front of the houses of priests, seigneurs, and young women with eager suitors, and maypoles could honor the election of aldermen. Those honored with a maypole were required to provide treats in the form of food or alcohol.[11] Anthropologist Arnold Van Gennep suggested that the maypole ritual was a reciprocal exchange that could mark the successful completion a relationship of obligation. For example, at the end of a harvest, agricultural laborers sometimes erected a maypole for their employer, who then provided them with a banquet, signifying that both parties were satisfied.[12] French settlers brought the practice of putting up maypoles to the St. Lawrence valley. As in France habitants honored seigneurs with maypoles placed in front of their residences in return for feasts. Not all seigneurs were so honored, and by the eighteenth century seigneurs began inserting clauses in deeds requiring habitants to erect maypoles for them. In the tumultuous years before the 1837 rebellion in Lower Canada, habitants used maypoles to honor militia captains. Like Van Gennep, Allan Greer asserts in these cases that the meaning of maypole ceremonies was reciprocity: "[T]he men presented their captain with a symbol of his authority, while he for his part had to make a gesture of repayment. In accepting the symbol of power, the captain also accepted the responsibility it implied, responsibility, that is, towards the men under his command, rather than towards his superiors."[13]

Poles had a variety of meanings among Aboriginal peoples encountered by voyageurs. Poles were most commonly used in dwelling constructions, such as tepees (made of straight poles and covered with birch bark) and tents (smaller and more temporary tepees covered with brush), and the Ojibwe *wáginogans* (hemispheric structures made of bent poles and covered with birch bark) and *cäbandawans* (elongated wáginogans).[14] Architectural debris of abandoned Aboriginal campsites was probably often seen along fur trade routes.[15] But some poles had a deeper significance. One of the best-known examples of sacred poles is that among the Omahas. Called Umon'hon'ti, the Sacred Pole of the Omaha tribe was not only a physical object made from cottonwood but a living person. Robin Ridington and Dennis Hastings (In'aska) explain that the Sacred Pole "served to symbolize the tribe's unity at a time when they were moving from one place to another. He continued to stand for their tribal identity during the good times when they controlled the trade up and down the Missouri River."[16] Did Aboriginal perspectives on and uses for poles influence practices among voyageurs, or did voyageurs use of poles influence Aboriginal peoples?

The meaning of maypoles in the fur trade was not clear-cut. As with seigneurs not all bourgeois received the honor of a maypole. Although some fur traders mentioned seeing clusters of maypoles along fur trade routes, few have written about the ceremony. Presumably a symbol as dramatic as a maypole constructed in one's honor would have occasioned comment. Who, then, received the honor of maypoles? Some traders, like the abovementioned Mr. McKay, ordered voyageurs to construct a maypole for them. In 1790 trader Peter Pangman created a lobstick for himself at Rocky Mountain House in sight of the Rocky Mountains to mark the spot of the farthest extent of traders' discoveries along the Saskatchewan River. The lobstick came to be known as "Pangman's Tree."[17] On an expedition to explore the prairies in 1857, Henry Youle Hind described a site near Cat Head on Lake Winnipeg: "A spruce tree growing on this peninsula has been trimmed into a 'lopstick,' by Angus Macbeth, from which the locality has derived the name of Macbeth's point."[18]

Travelers in voyageur canoes, who owed voyageurs nothing except payment of safe passage, could be honored with a maypole. The ceremony was not restricted to traders operating out of Montreal. One intriguing example was the wife of Sir George Simpson, the governor of the HBC after the 1821 merger with the NWC. A maypole was raised in honor of Frances Simpson in 1830 at Norway House while she journeyed from Red River to York Factory. She wrote in her diary:

> *[T]he Voyageurs agreed among themselves to cut a "May Pole," or "Lopped Stock" for me; which is a tall Pine Tree, lopped of all its branches excepting those at the top, which are cut in a round bunch: it is then barked: and mine (being a memorable one) was honored with a red feather, and streamers of purple ribband tied to a poll, and fastened to the top of the Tree, so as to be seen above every other object: the surrounding trees were then cut down, in order to leave it open to the Lake. Bernard (the Guide) then presented me with a Gun, the contents of which I discharged against the Tree, and Mr. Miles engraved my name, and the date, on the trunk, so that my "Lopped Stick" will be conspicuous as long as it stands, among the number of those to be seen along the banks of different Lakes and Rivers.*[19]

Frances Simpson was among the first white women to live in the Northwest. Sylvia Van Kirk explains that "with the arrival of Frances Simpson, the [HBC] Governor [George Simpson] seemed determined to create an all-white elite in the [Red River] settlement. Mrs Simpson's female society was restricted to those few white women whose husbands possessed social standing."[20] Were the voyageurs trying to make a good impression on the governor? Perhaps the voyageurs were awed with the exotic Mrs. Simpson, who represented an alien world of upper-class British society. Another traveler deemed worthy of a maypole was Paul Kane, an artist from Toronto, who traveled through the Northwest in the late 1840s, sketching Indians and the environment. Kane makes clear, however, that the men in his brigade carved a maypole for him simply because they were bored and trying to pass the time while they awaited the arrival of another brigade.[21] While traveling with the HBC in June 1842 close to York Factory, the "old voyageurs" honored traveler John Birkbeck Nevins with a lobstick. Nevins reported: "This is a complimentary ceremony, which is performed for most strangers, the first time of their traveling up the country . . . which the stranger returns, by making them a present of a gallon of rum, or something of equal value, on arriving at the first fort." Nevins goes on to describe a case where two men, who "professed tee-total principles," refused to provide alcohol to the men who cut them lobsticks. The next time they traveled by the site of their lopsticks, they had been cut down. When they expressed indignation, the canoemen retorted, "They were not yours; you never paid for them."[22] The ceremony resembled other common rituals in the trade, such as the firing of guns and cheering. In Simpson's case, adding feathers and streamers to the maypole suggests Aboriginal influences.

In addition to honoring an eminent person and creating occasions for treats, maypoles helped to mark canoe routes. On August 16, 1793, John McDonell reported seeing a maypole, which he referred to as "the *Mai*" about fifty miles west of Lake Superior on the route to Lac La Pluie.[23] The famous explorer John Franklin sighted a maypole at White Fall along the Hayes River in between Hudson Bay and Lake Winnipeg. On October 2, 1819, he remarked that at the falls that they "observed a conspicuous *lop-stick*, a kind of landmark, which [he had] not hitherto noticed, notwithstanding its great use in pointing out the frequented routes."[24] The site was ever after referred to by the name of the person honored. The maypoles reminded voyageurs of those who had traveled that way in the past. As Alexander Ross's brigade passed a maypole at the mouth of Berens River in the 1820s, one of the men in his crew recalled creating it eighteen years earlier.[25] Almost sixty years later the site at the mouth of the Berens River was known as "Lobstick Island."[26] Other landscape features were thus named. An island in Rainy Lake is still known today as Maypole Island. In 1872 George M. Grant, traveling with the engineer-in-chief of the Canadian Pacific and Intercolonial Railways, wrote about "Lobstick River" flowing into the Pembina River on the prairies. Grant attributed the name to an Aboriginal practice: "[L]obstick is the Indian or half-breed monument to a friend or a man he delights to honour. . . . You are expected to feel highly flattered and make a handsome present in return to the noble fellow or fellows who have erected such a pillar in your honour."[27] Did Aboriginal peoples adopt the practice from voyageurs, or was the practice passed down to the métis children of voyageurs?

As recently as 1941, Grace Lee Nute reported that "[l]ob pines are said to be standing on the Kaministikwia route between Fort William and Lac La Croix, on Knife Lake, Cecil Lake, and at other points, lone survivors of a picturesque era now gone forever."[28] To the best of my knowledge, none remains today.

The Short Arm of the Law

At the center of the master-servant relationship was the legal compact of voyageurs' engagements (discussed in chapter 2). The principal tenet of the contract dictated that servants obey their masters in exchange for board and wages. To enforce the terms of the legal contracts, the bourgeois tried to regulate their servants through legal and governmental sanctions. In January 1778 the NWC sent a memorandum to the Quebec governor Sir Guy Carleton requesting "that it be published before the Traders and their Servants that the latter must strictly conform to their agreements, which should absolutely be in writing or printed, and before witnesses if possible, as many disputes [arose] from want of order in this particular."[29] The memorandum goes on to ask that men be held to pay their debts with money or service and that traders hiring men already engaged to another company should purchase their contracts. Lower Canadian law eventually recognized the legality of notarial fur trade contracts, and a 1796 ordinance forbade voyageurs from transgressing the terms or deserting the service.[30] In Lower Canada, the legislature empowered justices of the peace (JPs) to create and oversee the rules and regulations for master-servant relations in the Montreal trade.[31]

In addition to seeking governmental support, the bourgeois and the clerks turned to courts of law to enforce the terms of voyageur contracts and charged voyageurs for breaking contracts through desertion, insolence, and disobedience.[32] The files of the Court of Quarter Sessions in the District of Montreal reveal a range of cases: voyageurs accepted wages from one employer while already working for another, they obtained advance wages without appearing for the job, and they deserted the service.[33] Cases of voyageur desertion and theft can also be found in the records of the Montreal civil court.[34] In 1803 the British government passed the Canada Jurisdiction Act stipulating that criminal offenses committed in the "Indian territories" could be tried in Lower Canada. The five JPs named were all prominent fur trade bourgeois.[35] The effectiveness of court actions to control workers is obscured because prosecution rates have not survived in most of the records. Presumably the bourgeois would not continue to press charges if their efforts did not pay off. On the other hand, pressing charges against voyageurs did not seem to deter them from continuing to desert, cheat on contract terms, and steal from their employers. It is difficult to imagine bourgeois and clerks chasing a deserter, arresting him while in the pays d'en haut, and keeping him in bondage until he could be jailed in Montreal, while crews were racing against time to deliver their cargoes. If a bourgeois decided to file against a deserting voyageur, how would the courts deliver notification to the voyageur, who was probably still in the pays d'en haut?

The difficulties of apprehending and transporting contract breakers to Montreal led fur trade companies and partnerships to seek alternative methods of worker control. Fur traders sometimes cooperated to prevent voyageurs from jumping among different companies by compiling blacklists of deserters. In 1800 NWC officer William McGillivray wrote to Thomas Forsyth of Forsyth, Ogilvy, and McKenzie: "I agree with you that protecting Deserters would be a dangerous Practice and very pernicious to the Trade and fully sensible of this when any Man belonging to People opposed to The North West Company have happened to come to our Forts, we have told the Master of such to come for them and that they should not be in any way wise prevented from taking them back."[36] McGillivray assured Forsyth that he was not protecting deserters and that he would always contact their masters should any come to him looking for work. McGillivray was hoping to have the same assurances from Forsyth when he brought up the case of the NWC engagé Poudriés, who was allowed to return to Montreal because of ill health on the understanding that he pay his debt or return to the Northwest to serve the remainder of his time. When the NWC discovered that Poudriés engaged himself to Forsyth, Ogilvy, and McKenzie, they attempted to arrest him, but Poudriés was "smuggled out of the Country." McGillivray requested that Forsyth return Poudriés to NWC service or pay his debt. He went on: "With regard to paying advances made to Men I wish to be explicit, we have alwise made it a practice and will continue so to do to pay every shilling that Men whom we hire may acknowledge to their former Master such Men *being free on the Ground*. We hire no Men who owe their Descent considering this a principle not to be deviated from in determining to adhere strictly to it we cannot allow others to treat us in a different manner—if a Man was Free at the Point au Chapeau we do not consider him at liberty to hire until he has gone to it."[37] McGillivray decided to purchase voyageurs' engagements from their previous masters rather than pay their wages and warned other fur trade companies against hiring any deserters.[38] The other fur trade companies soon followed suit.[39]

Concurrently voyageurs often sued their bourgeois for wages by filing petitions with courts.[40] Cases of this kind were widespread in all sorts of labor contracts in New France and Lower Canada. Most voyageurs would have had some exposure to the power of courts while they lived in the St. Lawrence valley. Voyageurs were not usually successful, however, in claiming wages for jobs they had deserted or where they had disobeyed their masters.[41] Even in courts where the JPs were not all fur traders, the Montreal middle-class establishment supported the fur trade merchants, who belonged to their own social class.

The Beaver Club

The fur trade bourgeois were able to prevail in the Canadian court systems because they belonged to the ruling classes of colonial society. The fur trade masters created their own niche by founding the Beaver Club, one of many dining clubs for Montreal's merchant class. Membership in this all-male club was restricted to NWC bourgeois who had spent at least one winter in the pays d'en haut. But members frequently brought guests, who included militia officers, government officials, businessmen, and professionals, such as judges, lawyers, and doctors, and distinguished visitors to Montreal, such as John Jacob Astor, Washington Irving, and Thomas Moore. The Beaver Club dinners were part of a large continuum of vigorous socializing among fur traders and Montreal's bourgeoisie. Fraternization among men was formalized in clubs and associations, many of which had overlapping memberships. Other men's dining clubs in Montreal included occupationally defined groups, such as the Brothers-in-Law Club; clubs based on family status, such as the Bachelors' Club; clubs based on hobbies, such as the Montreal Hunt Club; and clubs of volunteer community service, such as the exclusive Montreal Fire Club. During these club dinners, the bourgeois mingled with other merchants and colonial elites to forge business alliances, exchange information, share ideas, and cement social ties.[42]

The Beaver Club met fortnightly in the off-season of the fur trade, between December and April, with dinners beginning at four in the afternoon and often lasting until four in the morning.[43] Dinners were held in various Montreal hotels and taverns, such as the City Tavern, Richard Dillion's Montreal Hotel, Palmer's Hummums, and Tesseyman's, as was usual for private parties, business and political meetings, and gatherings of male friends in the eighteenth century.[44] The passing around of a calumet, or peace pipe, marked the beginning of the club's formal rituals, which were continued with a speech, or "harangue," made by the evening's president, and formal toasts.[45] Dinner fare included country food, such as braised venison, bread sauce, "Chevreuil des Guides" (stew), venison sausages, wild rice, quail, and partridge "du Vieux Trappeur," served with crested glass and silverware.[46] After dinner the club became more informal, as men began to drink more heavily, sing voyageur songs, and reminisce about the good old fur trading days. Festivities continued until the early morning, with men dancing on the tables, reenacting canoeing adventures, and breaking numerous bottles and glasses.

The club served as a forum for retired merchants to reminisce about the risky and adventurous days of fur trading and for young fur traders to enter Montreal's bourgeois society. In this setting elder fur trade masters could teach new masters how to assert authority over their servants. Virtually no fur trade laborers (and very few clerks) were ever invited to the Beaver

Club. In the mid-eighteenth century some men were able to rise from the rank of worker to manager, but by the time of the emergence of the NWC in the 1780s, the social and occupational hierarchies were firmly in place. Attitudes toward the lower orders, however, covered a complex and contradictory range, especially for fur traders who had lived and worked alongside their labor force in isolated and dangerous settings for long periods. Although fur trade bourgeois often admired voyageurs for their strength and skill and established relationships with them built on trust and interdependence, they also considered voyageurs to be thoughtless, irrational, and rude.[47] Club rituals imitating voyageurs helped the bourgeois to distance themselves from their workers. One of the most frequently mentioned amusements was the singing of voyageur songs.[48] Club member James Hughes told stories of the men arranging themselves on the floor, imitating the vigorous paddling of a canoe, and mounting wine kegs to "shoot the rapids" from the table to the floor.[49] The romanticization of voyageurs' activities cast them as exotic curiosities. At the same time, bourgeois appropriated voyageurs' experiences in the fur trade. The bourgeois reminisced about paddling canoes and running through rapids, even though this was the work of the voyageurs. The bourgeois did not regularly risk their lives in rapids and portages, carry back-breaking packs, paddle at outrageous speeds, nor survive on minimal food, as did the voyageurs. Rather, bourgeois directed crews, managed accounts, distributed food, and had better rations than their voyageurs. The bourgeois distanced themselves from their men in the pays d'en haut to assert their superiority, and yet in Montreal they appropriated voyageurs' rugged behavior to bolster their sense of manhood in the eyes of urbane Montreal merchants.

Scenes of Rule in the Pays d'en Haut

The bourgeois also tried to distance themselves from their servants while actually working in the trade. Junior clerks in particular, whose authority in isolated wintering posts was threatened by experienced laborers, were encouraged by more senior masters to establish firm lines of control. When the NWC clerk George Gordon was still a novice, he received advice from a senior clerk, George Moffatt, to be independent, confident and very involved in the trade; Moffatt also advised: "[You should] Mixt. very seldom with the Men, rather retire within yourself. than make them your companions.—I do not wish to insinuate that you should be haughty—on the contrary—affability with them at times, may get You esteme, while the observance of a proper distance, will command respect, and procure from them ready obedience to your orders."[50] In 1807 John McDonald of Garth was sent out as a novice to take over the NWC's Red River Department, which was notorious for its corruption and difficult men. A French Canadian interpreter named Potras, who had long been in the district and had great authority among voyageurs and Aboriginal people, had to be reminded by McDonald: "You are to act under me, you have no business to think, it is for me to do so and not for you, you are to obey."[51]

Masters also enacted a "theater of authority" in material ways. The bourgeois and the clerks performed less physical labor than the voyageurs. They were usually passengers aboard canoes and only helped their men paddle and portage in cases of extreme jeopardy. At times the rituals of travel situated masters at the head of great processions. In his reminiscences of his fur trading career, Alexander Ross described how the light canoe, used for transporting men and mail quickly through the interior, clearly positioned the bourgeois as a social superior: "The bourgeois is carried on board his canoe upon the back of some sturdy fellow generally appointed for this purpose. He seats himself on a convenient mattress, somewhat low in the centre of his canoe; his gun by his side, his little cherubs fondling around him, and his faithful spaniel lying at his feet. No sooner is he at his ease, than his pipe is presented by his attendant, and he then begins smoking, while his silken banner undulates over the stern of his painted vessel."[52] HBC surveyor Philip Turnor both envied and criticized the Montreal traders: "[They] give Men which never saw an Indian One Hundred Pounds pr Annum, his Feather Bed carried in the Canoe, his Tent which is exceeding good, pitched for him, his Bed made and he and his girl carried in and out of the Canoe and when in the Canoe never touches a Paddle unless for his own pleasure all of these indulgences I have been an Eye Witness to."[53] Likewise, the bourgeois did not participate in the vigorous round of activities that kept the post functioning smoothly, such as constructing and maintaining houses; building furniture, sleighs, and canoes; gathering fire wood; hunting; and preparing food. Rather, they kept accounts, managed the wares and provisions, and initiated trade with Aboriginal peoples.

Masters provided themselves with larger quantities and more varieties of food, fancier clothing, and better sleeping conditions than they provided voyageurs.[54] In the Rocky Mountain fur trade after 1821, Cole Harris describes the display of hierarchy at the HBC posts:

> *[F]ort routine and work were inserted in a close theatre of power, with calculated disciplinary intent. Men ate rations issued every Saturday, dried fish and potatoes more often than not, which they or Native women prepared in their quarters. Officers and clerks ate in the dining room of the officers' residence, the Big House, where they sat in order of rank and dined handsomely. Men were issued striped cotton shirts and a few yards of cloth; officers often dressed elegantly. . . . Officers' quarters were spacious and commanded the fort; men lived in barracks along the lateral walls, several men to a room if they were single, in small rooms of their own if they lived with Native women.*[55]

Probably the greatest challenges the bourgeois and the clerks faced in asserting authority and controlling their workers came from the circumstance of the fur trade itself—the great distances along fur trade routes and between posts and the difficulties of transportation and communication. Thus, the further they penetrated the interior, away from the larger fur trade administrative centers, the more the bourgeois had to rely on inexpensive symbols and actions to enforce their authority, such as carefully maintained social isolation, differential work roles, control over scarce resources, reputation, and ability.[56]

Accommodation between voyageurs and bourgeois and clerks made up a necessary part of the master-servant relationship. They worked very closely together for long periods of time, often shared living quarters, and faced many calamities and adventures together. The surest way for bourgeois and clerks to ensure loyalty was to provide plenty of good food for their men, as many disputes were caused by shortages of provisions. Bourgeois and clerks fostered good will by meeting other paternal duties, such as attempting to protect their men from dangers in the workplace, providing medicines, and treating men with respect.

Obligations

In paternalist contexts the masters' material advantages came with a symbolic and substantive price. As in maypole ceremonies servants expected that masters share the scarce resources of drink and food. On a symbolic level servants insisted their masters perform the paternalistic obligations that went hand in hand with authority.

Masters commonly met paternalistic obligations by providing voyageurs with drams (shots of alcohol) or regales (treats of alcohol, food, or tobacco). The frequency of providing drams or treats varied among masters and was affected by the availability of resources and the morale of a crew. Masters provided regales when settling accounts with servants and signing new engagements.[57] Voyageurs were awarded drams when they completed significant duties, such as building houses or erecting flagstaffs, the last task in constructing a post.[58] Drams marked arrivals to and departures from posts.[59] Masters were inclined to reward exhausting tasks such as the constant travel in winter between posts, hunting camps, Aboriginal people's lodges, and traps. Traveling in the company of Aboriginal people was often perceived as hazardous or risky, and masters frequently provided these travelers with drams as extra incentive, especially to those who were camping at Aboriginal lodges.[60]

Historian Craig Heron observes that in preindustrial Canada "booze was obviously intended to fortify the manual worker for heavy toil, or to sustain him in carrying it out."[61] Likewise, in the fur trade masters incorporated routine "rewards" into the tedious and trying aspects of fur trade work, such as portaging.[62] Voyageurs also rewarded themselves after difficult portages by saving their regales for such occasions.[63] Constructing furniture or snowshoes could be rewarded with a dram.[64] Sometimes the giving of gratuities was self-interested, such as when Alexander McKay gave his men moose skins to make themselves shoes, mittens, and blankets to last them through the winter, warning them that they had "a strong opposition to contend with" that year and they must be ready to go at a moment's notice.[65] He apparently believed his gift would help the voyageurs to perform their duties more effectively.

As part of this general encouragement, masters treated their men with drams at the end of a day of hard work.[66] Masters also could provide drams at the start of a day or of a difficult task as added incentive.[67] The promise of a dram as a reward was often made explicitly to coax voyageurs to work harder and faster.[68] In one case during a particularly grueling canoe journey, Alexander Mackenzie became fearful that his men would desert, so he cajoled them with a "hearty meal, and rum enough to raise their spirits," before resorting to threats and humiliation.[69] While on the Columbia River in the early nineteenth century, Ross Cox's party encountered hostile Aboriginal people. The bourgeois in charge, Stuart, gave "each man a double allowance of rum, 'to make his courage cheerie.'"[70] Masters also gave the Aboriginal wives and families of voyageurs gifts.[71] Including families in gift giving was a tacit acknowledgment of their importance at interior posts. Maintaining the goodwill of Aboriginal wives was essential to traders dependent on their knowledge and skill. Providing men with drams and regales seemed to mirror the custom of gift giving in trading with Aboriginal peoples.[72]

John Thomson's journal illustrates how some masters used drams at posts. When his crew arrived at Rocky Mountain Fort along the Mackenzie River in mid-October 1800, he provided his men with a dram each after they had set up the encampment. He gave them another dram five days later after they had constructed a warehouse and secured the trade goods inside. In the following week he gave his men drams while they were building houses and when they planted a flagstaff. He gave the voyageurs "a little Liquor to

Divert themselves. . . . Not merely on that Consideration, but more particularly on that of their Having exerted themselves & did their duty as well as [could] be expected from any Men."[73] Some bourgeois tried to restrict the provision of alcohol to their men to save money and to improve their performance, but as Archibald Norman McLeod explained, voyageurs needed "a little debauchery" now and then. He broke with custom by not providing his men drams when they finished constructing houses and erected the flagstaff at Fort Alexandria but gave them a quart of high wines on St. Andrew's Day.[74] Perhaps his men made it clear that they would not work effectively without this incentive.

Scenes of Resistance

Despite these points of accommodation, the fur trade workplace was infused with voyageur resistance to their masters' authority. Although voyageurs rarely challenged the structure of power, they constantly tried to shape the workplace to improve their lot. Voyageurs' discontents focused sharply on unsuitable working and living conditions, such as poor rations or unreasonable demands by bourgeois or clerks. They employed a number of tactics to initiate change, ranging from the relatively mild strategy of complaining to the extreme of deserting the service.

Voyageurs' complaining became a form of countertheater that contested the masters' performances of their hegemonic prerogatives. Just as masters asserted their authority in a theatrical style, especially in canoe processions, voyageurs asserted their agency by "a theatre of threat and sedition."[75] In one illuminating example, in the summer of 1804 while trying to travel through low water and marshes, Duncan Cameron's men ceaselessly complained about the miserable conditions and difficulty of constantly portaging. They cursed themselves as "Blockheads" for coming to that "Infernal Part of the Country," as they called it, damning the mud, damning the lack of clean water to quench their thirst, and damning the first person who attempted that road. Cameron tried to be patient and cheerful with them, as he knew that complaining was their custom.[76] Voyageurs sometimes chose to limit their resistance to complaining to their bourgeois or clerk in private, so that they would not appear weak in front of the other men. During a difficult trip from Kaministiquia to Pembina, Alexander Henry the Younger commented that little or nothing was said during the day when the men had "a certain shame or bashfulness about complaining openly," but at night everyone came to gripe about bad canoes, ineffective coworkers, and shortages of gum, wattap, and grease.[77] But depending on the attitude of the bourgeois, voyageurs could also restrain their complaining in front of their master in order to avoid losing favor. In many cases their demands were more likely to be met if they approached their master individually with strategic concerns rather than openly abusing their masters for unspecified grievances. For example, a blacksmith named Philip earned the wrath of his bourgeois, McKay, when he abused him both behind his back and to his face.[78] In another case clerk George Nelson felt pressured by the continual complaints made by his men about their rations. He worried that his men were spreading discontent among themselves and preferred that they approach him directly with their concerns.[79]

When labor was scarce, men often bargained for better wages, both individually and collectively. In a large and organized show of resistance in the summer of 1803, men at Kaministiquia, on the western tip of Lake Superior, refused to work unless they received higher pay.[80] Group efforts to increase wages were much rarer than the relatively common occurrence of men individually bargaining for better wages. Daniel Sutherland of the XYC instructed his recruiting agent in Montreal, St. Valur Mailloux, to refuse demands made by a couple of engagés for higher wages and to appease the men with small presents. One engagé named Cartier caused turmoil by telling the XYC wintering partners that Mailloux was hiring men at significantly higher wages and asking for his pay to be increased to that amount. Sutherland became angry with Mailloux, warning him: "Always [offer more to] oarsman and steersman, but never exceed the price that I told you for going and coming [pork eaters]."[81] Voyageurs could refuse to do tasks outside the normal range of their duties without extra pay as another means of increasing their wages.[82] Demands for better working conditions often accompanied men's demands for more pay. Most often their concerns centered on safety, and they could refuse to take unreasonable risks. During a moment of intense company competition in 1819 at Great Slave Lake, the NWC had taken into custody HBC officer Colin Robertson because the voyageurs insisted on it. NWC master W. F. Wentzel complained to Roderick McKenzie: "Several of our men informed that [Robertson] had threatened to excite the Natives to Massacre the North West Companys Servants at Fort Chipewyan, and our men refused to do their duty unless he was apprehended & detained in Safe Custody—This occasioned his arrest and has been Kept confined ever Since, but treated with every attention he could expect in Such a Situation."[83] The NWC bourgeois evidently decided it was worth inflaming the HBC so that his servants would continue to work.

French Canadian laborers had a reputation among all fur trade companies in North America as very skilled canoemen, and Montreal companies and the HBC often competed for voyageurs' contracts.[84] In a letter to the governor and the committee of the HBC, Andrew Graham, master at York Fort, wrote: "The Canadians are chosen Men inured to hardships & fatigue, under which most of Your Present Servants would sink, A Man in the Canadian Service who cannot carry two Packs of eighty Lbs. each, one & an half League losses his trip that is his Wages. But time & Practice would make it easy, & even a few Canadians may be got who would be thankful for Your Honours Service."[85] Their reputation made it easy for voyageurs to switch fur trade companies if they wanted to increase their wages or change their posting or if they were angry with their master.[86] Alexander Henry the Younger was disgusted by some men's lack of loyalty:

> *[T]he voyageurs southward, about Michilimackinac, the Mississippi, etc., are in the habit of changing employers yearly, according to wages offered, or as the whim takes them, which, with the spirit of competition in the South trade, and the looseness and levity they acquire in the Indian country, tends to make them insolent and intriguing fellows, who have no confidence in the measures or promises of their employers. Servants of this description cannot be*

> *trusted out of sight; they give merely eye service, and do nothing more than they conceive they are bound to do by their agreement, and even that with a bad grace.*[87]

Voyageurs who had worked in the service for some time often became expert bargainers, frustrating bourgeois and clerks who expected to be obeyed without hesitation. Clerk George Nelson expressed his frustration with servants: "The common men of all companies, places, who, or whatever they are, are always fretful, jealous, dis-contend & gluttonous, let the places or country be what it may, rich or poor, be the master ever so kind & indulgent, unless he be prudent & severe, not a little, the men will be always found the same, men; and only want an opportunity for shewing themselves so:—it is still worse where the country is hard."[88] The fretful, jealous, discontented, and gluttonous voyageurs were most likely those who negotiated for the best terms in their contracts and knew their worth. Their loyalty to their masters did not extend past their contract, and some of the men who went to work for the HBC did not hesitate to apprise HBC officers of the business plans of the NWC to please their new masters.[89] Men with uncommon skills and knowledge, such as interpreters and guides, were in the best position to bargain for better working conditions and more pay.[90] Because fur trade labor was often scarce, and the mortality rate was high, skilled men were valued. Masters often overlooked servant transgressions and met servant demands in an effort to maintain their services.

Another common strategy voyageurs employed to improve their working conditions was to deceive their bourgeois or clerk by pretending to be ill or by lying about resources and Aboriginal peoples in the area in order to evade work. It is difficult to judge the extent to which voyageurs tried to trick their masters, especially when they were successful. However, hints of this practice and suspicions of masters appear frequently in fur trade journals, suggesting that the practice was widespread. In December 1818 George Nelson, stationed near the Dauphin River, became frustrated with one of his men, Welles, who frequently sneaked in "holiday" time by traveling slowly or claiming to be lost.[91] Less-suspicious bourgeois and clerks probably did not catch half of the "dirty tricks" more careful voyageurs regularly played on them. Some masters, however, questioned their men's dubious actions and sent out "spies" to ensure that voyageurs were working honestly.[92] Other deceptions were more serious. Alexander Mackenzie was suspicious that his interpreters were not telling Aboriginal people what Mackenzie intended, which could have had serious repercussions for the trade.[93]

When efforts to deceive their masters were frustrated, voyageurs could become sullen and indolent, working slowly and ineffectively, and even openly defying their masters' orders. In one case in the fall of 1800, while trying to set out from Fort Chipewyan, James Porter had to threaten to seize the wages of a man who refused to embark. When the voyageur reluctantly complied, he swore that the devil should take him for submitting to the bourgeois.[94] More serious breaches of the master-servant contract included stealing provisions from cargo. Though Edward Umfreville kept a constant watch over the merchandise in his canoes, a father and son managed to steal a nine-gallon keg of mixed liquor.[95] George Nelson described the pilfering of provisions as routine.[96] Men stole provisions to give extra food to their girlfriends or wives.[97] For the Orcadians working in the HBC service, Edith Burley characterizes this type of countertheater—working ineffectively and deceiving masters—as both a neglect of duty and an attempt to control the work process.[98] The same applies to the voyageurs.

One area of particular unease between voyageurs and masters was the issue of voyageurs free-trading with Aboriginal peoples. Unlike the HBC the Montreal fur trading companies did not strictly and universally prohibit voyageurs from trading on the side with Aboriginal peoples to augment their income; a few bourgeois and clerks even expected voyageurs to do so as long as they did not abuse the privilege.[99] Most bourgeois and clerks, however, were upset to find their men trading with Aboriginal peoples because they wanted to concentrate the profit into their company's hands and considered free-trading "contrary to the established rules of the trade and the general practice among the natives."[100] In an 1803 trial over trading jurisdiction NWC clerk John Charles Stuart testified that when any men brought skins from the wintering grounds for the purpose of trading on their private account, "it was by a Special Favour" granted by their bourgeois, supported in the clause "Part de pactons" in their contracts. Although the practice was customary, the bourgeois retained the right to grant or refuse it.[101] After the 1804 merger of the XYC and NWC, the bourgeois decided to restrict private trade to increase profitability in the newly reformed company. Any man caught with more than two buffalo robes or two dressed skins, or one of each, would be fined fifty livres NW currency, and any employee caught trafficking with "petty traders or Montreal men" would forfeit his wages. The bourgeois were able to enforce this new restriction because the merger had created a surplus of men; employment became tenuous and many voyageurs were concerned that their contracts would not be renewed.[102] In the minutes of the 1806 annual meeting, NWC partners agreed to ban men from bringing furs out of the interior in order to discourage petty trading.[103]

If voyageurs became frustrated with small acts of daily resistance, they engaged in direct action against their masters' rule. Deserting the service was an outright breach of the master-servant contract.[104] Voyageurs deserted the service for a variety of purposes. Temporary desertions could provide a form of vacation, a ploy for renegotiating terms of employment, and an opportunity to look for a better job. The act of deserting the service shows that voyageurs had a clear notion of their rights as workers, which was instilled by the reciprocal obligations of paternalism. This may be one of the more significant differences between voyageurs and laborers from the Scottish Orkney Islands who worked for the HBC. Orcadians did not desert very often because they had nowhere to go once they left the service. It was virtually impossible to find passage on a ship back to Great Britain because most ships belonged to the HBC. Orcadian laborers had fewer opportunities to form close ties with Aboriginal peoples in the Northwest because the fur trade officers conducted most of the trade, and HBC employees mainly lived within the confines of trading posts. Possible refuges for deserting Orcadians were posts of competing traders, such as the NWC and XYC, where they could look for alternative employment or find passage to the Canadian colonies.[105] Conversely, voyageurs working in the Montreal trade had the options of becoming freemen, joining Aboriginal families, or returning to the St. Lawrence valley.

Discipline

As part of the continual negotiations between masters and servants, the bourgeois responded to voyageurs' acts of resistance with intense performances of authority. The bourgeois and the clerks disciplined their men for transgressions of the master-servant contract and as a means of encouraging voyageur obedience. They withheld servant privileges, such as regales, drams, and liquor for purchase.[106] They frequently humiliated and intimidated their men. In one case during a journey to the Peace River in the summer of 1793, Alexander Mackenzie was confronted with a man who refused to embark in the canoe. He wrote: "This being the first example of absolute disobedience which had yet appeared during the course of our expedition, I should not have passed it over without taking some very severe means to prevent a repetition of it; but as he had the general character of a simple fellow, among his companions, and had been frightened out of what little sense he possessed, by our late dangers, I rather preferred to consider him as unworthy of accompanying us, and to represent him as an object of ridicule and contempt for his pusillanimous behaviour; though, in fact, he was a very useful, active, and laborious man."[107] Mackenzie also confronted the chief canoe maker during the same trip about his laziness and bad attitude. The voyageur was mortified by being singled out.[108] This kind of ritualized public shaming reinforced masculine ideals of effectiveness and skill. On an expedition to the Missouri in 1805, one of Antoine Larocque's men wished to remain with Charles McKenzie's party. Larocque became angry and told the voyageur his courage failed him like an old woman, which threw the voyageur into a violent fit of anger.[109] On occasion a voyageur was whipped for delinquency. For example, at Fort Alexandria Archibald McLeod became frustrated with voyageurs La Rose and Ducharme for leaving part of a cargo of meat and some blankets behind at an Aboriginal lodge. McLeod recorded in his journal: "La Rose being the only one I saw, got Seven reprehensions for his carelessness, in respect of the Blanket & their leaving a part of the meat, I told him I Should charge the Blanket to his At [account] untill I learned whether it is lost or not. he means to return tomorrow, to learn the fate of the Blanket, & fetch the remainder of the meat."[110] Bourgeois and clerks sometimes played on the fear of starvation as a means of asserting authority over their men.[111]

In cases of severe dereliction bourgeois had the power to fire their employees.[112] In some cases voyageurs were happy to be dismissed because they desired to become freemen, as in the case of Joseph Constant, whom Nelson fired for his "fits of ill humour without cause."[113] It was a very serious matter when voyageurs decided to quit. Masters made efforts to recoup deserters and could punish deserters with confinement. In 1804 in the Rainy Lake area, NWC clerk Hugh Faries spotted a deserter named Gâyou from the Athabasca River brigade at an XYC post. Faries reported that the principal NWC clerk of the Rainy Lake District, Archibald McLellan "sent Jourdain [a voyageur] up with a note, desiring Lacombe [the head of the XYC post] to send [Gâyou] down. he told him, he might go if he pleased, but the fellow would not come down. Mr McLellan went himself, & Richard [a voyageur] and [Faries] followed him. the fellow made no resistance but came down immediately. Mr McLellan put him into a cellar swarming with fleas for the night."[114] Relations between masters and voyageurs were often tense, and on rare occasions the relationship could become violent. The usual difficulties of the weather, accidents, and the constant challenge of the strenuous work could lead to high levels of stress and anxiety. Voyageurs' blunders, lost and broken equipment, and voyageur insolence often resulted in tense situations.[115] Alexander Henry the Younger grew frustrated with one of his men, Desmarrais, for not protecting the buffalo he had shot from wolves. He grumbled: "My servant is such a careless, indolent fellow that I cannot trust the storehouse to his care. I made to-day a complete overhaul, and found everything in the greatest confusion; I had no idea matters were so bad as I found them. . . . Like most of his countrymen, he is much more interested for himself than for his employer."[116] Mutual resentments could lead to brawls between the masters and the servants. One NWC master named McDonald often challenged his men to fights. Cox recorded:

> *One of our Canadian voyageurs, named Bazil Lucie, a remarkably strong man, about six feet three inches high, with a muscular frame, and buffalo neck, once said something which he thought bordered on disrespect. Any man under five feet ten might have made use of the same language with impunity, but from such a man as Lucie, who was a kind of bully over his comrades, it could not be borne; he accordingly told him to hold his tongue, and threatened to chastise him if he said another word. This was said before several of the men, and Lucie replied by saying that he might thank the situation he held for his safety, or he should have satisfaction sur le champ. McDonald instantly fired, and asked him if he would fight with musket, sword, or pistol; but Lucie declared he had no notion of fighting in that manner, adding that his only weapons were his fists. The pugnacious Celt [McDonald] resolving not to leave him any chance of escape, stripped off his coat, called him un enfant de chienne, and challenged him to fight comme un polisson. Lucie immediately obeyed the call, and to work they fell. I was not present at the combat; but some of the men told me that in less than ten minutes Bazil was completely disabled, and was unfit to work for some weeks after.*[117]

More typically tensions between masters and servants were expressed in unfair treatment rather than violence. Motivated by the desire to save money and gain the maximum benefit from their workers, the bourgeois and the clerks pushed their men to work very hard, which could result in ill will. Most serious cases of ill will and injustice concerned bourgeois selling goods to voyageurs at inflated prices and encouraging voyageurs to go into debt as soon as they entered fur trade service. It is difficult to find many cases of "bad faith" in the bourgeois' own writings, as they would not likely dwell on their cruelty as masters or reveal their unfair tricks. However, travelers, critics of fur trade companies, and disgruntled employees provided clues.

The French Duke de La Rouchefoucauld Liancourt and Lord Selkirk charged that the NWC deliberately tried to ensure that their men went into debt by encouraging them to drink and throw their money away on "luxeries" and then charging their men highly inflated prices for these goods.[118]

Insurgency

Voyageur responses to masters' cruelty could reach intense levels of resistance. Ill will between servants and masters usually impeded work. Sometimes the tensions were so strong that voyageurs refused to share with masters the food they obtained hunting and fishing.[119] The more outrageous instances of masters abusing servants could lead to collective resistance among the voyageurs in the form of strikes or mass desertion. When a voyageur named Joseph Leveillé was condemned by the Montreal Quarter Sessions to the pillory for having accepted the wages of two rival fur trading firms in 1794, a riot ensued. A group made up largely of voyageurs hurled the pillory into the St. Lawrence River and threatened to storm the prison. The prisoner was eventually released, and no one was punished for the incident.[120] Voyageurs seemed to have developed a reputation for mob belligerence in Lower Canada. Attorney general Jonathan Sewell warned in a 1795 letter to Lieutenant Colonel Beckworth that officers in Lower Canada should be given greater discretionary power to counter the "riotous inclinations" of the people, especially of the "lawless band" of voyageurs.[121] Mass rioting and collective resistance sometimes occurred in New France and Lower Canada.[122] However, the small population, diffuse work settings, and not too unreasonable seigneurial dues usually restricted expressions of discontent to individual desertions or localized conflicts.[123] Yet instances of collective action created a precedent for mass protest.[124] On occasion voyageurs deserted en masse during cargo transports or exploration missions. In these cases their tasks were difficult and dangerous, and men worked closely together in large groups, performing essentially the same type of work. Communication, the development of a common attitude toward work, and camaraderie fostered collective consciousness and encouraged collective action.

In the summer of 1794 a Montreal brigade at Lac La Pluie attempted to strike for higher wages. Duncan McGillivray explained: "A few discontented persons in their Band, wishing to do as much mischief as possible assembled their companions together several times on the Voyage Outward & represented to them how much their Interest suffered by the passive obedience to the will of their masters, when their utility to the Company, might insure them not only of better treatment, but of any other conditions which they would prescribe with Spirit & Resolution."[125] When they arrived at Lac La Pluie, the brigade demanded higher wages and threatened to return to Montreal without the cargo. The bourgeois initially prevailed upon a few of the men to abandon the strike. Soon afterward most of the men went back to work, and the ringleaders were sent to Montreal in disgrace.

Efforts at collective action in the Northwest did not always end in failure. In his third expedition to Missouri Country in the fall of 1805 and the winter of 1806, Charles McKenzie's crew of four men deserted. They had been lodged with Black Cat, a chief in a Mandan village, who summoned McKenzie to his tent to inform McKenzie of their desertion. The men had traded away all of their property to the Mandans and intended to do the same with McKenzie's property, but Black Cat secured it. When McKenzie declared he would punish his men, Black Cat warned that the Mandans would defend the voyageurs. McKenzie tried to persuade the men to return to service, but they would not yield.[126] As this shows, men who spent their winters in the pays d'en haut became a skilled and highly valued labor force; they felt entitled to fair working conditions and were not afraid to work together to pressure the bourgeois.[127]

Despite the occasions of mass action, voyageurs acted individually more often than collectively, like the Orcadians working for the HBC.[128] Their most powerful bargaining chip in labor relations was the option of desertion. Although the bourgeois took voyageurs to court for deserting their contracts, the measure had little effect because voyageurs continued to desert anyway. The option to desert acted as a safety valve, relieving pressure from the master-servant relationship. If voyageurs were very unhappy with their master, they could leave to work for another company, return to Lower Canada, or become freemen. Collective action was also hindered because voyageurs seemed to idealize freedom and independence.[129] Desertion of individuals worked against a collective voyageur consciousness.

Some permanent deserters maintained a casual relationship with fur trading companies, serving the occasional limited contract or selling furs and provisions. One man, Brunet, was pressured to desert because his Aboriginal wife wanted to join her relatives rather than stay at the post. George Nelson negotiated with Brunet to provide him with a more informal contract and allowed Brunet and his wife to leave if they helped the company make trading contacts with her family.[130] Conversely, another man named Vivier decided to quit his contract in November 1798 because he could not stand living with Aboriginal people, as he was ordered to do by his bourgeois, John Thomson, who noted: "[H]e says that he cannot live any longer with them & that all the devils in Hell cannot make him return, & that he prefers marching all Winter from one Fort to another rather than Live any Longer with them."[131] Thomson refused to give him provisions or equipment because in the fall he had provided him with enough to pass the winter. Thomson had been frustrated with the man's behavior all season, as he had refused to return to the fort when ordered. Vivier had become so disenchanted with the trade that he offered his wife and child to another voyageur so he could return to Canada, but his wife protested. Thomson finally agreed to provide him with ammunition, tobacco, and an axe on credit, and Vivier left the post. A month and a half later Vivier returned to the post to work.[132] Voyageurs may have returned to work for fur trade companies because they could not find enough to eat or desired the protection that a post provided. Fear of starvation and the dangers of the Northwest may have discouraged voyageurs from deserting in the first place. In one case Alexander Henry the Younger came across a pond where Andre Garreau, a NWC deserter, had been killed in 1801 with five Mandans by a Swiss party.[133]

Despite the efforts of the bourgeois to impose a system of organization on the Montreal fur trade, the terms of work for voyageurs were not fixed. The changing needs of the fur trade companies and the habitants led to fluctuations in recruitment, engagements, and wages. The instability in the system was probably key to providing the flexibility necessary to the growth of the fur trade companies, especially in the context of the fierce competition for furs in the interior.

Although it is difficult to quantify the occurrence of turbulence and accommodation in the relations between masters and servants, negotiations over acceptable labor conditions dominated the Northwest fur trade. Masters tried to exert control over the workforce by encouraging men to become indebted to their company and by being the sole providers of European goods in the interior. Masters also capitalized on risk taking and the tough masculine ethos to encourage a profitable work pace. However, their most successful way to maintain order was to impress their men with their personal authority, generated by a strong manner, bravery, and effective management of servants and limited resources. Formal symbols, such as dress, ritual celebrations, access to better provisions, and a lighter workload, reminded voyageurs of the superior status and power of masters. This theater of daily rule helped to construct the hegemonic structure of paternal authority. Masters also turned to the courts to prosecute their men for breaches of contract and attempted to cooperate with other companies to regulate the workforce, but these methods were far from successful in controlling their voyageurs. The most effective means of asserting authority was through rituals and symbols. In turn voyageurs resisted master authority in their own countertheater in an effort to shape their working environment. Voyageurs generally had very high performance standards for work, which were bolstered by masculine ideals of strength, endurance, and risk taking. Nonetheless, voyageurs created a space to continually challenge the expectations of their masters, in part through their complaining. They set their own pace, demanded adequate and even generous diets, refused to work in bad weather, and frequently worked to rule. When masters made unreasonable demands or failed to provide adequate provisions, voyageurs responded by working more slowly, becoming insolent, and occasionally free-trading and stealing provisions. More extreme expressions of discontent included turning to the Lower Canadian courts for justice, but, like the bourgeois, voyageurs found that their demands were better met by negotiating for a better lot off the legal record. Their strongest bargaining chip proved to be deserting the service, which they sometimes did en masse. Overall voyageurs tended to act individually more than collectively, as the option to desert the service discouraged the development of a collective voyageur consciousness. Yet as we will see in the next chapter, the lack of a collective consciousness in regard to working conditions did not mean that voyageurs did not develop a shared mentalité.

6. Rendezvous

Parties, Tricks, and Friendships

> *Fort William is the great emporium for the interior. An extensive assortment of merchandise is annually brought hither from Montreal, by large canoes, or the Company's vessels on the lakes, which, in return, bring down the produce of the wintering posts to Canada, from whence it is shipped for England. . . . Fort William may therefore be looked upon as the metropolitan post of the interior, and its fashionable season generally continues from the latter end of May to the latter end of August. During this period, good living and festivity predominate; and the luxuries of the dinner-table compensate in some degree for the long fasts and short commons experienced by those who are stationed in the remote posts.* The voyageurs *too enjoy their carnival, and between rum and baubles the hard-earned wages of years are often dissipated in a few weeks.*[1]

The Montreal fur trade was a far-flung enterprise spanning thousands of miles. Central administrative posts were established in the interior of the pays d'en haut to facilitate the organization of trading and the transfer of goods. Ross Cox's description of Fort William quoted here, from his *Adventures on the Columbia River* (1831), conveys an image of a bustling and diverse center of commerce and cavorting. At these administrative nodes fur traders and laborers congregated in midsummer to exchange furs for European trade goods. These gatherings, called rendezvous, became a time of celebration and feasting. Arriving voyageurs were relieved to have survived their grueling journey, pleased to meet up with friends, and excited about fresh supplies of food and drink. In the 1770s trader Peter Pond described the rendezvous at Mackinac (at the junction of Lakes Michigan and Huron), where many "ware amuseing themselves in Good Cumpany at Billards Drinking fresh Punch Wine & Eney thing thay Please to Call for while the Mo[re] valgear Ware fiteing Each other feasting was Much atended to Dansing at Nite."[2] After 1803 the most famous rendezvous was at Fort William, at the western end of Lake Superior, which became a "great emporium," as Ross Cox aptly described it. Here pork eaters and northmen unloaded and loaded their ladings, the bourgeois held their annual meetings to plan business operations for the coming year, independent merchants set up shops to sell wares, and retired voyageurs who had settled in the area came to the fort to hear about the past year's adventures.[3] In the midst of all this activity, voyageurs' celebrations dominated the scene. When clerk George Nelson arrived at Grand Portage for the first time in 1802, he observed high levels of "Gambling, feasting, dancing, drinking & fighting."[4]

Although voyageurs were hired for extremely difficult work, a large part of their lives was occupied with celebrations, festivity, and play. The old voyageur working on Lake Winnipeg, described in chapter 1, reflected: "I wanted for nothing; and spent all my earnings in the enjoyment of pleasure. . . . were I young again, I should glory in commencing the same career again. I would [s]pend another half-century in the same fields of enjoyment."[5] Voyageurs enjoyed many aspects of their jobs, especially hunting and fishing, and sometimes engaged in these activities for fun in their spare time.[6] Perhaps play came to comprise a significant part of voyageurs' lives because they worked in a liminal space, on the boundaries between French Canada and Aboriginal societies, constantly moving through the pays d'en haut. Scholars have argued that liminality encourages playfulness and trickery; in particular cultural anthropologist Victor Turner asserted that "liminality is particularly conducive to play. Play is not to be restricted to games and jokes; it extends to the introduction of new forms of symbolic action . . . parts of liminality may be given over to experimental behaviour."[7] Voyageurs regularly moved across the thresholds of new worlds, and the thrill and adventure of traveling into the unknown were expressed in their parties, tricks, and friendships.

Following Turner's lead, this chapter takes a broad view of the concept of play, not simply as an opposite to work, but rather as a comprehensive term for festivities, pastimes, relief from work, and trickery. Parties, singing, dancing, gaming, and joking made up the play of voyageurs when they were working as well as resting. Play offered them amusement and diversion, but it also became a means through which they could shape their world.

Carnival on Canoe Journeys

Group celebrations were an especially revealing aspect of the play of voyageurs, and historians have developed lines of analysis to interpret the celebrations of lower orders of people, such as peasants and workers. In play Mikhail Bakhtin found a window to late medieval and early renaissance European folk culture. Bakhtin saw "carnival" as providing

> *[a] boundless world of humorous forms and manifestations opposed to the official and serious tone of medieval ecclesiastical and feudal culture. In spite of their variety, folk festivities of the carnival type, the comic rites and cults, the clowns and fools, giants, dwarfs, and jugglers, the vast and manifold literature of parody—all these forms have one style in common: they belong to one culture of folk carnival humor. . . . All these forms of protocol and ritual based on laughter and consecrated by tradition existed in all the countries of medieval Europe; they were sharply distinct from the serious official, ecclesiastical, feudal, and political cult forms and ceremonials. They offered a completely different, nonofficial, extraecclesiastical and extrapolitical aspect of the world, of man, and of human relations; they built a second world and a second life outside officialdom, a world in which all medieval people participated more or less.*[8]

In the fur trade the same applied to voyageurs, who constructed a world that differed dramatically from that of their masters. Voyageurs' distinctive identities and practices were not confined to specific celebrations, such as rendezvous, but permeated all their forms of play. Bakhtin observed that the concept of carnival is closely related to that of play: "Because of their obvious sensuous character and their strong element of play, carnival images closely resemble certain artistic forms, namely the spectacle. In turn, medieval spectacles often tended toward carnival folk culture, the culture of the marketplace. . . . [The carnival nucleus is] shaped according to a certain pattern of play. . . . Carnival is not a spectacle seen by the people; they live in it, and everyone participates because its very idea embraces all the people."[9] Carnival offered an easily identifiable mode in which peasants could create their own world separate from officialdom, where they could focus on bodily pleasures and radically subvert state ideology. Building on the work of Bakhtin, scholars have applied the theory of carnival in different contexts. Emmanuel Le Roy Ladurie found that in the French city Romans in the sixteenth century carnival became a vehicle for revolt against government, taxes, and nobility.[10] Others see carnival more broadly as a time of authorized transgression of any kind of norms.[11] Yet others look at carnival as a moment in which hierarchies are dissolved, popular culture of the masses rises to become the dominant discourse, and authority is dislocated.[12] In her study of early modern France, Natalie Zemon Davis found that "festive life can on the one hand perpetuate certain values of the community (even guarantee its survival), and on the other hand criticize political order."[13] Carnivals had many uses and meanings among lower orders that embraced the two extremes of forming of community bonds and deepening of cultural fissures.

As in other early modern folk settings, carnivals, and especially rendezvous, helped to shape the voyageurs' world. Literally translated as "meeting," rendezvous represented a time when fur traders came together to celebrate, encouraging camaraderie, competition, and social distinctions among everyone in the trade. Earlier we noted the omnipresent divisions between voyageurs and their masters. During rendezvous, however, divisions among voyageurs themselves became more pronounced. Throughout the rest of the year celebrations served the same functions: they unified men in camaraderie but also fostered social fissures.

In fur trade departures festivity pervaded the chaos of last-minute hirings, packing, and planning. This flurry of activity was most intense at the large annual leave-taking from the St. Lawrence valley at the beginning of a season.[14] People gathered around the crews at Montreal and Lachine, the departure point just west of the rapids near Montreal, to send off the brigades.

Clerk George Nelson reminisced that the young men bade farewell to their relatives and friends "with tears in their eyes & singing as if going to a banquet!"[15] Large parties were held at Lachine the night before the brigades intended to set out, and most people became intoxicated. In his biography of the voyageur Jean-Baptiste Charbonneau, Georges Dugas described the parties that were held before crews set out: "During fifteen days, it was, for these old wolves of the North, a series of celebrations and amusements; they invited all their friends, and reveled; one had to say that they kept spending down to the last cent, and left their gusset [pocket] completely empty. The drink was flowing in torrents; in the evening they had a dance. . . . . On the day of departure, a crowd of people went to Lachine to witness the spectacle."[16] Setting out from Montreal on April 25, 1833, explorer George Back commented on the festivities accompanying the departure to the interior:

> *[O]n arriving at La Chine . . . I found [the voyageurs] far too assiduous in their libations to Bacchus, to be subject to any less potent influences. Notwithstanding the alarm and confusion of the preceding night, a number of the officers of the garrison, and many of the respectable inhabitants, collected spontaneously together, to offer us a last tribute of kindness. We embarked amidst the most enthusiastic cheers, and firing of musketry. The two canoes shot rapidly through the smooth waters of the canal, and were followed by the dense crowd on the banks. A few minutes brought us to the St. Lawrence, and, as we turned the stems of our little vessels up that noble stream, one long loud huzza bade us farewell!*[17]

The event described by Back had long been a tradition in Montreal. Carousing was sometimes delayed until the first night of the voyage, when the men drank their allowances of rum paid to them upon departure.[18] The hangovers of both voyageurs and their masters could delay departures. While traveling with the NWC brigades in late April 1798, Colonel George Landmann described a wild party held at Lachine the night before his group intended to set out on their journey. He hid in the fireplace to protect himself as he watched the bourgeois Alexander Mackenzie and William McGillivray continue in their drunken frolics after everyone else had collapsed. After the delay Landmann described the parting: "[A]way we started, with hearty expressions of goodwill from those who remained. Our people reiterated Indian war-whoops as long as the windings of the waters we were on, allowed of our remaining in sight."[19]

The pageantry of departures and arrivals was heightened with "Indian war whoops" and firing muskets.[20] The yelling and musket fire were a form of salute to the brigades, a gesture of respect, and a wish of goodwill. "Indian war whoops" may have symbolized entry into a "savage world," unknown, exotic, and dangerous to voyageurs, and perhaps marked the beginning of the men's transition from French Canadian habitants to voyageurs who lived among Aboriginal peoples. The war whoops probably reflected both a fear of Aboriginal peoples as well as admiration for them. Dugas described the desires of new voyageurs to imitate Aboriginal people: "The savage life appealed to them; it seemed to them that down there, that they could be rid of all brakes, dressed like the Indian, sleeping with him under the tent, and hunting like him for livelihood."[21] The most common form of voyageur labor, canoeing, was a practice learned from Aboriginal peoples. The war whoops symbolized the extensive cultural borrowing of Canadians from Aboriginal peoples, but they also symbolized French colonists' view of Aboriginal peoples as an undifferentiated and exotic "other."[22] Philip Deloria has found similar cultural ambiguity in American appropriation of Aboriginal actions. He argues that "[t]he indeterminacy of American identities stems, in part, from the nation's inability to deal with Indian people. Americans wanted to feel a natural affinity with the continent, and it was Indians who could teach them such aboriginal closeness. Yet, in order to control the landscape they had to destroy the original inhabitants."[23] Voyageurs did not want to control the landscape to the same degree as American colonists, but they knew they were at the mercy of those who did. Thus voyageurs had to appease Aboriginal peoples, despite their fear. Imitating Aboriginal customs was a way in which voyageurs could familiarize themselves with these strange new people. Yet voyageurs' behavior was similar to that of American colonists in other ways. Deloria asserts that in the context of carnivalesque holidays, such as in Tammany societies, when the "real" world was suspended in favor of a topsy-turvy world of unstable power, the figure of the Indian became central. The Indian became a means through which to articulate a revolutionary identity separate from Europe and attached to the North American continent.[24] Likewise, "Indianness" or "Aboriginality" was evoked in the formation of the voyageurs' distinct identity.

The pattern of celebrations at departures carried over into the interior. Alexander Henry the Younger described his men's party in the summer of 1800 after the first day on the route from Grand Portage to Lake Winnipeg: "All were merry over their favourite regale, which is always given on their departure, and generally enjoyed at this spot, where we have a delightful meadow to pitch our tents, and plenty of elbow-room for the men's antics."[25] This treat was especially appreciated after the arduous portage at that site.

Arrivals were marked with the same festivity and pageantry as departures. A sense of relief rather than excitement dominated the occasions, as the men celebrated the completion of a safe and successful journey. Arriving back in Montreal was an especially momentous occasion, as it marked the passage out of the fur trade world. When Ross Cox's crew arrived at the Lake of Two Mountains, near Montreal, in September 1817, he presented his voyageurs with a keg of rum as a "valedictory allowance" and shook hands with each man.[26] At Fort William and Grand Portage men were treated with regales of bread, pork, butter, liquor, and tobacco, and usually held great parties.[27] At smaller posts men were treated with drams when they disembarked.[28] The fur trade arrivals were reminiscent of sailors reaching ports after long bouts at sea or lumbermen completing a river drive. Drunken merriment and unruly rioting were expressions of joy in finishing a round of grueling labor. Sailors arriving on transatlantic vessels combed the streets of port towns "in search of wine, women, and song."[29] In writing about nineteenth-century whalers, Margaret Creighton, however, warns that although some sailors engaged in irrepressible carousing, gaming, drinking, and sexual sport while on shore, others took pleasure in more quiet and pious ways. The whalers she studied were a diverse lot who did not fit stereotypes derived from legal records or the writings of moral reformers.[30] Likewise for voyageurs arrivals at posts probably included a range of activities, from drunken brawls to quiet prayers.

Incoming crews were usually met by the inhabitants of a post, including families that the men had left behind for the summer. Especially large crowds gathered at Grand Portage and Fort William.[31] Alexander Ross described the pageantry and pomp that could accompany the arrival of a crew: "On this joyful occasion, every person advances to the waterside, and great guns are fired to announce the bourgeois' arrival. A general shaking of hands takes place, as it often happens that people have not met for years: even the bourgeois goes through this mode of salutation with the meanest."[32] At smaller posts flags were raised and crews were saluted with musket shots.[33] Men were often sent out to meet expected canoes to help guide the crews into the posts.[34] Boisterous arrivals seemed to be a long-standing custom.[35]

At the major administrative centers along the Great Lakes, such as Michilimackinac, Grand Portage, and Fort William, departures and arrivals were similar to those in Montreal. The rendezvous in midsummer was particularly festive, and the men enjoyed abundant food and drink and the camaraderie of the large groups, which were hard to come by in the interior.[36] Ross Cox described the "good living and festivity" that predominated at Fort William, "the great emporium."[37] His account of voyageurs recklessly spending a year's wages was probably an exaggeration, but Cox's passage reflects the jubilation of rendezvous.

Traders mustered smaller though equally lively parties at interior posts, especially those that functioned as minor administrative centers, such as Fort Alexander, at the mouth of the Winnipeg River, and Fort Chipewyan, on Lake Athabasca.[38] At these posts, instead of saying goodbye to European Canadian families, men said goodbye to Aboriginal friends and families before departing.[39] As late as the mid-nineteenth century, travelers described interior rendezvous points, such as Grand Portage along the Saskatchewan River, a general Aboriginal meeting place, where voyageurs, métis, and freemen generally stopped on their way to Columbia. Their rendezvous gave the place "the animation and variety of a fair."[40] Celebrations occasionally occurred en route when crews passed each other, especially if they were in a particularly remote area, and if they were not in a great hurry.[41] Margaret Creighton found that "whaling ships sought each other out for company, and visits at sea, called *gams*, created a deep-sea society."[42] Like the whalers voyageurs used such occasions to visit, to share stories of risk, daring, and dangers on the rivers, and to commiserate with one another about the *misère* of the work.

Parties at the start and the end of journeys were not unique to voyageurs or French Canada in the eighteenth century, but these celebrations became distinctive social markers of the voyageur's journey, underscoring the journey's importance to the trade, its danger, as well as its defining status for voyageurs. The pageantry and festivities helped to separate the voyageur social order from French Canada and marked the transition between the distinct social spaces and the emergence of a new voyageur world (see chapter 3). The designated (though limited) space for revelry allowed voyageurs an opportunity to express their fear, anxiety, sadness, and excitement at traveling between these different worlds. By "letting go" or "going wild" at the parties, men were then better able to focus on the task of efficient traveling, so necessary to the effective functioning of the trade.

The rendezvous, on the other hand, was unique to the fur trade. It assumed great significance because it brought together most parts of the disparate trading operations and underscored the extreme division of times of plenty from times of want in the trade. Some rendezvous may have been modeled on Aboriginal trading fairs, such as those at Montreal in the second half of the seventeenth century.[43] In the continental interior many Aboriginal peoples met with one another in large groups on an annual basis.[44]

Among the most significant of these gatherings on the plains were the annual summer trading fairs at the Mandan-Hidatsa villages, but smaller fairs also occurred among the Crees, the Ojibwes, the Assiniboines, the Shoshones, and the Blackfeet.[45] David Meyer and Paul Thistle contend that fur traders built their posts along the Saskatchewan River in the vicinity of annual religious gatherings of Cree people.[46] Ironically the fur trade rendezvous could become a source of consternation for Aboriginal peoples. Victor Lytwyn has shown that Ojibwe hunters and trappers were intimidated by traders at Grand Portage, especially during the rendezvous, when revelry got out of hand.[47]

Annual Cycle of Carnival at Trading Posts

Voyageurs had much more leisure time during the winter months spent at interior posts than they did during the canoe journeys of the summers. Yet here they also had more time to feel homesick and anxious in the midst of a foreign world. Much of their play was reminiscent of French Canada, such as celebrating annual holidays, drinking, and holding balls; these festivities helped voyageurs create a sense of home away from home. Voyageurs also had the time to create new connections, form new families, and solidify a distinctive society in the Northwest. Their celebrations helped them create new memories and new traditions rooted in their new locations.

An annual schedule of holiday celebrations accompanied the yearly round of labor, which was especially important to the men living at isolated posts, away from their families and friends. Men often journeyed from outlying posts to congregate at larger central forts to celebrate the holidays and gladly risked the dangers and discomfort of winter travel, even a week of walking with snowshoes, to avoid spending a holiday alone.[48] Holidays helped to mark the passage of time and provided structure during the long, dreary, and often lonely months at the interior posts. Coming together to celebrate at specific times helped to generate camaraderie and fellow feeling with one another, their masters, and Aboriginal peoples.

Christmas and New Year were the most popular holidays for the fur traders and were rarely forgotten or ignored. Other holidays that were sometimes celebrated included All Saint's Day on November 1, St. Andrew's Day on November 30, and Easter in early April.[49] Similar celebrations occurred at HBC posts.[50] The occasional mention of celebrations occurred on Palm Sunday, the king's birthday (June 4, George III), and Epiphany, or "Little Christmas" (January 6).[51] Men seemed willing to commemorate any day, regardless of its origins or significance to them, because it served as an excuse for a celebration and drams from the bourgeois. Commemorating St. Andrew, the patron saint of Scotland, and observing the birthday of George III, king of Great Britain, were probably holidays introduced by the Scottish and English bourgeois and clerks, while Christmas, New Year's, All Saint's Day, and Easter would have been common celebrations in French Canada.[52] George Landmann noted that in late eighteenth-century Montreal, New Year's Day was "a day of extraordinary festivity, which was extended to the two or three following days. Amongst the Canadians it was . . . the fashion for everybody to visit everybody during one of the three first days of the year, when a glass of noyeau or other liquor was, with a piece of biscuit or cake, presented to the visitor, which, after a hard day's work in calling at some twenty or thirty houses, frequently terminated in sending a number of very respectable people home in a staggering condition toward the close of the day."[53] Feasting, drinking, and levees, or paying courtesy calls on masters (particularly on New Year's Day), were characteristic of celebrations in fur trade society.

The holiday celebrations seemed to follow a formula. Specific rituals and ceremonies, giving the day a sense of orderly formality and tradition, were followed by chaotic parties, where wild abandon and heavy drinking predominated. Alexander Henry the Younger complained on New Year's Day in 1803 that he was plagued with ceremonies and men and women drinking and fighting "pell mell."[54]

During most holiday celebrations at fur trade posts, men generally did not have to work.[55] During the Christmas and New Year's holidays, voyageurs and bourgeois frequently arranged to visit other posts or invited visitors to their post for the day or for the entire holiday season.[56] Many men tried to organize their work schedules so they would not miss any of the festivities. In December 1818 at Tête au Brochet, George Nelson was frustrated by one of his voyageurs named Welles. Nelson had sent Welles to Falle de Perdix on December 23, but Welles returned to the post on December 30, claiming that the snow and ice prevented him from reaching his destination. Nelson suspected that this was a lie and that Welles really wanted to be back at the post for the New Year's celebrations.[57] Men of different companies sometimes put aside their different allegiances to celebrate together. During the Christmas holidays in 1805, XYC employees celebrated with their NWC neighbors at Lac La Pluie.[58] Frequently Aboriginal people came to the posts to participate in the festivities, which helped the traders solidify trading ties and foster goodwill with them.[59] Donald McKay noted that it was customary for Aboriginal people to arrive at the post on all feast days.[60] Voyageurs sometimes visited Aboriginal lodges as part of the day's celebrations.[61] Those Aboriginal people who were closely involved with provisioning and fur trading, such as the "homeguard," celebrated with the traders.

The day's festivities on Christmas and New Year's usually began early in the morning. Voyageurs ceremoniously called on their bourgeois or clerk to formally wish him well and pay their respects.[62] The early morning firing of muskets or cannons usually woke the masters.[63] In 1793 Alexander Mackenzie wrote: "On the first day of January, my people, in conformity to the usual custom, awoke me at the break of day with the discharge of firearms, with which they congratulated the appearance of the new year. In return, they were treated with plenty of spirits, and when there is any flour, cakes are always added to the regales, which was the case, on the present occasion."[64] Like the firing of muskets when a brigade arrived at a post, this salute was a symbolic welcome and a formal honoring of the holiday.

After the firing of muskets, all the residents of the fort gathered together in a general meeting where the bourgeois or clerk would provide regales or gifts to the voyageurs. Depending on the wealth of the post, regales could be as little as a single dram or as much as great quantities of alcohol, especially if there was a shortage of food.[65] At the beginning of 1802, Daniel Harmon gave his men a dram in the morning and then enough rum to drink throughout the course of the day, to help distract them from the scarcity of meat.[66] In an effort to secure more alcohol for the day's festivities, men would go to great lengths to salute their bourgeois or any passing visitor or dignitary, in hopes of gaining a treat.[67] Regales on New Year's seemed to be slightly more generous than those at Christmas, as men were frequently given tobacco in addition to drams.[68] At wealthier posts the men's regales included food, usually specialty items that were hard to procure, such as flour and sugar, though the regale could include meat and grease.[69]

Regardless of wealth most posts mustered some kind of feast on Christmas and New Year's as part of the day's ceremonies. Voyageurs took great pleasure in their food and in feasting, especially since survival could be so precarious in the pays d'en haut, and their victuals were often mundane and limited. In 1812 Gabriel Franchère commented: "The 25th of December, Christmas Day, was spent most pleasantly. We treated our men to the best that the post could offer, which delighted them as they had lived for nearly two months on fish dried by fire, which is very poor food."[70] Bourgeois were not always so generous. Alexander Henry the Younger wrote on January 1, 1814, that the bourgeois could scarcely collect liquor enough out of the kegs to give the men one dram each, so they provided them with rice, salt beef, and swans as well. The bourgeois, however, provided themselves with a great feast of rice soup, boiled swans, roast wild fowl, roast pork, potatoes, rice pudding, wild fruit pie, cranberry tarts, cheese and biscuits with porter, spirits, and two bottles of Madeira.[71] However, it seemed to be more usual for the bourgeois and the voyageurs to celebrate the day together.[72] This temporary lowering of class barriers probably stemmed from the loneliness of the bourgeois and the clerks who were isolated from other masters. Sometimes all hands pitched in and worked together in preparation of the feast. While in the Athabasca District in 1799–1800, bourgeois James McKenzie recorded the post's cooperation in preparation for celebrating the New Year. On December 31, voyageur Dusablon made fish soup, and voyageur Lambert made fish cakes and dried meat, while voyageur Masquarosis drew water and tended the fire. McKenzie and bourgeois George Wentzel oversaw the preparations and pitched in where needed. "In short," Wentzel wrote in his journal, "every body in the House had a finger in the pie & were busy all night as *une queu de veau* [the switching of a calf's tail]."[73] By providing voyageurs with a decent feast, masters could ensure goodwill from their men. Working together to create a celebratory feast fostered a feeling of fellowship among the men.

After the formal ceremonies of honoring the day, exchanging gifts, and feasting, the real party began. Men celebrated by drinking liberally.[74] Serious drinking could last for several days after the holiday.[75] Both Edith Burley and Anne Morton found that at HBC posts, Christmas and New Year's could be celebrated with almost a week of "incessant carousing."[76] Drinking heavily usually led to fighting among the men.[77] Duncan McGillivray commented that "the Holidays [had been] spent as usual in dissipation & enjoyment, intermixed with quarreling and fighting- the certain consequences of intoxication among the men."[78] Dancing, fiddle playing, and singing were also significant ingredients of the parties.[79] During this part of the day's festivities, disorder and subversion dominated. In the words of Mikhail Bakhtin, "[w]hile carnival lasts, there is no other life outside it. During carnival time life is subject only to its laws, that is, the laws of its own freedom."[80] Yet the chaotic mayhem was constrained and limited by its designated site and meaning. It was a socially sanctioned time where voyageurs as well as their masters were allowed to carouse to the extreme.

This style of celebrating holidays—starting with formal ceremonies and then moving on to wild abandon—lasted well into the mid-nineteenth century at the interior fur trade posts. Upper Canadian artist Paul Kane described the Christmas festivities at Fort Edmonton in 1847. A flag was raised at the post. An enormous feast of buffalo, white fish, beaver tails, geese, potatoes, and turnips was served to all inhabitants of the post. In the evening a dance was held in the great hall, "filled by the gaily dressed guests. Indians, whose chief ornament consisted in the paint on their faces, voyageurs with bright sashes and neatly ornamented moccasins, half-breeds glittering in every ornament they could lay their hands on; whether civilized or savage, all were laughing, and jabbering in as many different languages as there were styles of dress."[81] British scientist John Lefroy described the 1844 New Year's celebrations at Fort Chipewyan:

> *[L]a bonne année as the Canadians say . . . which according to their custom every person in the Fort came to wish me, and the rest of us, this morning. It is a day of great fête, in which the gentlemen hold a kind of levée in the morning, and give a dance in the evening—for the latter I hear the fiddle tuning while I write—and which is the one holiday of the year to young and old. A separate levée or drawing room is held for the ladies in which a laudable custom exists of giving them a kiss in wishing la bonne année (this old fashioned salute is general in the country on other ceremonial occasions). . . . After this they have a 'régale' of which I must not lower your idea by revealing what it consisted in, but one item is always a glass of wine, if there is any. Our ball went off with great éclat. Many of the Canadian dances are amusing enough, particularly one called the Chasse aux Lièvres. . . . The voyageurs have an amusing custom of pressing the gentlemen to dance in such a way as this 'Ah! Monsieur, wont you dance, and you shall have my partner!' the lady takes it as a compliment. 'Voulez vous pas dancer, et avec cette dame icit' handing to you the lady who has just stood up with himself. We mustered six or eight women to about three times that number of men, and they enjoyed themselves until about 1 in the morning to an old fiddle and an Indian drum.*[82]

French Canadians brought not only their songs and tunes but also their dances and social customs of kissing women to the far Northwest. The fiddlers may have adopted the Indian drum or adapted their drums to an Aboriginal style to extend their musical range. Ross Cox described one dance at Lac La Pluie in 1817:

> *We had two excellent fiddlers; and as several of the gentlemen had wives, we got up three or four balls, in which the exhilarating amusement of the 'light fantastic toe' was kept up to a late hour in the morning. We walked through no lazy minuets; we had no simpering quadrilles; no languishing half-dying waltzes; no,—ours was the exercise of health; the light lively reel, or the rattling good old-*

> *fashioned country dance, in which the graceful though untutored movements of the North-west females would have put to blush many of the more refined votaries of Terpsichore.*[83]

The practice of respecting women, regardless of their race, existed to some degree in the Northwest before the arrival of European women. This attitude was apparent at Beaver Club dinners held for the fur trade bourgeois in Montreal. One of the formal toasts that began each dinner was to wives and children in the Northwest.[84] Historian Michael Payne provides an almost identical description of balls at the HBC post of York Factory. Amid the fiddle music and Scottish dancing, company employees lined up to be kissed by all Aboriginal women present at the ball.[85] But this ritual was not always carried out willingly. At York Factory, Robert Ballantyne admitted to his horror of kissing *all* the women:

> *[T]he moment we entered, the women simultaneously rose, and coming modestly forward to Mr W———, who was the senior of the party, saluted him, one after another! I had been told that this was a custom of the ladies on Christmas day, and was consequently not quite unprepared to go through the ordeal. But when I looked at the superhuman ugliness of some of the old ones, when I gazed at the immense, and in some cases toothless chasms that were pressed to my senior's lips, and gradually approached, like a hideous nightmare, towards me; and when I reflected that these same mouths might have in former days demolished a few children, my courage forsook me, and I entertained for a moment the idea of bolting.*[86]

Many groups of all-male sojourners seemed to enjoy music and dances in their leisured moments. Nearly all shanty camps in northern Ontario had a fiddler, and singing and dancing were popular Saturday-night pastimes.[87] Creighton argues that some of the most popular activities on the forecastles of whaling ships were singing and dancing, which helped forge bonds among the different classes and ethnicities of men and accommodate social differences.[88] The same seemed to be true at the interior fur trade posts.

Holding a formal ball was an importation from French Canada, but the dancing and music were culturally distinctive. The "old fiddle and Indian drum" symbolized the mixing of European and Aboriginal forms.[89] Dancing was not restricted to holidays but continued throughout the seasons at fur trade posts. Having dances or "balls" was a fairly common occurrence both at the Great Lakes posts and in the interior.[90] Either fiddlers or singers provided the music. Fast and spirited dancing predominated. The descriptions of the "lively reels" of country dances reflected a rough and tumble joie de vivre that was characteristic of many voyageurs' activities. Balls at Grand Portage during the rendezvous, however, were genteel affairs for the benefit of the bourgeois, with music from the bagpipe, violin, flute, and fife.[91] Yet even at these balls, "country music" combined musical forms from Canada, Scotland, England, and Aboriginal peoples. Dances were often held to celebrate specific events, such as the coalition of the XYC and the NWC in 1804, but the most common occasions were weddings and to honor visitors to the post.[92] Men from different companies frequently attended each others' dances.[93] Sometimes dances were held for no particular reasons other than to have fun and enliven the monotony of post life, especially during the long winters.[94]

Alcohol

In eighteenth-century European and colonial settings, most people drank a significant amount of alcohol.[95] Historian Craig Heron explains that "alcohol was regularly consumed in the home as a beverage and a tonic, and to a degree now unimaginable it also saturated almost all arenas of work and leisure. European settlers, especially men, drank often, though only occasionally to get drunk."[96] The voyageurs' use of alcohol or attitudes toward it probably did not differ from those of habitants or other groups of laboring men. A key difference, however, was that alcohol was restricted and controlled by the bourgeois, and voyageurs did not have habitual access to it as they would have had in French Canada. The bourgeois and the clerks controlled the rations of alcohol to save money and to exert control over their men (see chapter 5). Although the bourgeois and the clerks probably drank as much as their men, they often disparaged voyageurs as useless drunks. They frequently reprimanded their men for drunkenness.[97] Bourgeois and clerks sometimes refused to sell alcohol to their men in an effort to curb their drinking practices, especially when the bourgeois wanted voyageurs to pay their debts.[98] Seeing themselves as distinct from their men in regard to drinking helped the bourgeois to distance themselves socially from their voyageurs, which helped them maintain authority. These attitudes are ironic when compared to the behavior of the bourgeois at the Montreal Beaver Club and annual rendezvous, where the dinners were notorious for excessive drinking and revelry.[99] After the merger of the HBC and the NWC in 1821, the new governor, George Simpson, imposed stringent temperance regulations on posts but met with little success.[100]

Drinking also occupied a central place in seafaring culture. Unlike the Northwest, where cargoes had to be physically hauled over unending portages, deadly excesses of drinking were common. Drink offered respite from an often punishing life on ship. Marcus Rediker speculates that "[t]oo much plain dealing, with the elements and with the conditions of life at sea, led to a lot of plain old drinking."[101] Unfortunately for the voyageurs, they could not carry enough liquor to offer respite from their journeys. Yet, as for sailors, drinking served critical social functions for voyageurs, allowing the men to bond with one another and form enduring friendships.

The masters' control over supplies and the frequent shortage of alcohol on canoe voyages and in the interior probably encouraged voyageurs to develop a "feast-famine" attitude toward drinking. If they knew that the supply of alcohol was precarious, they would drink with abandon while it was available. Although these occasions were described in considerable detail in the journals of the bourgeois and the clerks, limited supplies of alcohol made them exceptional rather than routine.

In some extreme cases voyageurs were drunk when they worked.[102] Periodically a master mentioned that the drunkenness of the voyageurs had impeded their work. One bourgeois could not send off his goods as early as he wished because his men "were amusing themselves and not fit to travel."[103] Voyageurs sometimes began to drink their regales while paddling, and journeys had to be interrupted because the voyageurs were not fit to continue.[104] A few posts were known for general drunkenness, but more commonly heavy and raucous drinking had a designated time and form at all posts, such as during holiday celebrations.[105] On canoe journeys and at interior posts men usually confined their heavy drinking to the occasional evening.[106] The bourgeois and the clerks sometimes used alcohol as a means of maintaining good faith among their men on a particularly difficult journey. In the summer of 1793 while on an arduous mission to find an overland passage to the Pacific Ocean, Alexander Mackenzie described the end of one hard day of work: "At the close of the day we assembled round a blazing fire; and the whole party, being enlivened with the usual beverage which I supplied on these occasions, forgot their fatigues and apprehensions."[107]

Heavy drinking was reserved for special occasions, such as when supplies arrived and during parties and "balls," and especially the rendezvous, where voyageurs received generous *regales*.[108] Some instances of "wild excess" are to be found further in the interior. One small creek near the Red River earned the name "Drunken River" when a carousing group of voyageurs had a particularly memorable party.[109] At least one voyageur was nicknamed "the Drunkard," and this mark of notoriety made it into official correspondence.[110]

Often excessive drinking led to violence. A voyager named Voyer, between forty and fifty years of age and described as "a great drunkard," went to Grand Portage to visit friends. When he became drunk, some of the clerks and bourgeois smeared his face with "caustie" (encaustic?) and drew lewd figures on it. Voyer became enraged when he sobered and swore revenge on those who had marked him. The following summer, when the same bourgeois denied him alcohol and chided him for his drunkenness, he killed several of their horses and threatened them with a knife.[111] These exceptional cases of "drunkards" can be found in most early modern societies; they represent the edges of social acceptability rather than the norm.

Despite the outbreaks of violence, drunkenness was contained rather than excessive. Drinking did not seriously threaten the social order of the fur trade; rather it provided an outlet for debauchery and disorder. Michael Payne found the same pattern at York Factory—although excessive drinking caused some social tensions, alcoholism was not widespread and fatalities resulting from drinking were limited.[112] The "boundaries of containment" were set by the availability of alcohol and the commonly accepted social sites for heavy drinking. Voyageurs became apprehensive when violence became excessive, when the functioning of the fur trade was disrupted for a great length of time, and when food was in short supply. In one extreme case a bourgeois named Duncan Campbell, charged with drunkenness by the NWC in 1809, had allowed his trading post to become a corrupt, filthy, and starving "heart of darkness." He lost all his trade goods, ran out of food, drank himself into oblivion, and neglected his paternal duties to his servants. He was court-martialed, and his voyageurs testified that they were disgusted by his behavior.[113]

Games and Contests

The voyageurs' ethic of nonaccumulation (see chapter 2) derived in part from the fact that they could not carry many material goods while working in the fur trade. But for many money became less important the longer they worked in the trade and were away from their families in French Canada. Wealth became measured in different ways. Pierre Bourdieu's economic metaphor of "capital" provides a way to understand voyageurs' notions of wealth and how this connected to their play.[114] Bourdieu expands the notion of capital beyond its economic conception to the realm of the cultural, social, and symbolic. Different types of capital can be acquired, exchanged, and converted into other forms. Cultural capital refers to the value that can be found in family background, social class, education, and other factors that may lead to success. For voyageurs cultural capital would have included knowledge of skills such as making canoes and snowshoes. Cultural capital can be inherited, purchased, or earned. Bourdieu defines social capital as connections among people. Voyageurs could enhance their social capital through their relationships with Aboriginal people, with the bourgeois and clerks, and with each other. Symbolic capital represents prestige and honor, which voyageurs could earn by demonstrating their manliness. The masculine values of strength, courage, and risk taking became expressions of symbolic or masculine capital. Play, especially games and contests that demonstrated these qualities, became a means of accumulating masculine capital.

Because voyageurs had few possessions and could not carry many personal belongings with them into the interior, games could not involve elaborate equipment.[115] Playing cards and gambling were common pastimes.[116] Michael Payne also found small board games such cribbage and dominoes at York Factory.[117] Voyageurs played games from French Canada, such as those with a ball.[118] Other games or amusements, such as "pagessan" or "le jeu au plat" and body tattooing, were learned from Aboriginal peoples.[119] John Richardson, a surgeon in the Royal Navy and a traveling companion of John Franklin, described games played by Crees at Cumberland House. The game *puckesann* involved betting on the number of stones tossed out of a small wooden dish. In the "game of the mitten," one marked and three unmarked balls were placed under four mittens, and contenders had to guess under which mitten the marked ball lay. These games, along with lacrosse, required little equipment, which could be easily made from materials in the surrounding environment.[120]

Voyageurs gained symbolic currency both by enhancing their reputations for toughness and skill and by their own belief in their strength and ability. In reminiscing about his life, the elderly voyageur on Lake Winnipeg bragged to Alexander Ross: "I beat all Indians at the race, and no white man ever passed me in the chase."[121] The value of beating Aboriginal peoples implies that Aboriginal men were faster and stronger and thus more manly than European Canadians. The desire to excel at skills necessary for survival in the Northwest, skills that were usually learned from Aboriginal peoples, was a clear example of shifting cultural values among voyageurs.

Being more "Indian" than the "Indians" was a measure of manliness and success in adapting to new social and physical spaces.

Currency could also be earned in physical contests among voyageurs. In canoe races, a popular form of competition, crews would race against one another within a brigade or race against other brigades.[122] These contests built a sense of fellowship, trust, and cooperation among the crews. Masters encouraged their men to race, and they often set out to break one another's records for the fastest time between major posts. Recall George Landmann's record for the journey from St. Joseph's Island, near Detroit, to Montreal, which his crew completed in seven and one-quarter days.[123] After the 1821 merger, Montreal canoes and York boats frequently raced at York Factory.[124]

Brawling was a common social activity and had a variety of meanings among the voyageurs. Fighting frequently accompanied parties and heavy drinking, and in these contexts hostilities and maliciousness sometimes led to mayhem or riots.[125] However, brawling was often an organized event or competition in which men sought to demonstrate their prowess, boost their reputations, and amuse their mates.[126] They often "fought for a set," and a "drawn battle" could be decided with "fair boxing at head quarting."[127] Brawling could demonstrate strength and toughness, and it underscored the dimension of physicality in voyageur culture, which was encouraged by the nature of the job. One Métis voyageur, Paulet Paul, achieved fame as a fighter after the 1821 merger.[128]

Fur trade journals are filled with stories about the difficulty of fur trade work and the almost mythical strength, endurance, and joviality of the voyageurs. The literate in the fur trade frequently referred to voyageurs as "beasts of burden," which both reduced them to animals and elevated them to "hyper-masculine" superheroes. Clerk George Nelson wrote: "[Voyageurs] seem to do more than ever was meant for human nature; . . . [they] rise at dusk in the morning and until near sunset, are either pulling on their paddles, or running with 180, or 200 lbs wt. on their backs, as if it were for life or death; never stop to take their meals peacably, but with a piece of pemmican in their hands eat under their load."[129] He went on to marvel that voyageurs seemed tougher, stronger, and swifter than dogs or horses. Voyageurs tried to outperform one another to demonstrate their masculine capital. Contests were not limited to physical prowess but extended to almost any area. Competing to see who could eat or drink the most functioned like gaming; voyageurs could gamble small amounts of their symbolic capital for entertainment's sake. In the spring of 1808 while journeying between interior posts, two of George Nelson's voyageurs, Leblanc and Larocque, decided to see who could eat the most during one of their meals. Both unfortunate men began to feel ill and shake, when lynx excrement was discovered at the bottom of the pot, which elicited "many coarse & filthy jokes."[130]

Tricks

Were the feces in the pot an accident or a joke? The predominance of jokes and trickery among voyageurs leads one to think that the latter was the case.[131] Humor is difficult to translate across cultures, both for historians trying to understand voyageurs and for voyageurs trying to have fun with one another, their masters, and their Aboriginal friends and families. For example, at Rocky Mountain Fort in fall 1799 a voyageur named Gagnon threw his recently deceased dog on the side of a riverbank. The men of the post then sent out a "simpleton" named Borriard to see if the dog had to come to life.[132]

Cruelty to animals was a strain of humor that voyageurs shared with other early modern peoples. It is surprising that voyageurs focused on dogs in the Northwest. Sled dogs were important assets for winter travel. Voyageurs collected and cherished dogs, decorating them as they would their canoes and paddles. Yet they occasionally abused dogs for fun. In complaining about traveling in the interior, John Franklin commented: "The next evil is being constantly exposed to witness the wanton and unnecessary cruelty of the men to their dogs, especially those of the Canadians, who beat them unmercifully, and habitually vent on them the most dreadful and disgusting impreciations."[133] Perhaps because voyageurs were so highly dependent on dogs for winter travel, those dogs that could not be properly trained for pull-

FIRST STAGE OF CRUELTY.
While various Scenes of sportive Woe
The Infant Race employ,
And tortur'd Victims bleeding shew
The Tyrant in the Boy;
Behold a Youth of gentler Heart,
To spare the Creature's pain
O take, he cries—take all my Tart,
But Tears and Tart are vain.
Learn from this fair Example—You
Whom savage Sports delight,
How Cruelty disgusts the view
While Pity charms the sight.

Fig. 8. *The Four Stages of Cruelty*, plate 1, *First Stage of Cruelty*, by William Hogarth, 1751 (reprinted ca. 1822). Courtesy of the Charles Deering McCormick Library of Special Collections, Northwestern University, Chicago.

ing sleds were scorned. Alexander Henry the Younger recorded that his men sometimes amused themselves by "watching dogs copulate, and then rushing upon them with an axe or club."[134] Voyageurs clearly found it amusing, although the bourgeois did not. Common notions of trickery and jokes are significant signs of a cohesion among voyageurs. The humor in torturing dogs may be part of what Bakhtin has termed "grotesque realism" in medieval and early modern European folk humor. Bodily elements were deeply positive, not repulsive, and all that was "bodily" became "grandoise, exaggerated, immeasurable." Dogs assumed a symbolic value as that which expressed "base" animal (and human) needs in an immediate way. Bakhtin goes on to explain that "the essential principle of grotesque realism is degradation, that is, the lowering of all that is high, spiritual, ideal, abstract."[135] Abusing dogs may have been a form of debasing that which voyageurs considered "high." Dogs were valued by voyageurs not only for sled travel but also as food when provisions became scarce. Voyageurs probably learned from Aboriginal peoples that eating dogs was both a good source of food and a potential source of spiritual power.[136] Dogs thus became visible targets for debasement. These forms of amusement are echoed in paintings by William Hogarth, such as "The First Stage of Cruelty" (see figure 8).[137]

In this image dogs are being tortured by on the streets of eighteenth-century London for the amusement of men. This cruel abuse of dogs is reminiscent of what historian Robert Darnton coined as the "great cat massacre," where apprentices in an eighteenth-century printing shop captured and charged most of the cats in the neighborhood in a mock trial and strung them up on a makeshift gallows. The apprentices did not depend on cats, as the voyageurs relied on dogs. Yet, as with the cat massacre, modern readers' inability to see the humor in torturing dogs underscores the cultural distance that separates us from voyageurs.[138]

Symbolic and social capital was exchanged in acts of trickery among voyageurs by efforts to garner respect and mete out humiliation. Excessive joking and teasing could cause ill will between men.[139] In one case, at the Park River post near Pembina in the fall of 1800, all the men were edgy because they feared an attack by the Sioux. One of the voyageurs, Charbonneau, earned the ire of the post for his tomfoolery. He fired his gun at the bourgeois, Alexander Henry the Younger, and then hid, leading everyone to believe that the Sioux had begun an assault.[140] Sometimes jokes could end in tragedy. At Pembina River in the summer of 1803, voyageur Joseph Rainville accidentally killed voyageur Venant St. Germain when, in play, he shot him with a gun he thought was not loaded.[141]

Playing tricks on their bourgeois and clerks was a way for voyageurs to express dissatisfaction or to try to gain the upper hand in the relationship. George Nelson seems to have fallen victim to many of his men's tricks. Early in his career, while he was still a novice, Nelson's voyageurs shook his house in the middle of the night, made Nelson believe that it had been caused by an animal, and then refused to stay in the house with him for mutual protection. His men grabbed him when he went out to inspect the post at night, which amplified Nelson's fear of the dark, and they fabricated stories of ghosts to scare him.[142] These tricks probably extended to novice voyageurs as well.

Nelson's suspicions of his men playing "derty tricks" on him lasted into the later years of his career.[143] Nelson may not have been a typical clerk; his insecurity in wielding authority over his men may have made him appear weaker than most and thus made him particularly susceptible to tricks played by his men. Other bourgeois and clerks may have been more hesitant than Nelson in recording tricks played on them because of the humiliation they undoubtedly endured. Robert Darnton found that early modern artisans used symbols to make fools of masters for the benefit of other workers, but kept jokes ambiguous enough to avoid being fired. Along the same lines, voyageurs' abuse of dogs may have been funny to them because it paralleled how they felt about being under the rule of their masters. Their "symbolic horseplay" might have been an attempt to chastise a harsh bourgeois for his ill-treatment.[144]

Masters sometimes held the upper hand in jokes and trickery. Alexander Henry the Younger mercilessly teased two of his men, Langlois and Desmarais, one day in the early fall of 1800. He pretended generosity by giving them some bad West India rum but telling them it was fine French brandy.

After the men praised the liquor and boasted their expertise in assessing the quality of cognacs, Henry revealed his trick. The next day he gave the same men some colored high wines (undiluted, overproof rum), who praised it as the best West India rum they had ever drunk and esteemed it far better that "that nasty strong stuff, high wine." Henry had a second laugh and secured the promise from the men that they would never again pretend to judge liquor.[145] The bourgeois and the clerks tried to reinforce their social distance from voyageurs by demonstrating greater knowledge and sophistication. However, sometimes they employed the rough and cruel antics that they usually attributed to their men. In a malicious and exceptional case, one bourgeois, the notably "eccentric" Alexander McKay, set fire to a tree that a voyageur was turning into a maypole (see chapter 5). The unfortunate man, caught at the top of the blazing tree and enveloped in smoke and heat, barely saved his life by jumping to another tree.[146] Most masters and voyageurs would hesitate in taking jokes so far that they would permanently alienate their employees and peers.

Joking and trickery took on interesting dimensions with regard to Aboriginal peoples. Voyageurs were fascinated by Aboriginal people's "antics" and enjoyed Aboriginal singing and dancing.[147] Aboriginal peoples were also frequently amused by the voyageurs, as at Spokane House in the summer of 1814, where the Aboriginal people were delighted when the voyageurs managed to domesticate and train a young bear.[148] In another instance some starving voyageurs amused a group of Ojibwes with their efforts at imitating Ojibwe chanting, singing, and dancing. The Ojibwes took pity on the voyageurs and gave them food.[149] Teasing and joking were also common among Aboriginal women who married voyageurs. Aboriginal women often asserted their power over the traders by playing tricks on them. In the winter of 1810 an old voyageur named Desrocher pretended to sell his wife to another voyageur named Welles. As part of the elaborate plot, the wife played along. When Welles awaited his new bride in their marriage bed, rather than joining him, she threw a kettle of ice water all over him.[150] This incident is reminiscent of the trickster figure (discussed in chapter 3). Voyageurs would have learned about the trickster from their Aboriginal wives.

Even if voyageurs had no understanding of Aboriginal spirituality, the similar appreciation of tricks as a form of humor probably provided a cultural meeting ground.

The social life and play of voyageurs at the interior posts reveals an interesting tension between old and new social practices. Voyageurs preserved social traditions from French Canada to create a sense of home in the pays d'en haut, which could be overwhelming in its strangeness. Celebrating annual holidays, drinking, and dancing reminded voyageurs of their lives in rural French Canada and allowed them to continue to be part of that social world. Yet the circumstances of the fur trade led to the emergence of new behaviors. Contests and trickery became important because they bolstered the heightened masculinity of the male-dominated workplace, which valued toughness and strength, and the liminal social spaces of canoe journeys and post life. Men made every effort to demonstrate their strength, endurance, and good humor, especially in the face of hardship and privation. They were influenced by the cultural practices they observed among Aboriginal peoples, and imitating Aboriginal peoples became a way of increasing symbolic capital.

Camaraderie

How did the liminal position of voyageurs working in the fur trade affect their relationships with one another? How did the men work out the social conventions of their new cultural locations? How were their friendships with fellow voyageurs different from their friendships with men in French Canada? These questions are difficult to answer. The dearth of work on male friendships among habitants makes comparisons especially challenging. A significant drawback in assessing the shape and nature of voyageur friendships is that their lives are mainly visible in the writings of their bourgeois and clerks, who were probably not aware of many of the relationships among their men, and would have little reason to record them in their letters and journals unless the behavior directly affected fur trade work. The documentary record contains descriptions of extremes in behavior, situations that were remarkable or abnormal, and conduct that hindered the workings of the trade. Despite these daunting drawbacks, it is possible to trace the outlines of voyageur camaraderie. In friendships between the men we can see expressions of a voyageur social order, such as an emphasis on good humor, generosity, rowdiness, and strength. In a culture where money and material possessions had limited significance, the quest for a strong reputation became more important.

Politeness was a social convention brought from French Canada. Traveling through the Canadas in the early nineteenth century, John Lambert noted that French Canadians were generally "good-humoured, peaceable, and friendly" and remarkably civil to one another and to strangers. People bowed to each other as they passed on the streets, and men sometimes even kissed each other on the cheek.[151] Similarly writers remarked on the good humor and affection that voyageurs showed to one another and even to their masters. Ross Cox marveled that the men referred to each other as *mon frère* (my brother) or *mon cousin* without being related and that they made up pet names for their bourgeois.[152] Bestowing kinship names on one another may have been a practice borrowed from Aboriginal peoples, who frequently adopted outsiders or assigned them kinship designations to incorporate them into their social order.

Yet civility among voyageurs was often described as "rough," and verbal exchanges were described as the "coarse & familiar language of brother voyageurs."[153] Swearing or blasphemy was not restricted to expressions of anger but was common in many different contexts. Expressions of profanity usually had to do with religious imagery, such as *sacré* (sacred), *mon Dieu* (my God), and *baptême* (baptism), which probably eased tension and poked fun at serious situations.[154] Masters' characterizations of voyageur familiarity and camaraderie as "rough" may reflect the bourgeois' desire to be "civilized."[155] Peter Moogk asserts that verbal and physical abuse among "the lower orders" in New France was commonplace, but it did not mean that habitants were particularly vulgar or wanton people. Bakhtin notes that billingsgate, or curses, oaths, and popular blazons, figured prominently in folk humor in early modern Europe. Abusive language was a mark of familiarity and friendship.[156] The "rough" civility may have found a particularly exaggerated expression in the pays d'en haut. Because the men worked in harsh and dangerous conditions, they wanted to be especially jovial and rowdy to demonstrate their lack of fear and their great strength in living amidst adversity. Rediker suggests that at sea "rough talk" was a way for sailors to express an opposition to "polite" bourgeois customs and their ideals of gentility, moderation, refinement, and industry. He asserts that "rough speech" was a transgressive means to deal with shipboard isolation and incarceration.[157] Likewise rough talk among voyageurs was probably a verbal cue for a distinct masculine identity.

Fraternity among voyageurs was aided by the values of charity, generosity, and good cheer, especially in the interior, where many unknown dangers could befall travelers and life was often precarious.[158] Canoes invariably stopped to help others if they were in need or short on food.[159] These values became a kind of "insurance" for cases when voyageurs were in need of assistance. They protected one another from hostile Aboriginal people, dangerous animals, and a treacherous environment. In a case near Fort Vermilion, at Plante's River in February 1810, a couple of voyageurs were robbed and threatened by a party of thirteen Crees and three Assiniboines. The Aboriginal people agreed not to hurt one of the voyageurs, Cardinal, whom they knew from previous trading, but they wanted the scalp of the other voyageur, Clément. Alexander Henry the Younger related that "Cardinal, who [was] a most loquacious person, was exercised to the utmost of his ability, and by his fluency of speech saved the life of Clément from these scoundrels." In the end Cardinal had to appease the Aboriginal people by relinquishing all of his and Clément's trade goods, including a valuable pistol.[160] Voyageurs on occasion were also able to save one another from bears, snakes, and other dangerous creatures.[161] The most common danger of travel was canoe accidents, and many men were rescued from near drowning by their fellow crew members.[162] The voyageurs took great pride in being cheerful and good-spirited in the face of hardship, toil, and danger. This kind of stoic and blithe endurance of adversity was reinforced by Aboriginal peoples. Voyageurs were impressed by Aboriginal peoples, who always shared with others and laughed and jested when they were starving.[163]

No doubt many genuine friendships emerged among voyageurs. A sense of intimacy was often the result of working closely together, especially in difficult circumstances. Alexander Ross wrote: "There is, perhaps, no country where ties of affection are more binding than here."[164] However, it is hard to determine the depth and longevity of friendships. Men often changed posts from year to year, a factor that could undermine friendships. The overall fluidity of the workplace worked against the development of long-lasting relationships. Men were always moving into the job, leaving to live with Aboriginal people, leaving to live as freemen in the interior, returning to Canada, or dying.

Personality differences and workplace incidents caused strains among voyageurs.[165] Sometimes men disliked a particular voyageur because he did not work as hard as everyone else or was a bully.[166] At the Pembina River post under the direction of Alexander Henry the Younger in fall 1800, one man was abusing some of the weaker men at the post, physically intimidating them and treating them as his personal slaves. By mid-November one of the other men, who was as strong as the bully and had been on friendly terms with him, was so appalled by the situation that he defended the weaker men and challenged the bully to fight. To the delight of everyone, the bully received a beating and was put in his place.[167] Animosity between voyageurs was sometimes so strong that the bourgeois deliberately placed them at different posts.[168] Men of different companies frequently quarreled and fought, probably as a result of direct competition for furs and favor among the Aboriginal people.[169]

Instances of brutality and cruelty among voyageurs seem to be confined to individuals, rather than characterizing the social order. Yet voyageurs may have become hardened as they tried to toughen themselves to survive in the often cruel environment. Voyageurs could steal from and severely beat one another with little apparent provocation.[170] Men who became ill during a journey were especially vulnerable to cruelty. Voyageurs generally did not want to be put at risk themselves by being left behind to care for those who could no longer travel or were dying. In several recorded instances ill and dying men were deserted by those who were chosen to care for them.[171]

However, most instances of recorded cruelty occurred under especially difficult or crisis conditions, such as when men were starving.[172]

Despite the "rough talk" social conventions among voyageurs stressed charity and generosity, especially in the face of hardship. Voyageurs could demonstrate that they were tough and strong enough to be kind in a brutal environment. If the difficulty of life in the fur trade sometimes caused men to be harsh and cruel to one another, much of this ill will could be expressed in the frequent and usually organized "sport" of fighting. The tension between a desire for equality and the centrality of social ordering influenced relationships among men in both good and bad ways. Voyageurs worked very closely together and relied on one another for survival. Their often deep friendships, however, were threatened by the transience of the job.

Sexuality

How deep did friendships among men develop? Did the homosocial environment, especially on canoe journeys, lead to the development of homosexuality as a normative expression of affection? Did sex between men become a common voyageur pastime? How would this affect the ideal of masculinity central to voyageur culture? Some scholars have argued that masculinity or gendered identities cannot be separated from sexuality and that heterosexuality is often a key part of working men's masculine identity.[173] This construction of masculinity becomes especially problematic in homosocial working environments when men do not have access to women for erotic pleasure. The situation of the voyageurs is historically unusual: they often worked in all-male environments, yet they had access to women of a "savage race." Was heterosexuality constructed in the same way when the sexual "other" was also the racial "other"?

The bourgeois and the clerks portrayed voyageurs as heterosexual and were conspicuously silent on homosexual practices. Masters may have consciously chosen to overlook the occurrence of homosexuality, considering it an unmentionable deviance. The silence may also indicate an ignorance of homosexual practice among voyageurs and Aboriginal men. Or homosexuality may not have existed as a social option for voyageurs who had easy access to Aboriginal women for sex. In any case, the silence demands close scrutiny.

Many all-male sojourners, most notably sailors, have a documented history of practicing sodomy, although it remains a clouded issue.[174] Without being essentialist about the nature of erotic desire, one is not unreasonable to assume that voyageurs sometimes had sexual feelings for each other or participated in sexual acts together. If sexuality is understood to be situational, then men working together in isolated groups probably developed sexual and emotional relationships with one another.[175] The voyageurs who transported goods and furs on the arduous route between Montreal and Lake Superior worked in isolated settings and had limited contact with Aboriginal peoples. These men, however, worked in the trade only during the summer months and returned to their French Canadian parishes, where not only homosexuality but any kind of nonmarital sexual practice was prohibited.[176] Is it possible that in the isolation and freedom of their summer jobs they experimented with different kinds of sexual pleasure? Or were they simply too tired to be interested in sex? Voyageurs who worked in the interior were often cooped up in trading posts, far away from the regulative forces of the Catholic Church and the scrutiny of social peers, and they had the time and leisure to pursue erotic pleasure. Here one might expect to find significant emotional and possibly sexual bonding. The difficulty of fur trade work and the great risks in canoeing and portaging often created intense bonds of friendship and trust between men.[177] One clue to homosocial practice in the interior may lie in the patterns and rates of marriages between voyageurs and Aboriginal women.

Documentation on sodomy in early modern settings has been found mainly in legal records. I have found no prosecutions for voyageur buggery, or sodomy, in French Canadian courts. The Montreal traders did not impose rigid military discipline on their workers as did the HBC, and thus voyageurs were less socially regulated and freer than HBC laborers.[178] Edith Burley has found a few prosecutions for sodomy among the Orkney men working at HBC posts, but she asserts that "officers appear to have had little interest in the regulation of their men's sexuality and were probably content to overlook their improprieties as long as they did not interfere with the company's business."[179] Was the same true for the Montreal bourgeois? Many violations of contracts and other crimes were not formally punished because legal systems did not exist in the interior. Perhaps because the bourgeois knew they could neither prosecute buggery nor prevent it, they turned a blind eye to it. The silence regarding sodomy in bourgeois writings may reflect that the practice was considered deviant, amoral, illegal, and possibly unimaginable. If sexual contact between voyageurs and masters occurred, it would have been silenced by masters, who did not wish to be incriminated.

Masters may have chosen to overlook sexual relations between voyageurs and Aboriginal men so that they would not threaten trading alliances or create enemies. A substantial group of scholars have explored homosexuality among Aboriginal societies in the cultural form of berdaches.[180] Berdaches occupied "third sex" roles and were sometimes called "two-spirited people." They were most often people who played opposite or both male and female roles and held significant spiritual power, and they often became culture heroes. Although berdaches represented many different configurations of gender roles and sexual practices in different Aboriginal cultures, their widespread presence may indicate that sexuality was not dichotomous in many Aboriginal societies and that there was space for the expression of homosexual desire. Some scholars suggest that berdaches represented forms of "institutionalized" homosexuality. It is possible that the presence of berdaches indicates that homosexuality was permissible in some Aboriginal societies and thus permissible among voyageurs and some Aboriginal men.

It is difficult to know the extent to which the intense physicality of voyageur culture, the worship of masculine qualities of strength and physical endurance, and the scarcity of women enabled experimentation at a sexual level. If such relations among self-identified heterosexual men occurred in this liminal setting, like other forms of play they probably fortified friendships, and increased a sense of collectivity among voyageurs. At the same time, competition over partners and rejected advances probably created tensions and facilitated cultural divisions.

Because voyageurs lived between worlds, they found opportunities to transcend social restrictions learned at their homes in French Canada. In the process of trying out or "playing at" new ways of living, they could reinvent or refashion themselves. The play of voyageurs was influenced by customs brought from French Canada, by new practices learned from Aboriginal societies, and by the everyday life of the fur trade workplace. The working environment especially encouraged new "experimental" behavior because voyageurs were constantly traveling and thus isolated from established communities. Voyageurs' penchant for trickery and play became a tool for carving out the contours of their workspace. Play also became a social space where voyageurs could assert their particular ideal of manhood and where they could appropriate the behavior of Aboriginal peoples in order to be successful voyageurs. By providing a space for voyageurs to test new forms of social behavior, play strengthened voyageurs' social bonds with one another and encouraged camaraderie and a unified identity. At the same time, play became a vehicle through which voyageurs distinguished categories among themselves and deepened occupational fissures determined mainly by job status. It thus had a simultaneously homogenizing and diversifying effect on the voyageurs' world.

Although play became an area for the expression of new social practices that made voyageurs distinct from habitants and other early modern peasants, it did not threaten the paternalistic order of the fur trade or the masters' subordination of the voyageurs. Most of the play of voyageurs was highly structured and occurred within designated and contained contexts. It provided a safe space for voyageurs to express their anxiety and fear of entering the exotic pays d'en haut, their anger at unfair masters and unreliable colleagues, and their excitement at setting off on new adventures. Forms of play generally sanctioned by the bourgeois allowed voyageurs to frolic without threatening the pace or effectiveness of their work and encouraged values that were consistent with effective working skills, such as strength, bravery, risk taking, and perseverance.

Play and sociability were central to voyageurs' working lives. All forms of play, including carnivals, games, contests, tricks, and friendship, helped to create and support a distinctive voyageur world by both encouraging social bonding and facilitating the growth of social fissures and divisions. Three dominant themes emerged in the play of voyageurs. Contests provided men with "symbolic capital" in their efforts to bolster their reputations as strong men. The liminal space particularly encouraged jokes and trickery. Finally, voyageurs tried to form a unified and somewhat collective culture in the face of centrifugal forces caused by their transience and the mobility of the job. These ideals and themes distinguished voyageurs from habitants in French Canada, fur trade bourgeois and clerks, and Aboriginal societies. In the next chapter we shall examine the context in which Aboriginal peoples had the greatest impact on voyageurs: at the interior trading posts staffed year-round by voyageurs and at Aboriginal lodges where voyageurs occasionally spent a winter while trading en dérouine.

7. En Dérouine

Life at Interior Fur Trade Posts

Nicolas Landry a lesquels cest Volontairement Engage est Sengage par Cest Cest presents avec Charles McKenzie &Co a ce present est Acceptant pour la dite Compagnie pour Hyverner pendant deux Années dans les dependences du Lac Ouinipique en Qualite d'Interprette exempt de Batire[,] Bucher[,] Nager [pagayer] dans les Canots et de porter, oblige de Courrire la derouine.

Nicholas Landry agrees, and by the present [contract] binds himself to Charles McKenzie & Co, here present and accepting for the said company, to winter for two years in the region of Lake Winnipeg in the capacity of interpreter, with exemption from building[,] chopping[,] paddling canoes and portaging[.] Obligation to go about [trading] en dérouine.[1]

There is no English equivalent of the phrase "la derouine" that Nicolas Landry was obliged to do in this 1803 contract signed at Fort William.[2] According to the linguist Robert Vézina, it is a term original to the fur trade and became a part of the specialized vocabulary of voyageurs.[3] It roughly translates as traveling with a small complement of goods to Aboriginal homes or hunting lodges, singly or in pairs, to trade for furs on a small scale on behalf of a fur trade company. The term signified the uniqueness of voyageurs in several ways. Voyageurs developed a specialized vocabulary. They constituted the majority of non-Aboriginals to trade with Aboriginal peoples in the fashion of en dérouine, and few voyageurs who wintered west of Lake

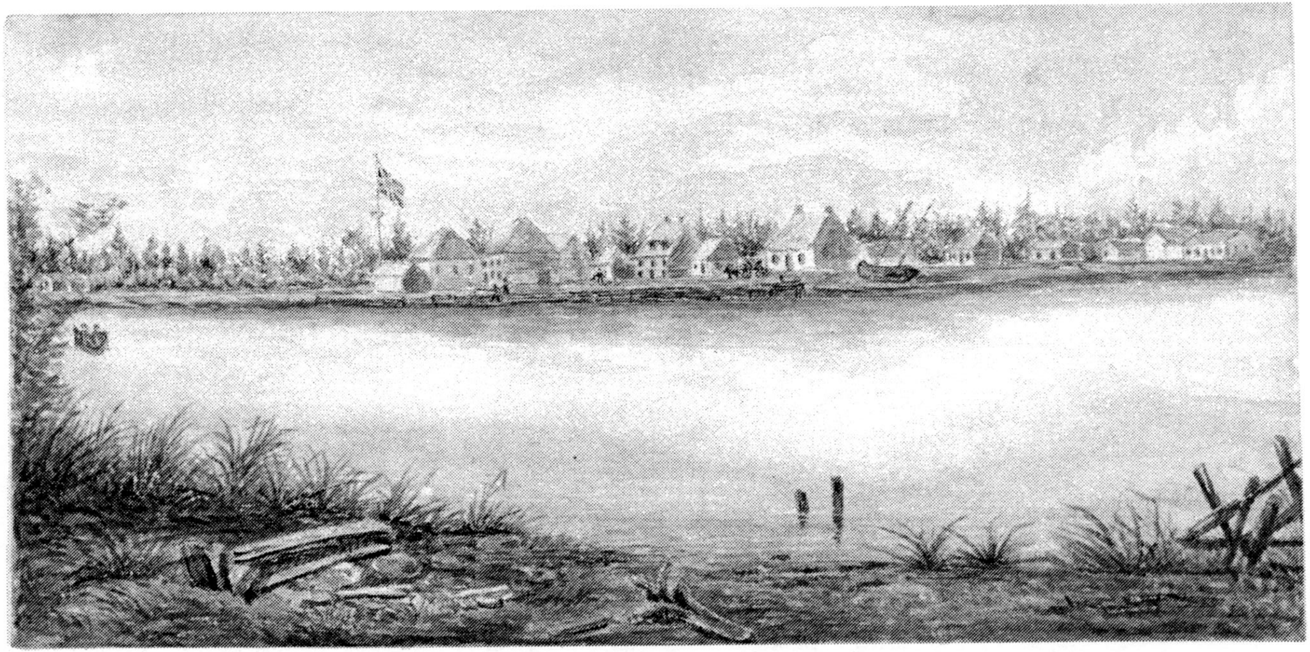

Fig. 9. *Fort William N.W.* (1811 or 1812), by Robert Irvine. Accession R9266-290, reproduction C-001464. Courtesy of the Library and Archives Canada, Ottawa.

Superior were exempt from the practice. In the process of trading en dérouine, voyageurs entered Aboriginal worlds, developed relationships with Aboriginal peoples, and created conduits for cultural transfer.

In the world voyageurs inhabited in the interior posts beyond Lake Superior, they encountered Aboriginal peoples on a sustained and intimate basis and performed a wide range of duties that included trading, trapping, hunting, building, and canoeing. Work at posts was less demanding and dangerous than working in canoes, but it required a much broader range of skills. Here voyageurs were able to draw widely on their experiences of growing up on farms in the St. Lawrence valley, especially in construction, hunting, and cultivating gardens. Bourgeois Benjamin and Joseph Frobisher commented: "In winter Quarters . . . [voyageurs] are at ease, and commonly in plenty, which only can reconcile them to that manner of life, and make them forget their Sufferings in their Annual Voyage to and from the Grand Portage."[4] Like canoeing post life had its own rhythms of hard work, rest, tedium, and excitement. The dominant goals were trading with Aboriginal peoples and winter survival rather than traveling.[5]

Fur traders constructed three kinds of posts: large permanent ones usually at transportation hubs, small impermanent posts away from well-traveled routes, and satellites in the most remote regions.[6] Large posts were much busier than smaller and isolated ones. The largest administrative post, at the site of the annual rendezvous, was the interior headquarters of Grand Portage, located at the western tip of Lake Superior. This post was moved fifty miles northwest in 1803 in order to access routes north of the new international boundary. It was called Fort Kaministiquia in its first few years, because it was located on the Kaministiquia River, but in 1807 it was renamed Fort William in honor of NWC head William McGillivray.[7]

Rainy River House on Lac La Pluie (Rainy Lake) acted as a secondary administrative center to Fort William and was sometimes the site of exchange of trade goods and furs between the Montreal and the interior brigades, especially those coming from distant regions such as the Athabasca District. Bas de la Rivière, renamed Fort Alexander in 1807, at the mouth of the Winnipeg River, served as an interior summer rendezvous site. Other major interior posts included Cumberland House, Ile à la Crosse, and Rocky Mountain House (see map 3).[8] Furs, provisions, and transport supplies were often stored at these interior administrative centers, and men were employed in sorting, packing, and caching the goods. These larger centers also served as employment sites. Here men were exchanged between brigades, and freemen congregated if they were looking for work.

Most of the interior posts were small and had short lives, some spanning only a few years.[9] These posts, located off the main transport routes, did not receive nearly as much traffic as the major posts. Usually one or two north canoe crews became their core populations. In 1795 the NWC decided to begin trading in the Mackenzie River District and sent clerk Duncan Livingston, who established Trout River post about eighty miles down river from Great Slave Lake. The post served the Mackenzie River Slaveys until 1802, when it was abandoned. The NWC also established a trading post on Slave Lake, near the mouth of the Slave River in 1786, which was moved at least three times in the ensuing eighteen years in efforts to find good fishing.[10] At posts such as these, voyageurs spent more time on construction and post maintenance than on packing and transporting ladings. Much energy was also devoted to developing relations with Aboriginal people in the area, either establishing trade or securing food from them. In these small settings voyageurs often became very close to one another and to their bourgeois.

Satellite posts formed a third category. They were usually very small and rarely lasted more than a year. Men were often sent out in pairs or small groups to reach Aboriginal communities far from regular fur trade routes. Lac La Martre, a satellite of the Slave Lake post, was set up for the Dogribs.[11] In the Red River valley, south of Lake Winnipeg, Alexander Henry the Younger set up Park River post in 1800 and immediately established a satellite post in the Hair Hills.[12] In these settings a few voyageurs worked closely together and depended on one another for survival. These men often developed intimate relationships with the Aboriginal people with whom they traded. Some became the voyageurs best suited to trade en dérouine, and many created and maintained alliances with Aboriginal peoples.

At all types of posts work was divided into four main areas. The first was post construction and maintenance, and artisan craftwork, such as blacksmithing, coopering, and carpentry. In Lower Canada habitants were accustomed to the wide range of duties and skills needed to run a farm and household, but they usually turned to skilled craftsmen for iron, metal, clay, and some wood products.[13] At the posts men were expected to perform a far greater range of jobs, and there were only a few skilled craftsmen in the trade. The second type of work for voyageurs was trading with Aboriginal peoples. The third type of work was the quest for food. Survival was often precarious, and men were highly motivated to maintain decent diets. Even in times of plenty, men devoted much energy to finding a variety of good food. Fourth, voyageurs traveled throughout the year between interior posts to carry furs, provisions, news and mail, creating an information net that reinforced the interior fur trade community.

Arrival at Interior Trading Posts

At the annual summer rendezvous, the partners of the Montreal fur companies met to decide where to send traders for the coming year. Crews were assigned to specific posts or assigned to establish new posts in areas deemed to have trading potential. In the latter case the bourgeois or clerk in charge of the brigade would choose the precise location for the new post.[14] Crews felt a tremendous relief when they arrived at a post in the fall after a long and hard journey racing against the freeze-up of waterways. However, post duties immediately became pressing concerns. Contact with Aboriginal people in the area was the first order of business, even before unpacking from the long journey and building shelter. Trade was the main reason for traveling into the interior, and trading rituals commenced at the earliest opportunity.[15]

Once contact had been established with Aboriginal trading partners, or if Aboriginal people were not in the area upon their arrival, traders turned their attention to establishing the post. When returning to a post, men were directed to unpack, clean up the site, repair old buildings, and possibly build new ones. Sites were often neglected over the summer or abandoned for several years.[16] Construction for new posts became the next priority. When John Thomson's party arrived at their designated site in the Mackenzie River District in mid-October 1800, he decided to set up his post near an Aboriginal settlement. The first day, "[t]he Men Delivered their Baggages, & made our Encampment &c—which done gave them a Dram—" and early the next morning "[I] gave the men 4 large Axes & a file in order to set about Building as quick as possible."[17] In their letters and journals the bourgeois and clerks frequently reported the rate of post construction and their efforts to encourage their men to build quickly.[18] Voyageurs could build posts very quickly, especially if the crew feared an attack by Aboriginal people. When Alexander Henry the Younger arrived on September 9, 1800, at Park River post he quickly chose a site. Fear of Sioux attacks encouraged the voyageurs on the same day to unload canoes and arrange camp in a way best suited for defense. The next morning Henry gave each man a large axe and supplied the men with drams of high wine in order to encourage them to build the storehouse for the trade goods as soon as possible.[19] Bad weather and shortages of food also acted as an incentive to build shelter quickly. During the fall of 1798 at Grand Marais near the Peace River, John Thomson lamented that it had started to snow and the houses were not yet finished. He had to send the Aboriginal hunter's wife to retrieve meat because there was too much work to be done to spare any of his men for the task.[20]

Community

The communities formed at the interior posts were made up of a range of people. Each post generally had at least one bourgeois or clerk to oversee the operations and trading in the area. Bourgeois were frequently assigned to a post or a region for several years at a time.[21] Many of the bourgeois married Aboriginal women and had families that moved around with them from post to post.[22] Voyageurs were usually assigned to different posts every year, depending on which brigade they accompanied into the interior. The men in a crew made up the labor force of the post for which they were destined. However, on occasion some members of the crew were sent to live off the land for the winter if the company could not afford to provide for their welfare or if there was an abundance of labor. Duncan McGillivray commented that at Fort George on the North Saskatchewan River in 1794, about fifteen of his men were "permitted" to spend the winter on the plains and were provided with ammunition and allowed to trade with Aboriginal people for their sustenance.[23] In 1797 John McDonald of Garth wrote that he sent some of his men to live in twos and threes along the river to survive the spring because the buffalo were scarce.[24] In another example at Fort Alexandria along the Swan River in 1801, Daniel Harmon could not afford to feed the post's population. He directed voyageurs and their wives and children to spend the winter on the plains, where they could hunt buffalo.[25]

Like the bourgeois many voyageurs married Aboriginal women in the interior and had families that lived with them at the interior posts (discussed in chapter 8). The number of people at a post varied greatly, depending on the season, its location, and its relative importance to trade operations. Table 4 shows the great diversity of populations at interior posts. The population at other fur trade posts matched these variations. At Fort Dunvegan, an important supply post for furs and provisions in the Athabasca District, numbers of employees (including women and children) varied from seventy-five in 1805 to about fifty in 1808 and dipped significantly after the 1821 merger to nineteen in 1822 and twenty-four in 1839.[26] In the Cordillera region the number of officers and men at fur trade posts varied from as few as six to as many as forty or fifty in the larger establishments.[27]

At posts the bourgeois and the clerks usually lived in their own houses, and voyageurs lived all together with their families in a larger house. Voyageurs sometimes lived alone or with their families in separate small dwellings. For example, in 1792 at the Peace River fort, or "Old Establishment," two canots du nord of about sixteen men built five houses seventeen by twelve feet for themselves.[28] On occasion one or two families shared a house, depending on the length of time they planned to spend at the post.

However, in most posts, such as Fort Vermilion, shown in table 5, single men shared housing with married men and their families. Although the

Table 4. Composition of Posts in the Northwest Interior

Date	Post & head	No. of bourgeois	No. of clerks	No. of interpreters	No. of guides	No. of engages	No. of women	No. of children	Total
1798[a]	Fort George, John McDonald of Garth	1				16			17
1798	Fort Augustus, Hughes	1				16			17
1800[b]	Reed River & Red River, Michel Langlois					7	3	3	13
1800	Park River, Alexander Henry the Younger	1				8			9
1801 summer	Fort Alexander, Daniel Harmon	2	1	2		5	6	13	29
1801	Bird Mountain on Swan River, Daniel Harmon	1		3		6	2		12
1802[c]	Fort Alexander, Frederick Goedike	1		2		3	UN	UN	6
1802	Bird Mountain, Daniel Harmon	1		I		6			8
1803[d] summer	Fort Alexander, Daniel Harmon	1		1		UN			ca. 30
1803	Unnamed satellite post of Fort Alexander, Frederick Goedike	1				2			3
1803	Hair Hills, Michel Langlois				1	20	5	5	31
1804[e]	Lac La Peche on Qu'Appelle River, Daniel Harmon	1				12			13
1804 summer	Fort Alexander, Daniel Harmon	3		1		UN			UN
1805[f]	Lac La Pluie		6	3	2	28			39
1806[g] summer	South Branch House, Daniel Harmon and Smith	2		3		4	UN	UN	9
1806	Moose Lake, Pierre Pérâs [or Perra]	1				4			5
1807[h]	Dauphin River, George Nelson		1	1		5	2		9
1808[i]	Broken River, Crebassa		1			4	1		6
1808	Pigeon River, John McDonell	1		1	1	4	4	2	13

1808	Grand River, Robert Campbell	1		1		5	2	4	13
1808	Dauphin River, George Nelson		1			4	1		6
1808	Dunvegan, Frederick Goedike	5				32	9	UN	46
1809[j]	Fort Vermilion, Alexander Henry the Younger	3				33	27	67	130
1810[k]	New White Earth House, Alexander Henry the Younger	5				20	36	68	129 & 85 HBC people
1810	Stuart's Lake in New Caledonia, Daniel Harmon	2				13			15
1812[l]	Fort Astoria	5	9			90			104
1813[m]	Athabasca	5	13	8		162			188
1813	English River (upper)	1	3	3	2	37			46
1813	English River (lower) or Rat River & Cumberland House	1	3	1		36			41
1813	Saskatchewan River (Fort des Prairies)	2	4	7	2	58			73
1813	Athabasca River & Lesser Slave Lake	1	1	1	1	27			31
1813	Fort Dauphin	1	4	2	1	30			38
1813	Rocky Mountain Portage			1		5			6
1813	Lac Ouinipique [Winnipeg]	1	2	1	1	16			21
1813	Red River	1	4	3	1	32			41
1813	Lac La Pluie	1	2	1	1	16			21
1813	Fond du Lac	1	4			24			29
1813	Fort William	1	1			22			24
1813	Nipigon	1	4			24			29
1813	Michipicoten	1	3			16			20
1813	St. Marie's [Sault Ste. Marie]		1			6			7

continued

Table 4. Composition of Posts in the Northwest Interior

Date	Post & head	No. of bourgeois	No. of clerks	No. of interpreters	No. of guides	No. of engages	No. of women	No. of children	Total
1814[n] summer	Fort George, Alexander Henry the Younger	4				46			50
1814	English River (upper)	1	3	2	1	36			43
1814	Saskatchewan River (Fort des Prairies)	2	4	3	2	54			65
1814	Athabasca River & Lesser Slave Lake	1			1	24			26
1814	Fort Dauphin		4	2	1	27			34
1814	Lac Ouinipique [Winnipeg]	1	2	1		14			18
1814	Lac La Pluie	1	1	1		13			16
1814	Fond du Lac	1	3			26			30
1814	Fort William	1	1			15			17
1814	Nipigon	2	3		1	21			27
1814	Michipicoten	1	3			12			16
1814	St. Marie's [Sault Ste. Marie]		1			6			7
1817[o]	Slave Lake, John George McTavish	1				6			7
1821[p]	Winter Lake, Fort Enterprise near Coppermine River	5				20			25
Average									32

Note: UN=mentioned in sources but number unspecified. [a]Data for 1798 from NAC, MG 19 A 17, 57–58. [b]Data for 1800 from Henry (the Younger), *New Light*, September 3, 1800, 1:77. [c]Data for 1801 from Harmon, *Sixteen Years*, June 1, 1801, 48; October 2, 1801, 51–52. [d]Data for 1802 from Harmon, *Sixteen Years*, May 31, 1802, 58; November 11, 1802, 64. [e]Data for 1803 from Harmon, *Sixteen Years*, May 19, 1803, 66–67; May 19, and June 21, 1803, 66–67; Henry (the Younger), *New Light*, October 3, 1803, 1:225–27. [f]Data for 1804 from Harmon, *Sixteen Years*, February 22, 1804, 72; April 29, 1804, 80. [g]Data for 1805 from Faries, "Diary", 204–5. [h]Data for 1806 from Harmon, *Sixteen Years*, June 2, 1806, 100; September 17, 1806, 101–2. [i]Data for 1807 from TBR, S 13, George Nelson's journal "No. 5," October 27, 1807, 197–98. [j]Data for 1808 from TBR, S 13, George Nelson's journal, September 1, 1808–March 31, 1810, September 9, 1808, 2 (my pagination); and Harmon, *Sixteen Years*, October 10, 1808, 118. [k]Data for 1809 from Henry (the Younger), *New Light*, October 16, 1809, 5:554–55. [l]Data for 1810 from Henry (the Younger), *New Light*, 2:603; Harmon, *Sixteen Years*, November 18, 1810, 134. [m]Data for 1812 from Cox, *Adventures on the Columbia River*, May 1812, 54, 56. [n]Data for 1813 from NAC, MG 19 A. 35, 1815, 65. Simon McGillivray Papers, volume 7, Memoranda IV, 1815, 65–70. [o]Data for 1814 from Henry (the Younger), *New Light*, 2:868; and NAC, MG 19 A. 35, 65–70. [p]Data for 1815 from Cox, *Adventures on the Columbia River*, June 9, 1817, 257. MRB, MC, C. 27, March 26, 1821, 1.

Table 5. Housing Arrangements at Fort Vermilion, 1809

House	No. of bourgeois	No. of voyageurs	No. of wives	No. of children	Total
House 1		4	4	9	17
House 2		4	3	8	15
House 3		5	3	6	14
House 4		4	5	9	18
House 5		5	4	8	17
House 6		4	3	8	15
House 7		4	1	5	10
House 8	1				1
House 9	1				1
House 10	1		1	3	5
Tent		2	2	5	9
Total	3	32	26	61	122[i]

Note: Data from Henry (the Younger), *New Light*, October 20, 1809, 554–55. [i]Henry's calculations are 36 men, 27 women, and 67 children, totaling 130. Henry (the Younger), *New Light*, 555.

populations of forts varied throughout the years, it was not uncommon for children to constitute the largest demographic group.

Construction and Artisan Crafts

The material culture at fur trade posts was primarily European. Traders and voyageurs built permanent wooden and stone structures in a European model, rather than copying the Aboriginal styles of impermanent houses made of skin and bark. Because very few artisans were specifically employed to work at the posts, voyageurs were expected to perform a wide range of necessary duties. Voyageurs thus became "jacks of all trades," and they immediately applied their skills to constructing shelter. In New France and Lower Canada contracted carpenters usually built most houses, even those of simple frame and *pièce-sur-pièce* construction.[29] In the Northwest, however, voyageurs quickly had to learn the skills that went into building a house. Undoubtedly some of the voyageurs must have had a rudimentary knowledge that they shared with their fellow laborers. The most common type of house was probably post-on-sill construction, with horizontal logs resting on sills cut into the vertical log frames. This style came to be known as the "Red River frame" and was used widely in the Red River settlement, mostly because a single man with a few portable tools could construct such a house.[30]

Post construction and renovation were usually conducted in the fall, at the time of arrival at the trading site. During the summer months, the few men who did not accompany the travel brigades to rendezvous stayed behind to work on construction projects.[31] If weather permitted, construction projects spanned the winter months. For example, at the Rainy Lake post in early December 1804, engagés sawed logs, split shingles and then embarked on the construction of a new house, a project that lasted until the end of January 1805.[32]

Building a new post often required clearing trees.[33] Land was also cleared for gardens, and trees felled for construction. On Lake Temiscamingue NWC clerk Donald McKay established a post near Langue de Terre in the summer of 1805.[34] By the end of July he had two men sawing and two clearing ground along a little river. Throughout August his men sawed and squared wood for the store, the warehouse, and residences.[35] Cutting trees and squaring logs occupied much of the men's time. McKay's crew began sawing as early as April 8, 1805, and by May 22, 1805, had cut at least fifty-six trees for the first part of the construction.[36] To save energy men turned to existing structures in various states of disrepair, salvaging old material and building on previous foundations. At Tête au Brochet in the fall of 1818, the voyageurs set about repairing an old house, which had been made for George Nelson seven years earlier. They cleared out the rubbish, relaid the floors, and plastered.[37]

Posts in the northwestern interior usually consisted of a warehouse, a store, and houses.[38] The most important structure was the warehouse, and men were instructed to build it first. Usually the house for the bourgeois or the clerk or the store was built next. Last, voyageurs could turn to the construction of their own houses.[39] Voyageurs frequently worked on the shop and houses simultaneously.[40] Occasionally houses at the post were built before the shop.[41] Voyageurs sometimes defied bourgeois orders by concentrating on their own houses first, but the most common pattern was probably to work on the warehouse during most of the day before turning to their own houses in the latter part of the day.[42]

After building the frame of a structure, men plastered both the insides and outsides with clay.[43] Searching for clay and transporting it to the post was time-consuming.[44] Some houses were covered with mud and bark, which were easier to procure.[45] Plastering could take as long as twenty-five days.[46] The number of houses, the availability of material, and weather affected the pace. If food was not widely available in a region, men had to divert their attention to hunting and fishing, which slowed their construction pace. Injured men were assigned to plastering to allow other men to hunt.[47]

Once plastering was complete, men moved on to other tasks, such as roofing. Like plastering, splitting shingles was not as difficult a task as other aspects of house construction, so it was left to weaker men.[48] Next, floors were laid, and houses were whitewashed inside and out.[49] Chimneys were built from stone and secured with a plaster made of clay and hay.[50] Where stones were not available, men had to build chimneys solely from clay.[51] Hearths and sometimes ovens were built into the chimneys.[52] Men's carpentry skills were further developed in other aspects of house construction. Windows were cut and either left open or covered with skins, and shutters were added to keep out the weather.[53] Men frequently dug cellars, both inside and outside the houses, for food storage. Donald McKay reported that two men worked for one day digging the cellar for the house at Langue de Terre in the fall of 1799. But installing the floor, stairs, and a door for the cellar stretched out for almost a month.[54] Sometimes men built separate houses to store fish.[55]

The finishing touch on almost every post was a flagstaff, an overt symbol of colonial identity.[56] Cole Harris describes forts as "power containers" of the fur trade, imposing symbols meant to demonstrate power over Aboriginal peoples and over fur trade employees.[57] The flags represented an attempt to claim some kind of sovereignty in the pays d'en haut. They were supposed to signal to Aboriginal people or to their rivals a new presence on their land, and they instilled traders with a sense of legitimacy.

Some posts, especially the major ones, were fortified with palisades to protect them from attacks by Aboriginal people and rival companies. Although these kinds of assaults were not typical, fear of the unknown could lead fur traders to construct the palisades even before their residences. The Sioux, enemies of the Ojibwes and the Assiniboines, who traded regularly with the Montreal companies, caused much trepidation. When Alexander Henry the Younger's party arrived at the site of Park River post in September 1800, fear of the Sioux compelled them to post sentries and build palisades as soon as the storehouse was complete and the goods secure. Henry had each man cut fifty oak fence posts twelve feet long and arrange them around the post. It required the full strength of two men to carry one log at a time on their shoulders. He remarked that "fear was an excellent overseer, and the work went on with expedition." With relief he reported on September 10, 1800, that the stockade was complete. Only then did the men begin to fell trees for house construction.[58] Harris has noted that in the Cordillera when traders "did not build palisaded, well-defended forts, they took risks." In 1814 two NWC posts in the far west were overrun. "A characteristic fort in the Cordillera," according to Harris, "contained . . . [a] rectangular palisade of cedar, fir, or pine logs, usually squared on two surfaces (to fit tightly), planted four feet in the ground, standing fifteen to eighteen feet above it, and pegged to cross-pieces four feet from the top [and a] gallery six to seven feet wide on the inside of the palisades, four and a half feet below the top . . . from which men could fire through loopholes." Forts also contained bastions, usually square two-story structures, and a considerable armament of a variety of cannons, guns, muskets, bayonets.[59]

In areas where men feared attacks from hostile Aboriginal people or were suspicious of the subterfuge of competing companies, sentries patrolled the post during the night. At Fort George in the early nineteenth century, it was customary to keep a watch by night and a guard by day, and Alexander Ross asserted that it was run more like a military post than a trading establishment.[60] At larger depots where great quantities of goods and furs were stored, security was increased. For example, at Grand Portage the gates were always shut at sunset, and two sentries kept watch all night, chiefly for fear of fire.[61] Animals could pose threats to posts, especially to food stores and nets. Traps were frequently used to catch other intruding predators, such as wolves, wolverines, raccoons, foxes, and fishers, whose furs were also valuable to the trade.[62]

Large posts had more buildings than small posts and thus required more construction work from the voyageurs. Some had blacksmith shops.[63] Others had horse stables.[64] Given the importance of travel by horse on the open prairie, smaller prairie outposts also had stables, such as Alexander Henry the Younger's Pembina River post. By 1807, after the post was six years old, Henry had his men build a large stable to house fifty horses.[65] Some forts, such as Fort Alexandria in 1801 and the Forks on the Mackenzie River in 1807, had *glacières*, or icehouses.[66] The size and scale of construction projects were often dependent on the vision and zeal of the bourgeois in charge. For example, in 1807 Alexander Henry the Younger, a bourgeois with considerable drive, had his men build a bridge over a creek to haul firewood more conveniently.[67] Bourgeois and clerks sometimes directed their men to build houses for Aboriginal people in the area to improve trading alliances (though it is unclear if Aboriginal people chose to live in these houses).[68] On occasion voyageurs also had to build small houses near competitors' forts to facilitate spying on the competition.[69]

Frequent shortages of labor and the constant reassignment of men meant post communities were often haphazardly formed.[70] Most voyageurs were expected to perform an astonishing range of duties to keep a post functioning. For example, at the Rainy Lake post in the fall of 1804, in the space of eleven days voyageurs were building themselves beds, mending their clothing, chopping wood, constructing stables, laying floors, mending canoes, and catching and hauling thousands of fish.[71] At Fort Alexandria in the spring of 1801, over the course of three days voyageurs transported meat from the hunters' lodge, hauled ice and water for the icehouse, built sledges, hauled houses to new locations, made pemmican, hung up meat and tongues to salt, made kegs to store grease, and made nails.[72] Most voyageurs practiced carpentry, building furniture and fashioning tools, sledges, and snowshoes. They first gathered suitable wood for their projects.[73] The most common items constructed were beds and bedframes, tables, and chairs.[74] Men also made tools to help in other duties, such as wooden shovels, wheelbarrows, wedges to press packs, and fish baskets.[75] Barrels and containers for storage were very important at posts, and the skills of coopers highly valued. Talented coopers were employed to make barrels not only for their own posts but also for those in surrounding areas.[76]

The absence of artisans in the Northwest interior enabled some voyageurs with particular talent to specialize in crafts, such as blacksmithing, coopering, and making canoes. For example, some men were referred to specifically as carpenters, such as the unnamed engagés at Rainy Lake post in the fall of 1804 and Fort George in the winters of 1812–23.[77] These voyageurs probably skipped apprenticeships that could take many years in a colony.[78] Voyageurs who became experts at particular crafts were taught by fellow voyageurs in the Northwest or improved skills they brought from French Canada. In the spring of 1803 Alexander Henry the Younger wrote: "One of my men undertook to make a real pair of wheels on the plan of those in Canada; he finished them to-day, and they were very well done. I made him chief wheelwright, and we shall soon have some capital carts."[79] Often one man acted as a blacksmith while others helped him by cutting wood, making charcoal, and taking coals out of the kiln.[80] By helping, voyageurs probably learned some of the rudimentary skills of the craft. Blacksmiths made tools for post maintenance, traps for the trade, and helped repair guns.[81] The poor quality of firearms made gun repair a valued skill.[82]

After men had arrived at their post site and put the post in order, they began to prepare for the long winter months ahead. General preparations for the winter included building up stores of food and firewood and ensuring that all buildings were sound. In the late summer and early fall, men harvested wild hay and stored it for their horses, other livestock, and household use during the winter.[83] Throughout the fall men chopped, hauled, and stored cordwood.[84] Near Langue de Terre in October 1805, Donald McKay had his men chop and store firewood, collect and store hay, haul corn, repair the floor of the winter house, whitewash its ceiling, and collect flat stones for the hearth and pavement. In November his men squared logs and sawed boards to have on hand for construction and carpentry projects. They were ready to enter the wintering house on December 17.[85] Maintenance continued through the winter and the spring.[86] Snow removal could start as early in the season as mid-October, as it did at the forks on the Mackenzie River in 1807, and continue as late as March, as it did at the Rainy Lake post in 1805.[87]

Cleaning the forts was a year-round chore.[88] Garbage disposal and human waste management were challenges to maintaining sanitary conditions. Problems could arise early on. Alexander Henry the Younger's crew arrived at the site of the Park River post on September 9, 1800, and by September 24 Henry complained that "[t]he stench about [their] camp [was] so great from the quantities of flesh and fat thrown away since [their] arrival."[89] Voyageurs washed and mended their own and their bourgeois' and clerks' clothes.[90] They also participated in food preservation and preparation. They helped put cellars in order, baked bread, cleaned and cooked potatoes, boiled buffalo fat, made pemmican, and salted meat.[91] Some voyageurs were designated as cooks, but all were expected to know how to prepare food. In addition they made candles and soap out of bear fat and tallow.[92]

Aboriginal Laborers

Many opportunities arose for voyageurs to become close to Aboriginal people, who came to interior posts to trade and to work and frequently resided at posts for prolonged periods of time when hired as guides, interpreters, hunters, and general laborers. Although this phenomenon was more common at HBC posts, the HBC term *homeguard* was sometimes used to describe Aboriginal people living near the posts of other companies.[93] On occasion an Aboriginal person from the northwestern interior would be hired as a "regular" voyageur and sign a contract similar to that of the French Canadian voyageurs.[94] However, most interior arrangements did not involve formal contracts.[95] Labor of this sort was fluid and informal. Aboriginal people moved in and out of jobs to suit their personal provisioning and economic strategies. Their decisions of when and where to work were often determined by environmental factors, such as the abundance of animals in the area around the forts. Some Aboriginal people were engaged specifically to hunt hares, deer, and bears for a post, on both an individual and a group basis.[96] Aboriginal people were of crucial importance when a trader's knowledge of the environment was poor or when the voyageurs were too weak from hunger to hunt or fish.[97] In most arrangements the bourgeois supplied Aboriginal hunters with ammunition.[98] Aboriginal boys were often hired to deliver ammunition and tobacco to the adult hunters.[99] Aboriginal people were employed on a temporary, casual basis for tasks that included procuring bark, paddling canoes, transporting goods, making canoes, retrieving goods lost during canoe accidents, and hauling meat to the posts.[100] Aboriginal men delivered mail between posts, especially in the winter, when the journey was more dangerous than usual and voyageurs were reluctant to do this job.[101]

Aboriginal people were most often sought out to act as guides, interpreters, and negotiators. Aboriginal guides were frequently hired along trading routes in well-traveled areas, such as the routes between Lake Superior and Lake Winnipeg. Although traders were familiar with these areas, local guides allowed them to travel more quickly and avoid temporary environmental impediments, such as fallen trees or low water levels. In 1784 Edward Umfreville recorded hiring an Aboriginal guide from Lake Superior to Lake Nipigon even though some of his men had traveled the route several times before.[102] The services of Aboriginal guides were more crucial on unfamiliar frontiers, such as the Rocky Mountains, especially when bourgeois and clerks traveled to an area for the first time. Alexander Mackenzie's journals about his explorations in search of a passage to the Pacific Ocean are filled with descriptions of his efforts to procure guides in unfamiliar lands.[103] Sometimes Aboriginal people would be hired for several jobs, such as interpreting and hunting. On occasion bourgeois hired Aboriginal people to trade en dérouine.[104]

Although Aboriginal labor became important to the Montreal trade, there was little competition between voyageurs and Aboriginal people for casual labor. The bourgeois preferred French Canadian employees for long-term contracts of three to five years and treated Aboriginal peoples as a flexible and short-term labor force, hired during times of labor shortages or when their servants did not have the skills to perform the necessary tasks.[105] The bourgeois may have threatened to hire Aboriginal peoples to replace uncooperative voyageurs, but the threats were probably empty, as bourgeois generally considered Aboriginal people unreliable employees. Aboriginal people frequently threatened to quit and more often than not followed through on the threat.[106] However, in reference to a case where W. F. Wentzel, stationed at the forks of the Mackenzie and Liard Rivers in the summer of 1807, complained of an Indian who deserted his task of transporting a trader upriver, Lloyd Keith wisely cautions scholars that

> *[t]he perspective of the European fur trader is everywhere pervasive in these journals, much to the debasement of the Indian. Here the Native guide is seen as a 'rascal,' who has abandoned the bourgeois of the district while employed in a task that was 'much against his own inclination,' and such 'tricks' should not ordinarily be encouraged. . . . Nowhere is consideration given to the claim that he did not want to go in the first place and that he might be expected to abscond when opportunity presented itself. What might be reasonable for one was not allowed the other.*[107]

Sometimes Aboriginal guides bargained for better working conditions, such as demanding year-round contracts and food for their families. On his 1784 trip north of Lake Superior, Umfreville decided to fire his Aboriginal guide because the guide expected the trader to feed his family of eight; another Aboriginal guide he hired for the remainder of the journey insisted that he be granted a contract to last throughout the winter.[108] The bourgeois often lamented that they had to put up with outrageous demands and rascally behavior because they were so dependent on Aboriginal people. When animals were scarce and conditions poor, Aboriginal peoples often bargained for better terms in their contracts to hunt.[109] They threatened to stop hunting if not provided with enough rum, and bourgeois were compelled to comply with their request because the bourgeois feared starvation. In 1799 near Fort

Dauphin, Alexander Henry the Younger complained that the scarcity of animals obliged him to hire Aboriginal hunters on "extravagant terms." They demanded clothing for themselves and their families, liquor, guns, knives, ammunition, and tobacco. Henry griped, "[E]ven upon these terms I was obliged to consider it a great favor they did me."[110] Aboriginal agency and bargaining for better working conditions may have served as an example to voyageurs and introduced new ideas about their own potential freedom and power. Voyageurs probably knew that the bourgeois viewed Aboriginal workers as unreliable. This knowledge would have increased voyageurs' bargaining power, given them confidence about the security of their jobs, and increased their sense of self-worth as employees.

Trade

Voyageurs came into contact most often with Aboriginal people not as fellow workers but as fur trading partners. They met to trade in two settings: at trading posts and at Aboriginal lodges. The pursuit of furs dominated post life. Although the most expeditious way to obtain furs was by trading for them with Aboriginal peoples, all members of the post were required to secure furs in any context. The bourgeois and the clerks sometimes obliged their voyageurs to hunt for furs rather than for food. Aboriginal wives of traders were extensively involved in trapping and snaring.[111] Traps and snares were set out around posts throughout the year, and the animals caught ranged from beavers to martins, raccoons, foxes, fishers, and wolves.[112] Some steel traps were brought out from Lower Canada, but more frequently traps were made at the interior posts that housed a blacksmith and then exported to other posts.[113] Locales with blacksmiths also became important for the frequent repair required for traps.[114]

The bulk of furs from the Northwest were traded from Aboriginal people who traveled to posts to trade furs and to sell provisions.[115] Furs were also obtained when voyageurs were sent out individually or in small groups to trade en dérouine.[116] Voyageurs were frequently sent out in search of Aboriginal people to establish contact with them.[117] Scouting and reporting on Aboriginal movements continued throughout the course of the year. For example, at Fort Alexandria in mid-November 1800, voyageurs Collier and La Rose reported to bourgeois Archibald Norman McLeod on the local Ojibwes' and Crees' trapping activities and intentions to come to the post to trade. In early January the following year, Collier set out to collect Cree debts. In February Etienne Ducharme came to tell McLeod that six tents of Crees were encamped near his lodge and were loaded down with skins and provisions. McLeod sent voyageurs Roy, Girardin, Dannis, and Plante with provisions to trade with these prosperous Crees.[118] In addition to gathering information about Aboriginal peoples and trading with them, voyageurs also collected debts and conveyed messages between bourgeois and Aboriginal people.[119] Bourgeois and clerks sometimes sent men to watch Aboriginal people closely to prevent them from trading privately with free traders.[120] In other cases men were sent to stay with Aboriginal people to prevent them from trading with rival companies.[121]

Voyageurs were also dispatched to scout on the competing companies directly. Before 1805 the XYC and the NWC often had men spy on one another and attempt to impede one another's trading efforts.[122] In November 1804 at the Rainy Lake post, Hugh Faries sent out Laverdure and La France to follow the XYC men while they were out trading. Even after receiving the news of the merger of these two companies weeks later, on January 12, 1805, frictions continued. Faries continued to employ voyageurs to spy on the actions of the previous XYC clerk Lacombe, who Faries suspected was trying to cheat him.[123] Montreal fur traders were consistently suspicious of the dealings of the HBC before the 1821 merger and routinely ordered voyageurs to spy on them and attempt to interrupt their trading efforts. In 1807 a NWC voyageur named La Rocque, "a noted battailleur," was sent out to obstruct the trading of Peter Fidler of the HBC.[124] Throughout most of his career as a clerk for the NWC, George Nelson sent men out to spy on the actions of the HBC traders. In the fall of 1818 at Tête au Brochet, Nelson instructed a voyageur (possibly the same La Rocque) to build a house near the HBC fort as a permanent spy post.[125]

All men working in the fur trade, voyageurs, bourgeois and clerks included, participated in trading with Aboriginal peoples. Voyageurs could be employed simply to bring furs promised to the bourgeois or clerk.[126] But unlike most employees in the HBC, voyageurs were regularly entrusted with more responsibility. Voyageurs were sent to trade en dérouine without prearranged transactions.[127] Throughout the year voyageurs sought out furs, provisions, and materials to make necessary equipment.[128] They sometimes initiated trade with Aboriginal people in a new area, especially if they were experienced in the Northwest and in trading.[129] Voyageurs also traded with the English and with freemen, but most of their trading duties focused on Aboriginal peoples.[130] Large groups of voyageurs could be ordered to conduct the trade on their own, as was the case near the Assiniboine and Qu'Appelle rivers in the winter of 1794. John McDonell sent out Jean Baptiste Lafrance, Joseph Dubé, Joseph Tranquille, Hugh McCruchen, Louis Houle, Jean Baptiste Bertrand, and Antoine Bounuir Lanignes to Missouri "*en* traite."[131] Voyageurs could be singled out to head larger trading parties. For example, François-Antoine Larocque entrusted Azure with an equipment of goods at a Mandan village in the Missouri District.[132] When trading with Aboriginal people, voyageurs had to make difficult decisions concerning rates and prices and were obliged to haggle over the terms of trade. Duncan Cameron gave his voyageur Bellefleure "every instruction in dealing with the Indians" before allowing him to conduct trade.[133] Voyageurs Delorme and Desjarlais reported to Charles Chaboillez in January 1798 that they were forced to lower their prices to the level of the southern traders to remain competitive. Occasionally mishaps occurred that jeopardized the trade. Later that spring Delorme lost his way during a trading mission and consumed part of the liquor he was supposed to trade.[134] In March 1812 a voyageur named François Paradix severely damaged his relationship with Crees around Lake Winnipeg by stealing from them. When Paradix approached them to trade, the Crees refused and threatened Paradix's life. The Crees complained to George Nelson: "It is the fault of that curly headed lying dog. He too forsooth, must play his man, menaces us, beat us, steals our things and calls us liars. We were a little drunk, even if we were sober it would have been the same. He is a dog, a liar and a thief, Larocque know it. Let him go away we will not see the dog."[135] Despite these occasional problems voyageurs were usually adept at bringing Aboriginal peoples to the post to trade furs and provisions throughout the year.[136]

Voyageurs Residing with Aboriginal People

Voyageurs were also routinely sent out to stay with Aboriginal people for prolonged periods of time.[137] During these sojourns they traded with Aboriginal people at their lodges and encouraged Aboriginal people to trade at the posts and to hunt for furs and meat to provision the posts.[138] At Fort Alexandria in December 1800, Archibald Norman McLeod instructed Baptiste Roy and Jacques to separate the Cree hunters so that they might bring in more meat, and he sent rum and tobacco to appease them.[139] Staying with Aboriginal people was generally a duty of everyone employed at a post, and men took turns staying at Aboriginal lodges alone or in pairs.[140] Occasionally a master would visit Aboriginal lodges to check on his men and to provide additional encouragement for the Aboriginal people to cooperate with the voyageurs.[141] The length of time of a "turn" with Aboriginal people varied, depending on the distance from the post, the number of men available, and their relationship with the Aboriginal people. Some turns spanned a fortnight, but others could be longer, especially if the men took their families with them.[142]

If voyageurs did not get along with Aboriginal people, or if the Aboriginal people were demanding, indifferent, or even hostile toward the traders, staying with them could be the most unpopular task at a post. In late April 1815 at Manitonamingon Lake, George Nelson noted that a voyageur named LeBlond set off to inform his master Morrison that he refused to stay with the Aboriginal people any longer.[143] Men made excuses to skip their turns with Aboriginal people, as did Paradix at Dauphin River in the winter of 1808. When George Nelson sent him to go stay with the Ojibwes, he went spear fishing instead.[144] John Thomson had great difficulties convincing any of his men to stay with Aboriginal people at Grand Marais, along the

Peace River, in the fall of 1798. He initially sent out Vivier and Le Compte to stay with one group. Le Compte returned in a week, claiming that he was too ill to remain with them. Thomson was suspicious, describing him as "a most indolent Lazy fellow," but he had trouble convincing anyone to take his place. Eventually he managed to persuade Desrosier and Brousseault to join Vivier, but the voyageurs quickly became disgruntled and wished to return because the Aboriginal people were not cooperating with them. One wonders what the Aboriginal people thought of Vivier. By mid-November Vivier returned to the fort with his family, asserting that "he [could not] live any longer with them & that all the devils in Hell [could not] make him return, & that he prefer[ed] marching all Winter from one Fort to another rather than Live any Longer with them." Less than a month later Brousseault returned to the fort with his family as well, claiming that the Aboriginal people sent them back because there were no animals to kill for food.[145] Certainly more often than appears in the sources, Aboriginal people simply did not want voyageurs to stay with them, as was the case for the Mashkiegon (Swampy Cree?) band at Dauphin River in the fall of 1810.[146] Part of the reason may have been the inconvenience and expense of having to take care of and feed the voyageurs, who were often unskilled and unsuccessful hunters and could not do a fair share of work. In November 1800 at Rocky Mountain Fort, which had been established by John Thomson that fall down the Mackenzie River from the Trout River post, Little Chief (Dene) sent the voyageur La Beccasse back to the fort because he did not want to feed him any longer. Little Chief insisted that Thomson pay for food before permitting voyageurs La Beccasse and St. Cir to spend the winter with his band. Later that winter a voyageur named La Violette had to be carried back to the post by the Dene because he was ill and his legs had swollen. He blamed the Dene for not taking care of him while he stayed at their lodges, and the Dene vehemently denied his accusations. The Dene were further insulted when Thomson gave one of them "a Twig [tweak] of the Nose to teach him better Manners" and bitterly complained that the Dene could not be relied on to bring provisions to the post. Thomson demonstrated remarkable hypocrisy here because he had previously described La Violette as a "Slow creaping Hare" who needed two days to get ready for a short journey.[147] Clearly Thomson's party gave the Mackenzie River Dene much grief, and their reluctance to aid the traders does not seem unreasonable.

Other instances where voyageurs stayed with Aboriginal people were more positive. Even one of John Thomson's men, St. Cir, was happy despite the general pattern of bad relations in the winter of 1800–1801 along the Mackenzie River. St. Cir was very pleased with the Dene at the lodge where he stayed and reported that they gave him plenty of hares to eat, unlike La Beccasse, who had to hunt for his own food, as "his Homme de Loge [host] [did] not take the least Notice of him." The men taking care of St. Cir agreed to host La Beccasse to save him from starvation.[148] Voyageurs often had better luck staying with Aboriginal people when they could utilize family contacts. At the Dauphin River in the fall of 1809, the two sons of Old Muffle d'Orignialle came to the post to pick up Larocque to pass the winter with them because he was married to their sister.[149]

Voyageurs Directing Trading Operations

Many voyageurs were entrusted with major tasks, such as setting up smaller or temporary satellite posts. In the fall of 1800, when Alexander Henry the Younger set out to establish the Park River post, he left half his crew at Pembina to start a post under the charge of Michel Langlois, one of his voyageurs. He directed Langlois to equip the neighboring Ojibwes to hunt and trap and send them inland as soon as possible. Henry then directed Langlois to make up a small assortment of goods for another small post at Hair Hills. On Henry's orders Langlois sent voyageur Lagassé with two other men to build a small hut there. The initial plan did not work, but Henry did not lose faith in all voyageurs. He sent another voyageur named Hamel to take the place of Lagassé, as "[n]one would remain under the command of Lagassé, nor [did he] think him a fit person to have property in charge." Three years later, when the Hair Hills post became more permanent, Henry sent Langlois to head that post.[150] The bourgeois in charge of Cross Lake in the fall of 1805 sent four of his men to run an outpost at Duck Lake at the request of the local Aboriginal people.[151] Sometimes the arrangement did not work out. At Rocky Mountain House in the winter of 1805–6, John Stuart entrusted voyageur Lammalice with the Trout Lake outpost. Lammalice abandoned the post without informing Stuart and later blamed the laziness and indolence of the other voyageurs sent to help him at the post.[152]

Bourgeois and clerks occasionally delegated to voyageurs responsibilities on par with setting up satellite posts. Individual voyageurs demonstrating trustworthiness and responsibility could be left in charge of posts when the bourgeois or the clerks had to be away.[153] James Porter was pleased in the fall of 1800 that Morin, left to take care of the post at Slave Lake during the summer, had been "very attentive and careful."[154] In the summer of 1800 on the Mackenzie River, John Thomson entrusted the charge of the Trout River post to a voyageur named Jean-Baptiste LaPrise, who had been Thomson's second-in-command the previous winter.[155] However, a voyageur left to take care of a post could meet with dreadful challenges, as did Louis Chatellain in 1805, who had to fight off a war party of 150 "Rapid Natives" with only the help of two other men.[156] Occasionally, when all the men were needed for a trip, one of the voyageurs' Aboriginal wives could be left to manage the post.[157]

Bourgeois and clerks sometimes left voyageurs in charge of posts for an entire season. In the winter of 1803 XYC clerk Chaurette left La Lancette with three men to pass the winter alone at Lac du Flambeau. With Chaurette's encouragement George Nelson decided to entrust voyageur Brunet with the post at Rivière des Saulteaux. By late December Nelson was pleased with Brunet's returns and his understanding of the Ojibwe language and felt Brunet was industrious enough to be in charge of the post for the rest of the winter, while Nelson wintered with Ojibwes.[158] Cooperation and mutual trust were not uncommon between voyageurs and their masters, and bourgeois and clerks could entrust their men with great responsibility, such as having men help with inventories. In the summer of 1805 in the Temiscamingue area, Donald McKay dispatched two voyageurs to inventory a post that had been forgotten in the spring. In another case a voyageur named Cloutier helped McKay put his cellar in order one winter.[159] Experienced voyageurs could also be valuable assets in helping new clerks. On the way to Grand Portage in the spring of 1792, bourgeois Angus Shaw left the young clerk John McDonald of Garth with the "faithful Guide Antoine" to help him manage the brigade.[160]

Sometimes bourgeois and clerks regretted trusting voyageurs to manage their post.[161] Voyageurs could have their responsibilities revoked if they did not perform to the satisfaction of their employers. Pierre L'Anniau was left in charge of Grand Portage in 1784, based on his extensive experience in the Northwest as a voyageur. However, when he did not get along with the surrounding Aboriginal people, he was fired and replaced by Roderick McKenzie, a young clerk at the time.[162] On September 19, 1800, Alexander Henry the Younger wrote in frustration: "My servant [Desmarais] is such a careless, indolent fellow that I cannot trust the storehouse to his care. I made to-day a complete overhaul, and found everything in the greatest confusion; I had no idea matters were so bad as I found them. I shall for the future take charge myself and find other work for him. Like most of his countrymen, he is much more interested for himself than for his employer, though he has a good salary for his abilities, which are not extraordinary, further than as interpreter."[163]

Aboriginal and Voyageur Friendships

During the early days of the postconquest Montreal fur trade, Thomas Hutchins, an HBC officer, commented: "The Canadians have great Influence over the Natives by adopting all their Customs and making them Companions, the[y] drink, sing, conjure, scold &c with them like one of themselves, and the Indians are never kept out of their Houses whether drunk or sober, night or Day."[164] Although Hutchins probably perceived voyageurs and Aboriginal peoples as close friends because he viewed both groups as part of a rowdy lower order, his observations had some truth. Some voyageurs, especially those working for many years in the pays d'en haut, became closer to Aboriginal people than did their masters. Voyageurs worked in a less-structured social environment than their masters and did not have the bourgeois' ambition for profit, large personal investment in the trade, and the expectation of high returns. The bourgeois were sometimes encouraged to marry Aboriginal and métis women (and sometimes voyageurs' daughters) to develop trading alliances.[165] Yet few created a permanent life in the Northwest. Conversely, many voyageurs lost touch with their families in the St. Lawrence valley, were eager to create new lives for themselves in the pays d'en haut, and naturally became more open to the influence of Aboriginal peoples.

This closeness was made possible primarily through trading contact. Friendships often emerged as Aboriginal people came to know individual voyageurs over the course of several years. Fur trade companies valued these voyageurs for their experience and trade networks. In 1825 bourgeois Roderick McKenzie did not want to send one of his men, Antoine SanRegret, to Duncan Clark, because SanRegret was the best voyageur to trade with the Aboriginal people, and McKenzie did not want to lose him.[166] Voyageurs sometimes used their personal friendships with Aboriginal peoples to trade outside the company for individual gain, which in turn led to closer relationships between voyageurs and Aboriginal people without master involvement. Goods that were "free-traded" primarily consisted of dogs, horses, and meat. At Rocky Mountain Fort along the Mackenzie River in 1801, bourgeois John Thomson complained that Martin, a man whom he sent out to get meat from Dene hunters, privately arranged to buy extra meat for his family and when caught claimed that it was a gift from a Dene friend.[167]

Voyageurs became closest to Aboriginal people when they lived and worked with them, such as when they wintered in Aboriginal lodges. Voyageurs helped Aboriginal hunters cache and haul their meat to the lodges and posts, and they traded en dérouine at Aboriginal camps.[168] Conversely, the bourgeois and clerks rarely lived alone with Aboriginal people in their lodges unless they were exploring new lands. Voyageurs "boarding" with Aboriginal people could sometimes be uncomfortable, as we have seen. Unfortunately the bourgeois and clerks more often recorded trouble between voyageurs and Aboriginal peoples than good rapport and trust. Clues to close friendships between Aboriginal people and voyageurs can be found by reading carefully through bourgeois reports. Offhand comments indicate that voyageurs frequently traveled with Aboriginal people back and forth from the lodges to the fur trade posts.[169] Voyageurs often socialized with Aboriginal people and welcomed them in their homes at the fur trade posts.[170] Marriages between voyageurs and Aboriginal women (discussed in the next chapter) were strong signifiers of amity. Signifiers of friendship can also be found in the incidence of voyageurs who chose to live most of their lives in an Aboriginal community. Alexander Henry the Younger described meeting among the Mandans in the summer of 1806 a Canadian named René Jussaume, who went on to work as an interpreter and guide for Lewis and Clark that fall. Henry commented: "This man has resided among the Indians for upward of 15 years, speaks their language tolerably well, and has a wife and family who dress and live like the natives. He retains the outward appearance of a Christian, but his principles, as far as I could observe, are much worse than those of a Mandane; he is possessed of every superstition natural to those people, nor is he different in every mean, dirty trick they have acquired from intercourse with the set of scoundrels who visit these parts."[171] Although Jussaume had not been a voyageur for fifteen years, Henry's description of him was typical of masters' disparaging remarks about the bad influence voyageurs and Aboriginal peoples had on each other. Reading between the lines, one suspects that Jussaume had adapted to Mandan culture very well. Other voyageurs lived in Aboriginal communities only on a temporary basis. Some chose to pass the summer with an Aboriginal hunting group instead of taking part in the summer frenzy of transporting goods and furs.[172] Sometimes wives pressured their husbands to live with their Aboriginal in-laws. One voyageur named Brunet, under the charge of George Nelson in the Lac du Flambeau and Chippewa River area, was repeatedly pushed by his Ojibwe wife to abandon the service. He and his wife occasionally left the post to spend time with her family.[173]

Living and working together often led to goodwill, cooperation, and knowledge exchange between Aboriginal people and voyageurs. Voyageurs very readily adopted Aboriginal customs to make their lives easier. A long history of borrowing from Aboriginal peoples in French Canada set an easy precedent. One of the most common areas of cultural borrowing was food. Of course voyageurs ate "country foods," or whatever was available in the pays d'en haut, but they frequently looked to Aboriginal people for new delicacies, such as dog meat, salmon berries, and particular oils and roots.[174] Voyageurs also frequently watched or participated in Aboriginal dancing and singing.[175] They helped one another build houses, canoes, and tools.[176] Aboriginal people also provided voyageurs with maps and information on travel routes.[177] They helped one another during accidents or illnesses by rescuing one another and sharing medicine and medical treatments.[178] Ross Cox recorded a case where some Flatheads made a sweat lodge for an old Canadian voyageur who had severe rheumatism.[179] The Dene who hosted La Violette near the Mackenzie River carried him back to his post when his legs swelled, despite La Violette's accusations that they mistreated him and neglected their hunting and trapping obligations to the NWC.[180] Sharing food was probably the most important means of demonstrating friendship.[181] Yet sometimes the "kindness" and "sharing" had a hard edge, such as when voyageurs compelled Aboriginal people to share provisions with them or vice versa.[182] Friendships between Aboriginal people and voyageurs were built on personal encounters. Voyageurs' reputations with Aboriginal people often depended on their personality, courtesy, honesty, and fairness. For example, at Tête au Brochet in 1819, clerk George Nelson commented: "[I]t is true La Roque [a voyageur] is a very Prudent man, respected & liked by the indians [Ojibwes] but Paradix is just the reverse."[183] Conversely, some voyageurs were disliked because they were considered liars, thieves, or cheats. The Ojibwes trading at Tête au Brochet disliked voyageur Paradix so much that they refused to trade with him and threatened to kill him.[184]

Conflict and Violence

Voyageurs were often sent out to follow Aboriginal people to dissuade them from trading with other companies, a tactic that impeded more than encouraged successful trade. In one case, at Cross Lake in 1805, two voyageurs helped their bourgeois change the directional markers left by Aboriginal people for the HBC. Later in the season the voyageurs could not find the Aboriginal people and complained that they did not leave markers.[185] Some Aboriginal people were afraid of French Canadians and claimed that they were subject to "constant ill usage & beatings" if they traded with rival companies.[186] Bourgeois Alexander Mackenzie described his voyageurs' relationship with the Beavers in the Athabasca District: "When the traders first appeared among these people, the Canadians were treated with the utmost hospitality and attention; but they have, by their subsequent conduct, taught the Natives to withdraw that respect from them, and sometimes to treat them with indignity."[187] Although the Beavers were probably wary of the bourgeois as well as the voyageurs, the reputation of Canadian traders as ruthless brutes could discourage Aboriginal people from trading with them.[188]

When voyageurs were given control of a post, they naturally became alarmed and frustrated when Aboriginal people refused to trade with them.[189] In one incident bourgeois Duncan Cameron recounted that a voyageur whom he put in charge of a trading expedition had "his pride . . . very hurt by the Osnaburgh Chief, who would not Acknowledge him to be a great Man."[190]

Most major disputes between Aboriginal people and traders were fomented by trading issues. Aboriginal people attempted to protect their position as major trading clients by preventing Europeans from moving inland to trade with other Aboriginal groups, especially those who were their enemies. For example, some Crees attempted to prevent the NWC from trading with the Slaveys in 1808.[191] Opposing companies sometimes encouraged Aboriginal people to attack the competition. Wentzel reported on the NWC's capture of HBC officer Colin Robertson near Great Slave Lake in spring 1819: "Several of our men informed that he had threatened to excite the Natives to Massacre the North West Companys Servants at Fort Chipewyan, and our men refused to do their duty unless he was apprehended & detained in Safe Custody."[192] Rumors of "Indian conspiracies" were recurrent. In 1808 George Nelson heard talk of a plot by Aboriginal people to attack fur trade posts. This conspiracy was linked to the spread into the Northwest of the nativistic teachings of the Shawnee Prophet, who counseled Aboriginal people to give up trade with Europeans and the use of European goods.[193] Rumors of Aboriginal conspiracies ranged from Crees and Sioux in 1810, Chipewyans and their neighbors in 1814, to Crees again in 1817.[194] It is hard to determine if the reported rumors were due to paranoia. Aboriginal people might have felt the pressures of dwindling resources and turned their anxiety into hostility against European traders.

Aboriginal people sometimes directly threatened to attack trading posts.[195] The threats were carried out on some occasions, which to some extent validated the rumors and suspicions. In 1781 Fort de Tremble, or Old Poplar Fort, on the Assiniboine River was attacked by a group of Crees. Alexander Henry the Younger recalled that "this unfortunate affair appeared to be the opening of a plan for the destruction of the whites throughout the North West." The attack took place early in the fall soon after the canoes had arrived, when the men were still building. Eleven of the men hid while the remaining ten defended themselves and drove off the Crees. Three Canadians and thirty Crees were killed in the battle. The post was immediately abandoned.[196]

Aboriginal people were often annoyed by the voyageurs' lack of experience in living in the interior, especially if they scared away fish and game that Aboriginal people were trying to hunt, or if they broke taboos and offended animal spirits.[197] Refusing to share food during times of scarcity violated Aboriginal social ethics. On one occasion some voyageurs refused to share their large supply of provisions and even preferred to feed their dogs very well before sharing even a bite with the Aboriginal people.[198] This behavior transgressed the social rules of "Indian Country," where everyone expected that food would be shared among all allies.[199] Traders' misunderstandings about the social ethic of sharing led to their widespread fear that Aboriginal people would steal their goods and furs.[200] Ironically the fear of pillaging often motivated bourgeois and voyageurs to trade fairly and generously with Aboriginal people, who in return often promised fair dealing.[201] In more cases, however, the fear of pillaging led to poor relations, mistrust, and unfair trading, which resulted in actual pillaging by Aboriginal people. They stole both trade goods and equipment from the bourgeois and the clerks and the individual property of the voyageurs.[202] Bruce White has found that pillaging was an important economic strategy for both Aboriginal peoples and traders. Pillaging or its threat by Aboriginal people encouraged traders to be fair and honest; at the same time, traders frequently pillaged Aboriginal people of their furs to prevent them from ending up in the hands of the competition. In any case, incidents of pillaging represented the breakdown of the social cohesion that best encouraged profitable trade.[203]

Traders took on the networks of friends and enemies of Aboriginal groups with whom they traded. For example, extensive trade with Algonquian-speakers on the plains led bourgeois, clerks, and voyageurs to hate and fear the Sioux, who were enemies of many Algonquian-speakers.[204] In the summer of 1810 at the Pembina River, a large party of Sioux visited the traders' establishment. They did not molest the fort inhabitants but were annoyed that the traders stayed behind the palisades. George Nelson recounts that "one night they observed the Sioux in large numbers around the fort and concluded they would certainly be attacked tho they had hitherto only sufferred annoyance and fear, and they prepared for the worst; whoops were heard and the death song." The Sioux probably wanted to simply intimidate the traders, as they could have attacked the post at any time, and their subsequent battle with Ojibwes and Crees did not involve the traders.[205]

More peaceable relations between Aboriginal peoples and traders were established when trading alliances were secured. Once harmony occurred on an official and diplomatic level, voyageurs and Aboriginal peoples developed personal ties. A system of rough justice reflected shared ideas about socially acceptable behavior in the Northwest. One voyageur feared that Aboriginal people would kill him because of his brutal conduct, recognizing that he had broken a social law of the pays d'en haut.[206] In the winter of 1810 two voyageurs met a party of thirteen Crees and three Assiniboines, who pillaged their furs, snowshoes, and guns. They seemed determined to kill one of the voyageurs, probably to avenge some previous injustice or feud. They had wanted the scalp of the bourgeois Alexander Henry the Younger but settled for that of voyageur Clément. The other voyageur, Cardinal, "who

[was] a most loquacious person, was exercised to the utmost of his ability, and by his fluency of speech [and by giving the Aboriginal people his pistol] saved the life of Clément."[207]

Revenge killing constituted one aspect of the rough justice of the pays d'en haut.[208] Even though it perpetuated cycles of violence that reinforced suspicion and mistrust between traders and Aboriginal people, it also represented personal connections and shared ideas of justice. In 1779-80 at Eagle Hill fort (Old Fort of Montagne D'aigle), a French Canadian trader poisoned a "troublesome" Aboriginal man with laudanum. In the ensuing fray both sides suffered several casualties. The traders were forced to abandon the post to avoid the wrath of the Crees, who subsequently pillaged the post.[209] Lord Selkirk described one of these cycles, which started in 1802 on Pike River near Lake Superior. Three Canadians running the post were murdered by some Aboriginal people, one of whom had helped them the preceding season. They then pillaged the post. In the following year the NWC and a competing company set up posts on that location. A "bataillier," or bully, from each of the posts together murdered an Aboriginal suspect and her husband, even though the husband had saved the life of one of the voyageurs on a previous occasion.[210] Most of the cycles of violence, however, did not lead to such significant rifts in trading relationships.

The Quest for Food

Another reason for conflict and violence between voyageurs and Aboriginal peoples was competition over food. The northwestern plains and subarctic areas were not rich in food sources and did not support large populations. Harvesting food resources required specialized skills that could be challenging to men accustomed to farming in a fertile river valley. Hunting animals for furs could have disastrous ecological consequences, leading to diminished animal populations and severe food shortages.[211] The quest for food dominated the fur trade and constituted a major concern for the men involved. When men arrived at a post, the hurried construction was accompanied by a scramble to build up the store of provisions for the winter. Food gathering, preparation, and preservation had its own cycle, which was affected by place and weather, and when fur traders were particularly competent, their cycles mirrored those of Aboriginal people in the area. Traders often relied on Aboriginal people for food or to teach them to procure it for themselves.[212]

The quest for food shaped post life and determined the ease or burden of voyageurs' work. Voyageurs were highly motivated to maintain a strong and varied supply of food, and food issues led to stresses in master-voyageur relations. Voyageurs often refused to cooperate with their bourgeois and clerks when they were not satisfied with the provisions. In times of hunger finding food was all-consuming and meant survival or death. In times of plenty a varied diet and high-quality food determined the standard of living at a post.

When fur traders first arrived in an unfamiliar place, they were dependent on Aboriginal people for food and were as anxious to trade for provisions as for furs. In times of dire need, men went in search of Aboriginal peoples for provisions. For example, in the summer of 1802 Daniel Harmon was concerned about the shortage of food at Bird Mountain, so he sent out seven men in several different directions in search of Aboriginal people to help them find provisions.[213] Traveling to Aboriginal camps for provisions was not restricted to times of crisis but was a regular post activity.[214] Men were also sent out to entice Aboriginal peoples with provisions to the post.[215] Aboriginal people often came to the fur trade posts without being sought by traders, especially once the word was out that the traders wanted provisions. At the Pembina River post in the winter of 1798, Ojibwes periodically visited and offered meat to sell. Charles Chaboillez, the bourgeois in charge of the post, recorded one day in February 1798: "Arrived an Old Woman, she brought four Pieces Dryed Meat, 3 Buffo Sdes, 2 Packs Cords & 2 Bladders grease, for which I paid her Ten Phiols Mixed Rum—gave her a Piece Tobo & she sets off."[216]

Traders often sought out Aboriginal people to hire as hunters as soon as they arrived at a post.[217] Some Aboriginal people were hired because they had reputations as excellent and reliable hunters.[218] At Trout Lake on June

21, 1806, Simon Fraser was excited to report that he finally convinced Little Head's brother-in-law to join their party, noting, "he is the most capable Indian to accompany us." He also employed Moise de dents de Biche, who seemed to be the best hunter in the area.[219] Traders felt more comfortable hiring Aboriginal people as hunters if they were widely known to other traders and also if they could serve multiple functions, such as guiding. When Alexander Mackenzie set off from Fort Chipewyan in early June 1789, he hired an Aboriginal man named English Chief as a guide and hunter. He had acquired the name English Chief because he was one of the Aboriginal people who conducted Samuel Hearne to the Coppermine River in the early 1770s and had been in the habit of carrying his furs to Churchill Factory on Hudson Bay ever since.[220]

Hiring Aboriginal people as hunters provided a post with security and provisions, but masters often did not trust them. Alexander Henry the Younger, stationed at Rivière Terre Blanche, near Fort Dauphin, in the winter of 1799, complained that the animals were so scarce, he had to hire his hunters on extravagant terms. After supplying his two hunters with whatever dry goods they wanted, he gave them, their wives, and their children each a full set of the best clothing in the store and provided "Saulteur [diluted] liquor," guns, knives, ammunition, and tobacco. Henry grumbled that "even upon these terms [he] was obliged to consider it a great favor they did [him]."[221]

Masters wished to be independent of Aboriginal people and thus urged their voyageurs to learn to hunt effectively. Generally most men working at a post were expected to hunt, but sometimes specific men were made responsible for hunting if they were particularly skilled, if there was a shortage of labor, or if the bourgeois or the clerk was trying to save on ammunition.[222] In the winter of 1809 Alexander Henry the Younger expected his voyageur hunters to make a *quart de loge*, which involved killing twenty animals, putting them on a stage, eventually hauling them to the fort, and collecting enough buffalo hide for twenty pemmican bags. The men's wives usually accompanied them on hunting trips to help them make their quart de loge and collect tallow and other offal, "which [were] of great service in their ménage."[223] Throughout the winter of 1784–85 at the Assiniboine–Rivière Qu'Appelle post, close to one hundred buffalo were killed by voyageurs stationed there.[224]

The prey men hunted varied according to the environment and time of year. For example, members of Alexander Mackenzie's crew near Slave Lake in June 1789 killed beavers and geese for food.[225] In the winter of 1800 at Terre de Langue, a voyageur named Lisé killed eight ducks, fourteen partridges, five muskrats, and a mink in one November trip, and during an eight-day December trip he returned with eighty hares and thirty-two partridges.[226] Some hunting trips could last a long time, depending on the availability of game. Etienne Charbonneau was away from the fort at Pigeon River for twenty-nine days on a hunting trip in November and December 1807.[227] Lengthy hunting trips, especially in times of scarcity or in dangerous territory, could cause men anxiety for both the safety of the hunters and the success of their trip. When Alexander Henry the Younger returned from a hunting trip in the fall of 1800 at the Park River post, close to hostile Sioux, he reported, "[M]y people had been uneasy about us, and were overjoyed when they heard us hallo."[228] Hunting techniques ranged from the use of guns and rifles to the use of snares, depending on the intended prey.[229] Aboriginal women were especially adept at hunting with snares, and often their yields could mean the difference between comfort and starvation.[230]

Storing and hauling meat from a kill site to caches and posts took much time and energy and was a constant job that dominated daily tasks at the posts.[231] After engagés were successful in a hunt, they usually cached the meat to preserve and protect it from wild animals until it could be transported to the post.[232] In the winter they used sleds to haul meat from the cache site to the post, and in the summer they used canoes or horses and carts.[233] Voyageurs also hauled the meat from Aboriginal hunters hired to work for a post and meat that had been purchased from Aboriginal lodges and caches.[234] Sometimes the task of hauling meat fell to women and children if a post was short on labor.[235] On occasion the masters hired Aboriginal people to haul the meat. For example, Alexander Henry the Younger found that it was "too troublesome to send [his] people daily for meat, so

[he] paid Indians more to transport the meat."[236] Caching was a risk, as wild animals or improper storage could damage the meat. In a comedy of errors at the Rocky Mountain House in January 1806, a voyageur named Forcier froze one his toes going to a cache for meat. The next day the master John Stuart sent voyageurs to retrieve more meat from a cache, but the men could not find it because they took the wrong road. When they finally returned a week later, they brought a small amount of meat that was almost too dry to eat, and they blamed the Aboriginal hunters. In an effort to prevent further mishap, Stuart had Aboriginal people guide his men to other caches and directed one of his men to stay with the Aboriginal people to secure the produce of their hunt in caches and to inform the men at the post of kills.[237] Sometimes the bourgeois or clerks would become so frustrated so with their men's incompetence that they set out themselves to retrieve meat. For example, George Nelson sent out one of his men to retrieve meat from Aboriginal lodges a few days after Christmas 1806, and he returned New Year's Eve with only one and half pounds and "a bunch of excuses about his woes." Nelson set off a few days later with his interpreter and three sleighs and had no trouble getting meat.[238]

Depending on the region fishing could be a productive way to obtain food. Fish were speared and hung up to dry.[239] Men also fished with lines.[240] It was most common to set nets in streams and rivers, which constituted a regular part of many post routines.[241] A successful operation could produce vast amounts of fish and act as the main provisioning source for a region. In the fall of 1804 at Rainy Lake post, an important provisioning center, voyageurs fished the "Chaudière" (Kettle Falls), and it was reported on October 22 that they caught 1,300 white fish, on October 28 they caught 1,050, on November 8 they caught 60, and on November 9 they caught 1,100. On December 10 four men went out to the *Pêche d'hiver* (winter fishing grounds) to set nets and began to catch pike.[242] On a smaller scale at James McKenzie's post in the Athabasca District in December 1799, Joseph Bouché "brought at different times upwards of 260 whitefish for himself & Cadien Le Blanc."[243] Many voyageurs combined fishing and hunting to maximize their food resources. For example, in the summer of 1809 a voyageur named Richard stationed at Dauphin River went hunting with his two youngest brothers, leaving the next oldest to fish and take care of the family.[244] It seems that most men stationed at posts participated in fishing, and usually men fished in groups (unlike hunting, which was frequently a solitary activity). In the southeastern part of Lake Winnipeg, George Nelson set up a semipermanent "fishery" and stationed men there on a continual basis.[245] Men also frequently went fishing with their Aboriginal wives and families.[246] Bourgeois and clerks sometimes participated in fishing with their men and on occasion took over for them when they were injured or ill.[247] At other times men fished for themselves and refused to share with their bourgeois or clerks. In a time of scarcity at Manitonamingon Lake in the spring of 1815, George Nelson reported that he was running out of food, and his men would only bring him fish when they had "too much to keep with decency."[248] Fishing could be impeded by weather and mishap. Thick ice prevented men from setting and retrieving the nets, and nets were often lost in the ice.[249]

Other threats to fishing (and hunting) came from hostile Aboriginal people and competing fur trade companies. Fear of impending attacks could lead men to desert their tasks and interfere with the provisioning of a post. In March 1805 both the NWC and the XYC men deserted the fishery near Rainy Lake post because they claimed that Aboriginal people in the area wanted to kill them. A voyageur named Richard went to investigate and found that the threat was a false alarm. The men resumed fishing and had a successful season.[250] Threats to men and fishing equipment were not always false alarms. In the Wisconsin Territory on Rivière des Saulteux, George Nelson had his men sleep out at the fishery to guard the nets from wolves and wolverines.[251] Maintaining a fishery also required caring for equipment and processing the catches. Men made and mended nets, made floats for nets, built fish houses, and dried and stored the fish.[252] Aboriginal women were usually involved in drying fish, lending their expertise in food preservation.[253]

In areas where the soil was fertile and the growing season reasonably long, traders planted gardens to supplement their diets.[254] Many posts fell into this category, and evidence of gardening can be found at posts as wide ranging as Langue de Terre, Lac La Pluie, Fort Alexander, Dauphin River,

Moose Lake, the Assiniboines–Rivière Qu'Appelle post, Cumberland, Fort Vermilion, Dunvegan, and the forks of the Mackenzie and Liard rivers.[255] The most common produce seems to be potatoes and turnips, but men also cultivated onions, cabbage, cucumbers, carrots, parsnips, and beets, using seeds brought from Canada.[256] Men began the gardens by clearing land in early spring, planting in the late spring, weeding throughout the summer, and harvesting in the fall.[257] Voyageurs also built fences around their gardens to guard against animals.[258] The soil was maintained by spreading manure and digging up stones.[259] In some locations men also experimented more extensively with crops, such as in the Lake Winnipeg area in 1805, where oats were cultivated, and at Tête au Brochet in 1818, where wheat was grown.[260] A more common activity was "making hay," or harvesting wild hay, used for beds, brooms, and stables.[261] Horses were the most common animals kept at fur trade posts, and their care constituted another aspect of voyageurs' varied duties.[262]

The men supplemented their diets with other foods available in their regions. Berry picking was common in the summer and fall months, and sometimes traders found more substantial fruit such as plums and grapes.[263] Other food sources obtained through gathering included the eggs of swans, geese, and ducks.[264] Aboriginal women were crucial to the traders in learning to reap the benefits of the environment of the Northwest and frequently helped their husbands by gathering food from the land.[265]

Transportation and Communication

Along with construction and craftwork, trade, and seeking food, voyageurs at interior posts transported goods, news, and information among the posts throughout the year.[266] The most common form of travel was by canoe, but travel by horse, and in the winter, by dog-team, became popular. Travel over difficult terrain in harsh winter conditions was risky, and voyageurs looked to Aboriginal peoples for help with routes and gear.

Preparation for the annual journey to Lake Superior was an important activity at the interior posts and dominated spring activities. Men prepared to ship back the furs they had collected during the winter and organized goods to be distributed for the coming year.[267] Goods were put together in packs of a manageable size and weight (between eighty and one hundred pounds) for effective canoe travel.[268]

During the fall, winter, and spring, considerable traffic moved between the interior posts in the Northwest to share provisions. Men were sent to obtain and deliver an array of foods, such as pork, grease, fresh meat, oats, and sugar.[269] The transport of provisions could be especially critical with the threat of starvation.[270] Posts commonly ran short of their own provisions once they had helped another post. For example, during the winter of 1808–9, Duncan Campbell left his post at Grand Rapids to travel to McDonell's post at Pigeon River and George Nelson's post at Dauphin River because he was short of provisions. Campbell's imposition drained McDonell's supplies, so that McDonell had to send three of his men, Desrocher, Boulanger and Larocque, to obtain supplies from Nelson and to fish at Tête au Brochet. Nelson himself had run out of provisions by late August 1809 and had to travel to Fort Alexander to obtain more.[271] Trade goods and other supplies such as horses and wood for construction were also shared among posts.[272]

In warmer months travel by water was the most efficient mode. Much time and energy at the interior posts were devoted to canoe building and maintenance (see chapter 4). Men gathered wood for constructing the canoe frame, bark to cover the body of the canoe, and gum to secure the bark and seal the seams.[273] They often relied on Aboriginal people to help them find these supplies.[274] The bourgeois and clerks usually hired Aboriginal people to construct canoes for the crew.[275] Traders also reclaimed old canoes left by Aboriginal people.[276] As with provisioning, traders helped one another obtain canoes. In May 1825 Roderick McKenzie, stationed at the Pic, wrote to Duncan Clark at Long Lake: "I wish you could get a small voyaging Canoe, made by Mondack; about the size of the one your men has here now, but a little higher in the ends—We are very badly off here for Canoes—The men must run about with Fishing Canoes, which are by far too large for two men."[277] Some engagés eventually learned to make canoes, especially with the help of their Aboriginal wives.[278] Men gained knowledge to construct canoes because they spent so much time mending them. The harsh weather and water routes caused cracks, rips, and leaks in even the sturdiest canoes.[279] Some voyageurs became well known for their canoe-making skills, and their expertise was requested by masters at other posts.[280] A few became master canoe makers, such as Amelle, who was stationed at the Rainy Lake post in 1804–5.[281] On occasion men learned on the spot how to construct European-styled boats to use on lakes and in large rivers. Archibald Norman McLeod commented in the spring of 1801: "I have no person here that ever wrought at a boat, but I fancy among us we may be able to make some sort of thing to float at least."[282] The simplest watercraft used for hauling goods short distances was a raft.[283]

During both summer and winter voyageurs used horses for travel, especially on the prairies, where horses could be traded from Lakotas, Assiniboines, Blackfeet, Snakes, and Plains Ojibwes.[284] Bourgeois, clerks, and voyageurs usually bought horses for themselves, although on occasion a bourgeois bought a herd of horses for his outfit.[285] Sometimes horses accompanied canoes during voyages and lightened their loads when passing through low water or against a strong current.[286]

One means of winter travel was by snowshoe, an item that became an important part of the trade.[287] Voyageurs, clerks, and bourgeois learned to make snowshoes from their Aboriginal wives, or relied on the women to make them.[288] Because snowshoes were difficult to make, voyageurs were proud when they developed the skill.[289] Men collected wood to make the frames, but they usually turned to Aboriginal people for *babiche* (rawhide) and parchment skins to net their snowshoes and moose skins for the soles.[290]

Another means of winter travel was a sled pulled by the men or by dog teams. Men built sleds or "trains" of *épinette rouge* (tamarac) or spruce, which was a technology learned from Aboriginal peoples.[291] Sleds were used to haul ice to the icehouse, *piquets* to construction sites, and meat from hunting and cache sites.[292] Sleds were also used to transport baggage between posts in the winter.[293] For long-distance travel sleds were pulled by dogs rather than humans, such as at the Red River post in November 1800 and the Pembina

River post in October 1801.[294] Dogs became a regular part of post life and at some posts equaled the human population.[295]

Guides were critically important to travel because it was easy to become lost.[296] Traders often tried to ease transportation by following well-established Aboriginal travel routes and by marking common roads wherever they could. At Fort Dauphin in 1808 George Nelson had one of his men, Fortier, plant bushes at intervals along the road to the fort to aid travelers.[297]

Accompanying trips to deliver food and supplies was the movement of information. News was often obtained informally from people passing by the posts. Voyageurs, freemen, and Aboriginal people always brought reports of business, politics, health, and deaths when they arrived at a post. For example, when two of McDonell's men arrived at Alexandria, they tattled to Archibald Norman McLeod that J. Sutherland at the Elbow was engaged in improper trade.[298] Men were also often sent out to seek news for their masters.[299]

Letter writing was not always more reliable than word of mouth. While en route to Rivière des Saulteaux, the young clerk George Nelson wrote a letter to his parents in Sorel and sent it via a trusted old voyageur named Paulet who lived near his father. Nelson complained that, except for Paulet, voyageurs were generally unreliable carriers of letters: "For people in this Country when they wish any thing to go or come safe to or from their friends it is always best by far to put it in charge of the Gentlemen of the concern which not for mere Gratitudes sake I must say they always take Great care to have every thing safely delivered. When I wrote this letter I little thought of what was soon to happen [to] me. This old Paulet a very honest man being desirous of taking a letter from me to my parents I gave it him without hesitation as I knew that it would be safely deliver'd unless accidents."[300] However, rarely could a letter writer be so choosy. Generally people sent letters with anyone traveling to a similar destination, and everyone traveling through the interior was expected to carry mail, including Aboriginal peoples, freemen, voyageurs, clerks, and bourgeois.

Jane Harrison has described the form of mail delivery in early Canada before the introduction of a unified postal system, used commonly in Europe, which was copied by traders in the Northwest. Letters contained an inventory on the flow of the mail, reported on who delivered a previous letter, and who was designated to carry the current letter.[301] The first line of a letter to Duncan Clark at Long Lake from Donald McIntosh at Michipicoten read: "This article will be handed to you by old Le May."[302] Another letter to Clark, this one from Roderick McKenzie at the Pic, reported: "Your favor of the 12th Inst. was handed to me by my son, who arrived here yesterday, along with two of the Pic Indians, they will leave this to morrow, with half a dozen of Pieces, belonging to Michipicotton, which you will endeavour to forward, to the latter place, as possible. . . . I received your letter by the Lake Nipisingue Indians."[303] In May 1815 John Pruden in the Carleton District wrote to Robert McVicar at Cumberland House: "[B]y the return of the 2 canadians to this place I had the pleasure of receiving your kind Letter."[304] People sometimes left letters for each other in various places. For example, in August 1805 Daniel Harmon was given a letter near the mouth of the Red River addressed to him, left by Frederick Goedike, informing him that Goedike was in good health and on his way to Athabasca, so that they would probably not meet again for several years.[305]

Letters were sent with voyageurs on most of their trips.[306] Bourgeois and clerks often scrambled to quickly dash off letters before a voyageur departed.[307] The major trip from interior posts to district headquarters every year involved sending substantial packages of letters and reports.[308] Letters usually accompanied post visitors and returning men.[309] Mail was also delivered by freemen and Aboriginal peoples.[310] Alexander Henry the Younger sent the 1810 "North West winter packet" to the South Branch on the Saskatchewan River with a western Ojibwe and an Odawa, as he felt they were the only two men in the fort who would undertake this dangerous journey.[311] Sometimes Aboriginal people acted as guides for men sent out to deliver the mail.[312]

Many trips were planned for the sole purpose of delivering letters.[313] John McDonell, stationed at Assiniboines–Rivière Qu'Appelle, frequently sent his men out to deliver mail, especially to report on important news, such as informing other masters of lost men.[314] Voyageurs were sometimes sent with important orders as well as the mail. In September 1808 Ferguson sent two men to Dauphin River with letters from their bourgeois and orders to take back his wife and two children, who had passed a part of the summer there.[315]

The sending of mail and the sharing of information were such an important part of the fur trade that a "general express" and "winter express" constantly traveled about the Northwest delivering mail and news.[316] Alexander Ross described its workings: "From every distant department of the Company, a special light canoe is fitted out annually, to report on their transactions."[317] Daniel Harmon noted that the winter express left Athabasca every year in December and passed through the whole of the country, eventually reaching Sault Ste. Marie at the end of March.[318] Men were sent out to meet the express or to intersect with it at major crossroads to save the express some time and distance.[319]

Like any travel in the Northwest interior, delivering mail could be treacherous. Threats from weather, wild animals, and hostile people could prevent its delivery and injure the mail carriers. Charles Chaboillez noted in February 1798 that two men who arrived with mail from Lac La Pluie were starving and could hardly walk. Chaboillez gave them each a dram, some tobacco, and a pint of rum to share.[320] The difficulties and danger that accompanied letter delivery often made masters sympathetic to the letter carriers. The men carrying the express were generally treated well as they passed through posts, which was usually a benefit reflecting the importance of their job. John Thomson habitually gave the express men tobacco, drams, provisions, ammunition, and one year even lent some express men an axe.[321] The importance of mail to the bourgeois and clerks also motivated them to treat mail carriers well. Masters often complained of loneliness in the Northwest interior, so that letters became especially important ties with the outside world. Daniel Harmon wrote of his joy in receiving mail: "[N]othing could give me half the real satisfaction, while thus *self-banished* in this dreary Country [and] at such a great distance from all I hold dear in this World."[322] Personal and business information passed on through letters also heightened their importance. In September 1806 Harmon received instructions that he was to pass the ensuing winter at Cumberland House and that his father had died.[323] Both the business and the personal importance attached to delivering news and mail made it a serious job for voyageurs to perform, and men were continually pressured to deliver news and mail swiftly and promptly.

The range of work described in this chapter demonstrates that voyageurs were highly skilled laborers who combined strength with dexterity and thought to survive the rigors of the Northwest. The dominant part of their jobs was to trade with Aboriginal peoples. When voyageurs traded with Aboriginal peoples, especially en dérouine, they had opportunities to develop close relationships and conduits for cultural exchange. Voyageurs adopted many practices from Aboriginal peoples that became crucial for survival such as methods of trapping, hunting, fishing, and food preparation. Even though Montreal company posts resembled European colonies in their architecture and artisan crafts, voyageurs adopted important Aboriginal technologies, such as snowshoes and sleds. Relations between voyageurs and Aboriginal peoples had implications beyond mere survival. Deep friendships and strong kin ties often developed. Some of these close relationships between voyageurs and Aboriginal women are explored in the next chapter.

8. Tender Ties, Fluid Monogamy, and Trading Sex

Voyageurs and Aboriginal Women

> *As . . . their [voyageur] husbands go home to Canada . . . these [Aboriginal] women must of necessity rejoin their respective tribes; where they generally remain in a state of widowhood during a year or two, in expectation of their return. If the husband does not return, the woman then bestows her hand on one of his comrades who has the good fortune to please her fancy the best.*[1]

> *[Voyageurs and Aboriginal women stay together] as long as they can agree among themselves, but when either is displeased with their choice, he or she will seek another Partner, and thus the Hymenial Bond, without any more ado is broke asunder—which is law here & I think reasonable also.*[2]

The previous chapter explored in detail the range of relationships that could develop between Aboriginal men and voyageurs. Romantic associations and kin ties between voyageurs and Aboriginal women and their families constituted important dimensions in voyageurs' lives. The relationships between voyageurs and Aboriginal women varied tremendously, although these two quotations found in the writings of NWC traders highlight their fluidity. In the first, Alexander Ross, in his *Fur Hunters of the Far West* (1855), observed the pattern of Aboriginal wives replacing departed husbands. In the second, Daniel Harmon's 1801 journal entry reveals the flexibility and choice open to both traders and Aboriginal women who stayed together as along as both were pleased with the arrangement. Other writers also documented the range of relationships that could develop between voyageurs and Aboriginal women.

Gender ideologies led traders, including voyageurs, to develop distinct intimate relationships with Aboriginal women, separate from those with Aboriginal men. These relationships spanned a wide range of configurations. Voyageurs encountered Aboriginal women traveling along canoe routes, during trading ceremonies, and while seeking provisions and directions. Pork eaters had time for only brief encounters with these women because they spent little time in the interior, while seasoned northmen who lived their whole lives in the interior could develop stable, long-term relationships. Between these two extremes lay the most common experience: voyageurs who spent only a few years in the trade developed brief and fluid relationships with Aboriginal women. Once voyageurs were posted in the interior, they often developed monogamous relationships with women who lived near their post. When voyageurs were sent out to live with Aboriginal families in hunting lodges or trade with them en dérouine, they met women outside the social confines of the post or the watchful eyes of the bourgeois. But most of these relationships were suspended or ended when the women's hunting groups moved away, or when voyageurs were re-posted to a different location or retired from the service and returned to the St. Lawrence valley. In systems of "fluid monogamy" unions were not always well defined, and relationships could be intermittent, short term, and concurrent.

In 1980 fur trade scholars Sylvia Van Kirk, Jennifer S. H. Brown, and Jacqueline Peterson convincingly demonstrated that numerous stable marriages existed between Aboriginal women and officers and masters of fur trade companies.[3] Following their leads, Tanis C. Thorne and Susan Sleeper-Smith have documented similar relations between French traders and Aboriginal peoples on the lower Missouri River and in the western Great Lakes, while Lucy Murphy has traced their descendants west of Lake Michigan.[4] Brown, however, has recently cautioned that indeterminacy characterized these relationships, as "[c]rossing profound gulfs of culture, language, and experience, they could not have had a clear sense of what sorts of unions they were getting into. Nor did they know at the outset what would happen to their relationships."[5] Similar patterns of stable and long-lasting relations with Aboriginal women can be found among voyageurs. The growth of a substantial métis population, fur trade company policies regarding the country wives and children of voyageurs, legal evidence, and the writings of the fur trade literate all point to the existence of long-term relationships between Aboriginal women and voyageurs. Yet such relationships were more fluid than unions between masters and Aboriginal women. Although such patterns are difficult to quantify because of fragmented sources, journals and letters produced in the fur trade suggest that voyageurs' mobility and limited wealth and power made their relationships more temporary and intermittent.

Sexuality played a central role in such encounters. Traders' encounters with Aboriginal peoples of the Northwest interior may be seen as part of a process of European Canadian sexual self-fashioning and the traders' writings as projections of European Canadian desire expressed in the discourse of Aboriginal promiscuity. Because sexual desire made up such a large part of the encounters between voyageurs and Aboriginal women, it became a site of cultural hybridity, as voyageurs and Aboriginal women forged sexual connections.

Gender Roles in French Canada and the Northwest

The categories of "male" and "female" were well defined both in French Canada and in Aboriginal societies, where work, diplomacy, social organization, and family arrangements were divided along gender lines. Yet ideas about the status of women and the range of power within gender categories differed between French Canadians and Aboriginal peoples. In forming unions voyageurs and Aboriginal women fashioned cross-cultural understandings and practices, resulting in the well-known *mariage à la façon du pays*, or marriage in the custom of the country.

As in France, French Canada was structured around patriarchy, where men ruled women, especially within the institution of the family.[6] This organization of power affected social systems such as divisions of labor and individual identities. In New France after the arrival of the *filles du roi* (young French women sponsored by the French Crown to immigrate to New France to marry, starting in the 1660s), the institution of marriage became pervasive. Historian John Bosher has shown that virtually everyone outside the clergy married, and widows and widowers remarried soon after their spouses died.[7] Did this lead to a society dominated to a greater extent by patriarchy? Jan Noel has argued to the contrary, asserting that women in New France enjoyed an unusually privileged position with access to superior education and roles in leadership and commerce. Most colonists migrated from France at a time when gender roles in New France were not as rigid as they later became. In the early years of the colony, the low number of women made them highly valued and respected. The women often took advantage of their unique demographic situation by choosing husbands carefully and asserting rights to work and to own property. By the eighteenth century men's frequent absences owing to involvement in warfare and the fur trade gave women more power and greater economic opportunities than they had in Europe.[8] Allan Greer cautions, however, that the variety of French Canadian women's experiences makes it hard to talk in universal terms. Noble women and religious women probably had the most power, habitant women had significant independence, especially when their husbands were absent, while servant women were the most subjugated. Yet all were subject to men.[9] In contrast, although Aboriginal men and women had clearly defined roles, they did not live in a system of omnipresent patriarchy. Women's economic roles and political status within Aboriginal communities are subjects of great debate, as is the question of whether Aboriginal societies were characterized by patriarchy or by equality between men and women.[10] Many scholars agree that though not all Aboriginal societies were egalitarian before contact, "relative equality" existed between men and women, and degrees of equality could vary. Contact with European traders, missionaries, and settlers led to or intensified the subordination of women.[11]

A common reaction of fur traders, or at least the literate elite, to Aboriginal societies was shock at how hard Aboriginal women worked and an assumption that Aboriginal women were treated as "beasts of burden" by Aboriginal men and forced to do hard labor.[12] Historian David Smits suggests that Europeans cast Aboriginal women as "squaw drudges" to signify Aboriginal savagery and thus help justify colonization.[13] The "squaw drudge" stereotype probably reflected European Americans' discomfort with women whose work seemed to overlap with what they believed to be men's domain. However, the stereotype can be read differently as an indication of women's importance within Aboriginal societies and in the fur trade. Priscilla Buffalohead sagaciously warns scholars that although "[s]ome observers began to fashion an image of [Aboriginal] women as burden bearers, drudges, and virtual slaves to men, doing much of the work but being barred from participation in the seemingly more important and flamboyant world of male hunters, chiefs, and warriors," their portrait of Aboriginal women "was based upon the premise that women should be shown deference precisely because they were biological and intellectual inferiors of men." European observers thus "failed to comprehend the full range of women's economic roles, the extent to which Ojibway women managed and directed their own activities, and perhaps most importantly, the extent to which women held ownership and distribution rights to the things they produced and processed."[14]

Voyageurs probably did not see Aboriginal women as beasts of burden in the same way as the literate of the trade. They had come from farms where all family members worked side by side. They would have closely identified with the clear division of labor based on gender roles within Aboriginal cultures. Both men and women contributed to the formation of a household, and women inherited their husbands' property. Men cleared land and worked in the fields, while women cared for domestic animals and took care of the home and children. In some ways this division of labor could be seen as egalitarian or balanced, even though French Canadian society was strongly patriarchal. Additionally, many French Canadian men were absent from their households while serving in the military, and when separated from each other, men and women each had to perform work that was usually the domain of the other sex. Yet legally men were the heads of the household during their lifetime. But beyond the legal strictures, patriarchy was, as Allan Greer explains, "a pattern of thinking and acting that had, over the centuries, entered into the customs and into the very languages of Europe, structuring relationships and shaping personal identities."[15] No doubt voyageurs attempted to rule their Aboriginal wives. Their efforts would have been doubly ineffective, not only because of Aboriginal women's unfamiliarity with European-style patriarchal rule but also because voyageurs were often dependent on their Aboriginal wives for survival in the Northwest.

Perspectives of Passion

Glimpses of the personal sentiment between voyageurs and Aboriginal women are deeply embedded in the writings of the fur trade literate, who had contradictory and often uncomfortable attitudes about unions with Aboriginal women. In addition, as Brown has eloquently explained, these glimpses are like little bits of fabric in a patchwork quilt that often do not convey much of their original pattern, and these glimpses need to be looked at from many different angles, much as land surveyors "triangulate" their observations by taking measurements at many different points in space and time.[16] George Nelson, though not by any stretch a typical voice of the bourgeois, provides some interesting clues from unusual angles. When he arrived to run the post at Fort Alexander in 1808, trader Duncan Cameron pressured him to marry one of the young women. He was adamantly adverse to "connexions of that sort," considering them to be adulterous and immoral and worrying about what his peers, parents, and God would think. He thought that those who married Aboriginal women did so to "serve craving lust," and when it suited them, they cast off their families "to linger in want and wretchedness." Yet he succumbed to pressure: "I was not, however, better than my neighbours; the Sex had charms for me as it had for others; But There always remained a sting, that time only wore away. I gave way, & went as the ox to the Slaughter."[17] Although Nelson was referring to Proverbs 7:22, his choice of a neutered animal as a metaphor highlights his discomfort with having relations with Aboriginal women, yet it also reflects an attitude to marriage as a conquering of men. Perhaps he felt that Aboriginal women "ensnared" European American men in their traps. By comparing Nelson's references to his two marriages to Ojibwe women written close to the time of the marriages with his later reminiscences, Brown suggests that Nelson and many fur trade officers came to accept marriages between Aboriginal women and European traders only after they spent time in the Northwest: "[t]heir definitions and meanings were commonly not fixed" and the sources offer only partial truths about the understandings between men and women.[18] Other traders, after they had spent more time in the Northwest, wrote of marriage to particular groups of Aboriginal women as if it were a matter of course. In describing the Spokanes of the Pacific Northwest, Ross Cox wrote: "Their women are great slaves, and most submissive to marital authority. They did not exhibit the same indifference to the superior comforts of a white man's wife as that displayed by the Flat-head women, and some of them consequently become partners of the *voyageurs*."[19] Cox thus did not view marriage as the diminishment of men's freedom or masculinity. Connections between traders and Aboriginal women were a common phenomenon, and the fur trade literate described these connections according to their own preoccupations with desire and its repression. These comments on the unions between voyageurs and Aboriginal women ranged from disgust at sexual promiscuity to sympathy for voyageurs "caught in a trap" to indifference. Fortunately some writers took more than a passing interest in connections between voyageurs and Aboriginal women and provided detailed descriptions.

Affection and love seemed to exist in many unions between voyageurs and Aboriginal women. In the Columbia district Alexander Ross wrote of all fellows: "[T]he tenderness existing between [Aboriginal wives] and their husbands presents one great reason for that attachment which the respective classes of whites cherish for the Indian countries."[20] Alexander Henry the Younger wrote about one voyageur who volunteered to work for free, as long he was allowed to marry his beloved and the company provided for their room and board. Henry commented that he had seen this "foolish" behavior before among voyageurs who "would not hesitate to sign an agreement of perpetual bondage on condition of being permitted to have a woman who struck their fancy."[21] James McKenzie was equally derisive about one of his voyageurs who was clearly devoted to his family: "Lambert went with his Bona Roba to gather Moss for their Son, the fruits of their Love and darling of their Lives. . . . Soon after He arrived with a Huge Load of Moss on his back while Madame walked slowly behind carrying nothing but her little Snarling brats."[22] Moss was used as a form of diapers and was wrapped around babies and stuffed into cradle boards. Many voyageurs cared deeply for their Aboriginal mates and demonstrated their devotion through gifts. Voyageurs often went into considerable debt to buy "finery" for their Aboriginal wives, and on one occasion a couple of men stole flour and sugar from HBC provisions in order to "feast their women."[23]

The writings of the fur trade literate also portray an image of the hypersexualized Jean-Baptiste, or North American Don Juan, like the elderly voyageur who had twelve wives. This seems surprising considering the overwhelming physical workloads of voyageurs. Perhaps voyageurs worried about their virility and so emphasized it even in the face of exhaustion. Not only was the acquisition of wives important but so was the way voyageurs treated them. The elderly voyageur bragged to Ross that all his wives had been as well dressed as the wives of a bourgeois. Providing expensive gifts to wives was a sign of wealth and signified skill, strength, and endurance, qualities of the hypermasculine voyageur. This seems to run counter to the ethic of nonaccumulation among the voyageurs, but spending money on clothing, jewelry, and good food for one's wife was a way to be lavish without the burden of amassing possessions that were difficult to transport. Some bourgeois remarked on how loyal and chivalrous voyageurs could be to their wives and lovers. Although they complained that voyageurs stole provisions and engaged in free-trading to provide extra rations for their wives, they also admired voyageurs' close attachments.[24] While serving in the War of 1812 as part of a voyageur regiment in the Great Lakes area, many voyageur soldiers sneaked off at night to sleep with their wives.[25] In one instance a couple of voyageurs chased some Aboriginal men in the middle of winter to retrieve their kidnapped wives, risking death from the cold and from their armed and angry Aboriginal rivals.[26]

The bourgeois and clerks often expressed surprise at the degree to which Aboriginal women were attached to their Aboriginal husbands, who seemed to treat them like slaves.[27] Duncan McGillivray speculated that Aboriginal women were treated so "barbarously" in the Northwest that they could not be expected to be fond of their husbands, Aboriginal or French Canadian.[28] Aboriginal women's voices are faint in fur trade documents, and we can catch only a few glimpses of their attitudes. George Nelson wrote of some women near Portage La Prairie who complained to the traders that the women's own people treated them badly. The women hinted that they would like to join up with the traders.[29] This may have been an economic strategy on the part of the women or the band to improve their circumstances and form valuable ties.[30]

Aboriginal men had varying attitudes toward unions between their wives and daughters and fur traders. Among many interior Aboriginal groups, marriages between tribes were encouraged as a way to cement diplomatic and trading relationships. Economic relations were based on actual or potential kinship links, and the establishment of marital ties with European American traders was a natural strategy.[31] Aboriginal fathers hoped for both trading advantages and a lasting commitment to their families. Thus some groups of Aboriginals frequently encouraged and even insisted that bourgeois, clerks, and voyageurs marry one of their women. Sexual liaisons and marital unions were expected as part of the ceremonies assuring a stable trading relationship.

Other Aboriginal men, owing to bad experiences, were opposed to sexual unions between Aboriginal women and fur traders. George Nelson recorded the opinion of one Ojibwe man who disapproved of his daughter's dealings with traders. He called her dirty and lazy because she liked the company of men too much:

> *[S]he is only good for white men, because with them she will have only snow shoes and moccasins to make, and can have as much of*

> *man as she desires; she is only good for the whites; they take women not as wives but only to use as sluts, to satisfy the animal lust, and when they are satisfied they cast them off, and another one takes her for the same purpose and casts her off again, and so she will go on until she becomes an old [woman] soiled by every one who chooses to use her[.] She is foolish, she has no understanding, no sense, no shame, she is only good to be a slut (bitch) for the white. I wish she would leave me.*[32]

Aboriginal men sometimes opposed foreign traders, as in the case of one voyageur named Joseph Constant, whom the Crees and the Ojibwes resented because of his "lavishness among the women."[33] Alexander Mackenzie found that the Beavers in the Athabasca District abhorred "any carnal communication between their women and the white people."[34] While crossing the plains in 1805 on an excursion of discovery in the Rocky Mountains, bourgeois Antoine Larocque reported that Aboriginal men were battling with traders and voyageurs over their wives, many of whom were running away to the mountains with their lovers: "Horses have been killed and women wounded since I am with them on the score of Jealousy."[35] In 1805 W. Ferdinand Wentzel reported that an Aboriginal man named Pouce Coupé decided to stop hunting for the post because he was displeased that his wife had an affair with the voyageur Little Martin Junior. Wentzel complained that despite his and his predecessor's best efforts, they could not keep their voyageurs from having sex with Aboriginal women, even when it led to quarrels with Aboriginal traders. He recalled one incident in the Athabasca in the summer 1804 when voyageurs raped some Dene women as well as insulting the group and stealing their furs. In retaliation all the Dene in the area refused to trade with the post and burned it to the ground, and at least six voyageurs were killed.[36] Some Aboriginal men were particularly jealous of any connections between their wives and traders, and in one case a Snake murdered his wife because she was having an affair with a trader.[37] These examples are specific cases, however, and do not represent the common pattern of relations between traders and Aboriginal peoples.

Generally Aboriginal men encouraged unions between Aboriginal women and traders as a means of securing alliances.

Aboriginal Women in the Fur Trade

Aboriginal women's voices, so faint in the writings of literate fur traders, have been amplified through the work of feminist historians in the 1970s. Sylvia Van Kirk's *"Many Tender Ties"* describes how Aboriginal women became integral to European traders as marriage partners because of their country skills and trading connections. Jennifer S. H. Brown's *Strangers in Blood*, published in the same year (1980), looks at women's roles in the formation of fur trade families. Also completed in 1980, Jacqueline Peterson's doctoral dissertation "The People In Between" explores fur trade families and the ethnogenesis of the Métis around the Great Lakes. These historians were able to sift through the writings of the male fur trade officers and masters to uncover the lives of Aboriginal women. Anthropologists and, in more recent years, historians have tried to explore the history of Aboriginal women independent of their relationship to fur trade officers and literate explorers, missionaries, and colonizers. For example, Susan Sleeper-Smith's *Indian Women and French Men* (2001) shows how in the western Great Lakes area, Aboriginal women were primarily responsible for integrating French mercantile capitalism with Aboriginal economies through kin networks.[38] Understanding Aboriginal women in their own cultural context is crucial to exploring how they interacted with European American traders. Unfortunately the paucity of sources has inhibited scholars to a large degree. In an article on gender and Aboriginal history, however, Gunlög Fur suggests that the paucity of these sources may be a methodological strength to the field because the fragmentary sources require such careful use and clearly show how gender is an important category of analysis in Aboriginal history.[39]

Although the writings of bourgeois and clerks either neglect Aboriginal women or portray them in subordinate positions, they reveal that Aboriginal women participated in the fur trade in key ways. Aboriginal women processed meat and furs to prepare them for trade and hunted and trapped small animals that were included in the fur and provisions trade. Like Aboriginal men Aboriginal women came to fur trade posts to trade furs and provisions.[40] Some women were quite astute traders, such as the white captive John Tanner's adoptive Odawa mother, Net-no-kwa. Net-no-kwa received large annual presents from traders, such a ten-gallon keg of spirits and a chief's dress and ornaments, presents that were usually reserved for the most influential and productive hunters.[41] When traveling across Grand Portage one summer, Net-no-kwa was determined to preserve her furs for the best prices. To prevent the traders from stealing her cargo, she did not use the traders' road to cross the portage. She resisted the traders' cajoling, gifts, and even threats to convince her to trade with them. She would only consent to trade when offered the prices she wanted for her furs. Her actions demonstrate agency and adeptness in dealing with the traders.[42] It is hard to know if Net-no-kwa was an exception among Odawa women; traders may have given her more respect because of her acuity and reputation and perhaps because she was an elder.[43] Jacqueline Peterson asserts that among Great Lakes peoples, social models existed of female hunters, warriors, celibates, prostitutes, and medicine women. Although these women were numerically uncommon, they were regarded with deference and respect, as their powers were thought to come from "other-than-humans" and spirits.[44] Priscilla Buffalohead describes gender differences in work roles among the Great Lakes Ojibwes, arguing that although normative gender ideology prescribed that men hunted and traded while women processed meat and furs from the hunt, on occasion women directly participated in the trade. She asserts that Ojibwe women probably had "ownership" rights to goods and could thus trade as did men, and that flexibility and the complementary nature of Ojibwe gender roles allowed women to participate in activities usually assigned to men in European American society.[45] Carol Cooper has found that among the Nishgas and Tlingits (which were matrilineal societies) on the Pacific coast some women participated in the fur trade and became intermediaries between the European trading companies and their tribes. One Nishga woman named Neshaki in the Nass River valley became an important trader, employed by the HBC to attract Aboriginal traders to their posts, and she became the wife of HBC officer Captain William McNeill.[46] The ritual baptism undergone by novices (discussed in chapter 3), stipulating that voyageurs could not kiss a wife against her will, suggests that Aboriginal women had some control in choosing sexual partners, whether or not they were married. In most northwestern Aboriginal cultures heterosexual couples were the norm for social organization, but marriages were fluid, and divorce and remarriage were routine.

Despite the incidence of Aboriginal women acting as independent traders, fur trade bourgeois and clerks tended to treat women differently from Aboriginal men, trivializing them as trading partners. George Nelson provided one of his voyageurs with high wines and tobacco to give to Aboriginal men and "several things of no value" to trade with the Aboriginal women.[47] Voyageurs probably also treated female traders differently because of the intense patriarchy and rigid gender divisions in French Canada. In her study of Ojibwes around the Great Lakes, Carol Devens asserts that the fur trade disrupted Ojibwe gender roles because "French traders wanted the furs obtained by men rather than the small game, tools, utensils, or clothing procured by women," causing women to become "auxiliaries to the trading process."[48] (Yet women's work increased because they had to prepare the furs for trade.) Women trading furs were probably underreported by the bourgeois because of prejudices against involving women in the trade or because the bourgeois simply did not see women as hunters, trappers, and traders. Despite this some Aboriginal women became important traders, and others were hired by the traders for short labor contracts and as interpreters and guides.[49] Some Aboriginal women were hired to dress skins and lace snowshoes, areas in which they had renowned expertise.[50] The most famous woman who aided Europeans in the fur trade was Thanadelthur, a Dene who acted as an interpreter and important peacemaker for the HBC in the early 1700s.[51]

The value of Aboriginal women's skills placed them in a unique position in the fur trade: they often became the central figures in alliances between fur traders and their Aboriginal trading partners. Numerous scholars have written extensively on the formation of long-lasting and serious marriages that took place between Aboriginal and fur trade partners and clerks, and the resulting families. As Van Kirk, Brown, and Sleeper-Smith have convincingly demonstrated, Aboriginal women's economic skills and kin ties, as well as the complete absence of white women, became a powerful incentive for traders to pursue them as wives. Fur trade officers desired Aboriginal women as wives to help them survive the rigors of the Northwest and profit in the fur trade. Aboriginal women played key economic and social roles in the emerging fur trade society by teaching their husbands to live off the land, by serving as diplomatic emissaries between the European and the Aboriginal traders, and by incorporating traders into Aboriginal kin networks.[52]

Sex in Trade and Trade in Sex

The fur trade was never simply a trade of furs for goods. At the very least it involved highly ritualized ceremonies and protocols with far-reaching political and social implications. In the 1960s and 1970s, fur trade history focused on the economic substance of trade between Europeans and Aboriginal peoples, debating the extent to which Aboriginal people were dependent on European goods.[53] Later scholars began to examine the ways in which Aboriginal people controlled the trade and began to uncover the larger sociocultural meanings of exchange, which could extend to arrangements such as marriage, ritual adoption, assistance in war, and participation in community ceremonies.[54] One area that has been neglected, however, is the role played by sexual liaisons. Sexuality was central to intercultural relations in the fur trade, and voyageurs were on the sexual front lines. Sexual liaisons between Aboriginal women and European American men often ratified ceremonies of trade and subsequent diplomatic and kin alliances and also created opportunities for a trade in sex.

Sex in trade and trade in sex probably existed among Aboriginal groups before the arrival of European American traders. Many scholars have found that wife sharing was common among allies and trading partners. Ruth

Landes attests that the freedom of sexual expression among the Ojibwes was common, although her descriptions reflect the early twentieth-century view of an association between licentiousness and "less civilized" peoples.[55] Yet more recent research supports the earlier contentions. Jennifer Brown describes a trade in female captives and slaves: "The Cree and Chipewyans urged both North Westers and Hudson's Bay men to accept women in the interests of friendship and alliance; but farther to the west among various Plains Indian groups, the North Westers frequently encountered societies that had for some time actively engaged in trafficking in women for profit. The pattern of selling female slaves to the Canadians, noted by Umfreville in 1790, went back at least to the 1730s and 1740s, in which period up to sixty Indian slaves a year had been sent to Montreal."[56] One can speculate that sexual relations played a part. Unfortunately most work on Aboriginal sexual practice focuses either on gender roles and male-female equality or on berdaches, a category for sexual "deviances," such as homosexuality, transsexuality, and third sex roles.[57] This neglects the seeming heterosexual hegemony and the presumption of hetero-erotic desire, which underlay reproduction and family structures. In most northwestern Aboriginal communities, social organization was dominated by heterosexual couples in stable marriages but instances of polygamy existed. Marriages were fluid, and divorce and remarriages were routine.[58] Most Aboriginal societies did not seem to have the same kind of moral regulation of sexuality as did Europeans. Adolescent sexual experimenting was encouraged in some cultures. Spousal sharing was common, but a strong distinction was made between open sharing and illicit affairs, which were not tolerated. Berdaches perhaps represented openness to diverse conceptions of the body. However, the sexual category of berdaches might also have reinforced heterosexual hegemony by defining and containing "deviance."

A similar paucity of research exists for the study of sexual desire and practice in early French Canada. The Catholic Church was the main regulator of sexual practice, and nonmarital sex was officially prohibited (and thus clandestine). Men and women usually married at a young age, depending on the availability of land and resources to start new family economic units.[59] Multiple kinds of sexual expression, such as autoeroticism, sexual coercion and abuse, and sex with children and animals were deemed deviant and usually punished and contained by the church. In addition nonmarital affairs and prostitution were not tolerated.[60] Thus the configurations of Aboriginal sexual practice must have appeared titillating to voyageurs entering the pays d'en haut. Sex was not confined to marriage, and though limits to sexual practice existed, sex was not as highly regulated as in French Catholic communities.

When traders first made contact with new groups of Aboriginal people, Aboriginal men frequently offered their wives or daughters for sexual relations to the traders who made first contact (usually masters, but sometimes voyageurs) as a means of cementing trading relationships.[61] Aboriginal people were often surprised and insulted at the prudish refusals of fur trade masters. In March 1795 at Qu'Appelle, John McDonell reported that the Aboriginal Grand Diable and his wife "were surprised and chagrined" at his refusal of Grand Diable's wife's "favour," "but the Lady much more so, and [McDonell] thought it prudent to make her some trifling presents to pacify her."[62] McDonell's concern over offending the Grand Diable's wife would imply that she was not simply her husband's token but rather was an agent in the trading relationship and had to be treated with dignity. In the following month McDonell commented that when he refused to trade for meat brought by two Assiniboines, one of them offered "the favours of his young wife & made use of strong arguments to convince [him] of the goodness of the lady in question—but to no purpose."[63] The bourgeois usually only recorded when sexual liaisons were offered to them, but no doubt the same held true for those voyageurs who initiated trading relationships. One wonders whether the voyageurs would have made similar prudish refusals to participate in sexual relations while visiting Aboriginal lodges to trade. European Canadian and Christian social prescriptions would have discouraged them from actively participating in the sexual relations, but voyageurs may have happily complied with sexual expectations in establishing trading alliances.

Although the fur trade writers portrayed Aboriginal women as passive objects who were bartered by the Aboriginal men, we cannot assume that such was the case. Women likely negotiated the conditions of sexual liaisons and played roles in building alliances through these sexual connections. Continued diplomatic and trading relationships were often accompanied by a prolonged sexual relationship that led to kinship ties. In this way women could become key arbiters of goodwill in the trade.

Contact between Aboriginal peoples and European American traders often led to both informal and highly organized exchange of women's sexual services for trade goods. Van Kirk argues that the traders had a great deal of difficulty comprehending the custom of wife sharing and corrupted Aboriginal generosity into "outright prostitution," and that Aboriginal men also exploited their women to "satisfy what appeared to be the Europeans' voracious sexual appetites."[64] This image hides the pervasiveness and normalcy of sexuality in the meeting of traders and Aboriginal peoples. European American traders were probably incorporated into existing Aboriginal diplomatic and social patterns. Trading sex did not usually become Aboriginal women's full-time livelihood. Nor did those who offered sexual liaisons become a separate social category, with trading sex as a primary social identifier (such as the category of "prostitute" in European societies). Carol Cooper asserts that among the Aboriginal societies on the Northwest coast, Aboriginal women often used sex as a form of payment for trade goods (and not for establishing kinship ties). This lowered the status of the Aboriginal women in the eyes of the European American traders, but not within their own societies. Among Northwest Coast societies there was no particular stigma attached to payment for sex, and adult women were free to determine their own sexual and reproductive lives. Cooper contends that "it is unlikely that many of the women who engaged in voluntary sexual activities for payment considered themselves as prostitutes by vocation, nor did their families regard them in this light." Conversely, slave women were treated as commodities and thus bought and sold, usually by men.[65]

The incidence of women trading sex for goods could suggest that women were seen as either "owners" or "instruments" of male hetero-erotic pleasure. In the former case women could use men's desire for them as a source of power. In the latter case women would be objectified and might come to think of themselves as commodities rather than agents. Some scholars have asserted that trading women instead of men as sexual partners may be explained by unbalanced sex ratios. There were often more women than men in Aboriginal societies, especially mobile Plains groups whose men were often killed in battle or who were more exposed than women to epidemics.[66] Women were offered to traders not only for alliances but also because they were plentiful and profitable. Wives came to be treated as commodities in some societies where polygamy was associated with wealth.[67] Another explanation not necessarily in contradiction to those offered here is that Aboriginal women participated in the sex trade of their own accord. Further ethnographic research is needed to reveal the specificities and divergences of attitudes toward sex among different Aboriginal cultures. Moreover, although the literate of the fur trade did not mention any kind of sexual relations between voyageurs and Aboriginal men, we cannot assume that everyone fit the heterosexual model.

Although the sources prevent us from measuring how common the trade in sex became around fur trade posts, they indicate that it was present along most of the fur trade routes, from the Ottawa River, around the Great Lakes, and into the interior.[68] The bourgeois and clerks often remarked when a group of Aboriginal people did not trade the sexual services of women, as though it were unusual, which may indicate that the practice was widespread.[69]

The trade in sex developed differently in local contexts. It could be informal or casual, with Aboriginal women individually offering sexual liaisons for goods. In many cases lines of trade were blurred when Aboriginal men offered their wives and daughters as an integral part of a trading alliance and establishing kinship ties. In other contexts the sex trade was more explicit and structured. Some Aboriginal men controlled and marketed women, selling them either individually, as prostitutes for an entire fort, or as permanent partners. At Rocky Mountain House in 1810, Alexander Henry the Younger noted one day that Piegans set off, "having several customers for their ladies during the night."[70] The sex trade could also be controlled by women, who traveled together in groups to posts offering their services. For example, when Meriwether Lewis reached the mouth of the Columbia River in November 1805 during his overland expedition, "an old woman who was the wife of a Chinook chief, came with six young women, her daughters and nieces, and having deliberately encamped near [them], proceeded to cultivate an intimacy between [their] men and her fair wards."[71] The bourgeois sometimes tried to keep the practice under control by banning the women from the post. Four years later at Fort George, Alexander Henry the Younger became irritated with women selling sex and refused to allow any of these women into the fort.[72] Prices for women are hard to determine. Some record that a woman could cost the price of one horse.[73] Yet at the Pembina River post in 1804, Henry recorded that one of his voyageurs "gave an expensive mare for one single touch at a Slave girl."[74]

The trade in sex could become a site of cultural misunderstanding among groups. Aboriginal men were often insulted at the refusal of bourgeois and clerks to accept the sexual services of their wives and daughters.[75] HBC officers criticized NWC traders for exploiting Aboriginal women. In 1792 Samuel Hearne wrote that the Chipewyans complained that Canadian traders abducted Aboriginal women by force and sometimes attacked elderly and infirm parents to steal their daughters. Hearne was appalled that "such . . . goings on in this Quarter . . . [are] encouraged by their masters, who often stand as Pimps to procure women for their men, all to get the mens wages from them."[76] Jennifer Brown suggests that women as items of trade could sometimes lead to "turbulent bargaining between North Westers and Indians and between the bourgeois or wintering partners and their own engagés. These employees, generally of French-Canadian backgrounds, were accustomed to female companionship and often placed an explicit economic value on that privilege, particularly if they were in debt."[77] In times of high levels of competition between trading companies, bourgeois encouraged the sex trade because it established closer ties with Aboriginal communities. The bourgeois also tolerated their laborers trading for sex because they had difficulty enforcing behavioral regulations. As the fur trade flourished and posts became more widespread, populous, and stable, the trade in sex perhaps grew to suit the new markets.

Much of the language of the fur trade literate portrayed Aboriginal women as economic commodities who were bought, sold, and pillaged. In one case at Fort George in the 1790s, a Beaver River Ojibwe complained to the trader Duncan McGillivray that his wife had been "pillaged," insinuating that the traders were the culprits.[78] Traders feared the same from Aboriginal peoples and freemen. While posted at Tête au Brochet and Moose Lake, clerk George Nelson commented that women were sometimes pillaged, yet his story implies the collusion of the women. He wrote: "[The sons of Old Lacorne were] all great bucks, I suppose they came sneaking about the house in hopes of finding some of our young women out and stealing them off—they can very easily do it, it is not but once that such things have happened. I cannot think that they had any other intention, for they could have very easily killed every soul of us. I communicated this to the men, who keep watch all night, and shut up the gates of our fort."[79] In other cases the Aboriginal women seem genuinely in danger. While traveling through the Okanagan, Alexander Ross feared greatly that nearby Aboriginal people would kidnap the wives in his party and counseled them to escape secretly in the night, without pausing for food, a guide, or protection, and to make their way home.[80]

How did the assumptions and attitudes of the fur trade literate color these portrayals? It is hard to believe that the Aboriginal women consented to be "bought and sold," but the instances in fur trade records are too numerous to dismiss. "Traffick in the fair sex" became a part of voyageur life in many areas. Voyageurs bought and sold their female sexual partners to one another and to company officers for personal pleasure, to increase their "social capital," and to pay off debts. In one New Year's joke described in chapter 6, a voyageur, Desrocher, pretended to sell his wife to another voyageur named Welles. But the joke lay in the fact that Welles did not have enough income or possessions to properly support a wife.[81] One voyageur named Morin asked bourgeois James McKenzie to sell his wife to the highest bidder and to credit Morin's account. Morin's wife did not idly consent to these dealings and refused any of the men to whom McKenzie tried to sell her.[82] The "traffick in the fair sex" was not only condoned but encouraged by the bourgeois, who often sold Aboriginal women to their servants.[83]

The "traffick in sex" was probably blurred with casual encounters between individual voyageurs and Aboriginal women and created the space for traders and Aboriginal women to become familiar with each other. No doubt voyageurs and Aboriginal women had sex with each other outside a formal union and where no money or goods exchanged hands. "Dating" rituals remain hidden from our view, probably because voyageurs tried to escape the gaze of the bourgeois. In any case the range of sexual relations encompassed sex in trading rituals, a trade in sex, and noncommodified sexual encounters.

Fur Trade Marriages

Families became very important for many voyageurs who worked for long periods in the trade and especially for those who decided not to leave the Northwest, settling down with their families in the interior and forming the foundations of métis communities.[84] NWC policy, legal testimony, and incidents recorded by fur trade literate all show that many voyageurs formed unions with Aboriginal women, and these "marriages" were often respected as serious unions even though they existed outside the Catholic Church. Although most of the evidence that relationships could resemble European conceptions of marriage involved the bourgeois and the clerks, these also occurred among voyageurs. Legal testimony indicates that some former voyageurs understood mariage à la façon du pays to be as serious and permanent as church marriages. But regardless of what those involved thought or said, these relations never corresponded exactly to Lower Canadian or bourgeois marriage where matters such as property and religion were concerned.

Early on some of the bourgeois of Montreal companies actively encouraged their servants to form unions with Aboriginal women because they knew Aboriginal wives' knowledge and kinship ties were important to the survival and prosperity of a post.[85] For more than thirty years before 1806,

Montreal traders provided sustenance for voyageurs' wives and children at interior fur trade posts. Although the Montreal traders accepted and encouraged these unions more than the HBC, they gradually became concerned with the number of dependents around their posts. The NWC's flexibility and tolerance of relationships diminished as the trade became more established in the Northwest. In 1806 the NWC partners placed restrictions on non-Aboriginal employees who wished to marry Aboriginal women. The minutes of the 1806 annual meeting record the following:

> *It was suggested that the number of women and Children in the Country was a heavy burthen to the Concern & that some remedy ought to be applied to check so great an evil, at least if nothing effectual could be done to suppress it entirely.—It was therefore resolved that every practicable means should be used throughout the Country to reduce by degrees the number of women maintained by the Company, that for this purpose, no Man whatever, either Partner, Clerk, or Engagé, belonging to the Concern shall henceforth take or suffer to be taken, under any pretence whatsoever, any woman or maid from any of the tribes of Indians now known or who may hereafter become known in this Country to live with him after the fashion of the North West, that is to say, to live with him within the Company's Houses or Forts & be maintained at the expence of the Concern. . . . It is however understood that taken [sic] the Daughter of a white Man after the fashion of the Country, should be considered no violation of this resolve.*

The NWC committee resolved that every officer should ensure that no men in his department become involved with Aboriginal (but not métis) women, and those who transgressed the rules be subject to a fine of one hundred pounds Halifax currency (which constituted at minimum one year's wages of a voyageur).[86] Van Kirk argues that this resolution was in part motivated "by the fact that in well-established areas marriage alliances were no longer a significant factor in trade relations."[87] Enforcement of the rule was selective. A clerk named Robert Logan at Sault Ste. Marie and a voyageur in the lower Red River were charged in 1809, but the important marriage alliances in the Columbia District were not affected, and some clerks and bourgeois continued to marry Aboriginal wives after this time, as did Daniel Harmon and George Nelson, but more married mixed-bloods.[88]

Despite these eventual restrictions, marriage to Aboriginal women was an important part of life at fur trade posts. French Canadian voyageurs who were occasionally hired by the HBC might insist on the right to have an Aboriginal wife.[89] It was customary for wives and families to be left behind at posts when voyageurs made their annual trips to Lake Superior.[90] These absences threatened the unity and strength of marital bonds. But longevity was encouraged when voyageurs were able to take their families with them as they moved from post to post and on their travels in the interior.[91] Voyageurs sometimes insisted on bringing their families with them on trading missions, threatening to desert if the bourgeois or the clerk did not consent.[92] Sometimes when voyageurs were forced to give up their wives either by their company or the refusal of their wives to travel with them, they insisted that their wives take no other husband and sought assurances from the company that they would not permit or approve any other voyageur marrying their former wives.[93]

A court case in Montreal provides an extraordinary insight into attitudes to marriage à la façon du pays in the Northwest. The 1867 case Connolly versus Woolrich and the 1869 appeal Johnstone et al. versus Connolly dealt with the legality in Canada of Chief Factor William Connolly's marriage to a Cree woman. Several voyageurs were called as witnesses to discuss their experiences in the pays d'en haut. The testimonies of the voyageurs called as witnesses for the plaintiff (Connolly's half-Cree son) are remarkably consistent. Seventy-two-year-old Amable Dupras, who had been a voyageur for fourteen years, testified: "The fashion in the country is that when one wanted to have a wife, *one asked her father, and if the father agreed to give his daughter, one buys something in recognition. Ordinarily, it was the fashion of the country to give a present to the girl's father.* One was not free to have more than one wife. . . . I often saw marriages in the country, and I speak of this custom with knowledge."[94] His testimony reveals the specific social regulations and rituals for forming relationships between voyageurs and Aboriginal women. Witness Pierre Marois corroborated the evidence of Dupras:

> *A man [in the Northwest] could not have more than one wife, we regarded this union like the union of a husband and wife [in Canada], and a sacred one. I myself have married [in the Northwest] in the fashion of the country. I lived twenty-three years with her, and she died eight years ago.* When one wanted to marry in the Northwest, one had to ask the [girl's] father and the mother . . . and if they consented, one asked the permission of the bourgeois to marry, and that was the only ceremony; and after that we were considered as a legitimate husband and wife as [in Canada], as if we were married in a church.[95]

When asked whether traders and voyageurs married women "pour toujours ou que pour le moment [for always or for the moment]," Joseph Mazurette replied, "Pour toujours."[96] Clearly these voyageurs considered mariage à la façon du pays as legitimate and serious as church marriages in the St. Lawrence valley. In contrast the defense witnesses (NWC traders Joseph Larocque and Pierre Marois, and Françoise (Fanny) Boucher, of French and Aboriginal descent, widow of HBC clerk Joseph McGillivray) claimed that marriage in the custom of the country was not a formal and binding agreement.[97] The diversity of views may have varied among individuals, communities, or classes of people.

In rural French Canada in the eighteenth and nineteenth centuries, weddings were joyful occasions that underscored the importance of the family unit in that society. Wedding day festivities were semipublic affairs with large parties witnessing the ceremony at the church, processions of carriages or sleighs carrying the families and guests through the countryside, and followed by long parties attended by neighbors and relations.[98] Traveler John Palmer saw several weddings in the French Canadian countryside in the fall of 1817 and noted: "[T]hey have a train of cabriolets, a clumsy sort of gig, according to the respectability or wealth of the happy pair; on returning the bride rides first, and far from appearing reserved on the occasion, she calls out to her acquaintance in the street, or waves her handkerchief in passing them; the market people, whom they take care to pass, greet them with shouts, which the party seem to court and enjoy."[99] This same spirit of celebration could carry over to voyageurs' weddings in the Northwest interior. At one extreme Fanny Boucher, testifying in the Connolly case, asserted that the only ritual to become married was simply to go to bed with a man.[100] Yet ceremonies and balls were often held to formally unite men and women in marriage and to celebrate their unions.[101] The wedding custom was a blend of Aboriginal and French Canadian practices. Additional testimony from the Connolly case shows that in some cases traders had to gain the permission of the girl's parents and pay the bride price. Some marriages included rituals, such as the smoking of a calumet and a public lecture by Aboriginal elders on the duty of a wife and mother. The new Aboriginal bride was then cleaned by other women at the post and then clothed in "Canadian fashion," which consisted of a shirt, short gown, petticoat, and leggings.[102]

An illustrative example is found in the case of a métis voyageur and highly respected interpreter named Pierre Michel. After aiding the Flatheads in one of their battles, he was awarded the wife of his choice for his bravery. His choice of bride was already promised to someone else, a warrior who loved her "ardently," but he agreed to allow Michel to have her. The happy Pierre presented a couple of guns, a dagger, cloth, and ornaments to his bride's relatives. In the evening the couple and her relatives and friends assembled at the chief's lodge, where they smoked and Aboriginal elders and the bride's mother lectured her on her duties as a wife and mother: "They strongly exhorted her to be chaste, obedient, industrious, and silent; and when absent with her husband among other tribes, always to stay at home, and have no intercourse with strange Indians." The new bride and her mother then retired to an adjoining hut, where she exchanged her leather chemise for one of gingham, a calico and green cloth petticoat, and a gown of blue cloth. The exchanging of clothes symbolized the changing of social identities, representing a new allegiance with the foreign traders. A procession was then formed by two chiefs and several warriors carrying blazing *flambeaux* of cedar, to convey the bride and her husband to the fort. They sang war songs in praise of Michel's bravery, and of their triumphs over the Blackfeet. The bride was

> *surrounded by a group of young and old women, some of whom were rejoicing, and others crying. The men moved on first, in a slow solemn pace, still chanting their warlike epithalamium. The women followed at a short distance; and when the whole party arrived in front of the fort, they formed a circle, and commenced dancing and singing, which they kept up about twenty minutes. After this the calumet of peace went round once more, and when the smoke of the last whiff had disappeared, Michel shook hands with his late rival, embraced the chiefs, and conducted his bride to his room. While [Ross Cox] remained in the country they lived happily together.*[103]

This marriage may have been more formal than usual, as Spokane women rarely married fur traders, and because Pierre Michel's bravery and importance among the Spokanes was exceptional. It illustrates, however, that marriage was represented by formal ceremonies, which combined Aboriginal and European practices.

Voyageurs treated marriage seriously. Polygamy was generally not tolerated in fur trade society. In addition Aboriginal men did not tolerate voyageurs mistreating their female kin. In the 1869 appeal, Joseph Mazurette testified: "It is not permitted to take *more than one wife in the country*. That sort of marriage is solemnly respected. . . . Almost all the nations are alike, as to these customs. One does not fool with an Indian woman just as one pleases. . . . One knows [not] to treat women badly. . . . There was the danger of having your head cracked, if you took [a wife] in the country, without the consent of the parents. It is the father and the mother who give the wives, and if they are dead, it is the closest to the parents . . . [One marries]

Table 6. Women at Fur Trade Posts

Year and post	Total no. of people	No. of officers	No. of voyageurs	No. of women	No. of children	% of men with wives
September 3, 1800						
Park River Post[a]	9	1	8	0	0	0
October 2, 1801						
Bird Mountain[b]	12	1	9	2	0	20
September 9, 1808						
Broken River[c]	6	1	4	1	0	20
October 10, 1808						
Dunvegan[d]	46+	5	32	9	"several"	24
October 27, 1807						
Dauphin River[e]	9	1	6	2	0	29
June 1, 1801						
Fort Alexandria[f]	28	2	7	6	13	67

Note: This table lists the posts where numbers of women are given, but the sources do not specify if they are wives of voyageurs or officers. [a]South of Pembina. Henry (the Younger), *New Light*, Park River Post, September 3, 1800, 1:77. [b]On bank of Swan River, 50 miles west of Swan Lake, north of Fort Dauphin. Harmon, *Sixteen Years*, October 2, 1801, Bird Mountain, 51–52. [c]TBR, S 13, George Nelson's journal, September 1, 1808–March 31, 1810, Broken River, September 9, 1808, 2 (my pagination). [d]Athabasca. Harmon, *Sixteen Years*, October 10, 1808, Dunvegan in Athabasca, 118. [e]TBR, S 13, George Nelson's journal "No. 5", Dauphin River, October 27, 1807, 13–14 (my pagination) / 197–98 (Nelson's pagination). [f]Harmon, *Sixteen Years*, Fort Alexandria, June 1, 1801, 48.

Table 7. Voyageurs' Wives at Fur Trade Posts

Year and post	Total no. of people	No. of officers	No. of voyageurs	No. of women	No. of voyageurs' wives	No. of children	% of voyageurs with wives
September 9, 1808 Dauphin River[a]	6	1	4	1	0	0	0
September 9, 1808 Grand River[b]	13	1	6	2	1	4	17
September 3, 1800 Reed and Red Rivers[c]	13	0	7	3	3	3	43
October 3, 1803 Hair Hills[d]	20	0	10	5	5	5	50
September 9, 1808 Pigeon River[e]	13	1	6	4	3	2	50
October 16, 1809 Fort Vermilion[f]	130	3	33	27	26	67	79
1810 New White Earth House[g]	129	5	20	36	20	68	100

Note: This table lists the posts where numbers of women are given and wives of voyageurs are specified. [a]TBR, S 13, George Nelson's journal, September 1, 1808–March 31, 1810, September 9, 1808, 2 (my pagination). [b]TBR, S 13, George Nelson's journal, September 1, 1808–March 31, 1810, September 9, 1808,2 (my pagination). [c]Near Pembina, Michel Langlois in charge. Henry (the Younger), *New Light*, September 3, 1800, 1:77. [d]Hair Hills Michel Langlois in charge. Henry (the Younger), *New Light*, October 3, 1803, 1:225–27. [e]Pigeon River, TBR, S 13, George Nelson's journal, September 1, 1808–March 31, 1810, September 9, 1808, 2 (my pagination). [f]Henry (the Younger), *New Light*, October 16, 1809, 2:554–55. [g]New White Earth House. Henry (the Younger), *New Light*, 1810, 2:603. In this case, assuming that men and women who shared tents with children were domestically involved, it seems that in one case two voyageurs shared one wife, and in possibly nine cases a voyageur had more than one wife.

Table 8. Alexander Henry the Younger's 1805 Census of the Northwest

Departments	"White" men	"White" women	"White" children	% men with wives
Athabasca	208	48	84	23
Athabasca River	37	12	15	32
English River	75	40	63	53
Rat River	25	7	10	28
Fort des Prairie	136	59	103	43
Fort Dauphin	45	22	18	49
Upper Red River	56	52	82	93
Lower Red River	75	40	60	53
Lake Winnipic [Winnipeg]	88	11	15	13
Lac La Pluie	46	10	10	22
Fond du Lac	128	29	50	23
Nipigon	90	20	20	22
Kaministiquia and Mille Lac and Lac des Chiens	62	16	36	26
Le Pic	16	2	3	13
NWC totals	1090	368	569	34
A K Co., men & c [old XYC]	520	37	31	7
Overall totals	1610	405	600	25

Note: Data from Henry (the Younger), *New Light*, 1:282. Fur trade officers not distinguished from voyageurs.

for always."[104] The number of voyageurs married or partnered with Aboriginal women is very difficult to discern, as the bourgeois kept no consistent record. Marriage rates seemed to vary tremendously between posts, but in many cases marriage was a visible and sometimes dominant part of post life. The emergence and growth of a substantial métis population in the Northwest interior and the widespread mention of voyageurs' wives in the writings of clerks and bourgeois suggest that the practice was common.

Aboriginal women are included with the annual listing of the post inhabitants in thirteen instances. In five of these cases the recorders did not specify whether the wives were married to officers or voyageurs. Percentages of Aboriginal women at these posts ranged from zero (where it was obvious that women would be mentioned if present) to 67 percent. Marriage rates varied tremendously among posts, but the sample group in tables 6 and 7 is too small to search for patterns or even a broad average. A census taken by Alexander Henry the Younger in 1805 for fourteen departments lists numbers of "Whites" as 1,610 men, 405 women, and 600 children (see table 8).

Henry determined the racial categorization of people by the "head of the household," so "White" wives and children "belonged" to the traders.[105] Assuming that all the "White" women were domestically involved with traders, an average of 25 percent of the combined officers and voyageurs had Aboriginal wives. This census also shows that partnerships with Aboriginal women were widespread throughout the Northwest. Jennifer Brown has argued that relationship rates between voyageurs and Aboriginal women were higher than those of laborers working for the HBC because the Montreal fur trade officers had less control over their men and could not prevent them from forming relationships with Aboriginal women.[106] Voyageurs had much more contact with Aboriginal women than did other fur trade laborers and thus had different attitudes toward them. Sylvia Van Kirk has convincingly portrayed the importance of Aboriginal wives to traders:

> *The economic role played by Indian women in fur-trade society reflected the extent to which the European traders were compelled to adapt to the native way of life. The all-encompassing work role of Indian women was transferred, in modified form, to the trading post, where their skills not only facilitated the traders' survival in the wilderness but actual fur-trade operations. At the North West Company posts and at Hudson's Bay Company posts especially, native women came to be relied upon as an integral if unofficial part of the labour force. Their economic assistance was a powerful incentive for the traders to take Indian wives; even within their own tribes, the women exercised a role in the functioning of the trade which has been little appreciated by historians of this period.*

Van Kirk describes Aboriginal wives supplying the traders with moccasins and snowshoes, dressing skins, helping in canoe construction and paddling, preparing food such as pemmican, curing and drying meat and fish, collecting rice and berries, and trapping small game.[107] The wives of voyageurs worked alongside their husbands, helping them with chores ranging from food procurement to trapping and dressing furs to cultivating trading contacts. Aboriginal wives helped their husbands make sugar from maple trees, gather wildfowl eggs, transport meat to the post from kill sites, fish, and attend to traps.[108]

Susan Sleeper-Smith has demonstrated that women played another role equally important in the fur trade. Those Aboriginal women who married French traders in the southern Great Lakes area in the early eighteenth century established elaborate kinship networks within fur trade families and connected to Aboriginal societies. These kin networks became crucially important for the successful functioning of the trade. She explains that "marital and kinship strategies transformed trade into a social process and mediated the disruptions inherent in disparate and competing economic systems. . . . Kinship transformed the impersonal exchange process characteristic of capitalism into a socially accountable process."[109] This pattern was especially important for voyageurs trading en dérouine because they were dependent on Aboriginal families for survival and success in the trade.

Like their husbands, voyageurs' wives were not always loyal and obedient to bourgeois and clerks; they sometimes helped their husbands in free-trading schemes. In the Athabasca District in the winter of 1800, two voyageurs named Martin and St. André sent meat from a cache to the post with some Aboriginal men. However, Martin instructed the transporters to give the meat not to John Thomson, the bourgeois in charge, but rather to Martin's wife, who would give them an awl and vermilion in exchange. Unfortunately for Martin, Thomson found out and became enraged, calling the voyageurs "a Dirty despicable set of fellows."[110] Van Kirk describes one particularly powerful Dene woman, Madame Lamallice, who was married to a French Canadian HBC brigade guide at Fort Wedderburn on Lake Athabasca. During the difficult winter of 1820–21, Lamallice was the post's only interpreter, had considerable influence with the surrounding Dene, and was accorded a favored position by the HBC. A young George Simpson complied with her demands for extra rations and preferential treatment to ensure that she stayed at the post. When the provisions ran low in the spring, the voyageurs were ordered to leave the post and support themselves at the fishery. Madame Lamallice refused and agreed to support her family with her own personal store of about two hundred fish. Simpson was not amused to learn that this "thrifty amazon" was carrying on a private trade in pounded meat, beaver tails, and moose skins, with a hoarded stock of trade goods. When the HBC officers attempted to limit Madame Lamallice's private trade, she threatened to turn all the Aboriginal people against them.[111]

Like Madame Lamallice voyageurs' wives could acquire significant power in the running of trade operations. They often accompanied their husbands on expeditions to trade with an Aboriginal group. Voyageurs left their wives with Aboriginal groups to act as liaisons between them and the traders, sometimes for as long as an entire summer.[112] On occasion voyageurs' wives went on expeditions to trade for their husbands.[113] As Van Kirk has noted, Aboriginal wives' knowledge and familiarity with the landscape and various Aboriginal tribes made them especially valuable as guides and interpreters. Aboriginal women taught their languages to European traders and travelers in the interior. They also acted as conveyors of information between Aboriginal groups and traders and often reported on the intentions and actions of various Aboriginal groups to help European Americans with their trading plans.[114]

Because of their economic and diplomatic importance, Aboriginal women could exert control over their voyageur husbands' careers in the fur trade. Aboriginal wives often encouraged their husbands to desert the service and become freemen or live with their Aboriginal families. In one case a voyageur named Chaurette, who was an expert canoe maker, deserted the service because his wife wished him to do so.[115] Aboriginal women could exert control over the distribution of food resources within a post, which sometimes caused jealously and resentment among traders.[116] George Nelson resented the wife of Brunet, one of his voyageurs, referring to her as "a vixen & hussy" who kept Brunet "in proper subjection by caresses, promises & menaces" and "sullen fitts or moodes." She persuaded him to disobey Nelson's orders and go to visit her relatives, and she constantly pressured him to quit the service.[117] Many voyageurs probably had to modify their presumption of patriarchal rule in marriage in order to maintain successful and stable unions with their Aboriginal wives.

Fluid Monogamy

How did the patterns of gender relations and marital unions differ between voyageurs and their masters? Van Kirk argues that the norm for sexual relationships in all ranks of the fur trade (officer, clerk, and servant) consisted not of casual, promiscuous encounters but rather of marital unions and distinct family units. She observes that voyageurs had much less money than clerks and bourgeois and thus did not have the resources to lavish gifts on their Aboriginal wives. Voyageurs also spent more time away from their Aboriginal wives than did the bourgeois. But she asserts that their relationships were fundamentally similar in that they were primarily marital.[118] Like Van Kirk's, Brown's study of the fur trade community in Rupert's Land and Sleeper-Smith's study of French traders in the Great Lakes area focus on men in the higher ranks of the fur trade. Brown also attests that similar patterns of intermarriage with Aboriginal women occurred among officers, clerks, and laborers in the trade.[119] But she differs from Van Kirk in her view that informality and flexibility were the dominant pattern in relations between traders and Aboriginal women. Brown suggests that British masters followed the pattern set by the earlier French and by their voyageurs and thus had intimate and yet often transient affairs with Aboriginal women.[120] Without rejecting their findings, especially where elites are concerned, I wish to emphasize that in addition to marriage a wide range of sexual relations could be found in the fur trade among the lower orders. Voyageurs entered the service with contracts for only three to five years, and initially they did not see the job as more than a temporary way to earn more money to supplement farming in the St. Lawrence valley. Because voyageurs' contracts only spanned three to five years, they probably did not see their relationships lasting longer. The voyageur would live with his partner's family in their lodges, or she would move temporarily to the post. If children resulted from these brief unions, they would either be absorbed into the Aboriginal woman's family, or the voyageur would leave the service and become a freeman so that he could form a long-lasting union with his Aboriginal family. Some couples managed to have long-term part-time unions if they could coordinate their yearly travels.

Although voyageurs came from a society where marriage was the norm, they did not automatically translate this attitude to the Northwest interior. If a voyageur fell in love with an Aboriginal woman, he would consider spending his life in the interior to stay with her. Some voyageurs may have brought their Aboriginal wives back with them to French Canada, but this would involve considerable expense and would require a dramatic change in lifestyle for the Aboriginal wife. The couple would have faced discrimination in French Canada. Miscegenation was not by any means an accepted practice, nor was there social mixing between habitants and their Aboriginal neighbors.

In the 1869 appeal of the Connolly case, the witnesses for the defense (Woolrich's children) provide interesting clues for the transience of marriage. NWC trader Joseph Larocque asserted:

> *It was very common to change women in the Indian country. The French Canadians, in the North-West company's employ and the English, did it too. . . . Some of the servants of the company brought women or wives with them to Canada and married them there according to the legal form of Canada. In the country, some lived with women in the interior and did not marry them but abandoned them, and others lived with them and abandoned them to marry white women in the civilized world. There were but very few of the servants of the company who did not take women when in the interior and lived with them, but there were very few who brought them into civilized society and married them.*[121]

The old voyageur, recorded by Alexander Ross, bragged that he had had twelve wives over the course of his career in the trade.[122] He probably had twelve successive wives, rather than many wives at once or wives in different places. All three voyageurs testifying in the Connolly case strongly asserted that polygamy was not tolerated in fur trade society, and the writings of the fur trade literate show that only very rarely did a voyageur have more than one wife or lover at one time, and that these instances were examples of voyageurs adopting Aboriginal customs when they could afford to do so.[123] If a voyageur was particularly prosperous, probably making money free-trading and garnering more symbolic capital, he could afford to have additional wives.

Unions between voyageurs and Aboriginal women were "seasonal" in nature because of the high mobility of voyageurs' jobs and of Aboriginal communities. Voyageurs usually did not bring their families when they made the annual summer trips to Lake Superior. During these summers Aboriginal wives often waited for their voyageur husbands to return, and some families congregated at central interior posts such as Fort Alexander at the mouth of the Winnipeg River. Some unions, however, probably ended during these periods, especially those that were less serious and had no children. Voyageurs were frequently relocated from post to post, especially when they renewed their three- to five-year contracts. Companies did not always pay for the maintenance of voyageur families, and voyageurs could often not afford to support them with their limited wages. Many of the men who developed serious relationships with Aboriginal women and deep commitments to their new families decided to "go native" and live with their in-laws or become freemen and travel with their families as independent traders. The short-term or temporary relationships among working voyageurs corresponded well with many Aboriginal cultures that were also highly mobile in their pursuit of economic resources and that sanctioned divorce and remarriage. The predominant pattern of relationships between voyageurs and Aboriginal women was fluidity. Aboriginal women sometimes had brief affairs with traders, lasting simply a season. Some affairs began when voyageurs arrived at a post for the winter and ended when they left the post for Lake Superior. Other relationships lasted several seasons or perhaps as long as the voyageur remained in the service and were often suspended during summer travel. The fluidity of unions is amply demonstrated by recurrent break-ups, the "buying and selling" of women by white traders, and serial monogamy.

Traders often passed their wives and lovers on to other traders with the woman's consent so that the woman was not left alone. This practice, which was called "turning off," was couched in tender language and revealed caring and respect for the women. When Daniel Harmon married a daughter of a Canadian man and a métis woman (Lisette Duval), he wrote: "[W]hen I return to my native land shall endeavour to place her into the hands of some good honest Man, with whom she can pass the remainder of her Days in this Country much more agreeably, than it would be possible for her to do, were she to be taken down into the civilized world, where she would be a stranger to the People, their manners, customs & Language."[124] Bourgeois and clerks often passed their wives on to voyageurs when they grew tired or annoyed with them.[125] Ross Cox commented: "When a trader wishes to separate from his Indian wife, he generally allows her an annuity, or gets her comfortably married to one of the *voyageurs*, who, for a handsome sum, is happy to become the husband of *la dame d'un Bourgeois*."[126] Voyageurs may have felt forced into some of these unions, but others may have been pleased.

Serial monogamy was also a common pattern among voyageurs. When voyageurs moved to different posts, they would sometimes end marriages and start new ones immediately at their new post, especially if their wives wanted to stay near their Aboriginal families and not move with the voyageurs. Van Kirk asserts that Aboriginal peoples "did not view marriage as a lifetime contract, nor did they consider it to be in their interest to have their women leave the district." Aboriginal women easily rejoined their Aboriginal families when "turned off" by European American husbands.[127] Likewise, if voyageurs frequently had a number of wives during their careers in the Northwest interior, their wives frequently had several European husbands.[128] Unlike their masters voyageurs had less control over their geographic mobility in their fur trade careers. Voyageurs thus ended relationships with greater frequency than their masters. Voyageurs may also have been compelled to end relationships that they highly valued and perhaps looked for opportunities to reunite with Aboriginal women whom they loved but had been forced to leave. In any case, movement in and out of relationships was fluid.

The range of relationships between voyageurs and Aboriginal women included casual encounters that could be pleasant or brutal. Mutually consensual sexual relationships outside marital unions certainly occurred between voyageurs and Aboriginal women. However, coercive sex and sexual violence was an occasional problem. Like other cultural conflicts this stemmed from misunderstandings and disrespect for moral codes.[129] Bourgeois W. Ferdinand Wentzel's disapproval of relationships between traders and Aboriginal women stemmed from his concern that the rape of Aboriginal women by voyageurs led to cycles of retributive violence.[130] Conflict was often augmented by adultery and rivalries over women between European Americans and Aboriginal peoples and within trading communities.

The fur trade literate recorded some cases of voyageurs sexually assaulting Aboriginal women. Direct references to rape or sexual violence are surprisingly rare, and mentions of "debauchery" are ambiguous regarding consent. It appears that a kind of moral code existed among voyageurs, clerks, and bourgeois. Obviously masters discouraged sexual violence because it led to retribution from Aboriginal families. But voyageurs also scorned men who committed acts of sexual assault. Bourgeois John McDonell records a case where an Ojibwe woman was able to rescue her daughter who was being raped by a voyageur by attacking him with a canoe awl. The voyageur received minor injuries and had difficulty walking, "a fate," observed McDonell, "he highly deserved for his brutality."[131] Vengeance by Aboriginal women on traders occurred occasionally, such as in the spring of 1792 when both Dene men and women attacked Canadian traders who had kidnapped the women.[132] The silence surrounding European American sexual violence may have been a deliberate or even unconscious oversight. Or sexual violence may have been limited in this context, where traders were highly dependent on Aboriginal peoples.

Voyageurs and Aboriginal women ended relationships for a variety of reasons. Most likely Aboriginal women ended relationships just as often as voyageurs. They could easily desert the post to rejoin their families.[133] Physical abuse no doubt contributed to Aboriginal women leaving relationships. Alexander Henry the Younger described one incident when a voyageur beat his wife, and afterward she went into the woods with a rope to hang herself but was discovered in time. Instances of suicide seem to have sometimes occurred among Algonquian women who were overwhelmed with grief.[134] Other Aboriginal wives simply left their husbands when they were abused, such as the wife of freeman François Richard, who complained of "ill treatment & jealousy."[135] Carol Cooper asserts that on the Northwest coast, maltreatment, such as beating, was a major factor in most cases of divorce between Aboriginal women and European husbands: "In 1842, a French-Canadian servant of the Company named Maurice gave his wife 'a drubbing because of her misconduct.' She quickly returned to her own people, taking her child with her. Families did not allow such abuse to go unchecked. One chief severely beat a Company servant named Turcotte when the man struck his daughter." In this context, at an HBC post near midcentury, abuse of Aboriginal wives may have been high because traders were far less dependent on Aboriginal women by this time. However, Cooper finds that on the whole fur trade servants valued their Aboriginal wives, and mistreatment was rare.[136]

Aboriginal women could run away with other voyageurs or Aboriginal men or simply decide to leave a post, and they were sometimes followed by their voyageur partners, who tried to beg or force them to stay. In a "heroic rescue" a voyageur named Cournager under the charge of Dominique Ducharme chased after "his bird [who] had flown" the nest and triumphantly "saved" her from some Aboriginal men. While posted at Great Bear Lake in 1806, three Aboriginal women deserted (the reason is not apparent). One of their voyageur husbands and a Dogrib trader caught up with them and brought them back.[137] When women deserted the posts and their husbands, they often took provisions and supplies with them, further demonstrating their agency and initiative in economic well-being. The three women who left the fort at Great Bear Lake, took with them "a Large ax of the Compys—Lines and fish hooks and 30 fish." When the women were brought back to the post, the voyageurs "gave the women a plenty full supper, in sted of Chastesing them."[138] In other cases break-ups were mutual, especially in openly hostile relationships. The wife of one voyageur was noted for having "fits," which Nelson suspected were feigned "to subdue the stubborn ill humour of her old husband whom she [said was] always quarrelling and disputing her on account of the illcare she ha[d] of his things and other qualities."[139] Disputes over custody of the children and cases of adultery often led to ugly partings.[140]

This chapter opened with quotations from Alexander Ross and Daniel Harmon that emphasize the temporary nature of relationships between voyageurs and Aboriginal women. But the overarching pattern of fluidity in these unions does not obscure the sincerity of the "many tender ties." Harmon's own life serves as a good example of how attitudes of women and men could change over time. While Harmon was serving in the Swan River Department in 1802, at the start of his career, a Cree chief encouraged him to marry one his daughters. Although Harmon could see the benefits ("I was sure that while I had the Daughter I should not only have the Fathers hunt but those of his relations also"), Harmon considered the marriage to be a snare laid by the devil and resisted "thanks to God alone." Four years later he married fourteen-year-old Elizabeth Duval, daughter of a French Canadian man and a Snare woman; Harmon explained, "[A]fter mature consideration concerning the step I ought to take I finally concluded it would be best to accept of her, as it is customary for all the Gentlemen who come in this Country to remain any length of time to have a *fair* Partner, with whom they can pass away their time at least more sociably if not more agreeably than to live a lonely, solitary life, as they must do if single." He planned to stay with her while in the Northwest, but when he retired, he intended to "place her into the hands of some good honest Man" to spare her the discomfort of trying to fit into the "civilized world." Yet when the time came for Harmon's retirement from the trade in 1819, he could not leave his family behind:

> *Having lived with this woman as my wife, though we were never formally contracted to each other, during life, and having children by her, I consider that I am under a moral obligation not to dissolve the connextion, if she is willing to continue it. The union*

which has been formed between us, in the providence of God, has not only been cemented by a long and mutual performance of kind offices, but, also, by a more sacred consideration. . . . I consider it to be my duty to take her to a christian land, where she may enjoy Divine ordinances, grow in grace, and ripen for glory.[141]

9. Disengagement

Going Home and Going Free

> *Nous l'avons dit en commençant, nos voyageurs du Nord n'ont jamais pu se faire dans la suite à la vie calme des champs. La vie nomade qu'ils avaient menée pendant leur jeunesse les avait tout à fait dégoûtés des travaux de l'agriculture. . . . A cette époque la chasse avait beaucoup plus de charmes que les travaux des champs.*
>
> *We have said it at the beginning, our voyageurs of the North never could have been able, afterward, to adapt to the calm life of the fields. The nomadic life that they had led during their youth had given them complete disgust for the work of agriculture. . . . At this time the hunt had much more charm that the work of the fields.*[1]

What happened to voyageurs when they left fur trade service? Did their "nomadic" lives as voyageurs ruin them for farming? Did they become frustrated with their station in life as indentured servants and feudal peasants and try to live freely away from royal and company control? The opening quotation, found in Georges Dugas's *Un Voyageur des pays d'en-haut* (1890), refers to a voyageur who had left fur trade service and remained in the pays d'en haut rather than returning to the St. Lawrence valley to farm under the control of a seigneur. The Roman Catholic priest, Father Georges Dugas, stationed at St. Boniface, wrote a biography of a former voyageur, Jean-Baptiste Charbonneau, who was released from his contract along with many other servants when the 1821 merger of the HBC and the NWC dramatically reduced the pool of labor that was needed when the companies competed with each other. Charbonneau had difficulty finding a satisfying means to earn a livelihood in the Red River colony. Was Charbonneau typical? Commentaries or accounts of former voyageurs who returned to the St. Lawrence valley to resume farming with their French Canadian families are rare, but this did not mean that voyageurs did not return to the St. Lawrence valley. Perhaps these men were too ordinary to merit discussion among literate elites of the colonies. This chapter will explore why men left the service and where they decided to settle to start new phases of their lives. It focuses on one option that received much attention in the literature of the fur trade: becoming a freeman in the pays d'en haut.

Previously we have seen that the broad contours of voyageurs' lives can be gleaned from a spectrum of observations made by their masters, explorers, and travelers in the pays d'en haut. The fragmentary records make it difficult to track individuals and discover what happened to voyageurs when they left the service. As exemplified by the excerpt at the beginning of this chapter, the literate elites made general observations on voyageurs' supposed characters and wrote about exceptional men who probably acted outside the norm. We can only speculate about the vast majority of voyageurs and outline their options for a post-voyageur life.

The absence of massive populations of French Canadians and their offspring in the pays d'en haut serves as the best evidence to show that most voyageurs did not stay in the interior but returned home to the St. Lawrence valley when they decided to leave the service. Pork eaters worked in the trade in the summer and were away from their farms for only part of the year. Many northmen probably returned to Canada after one term (three to five years) in the service, while others returned when they were no longer physically able to handle the demanding work. Bourgeois sent ill voyageurs back to Canada when they could not work. For example, in August 1803 George Nelson noted that one voyageur named Berthier was being sent back to Montreal because "he was subject to fits."[2]

A fascinating area that remains to be explored but is beyond the scope of this book is the influence of former voyageurs on the society and culture of Lower Canada.[3] The constant return of voyageurs from the Northwest interior and their numbers suggest that they had considerable impact. Some parish records in Lower Canada refer to men by their occupational status and include the designation "voyageur" though the men were clearly farmers in the parish, implying that the men had probably been voyageurs at one point in their lives.[4] When voyageur Joseph Leveillé (mentioned in chapter 5) was sentenced to the pillory for having accepted the wages of two rival fur trading firms, a group of voyageurs defended him by hurling the pillory into the St. Lawrence River and threatened to storm the prison. Leveillé was eventually released, and no one was punished for the incident.[5] In the following year (1795), Attorney General Jonathan Sewell complained about a "lawless band" of voyageurs in Lower Canada.[6] Did former voyageurs retain their identities as voyageurs for their whole lives? Did they maintain connections to other former voyageurs in Lower Canada and attempt to use these ties to shape their lives?

Most voyageurs maintained a connection to the St. Lawrence valley while in the pays d'en haut. The letters that voyageurs and their families wrote to each other (discussed in chapter 2) with the help of parish priests, bourgeois, and clerks, were sent across vast distances, entrusted to other voyageurs. In 1830 widow Marianne Duque wrote to her son, voyageur François Benoit: "I am profiting from this occasion of Mr. Athanase Felix for telling you the state of my health, which is not good." Unfortunately his father had died two and a half years earlier and had desperately wished to see his son before he passed away. Marianne Duque warned her son that she also would like "the consolation of seeing [him] before [her] death." Unfortunately she was too late, as her son had died in the service before he could receive her letter.[7]

In many cases these feelings of attachment were mutual. Homesickness led many men to return to Canada or to try to do so.[8] Sometimes voyageurs openly hated the interior and could not wait to return home.[9] In one case bourgeois Roderick McKenzie recalled voyageurs referring to the interior as "S_cci_e Pays M___d ___te ___" (Saccire or Sacre Pays Maudite, or this cursed awful country).[10] Voyageurs who had been in the service for many years frequently spoke about returning to the St. Lawrence valley.[11] The desire to return to Canada remained with some men who had established successful careers as freeman and had families in the Northwest. Charles Racette, one of the more successful freemen, who lived in the Northwest for more than thirty years acting as a guide, interpreter, and clerk for fur trade companies, is a good example.[12] In 1819 he was on his way to Canada with his Aboriginal family when he was waylaid at Grand Rapid (at the mouth of the Saskatchewan River) by the HBC and forced to participate in the kidnapping of NWC bourgeois Benjamin Frobisher and John Duncan Campbell.[13] It is unclear if Racette's journey to Canada was to be a visit or a permanent move or if he ever resumed the interrupted trip. Racette's life does not represent that of a typical voyageur because he was a freeman and thus able to travel as he pleased. But his desire to return to Canada represented a common trend. In another example a long-time voyageur named Louis La Liberté, who had a large family in the interior with an Aboriginal wife and became father-in-law to three bourgeois, spent a winter in Canada in his later years, although it is unknown whether he took his Aboriginal family with him.[14]

Yearnings to go back to the St. Lawrence valley were tempered with the voyageurs' desire to be in the interior and their fascination with and admiration for Aboriginal peoples and the landscape of the pays d'en haut. In one of his many romantic flourishes, Alexander Ross conveyed some of the sentiment of voyageurs in the Northwest in his description of masters' attitudes to their lives there. He wrote:

> *[Being posted in the interior] among the savages in the far distant wilds of North America, may appear to some as banishment rather than an appointment of choice in search of competency, which in a variety of ways fortune places more or less within our reach; yet of the persons who have spent any portion of their years in those countries, few or none are known who do not look back with a mixture of fond remembrance and regret on the scenes through which they have passed; preferring the difficulties and dangers of their former precarious but independent habits to all the boasted luxuries and restraints of polished society. In the wilderness they spend a long, active, and healthful life.*[15]

Artist Frank Blackwell Mayer was highly impressed by the life of Henry Belland, a voyageur from Montreal: "[F]or years he [Belland] roved the prairies and woods of the Northwest, through the wilds of Canada, th[e] lake country of Minnesota, the frozen regions of Pembina, and the trackless plains of Nebraska. He had visited the mouth of the Yellowstone, and on horseback, on foot, in the canoe, in winter or summer, he was at home in all situations of frontier life."[16] Many voyageurs became very attached to life in the pays d'en haut.[17] Some decided to spend most of their lives working in the trade and even to settle down in the interior. Men who were in heavy debt to their company and who had large Aboriginal families could settle around the Great Lakes, rather than return home and possibly face the shame of failure or discrimination. As early as 1750 Jesuit missionary Claude-Godefroy Coquart described a farm at Fort Michilimackinac where voyageurs worked as farm laborers to help them stay in the interior.[18] At Fort William in the second decade of the nineteenth century, Gabriel Franchère observed: "On the other side of the river the land is cultivated and inhabited by former servants of the Company who have not saved any money; married to Indian women and burdened with heavy family responsibilities, they dare not return to Canada but prefer growing a little corn, a few potatoes, etc., and living by fishing to going back to beg in a civilized country."[19] A. C. Osborne traced the movements of voyageurs who had settled around British garrisons in the Great Lakes in the early nineteenth century. Seventy-five voyageur families moved to Penetanguishene (in Simcoe County, Upper Canada) after Fort Michilimackinac and Drummond Island were ceded to the United States in 1821 and were each allotted twenty or forty acres.[20] The Red River valley was a popular place to settle, especially for those voyageurs who could not find work after the 1821 merger of the NWC and the HBC.[21] After working as a voyageur for fifteen years, Jean-Baptiste Charbonneau decided to settle in St. Boniface in the Red River valley to farm and work as a stonemason on the first Roman Catholic cathedral in the Northwest. After finding these occupations unsatisfying, Charbonneau decided to become a buffalo hunter and moved to the Minnesota Territory. His biographer, l'abbé Georges Dugas, explained, as cited in the opening quotation, that Charbonneau could not return to a life of farming because it was too peaceful.[22]

Some men who quit the fur trade service and stayed in the Northwest became absorbed into Aboriginal societies, such as René Jussaume, who lived with the Mandans in one of their great trading villages on the upper plains. Alexander Henry the Younger noted: "[This] man has resided among the Indians for upward of 15 years, speaks their language tolerably well, and has a wife and family who dress and live like the natives."[23] While traveling through North America, the Duke de la Rochefoucauld Liancourt observed that along the Missouri and Illinois rivers many French Canadians resided among Aboriginal peoples "and live[d] exactly as they [did]."[24] Another option for voyageurs was to become freemen, independently trading and hunting. Ross Cox described three freemen who had formerly been engagés in the NWC "who, after the expiration of their engagement, preferred the wild and wandering life of a trapper, to remaining in the Company's service, or returning to Canada."[25]

Freemen

While reminiscing about his career in the fur trade, clerk George Nelson described an eccentric "freeman" in the Northwest, the Charles Racette mentioned earlier, who "had his *amour propre* too (Self love) & did not chuse to associate with the Common labourers." According to a freeman named Lorrain, Racette thought and "stile[d] himself Lord of Lake Winnipick."[26] While complaining about freeman Antoine Desjarlais, who declared himself the "sovereign of Red Deer Lake," NWC bourgeois Alexander Henry the Younger bemoaned, "No dependence is to be placed on [freemen]; they have neither principles, nor honor, nor honesty . . . their aim is all folly, extravagance and caprice; they make more mischief than the most savage Blackfeet in the plains."[27] Alexander Ross despaired that freemen were "lost . . . to all the ties of kindred, blood, country, and Christianity." He continued:

> *These freemen may be considered a kind of enlightened Indians, with all their faults, but none of their good qualities; and this similarity to the Indians in their vagrant mode of life brings on them the contempt of both whites and natives. Indeed, they become more*

> *depraved, more designing, and more subtle than the worst of the Indians; and they instruct the simple natives in every evil, to the great detriment of traders: with whom, in consequence, they are never on a friendly footing.*[28]

Freemen seemed to be the scourge of fur trade officials.

Yet freemen were not unpopular with everyone. Many French Canadian voyageurs admired them. Because voyageurs worked in a vulnerable position as indentured servants, under the control of their masters and in a foreign land where Aboriginal peoples often determined life and death, they valued independence wherever they could find it. Freemen could be both the figurative and the literal ideals of voyageurs because they lived and worked outside the structures of seigneurialism and mercantile capitalism. Freemen relied on a variety of strategies for sustenance, which could include trapping, trading furs, subcontracting for fur trade companies, guiding, interpreting, hunting, fishing, gathering, and on occasion practicing horticulture. A few became prosperous merchants, such as Jean-Baptiste Boucher, who had a store and tavern at Fort William on Lake Superior, and Joseph Constant, who established his own trading post near Cumberland House and whose descendants founded the northern Manitoban community of The Pas.[29]

Like voyageurs freemen left little documentary record and are hard to trace. Unlike voyageurs they did not comprise an easily identifiable ethnicity or cultural group. Freemen could be métis, Orcadians, other Scots, English, and Iroquoians from the St. Lawrence valley, though this chapter is concerned primarily with French Canadians. Although they sometimes formed partnerships or communities that crossed cultural and linguistic lines, they usually lived alone or with their immediate families. Alexander Ross estimated that in the early nineteenth century there were fifty or sixty in the Columbia District alone, but in the other parts of the Northwest, they were far more numerous.[30] A census taken in February 1814 counted forty-two freemen living at Pembina, ten at Swam River, six at Rivière Qu'Appelle, and seven without a geographic designation, totaling sixty-five in the northeastern prairies.[31] In a general meeting of the NWC partners in 1812, the minutes record the presence of "freemen scattered all over the Country."[32]

Heather Devine has argued that freemen first emerged as a substantial population in the Northwest after the Seven Years' War, when many French traders and servants, alienated from the new British regime, sought independence outside trading companies. To become successful traders, they established influential relationships with Aboriginal hunting bands through marriage. Freemen living alongside local Aboriginal groups with whom they had kin ties were the fathers of the substantial Plains Métis communities that emerged in the nineteenth century. Ethnic identities, even within families, varied. Devine's close study of the Desjarlais shows how two brothers, Antoine (the sovereign of Red Deer Lake) and Baptiste "Nishecabo," portray the range of cultural options open to freemen. Antoine identified closely with his French Canadian heritage, while Baptiste chose to cultivate an Ojibwe identity and became a shaman.[33]

The quintessential French Canadian freeman and one of the most famous was Charles Racette, otherwise known as the Lord of Lake Winnipeg. He was born in 1765 or 1773 in the parish of St. Augustin, just west of Quebec City along the St. Lawrence River.[34] He entered the fur trade at least by 1790, joining a Michilimackinac-based group of Nipigon traders.[35] Racette's family had managed to provide him with an education because he entered the service as a youthful clerk rather than as a paddler. His start as a clerk may have explained his disdain for "common labourers." I suspect, however, that French Canadian voyageurs would have felt a strong connection to him because of their common origins and language, and that the bourgeois would have treated Racette in much the same way as voyageurs, especially during the times he worked on short-term labor contracts as a guide and interpreter. In the late 1790s the HBC hired Racette to establish a post on the upper Red River. This venture failed because the Orcadian English-speaking servants could not understand the French-speaking Racette and refused to work under his authority.[36] Some years later Racette tried again to work within the confines of a large company, this time for the NWC, whose workforce was primarily Francophone. He procured several hundred pounds to establish a post near Grand Portage, but this venture failed as well.[37] Early on, Racette became disillusioned with working for companies and began to trade on his own in the 1790s.[38] By 1807 he was living as a freeman with his family on the west side of Lake Manitoba, near Fort Dauphin, while continuing to work informally for the NWC.[39] Racette began a family in the Northwest sometime in the last years of the eighteenth century, when he would have been either twenty-five or thirty-two. He married a woman of Ojibwe descent, referred to in the records as Josephte Sauteux, who would have been about twenty, and had at least five children with her between 1787 and 1824.[40] Josephte, or "Mother," Racette was regularly mentioned in the writings of fur traders as an active part of the family enterprise.[41]

Like Racette many freemen came to the Northwest interior while working for a fur trade company, became disgruntled with their masters, and decided to live and work on their own. Another well-known and prosperous freeman, Joseph Constant, who began his working life as a voyageur, made no secret to his NWC masters that he desired to be free and settle with his family at The Pas, a community northwest of Lake Winnipeg. For years he had threatened to desert the service and probably used this as a bargaining tool for better work conditions and possibly greater pay.[42] Bourgeois James McKenzie offered the following description of a freeman named Piché who subcontracted for the NWC: "[He] always Complains to me of the hardship of having the Molly Gripes Continually owing to eating fish—a Common food he Says at this Morné Endroit—He Often Curses from the bottom of his heart both the place and the food and I dare Say the Bourgeois though I donot [*sic*] hear him—It is with regret he reflects on the fine times he used to have of it during the Summer Season at Slave Lake where he was his own Master and Chose his own meat while here neither is master nor eats meat without Choosing." Piché's strategy of manipulating McKenzie was successful: McKenzie gave him better food in hopes of keeping him happy and improving his work performance.[43]

A few exceptional men became freemen straight away, without first working for a fur trade company. One example was Jacques Hoole, a soldier from France who fought on the Plains of Abraham in the Seven Years' War, after which he settled as a farmer in the St. Lawrence valley. While he was fighting for the British in the American Revolution, the Republicans burned his farm, and his wife and children deserted him. He started a new life trapping furs to trade. He lived to the age of ninety-two, was called Père Hoole, and was treated with great respect by voyageurs.[44]

Other freemen were forced into their circumstances. When companies did not have the resources to feed their servants, they often released them from their contracts, leaving them to fend for themselves.[45] The French Canadian voyageur Antoine Desjarlais entered the fur trade in 1792 and worked with different firms affiliated with the NWC. He became a freeman after the NWC merged with the XYC in 1805.[46] When the HBC and the NWC merged in 1821, the large workforces necessitated by the fierce competition became redundant. Two-thirds of all company servants, approximately thirteen hundred employees, lost their jobs. About 15 percent of these men settled in the Red River valley, and small groups established communities along major fur trade routes, while most men returned to their homes in French Canada and Orkney.[47]

Like Charles Racette many freemen married Aboriginal women and had families. Immediate family members were crucial to economic survival. Charles Racette's wife regularly traded with fur companies and probably trapped with her husband. Joseph Constant started to include his sons in his fur trade work by the early 1820s and involved them in his undercover trading schemes. On one occasion in 1821 his son Antoine reported the NWC's trading activities to the HBC, thus helping his father act as a double agent between the two companies.[48] The marriages of freemen followed patterns similar to those of company officials: their Aboriginal wives provided kin ties of crucial importance to successful trading. George Nelson complained that Aboriginal people would always give food to freemen, but not to fur trade companies, even when the company men were starving.[49]

A large portion of the livelihood of freemen was earned while subcontracting with fur trade companies. They made temporary engagements for short periods, ranging from days to months, and worked as typical servants, transporting goods, trading with Aboriginal people, and maintaining posts.[50] Some were hired for a particular area of expertise, such as making canoes.[51] By far the most common arrangement was to hire freemen as guides or interpreters. For example, in 1804 near the Assiniboine River, NWC bourgeois Charles Chaboillez hired a freeman named La Fraise (also referred to as La France) as a guide, clerk, and interpreter, because he was the only Frenchman familiar with the route and had been a Missouri trader for several years.[52] Freemen were often well versed in Aboriginal languages and canoe routes, knowledge that was especially valued by trading companies. NWC trader Edward Umfreville was distressed in June 1784 when trying to find his way from Lake Superior to the Winnipeg River. He wrote is his journal: "Luckily that afternoon a Frenchman called Constant [arrived, who] is a guide in the service of Monsieur Coté, Constant says a Canadian is near hand, who is not at present engaged to any one, is well acquainted with the road, and he thinks will be willing to engage with us. This is a prize not to be lost, and we may see him as soon as possible, mean to send after him tomorrow." Two days later Umfreville engaged Pierre Bonneau to guide the crew to Sturgeon Lake. Umfreville lamented: "He is not content to go; we wished much to engage him to winter but found it impossible. . . . He has been a very good, quiet man and as he knows the way very well from Pais Plat to Sturgeon Lake, we would willingly engage him to winter, so that he may be employed as guide hereafter, if there should be occasion for him."[53] Freemen traveled extensively in the Northwest in all seasons and were often asked to carry mail between posts.[54] They became a source of important information to traders, passing on news such as successes in the trade, the passage of canoe brigades, and the movements of Aboriginal trading partners.[55] In especially close relationships the companies stored goods in a freeman's house, lodge, or encampment. In one case in 1805 trader William McKay entrusted a part of his year's outfit to the care of freeman Alexis Bercier to protect before the clerk in charge of the post arrived to take over.[56]

Freemen often had relationships with companies that mirrored those between Aboriginal peoples and companies. They exchanged furs for goods, sold country produce to the traders, and were often hired to hunt for a post.[57] Relations could be strained because freemen's trading defied company monopolies and undercut company profits. This strain could begin while freemen were still voyageurs. For example, while stationed at Moose Lake for the NWC, clerk George Nelson was outraged at Joseph Constant's "disloyalty" when Constant traded privately with Aboriginal peoples, against company policy. Moreover, Constant frequently gave away all the rum to bolster his reputation with the Aboriginal neighbors at Nelson's expense. According to Nelson, Constant was equally wily with the HBC. Constant traded privately with the HBC post under the charge of George Flett. To deflect suspicion he spread false rumors, telling Nelson that Flett was stealing Nelson's Aboriginal clients. Constant used his skills to cultivate trading relationships that benefited him personally, enhanced his reputation, and helped smooth the path for his switch from voyageur to freeman.[58]

Even when freemen were not nearly as successful or shrewd as Constant, fur trade officials were distrustful of them. Archibald Norman McLeod, a bourgeois working at Fort Alexandria in 1800, was convinced that the freeman La Frenier, who was trapping for the post, was "a trifler."[59] Alexander Henry the Younger complained: "Those freemen are a nuisance in the country, and generally scoundrels; I never yet found one honest man amongst them," and he made it a general rule to prevent his voyageurs from becoming freemen whenever possible.[60] Nelson described a freeman named Charles Grignon thus: "[He is] quite a blackguard—a drunkard, a boaster—& more than half a fool or a madman, & according to the usual character of such brutes as they are he would try to insinuate his bad maxims into others. . . . I was often disgusted with his conversation."[61] In 1811 Nelson wrote to his parents:

> *There is another set of people in these parts that truly deserve our pity, (compassion) & contempt alternately, —this tribe or set, is what we call free people, 'Gen libres!' . . . These are generally people, who are entirely masters & independant as they vainly imagine of the company's assistance or protection. Some . . . prefer entering in engagements with the Company in such a manner as to have leave of absence from the arrival of the canos in the fall 'till*

> *the latter end of April or beginning of may, giving all their hunt at certain fixed prices to the Compy. . . . Others are entirely free & roam & strole about the plains or hover about the forts like wolves, eating what they can eat & drinking what little remains while the women & Children as well as themselves are reduced to the most extreme wretchedness.*[62]

Groups of freemen often traveled and encamped together, usually in twos or threes, sharing resources among their families.[63] Bourgeois and clerks sometimes hinted at very large groups of freemen living and working together.[64] Nelson called one freeman named Swaine "the emporer of rascals," hinting that the freemen were organizing together on a large scale.[65] In 1807 while working in the Pembina area, Alexander Henry the Younger recorded: "This season we were troubled by an augmentation of freemen from Canada, etc. Their total numbers on this river amounted to 45; more worthless fellows could not be found in the North West."[66] Parts of the Desjarlais family lived together as an extended kin-based hunting band along the eastern slopes of the Rocky Mountains and on the shores of Lesser Slave Lake and Lac La Biche.[67]

Clues from the documentary record suggest that mixed freemen communities formed along many fur trade routes. A group of English, Scottish, and French Canadian retired servants began to farm along the Saskatchewan River, near Joseph Constant's post. In July 1833 passing explorer George Back complimented the former HBC ship captain John Turner on his large farmhouse, barns, fields, ten cows, and four horses.[68] When the Cree Anglican missionary Henry Budd arrived in the Cumberland area in August 1841, he reported that the Aboriginal people there had been farming and living in houses for some time, and that barley cultivated at the intended mission site looked "very well"; presumably this group included the freemen.[69] In the summer of the next year, a visiting Catholic priest, Joseph Darveau, noted Constant's field of turnips.[70] Historian Paul Thistle has found that many lower Saskatchewan Cree accepted the increasing number of freemen in the area and developed good relations with them.[71] Laura

Peers notes that between 1804 and 1821 some Ojibwes began to join with Cree, métis, and freeman groups to form mixed bands and comments on the presence of some mixed Cree-Ojibwe bands around Cumberland House in 1806–7. She asserts that the typical composition of these groups was a majority of Crees, with a minority of Ojibwes, freemen, and métis. Although these groups were beginning to compete with one another for resources, the complex web of kinship ties allowed them to combine their strengths. She also describes a group that had emerged around Lesser Slave Lake by 1810, made up of freemen, métis, Odawas, Ojibwes, Iroquois, and other eastern tribespeople, that wielded considerable power with the HBC.[72] Devine's work on the Desjarlais family confirms this pattern. Kinship ties lay behind the formation of these mixed bands.

Some freemen, however, eschewed the social rules of living with others. They chose to leave company service, they did not join Aboriginal communities, and they sometimes even shunned company servants. As George Nelson observed, Charles Racette did not choose to associate with common laborers.[73] Racette's nickname was the Lord of Lake Winnipeg. Despite Antoine Desjarlais's commitment to his extended family, he claimed sovereignty over Red Deer Lake. Another "lord" could be found at Cross Lake, north of Lake Winnipeg. An "Old Canadian fisherman," unnamed by bourgeois Gabriel Franchère, who passed by in 1814, called himself "*King of the lake*. He might [have] fairly style[d] himself king of the fish, which [were] abundant and which he alone enjoyed."[74] Joseph Constant appeared to reign over his domain. The Constant family had a house by January 1822, only six months after he left the fur trade service to settle at The Pas.[75] They were soon able to entertain passing traders and explorers. In 1833 HBC officer John McLean reported: "We arrived on the 5th of August at Rivière du Pas, where an old Canadian, M. Constant, had fixed his abode, who appeared to have an abundance of the necessaries of life, and a large family of half-Indians, who seemed to claim him as their sire. We breakfasted sumptuously on fish and fowl, and no charge was made; but a gratuity of tea, tobacco, or sugar is always given; so that M. Constant loses nothing by his considerate attentions to his visitors."[76] If freemen could thrive while living and working with only their immediate family, their dreams had been fulfilled, but not all were so fortunate. Bourgeois and clerks frequently reported on starving freemen who turned to both companies and Aboriginal people for help. Some freemen were forced to return to the life of indentured servitude, signing on for a full contract of three to five years at the same wages as a typical servant. The Desjarlais family suffered terribly from disease, declining fur resources, starvation, and the merging of the HBC and the NWC in the early 1820s.[77]

Regardless of their successes, freemen were admired by voyageurs because they carved out a distinct social, economic, and cultural space for themselves and their families and in doing so affected larger forces in the fur trade. The possibility of being free encouraged other servants to desert the service. Freemen can be seen as part of a long tradition in the fur trade that began with the coureurs de bois of New France, who worked independently and adopted the technology and social conventions of Aboriginal peoples, but they usually remained within the confines of mercantile capitalism.

In sum, when voyageurs left the fur trade service they could return to the St. Lawrence valley; settle in the interior to farm, especially near large settlements such as Fort William or the Red River settlement; join the métis buffalo hunters; join Aboriginal families; or become freemen, living and trading independently in the Northwest interior. A final option for voyageurs was to remain in the service. Some men spent the greater part of their lives working as voyageurs and died on the job. Of course, men died in the service while still young, but others lasted until well past the age of sixty. The elderly voyageur quoted by Alexander Ross on Lake Winnipeg, who so eloquently expressed the central values of the voyageurs' world, had worked as a voyageur for forty-two years; he maintained, "[W]ere I young again, I should glory in commencing the same career again. I would [s]pend another half-century in the same fields of enjoyment. There is no life so happy as a voyageur's life; none so independent; no place where a man enjoys so much variety and freedom as in Indian country."[78]

10. Conclusion

Carrying the World

> *This far, every thing was new & strange to me; wild, romantic & wonderful. No "falls", but at the Rideau & Chaudiere, but many rapids, at several of which many a poor canadian found his watery grave. Portages over rocks, hills & Swamps, mostly covered with dense forests. Not a few of them the theme of legends, stories & tales of adventures, accidents & miracles &c &c.*[1]

Voyageurs were always on the move, as conveyed by clerk George Nelson's journal entry from his first year in the trade, 1802. As pork eaters, their main priority was to transport goods between Montreal and Lake Superior during the brief months when the waterways were free of ice. Northmen had the additional responsibilities of staffing interior posts, securing provisions, and trading with Aboriginal people, all of which required travel over great distances in all kinds of conditions. Athabasca men traveled the greatest distances of all, across thousands of miles to the remote reaches beyond Lake Athabasca. For all these men (and voyageurs were always men), the hard physical reality of their annual journeys has shaped our historical understanding of them as a distinct group of laborers. But as I have argued in this study, their travels or journeys can also be considered metaphorically, in the work they undertook to navigate new social and cultural spaces. Along with passing through diverse landscapes, voyageurs met a wide range of peoples who differed dramatically from them in cosmology, world-view, language, and culture. They traveled across both geographic and social gulfs in order to transport and trade goods. Because voyageurs never stayed in any one place or with any one group of people for very long, they were forced to carry their world with them. This world, as we have seen, was made up of material objects, such as canoe cups and woven belts (*ceintures flèches*), rituals, such as Christmas celebrations and maypole ceremonies, and skills, such as paddling techniques and house construction. The quotation at the beginning of this chapter suggests another important part of their voyageur world: narratives that were expressed through oral means.

French Canadian voyageurs came from an oral world where systems of knowledge and meaning were shared through stories and songs. When French peasants crossed the Atlantic to settle in the St. Lawrence valley starting in the first quarter of the seventeenth century, they brought a rich oral tradition.[2] This oral tradition evolved among the habitants and came to reflect a distinct French Canadian identity, which was carried by voyageurs into the continental interior.[3] During their travels voyageurs encountered Aboriginal peoples, who also used oral systems as their primary expressive form. George Nelson's observation on the ubiquity of voyageurs' tales suggests that they were a central component of the voyageurs' world.[4] Through narratives, voyageurs could preserve their knowledge and memories of their working world, make sense of the landscape and Aboriginal cultures, and commemorate those who passed away. Although voyageurs appear to be virtually voiceless in the documentary record, they certainly were not in their own lives.

This book explores the world of French Canadian voyageurs working in the Montreal fur trade mainly during the period after the end of the Seven Years' War in 1763 until the 1821 merger of the NWC and the HBC, but the analysis stretches before and after this chronological framework. The period was characterized by fierce competition for furs between the English-chartered HBC and various partnerships based in Montreal, which largely merged into the NWC. Competition between the companies led to the rapid expansion of fur trade posts far to the north, south, and west. Growing numbers of servants were employed to transport the increasing volume of trade goods and to work at the posts. At the height of competition the number of voyageurs working in the trade at one time reached at least three thousand.

Voyageurs came primarily from parishes surrounding Montreal and Trois-Rivières, yet once in the trade they did not form distinct identities based on parish, region, or family ties. Rather, the men were inducted into a world organized along occupational lines. Voyageurs' identities were shaped by their habitant roots, the circumstances of their workplace, and by Aboriginal peoples they met in the pays d'en haut. Common customs and a specialized vocabulary emerged among the men as soon as they entered the trade and stayed with them throughout their careers.

This study begins with a look at the caricatures of voyageurs in popular culture, the silence surrounding them in scholarly histories, and voyageurs' apparent voicelessness in the historical record. It explains how their history can be uncovered from fragmented sources. The metaphor of voyage is the organizing framework to describe and explain their experiences working in the trade. Voyageurs became indentured servants in the fur trade to earn extra money for their farming families, and they usually sent their wages home. A handful of surviving letters written by families to voyageurs, and one letter from a voyageur to his wife, reveal the sentimental and economic attachments that stretched across vast distances and long absences. As soon as voyageurs began their contracts, they engaged in didactic rituals that helped them learn the customs of their new occupation and the rituals that helped them create and refine values to cope with their ever-changing locations. The ritual baptism at points of geographic distinction, for example, marked symbolic transformations from habitant to voyageur, from pork eater to northman, and from northman to Athabasca man. Each of these identities mirrored changes in landscape, increased risks and challenges in their jobs, and a greater sense of idealized masculinity based on the values of strength, perseverance, and daring. These rituals provide clues to voyageurs' behavior and world-view and dramatically augment the sources of voyageurs' voices.

The book next turns to the work performed in canoes, outlining the range of duties, working conditions, and another source of voyageurs' voices, their legendary singing. Singing helped voyageurs pace themselves while paddling and provided a means to reminisce about home and to commemorate those who lost their lives in the service. Voyageurs' work was not simply made up of mundane paddling but rather required a broad range of skills. These skills and voyageurs' aptness provided them with a means to bargain with their masters for improved working conditions. Although voyageurs regularly negotiated for better rations and higher wages, they did not challenge the paternalistic structures of the workplace en masse. The most common form of protest was to desert the service, and some voyageurs went on to become freemen, earning their livelihoods in a variety of ways outside the rule of masters or seigneurs.

When voyageurs reached the western tip of Lake Superior, pork eaters exchanged their ladings with northmen, and all participated in rendezvous, the largest celebration in the fur trade. Voyageurs' lives were not restricted to work, and many forms of play, especially encouraged by their ritualized workplace, helped them act out social values that reflected both the dramatically new worlds and the continued allegiances to life in the St. Lawrence valley. At interior posts voyageurs became jacks-of-all-trades, engaged in construction and artisan crafts, hunted for food, traveled among posts, and traded en dérouine with Aboriginal people. Voyageurs journeyed to Aboriginal lodges with small complements of goods to trade, and sometimes they spent winters there. Here voyageurs learned most about Aboriginal people and adapted to their lifestyles to survive. Many voyageurs formed romantic attachments with Aboriginal women.

The formation of close relationships led to a wide range of sexual and emotional ties, which mingled voyageurs' ideas of desire, pleasure, romance, and familial partnerships with those of Aboriginal women. Sexual relationships were fluid, and the rules and patterns were subject to constant negotiation. Sexual contacts could help ratify trade relationships and sometimes led to the emergence of a sex trade. Those voyageurs who desired stable and permanent families in the interior, such as the men who devoted their lives to the service and freemen, were able to establish long-term marriages, but "fluid monogamy" became the most common pattern.

Most voyageurs returned home after working for a term or two in the trade. Of those who stayed in the interior, some helped carve out new colonial spaces by settling and farming. The mere presence of European Americans and the mere act of farming did not make a space "colonial," but when voyageurs' farms became extensions of fur trade posts and subject to regulation by colonial authorities, they passed from being proto-colonial to extending European American control over Aboriginal land. Other voyageurs joined Aboriginal communities, and a significant portion became independent freemen. These men relied on a range of resources for their livelihood and challenged the efforts of the British government and the HBC to impose social and economic control over the continental interior.

This book contributes to scholarship on French Canadian history, the fur trade, cross-cultural encounters, and the process of *métissage*, sometimes called hybridization or cultural mixing. It highlights linkages between the St. Lawrence valley and the sites of fur (and cultural) exchange that spread over most of the northern parts of the continent and looks at how working men operated in a proto-colonial environment. It emphasizes cooperation rather than conflict between European Americans and Aboriginal peoples and as such, helps to illuminate the context in which the métis (people of mixed Aboriginal and European heritage) and the Métis Nation (an explicit assertion of ethnic identity) emerged.

This study of the extensive travel of French Canadian servants adds to the growing scholarship outlining the French imprint on early North America. It supports Gérard Bouchard's and Yvan Lamonde's formulation of a Québécois "collectivité neuve" (new settler society) that required French settlers to separate themselves from their mother country by adapting to the new continental space.[5] Voyageurs can be seen as agents of the North Americanization of French settlers in the St. Lawrence valley. More than most settlers, they faced the extremes of North American climate, weather, and geography and were exposed to a wide range of North American (Aboriginal) peoples. When they returned to the St. Lawrence valley, they brought their new skills, experiences, and attitudes with them. Although the book focuses primarily on voyageurs' experiences in the pays d'en haut, I hope that it will encourage further studies of the impact returning voyageurs had on their communities beyond their wages and absences. A few tantalizing hints of the voyageurs' continuing identity and collective actions in the valley suggest that this is potentially a rich line of inquiry. No discussions about former voyageurs are readily apparent in the correspondence of priests in customarily voyageur parishes, but baptismal records show that men continued to identify themselves as voyageurs after their return. Tracing the lives of former voyageurs and searching for specific skills and values brought back by voyageurs may provide clear pictures of how they shaped Lower Canada.

The cultural exchange did not just flow into the St. Lawrence valley. Voyageurs brought the customs and attitudes of the St. Lawrence valley inhabitants with them when they traveled across the continent, and we see their lasting influence in a myriad of settings. Placenames, such as Portage La Prairie (present-day town along the Assiniboine River) in southern Manitoba, Lac Ile à la Crosse in northern Saskatchewan, and Voyageur National Park in Minnesota reflect the presence of voyageurs and their experiences. Artifacts and the skill sets that produced them are evidenced in canoe cups, woven sashes, and post-on-sill houses. Songs and stories made their way from voyageurs' campfires into Aboriginal communities and were passed down through voyageur families. The most pronounced legacy left by voyageurs in the pays d'en haut is their offspring.

One of the most exciting and prolific fields in early North American history is the study of new peoples that emerged in cross-cultural encounters. Since the appearance of Marcel Girard's magisterial work, *Le métis canadien* (1945) and Jacqueline Peterson's ground-breaking 1980 PhD thesis on Métis ethnogenesis in the Great Lakes area, scholars have been engaged with questions of origins, diaspora, history during the fur trade, ethnic and political consciousness in the twentieth century, land claims, and métis women's history.[6] The exploding scholarship can be differentiated between studies that focus on the Métis Nation that matured in the Great Lakes region and Red River valley and those that examine the multiheritage (mixed-blood) communities that were created in the contact zones along fur trade routes.[7] In both of these cases understanding the background of the European fathers is of crucial importance, especially when the fathers took an active role in raising their children. I hope that this study will be helpful to scholars studying the offspring of French Canadian men and Aboriginal women.

In the field of fur trade studies, the book contributes to a growing interest in cultural studies and in particular introduces scholars to new questions of gender, masculinity, identity, and ritual. The book sketches the broad contours of the voyageur experience and provides a base for close and detailed studies of individuals and communities that focus particularly on working men. The Northwest during the time of the fur trade was a place of great diversity and fluidity, of which the voyageurs are perfect exemplars. Their lives were filled with change and movement. Although they preceded the waves of European colonists, and their activities in the trade paved the way for the process of colonization and commenced the long, damaging consequences of Aboriginal entanglements with European Americans, voyageurs do not fit a regular pattern of contact. Their impact on Aboriginal environments was light. They adopted many aspects of Aboriginal cultures, and some formed hybridized connections with them. Voyageurs represent a time of possibility, when the pattern of colonization was not inevitable or inexorable.

I began this study hoping to look past the stereotypical caricatures of voyageurs, rife in both the historical documentary record and contemporary popular culture, by finding and amplifying their voices as working men in a challenging workplace. What I found was a complex and diverse labor force negotiating its identity in the margins between well-established cultures, both European and Aboriginal. Although voyageurs left few conventional traces of their own voices in the documentary record, I was astonished by the extent of information that can be gleaned from these traces, especially in their recorded behaviors. I hope that this broad study will encourage more scholars to wander into the fluid world of the fur trade and examine the unusual sites of contact and hybridized communities that covered large swaths of time and space in early North America.

Notes

1. Introduction

1. Ross, *Fur Hunters*, 2:235.

2. Voyageurs National Park Index Page, http://www.nps.gov/voya/, visited June 1, 2002.

3. The full title (after a corporate merger) is Voyageur Corporation & Greyhound Canada Transportation Corporation.

4. Newman, *Company of Adventurers*, 2:23, 25.

5. Nute, *Voyageur*, vii. Later examples of romantic stereotyping of voyageurs include Campbell, *North West Company*, 22–24; and Francis, *Battle for the West*, 51, 61–62.

6. Innis, *Fur Trade in Canada*, 262.

7. For an excellent discussion of the history of textual representations of voyageurs, see Gross, "Voyageurs," 411–22.

8. Harmon, *Sixteen Years*, 197–98.

9. See especially the work of Ray, *Indians in the Fur Trade*, and the proceedings of the North American Fur Trade Conferences.

10. Voyageurs receive almost two pages in Woodcock, *Social History of Canada*, 99–100; one paragraph in Francis, Jones, and Smith, *Origins*, 377; one paragraph in Bumsted, *History of the Canadian Peoples*, 49–50; and no description, only brief mention in Friesen, *Canadian Prairies*, 56–57, 58.

11. Fur trade workers are mentioned briefly in some broader studies of labor and capital in early Canadian history, such as Pentland, *Labour and Capital in Canada*, 30–33; and B. D. Palmer, *Working-Class Experience*, 35–36. European traders first received significant attention by Brown, *Strangers in Blood*. Aboriginal laborers have been subject to some examination by Judd, "Native Labour and Social Stratification," 305–14. See also Swagerty and Wilson, "Faithful Service under Different Flags"; J. Nicks, "Orkneymen in the HBC"; Skinner, "Sinews of Empire"; Burley, *Servants of the Honourable Company*. Goldring first began to compile information on laborers in *Papers on the Labour System*. See also Bourgeault, "Indian, the Métis and the Fur Trade"; and Makahonuk, "Wage-Labour in the Northwest Fur Trade Economy."

12. Allaire, "Les engagements"; Allaire, "Fur Trade Engages," 19–20; Charbonneau, Desjardins, and Beauchamp, "Le comportement démographique," 125–26; Dechêne, *Habitants and Merchants*, 117–24; and Greer, "Fur-Trade Labour," 203–4.

13. Allaire, "Les Engagés de la Fourrure," 83–84.

14. On Iroquois voyageurs, see Grabowski and St.-Onge, "Montreal Iroquois Engagés"; Karamanski, "Iroquois and the Fur Trade"; T. Nicks, "Iroquois and the Fur Trade"; and Green, "New People in an Age of War."

15. In his study of voyageur contracts from 1701 to 1745, Allaire used the records of forty-eight notaries, who recorded roughly six thousand contracts, found in the Archives nationals de Québec. See Allaire, "Les Engagés de la Fourrure," 75–77.

16. Brown and Vibert, introduction to *Reading beyond Words*.

17. Podruchny, "Festivities, Fortitude and Fraternalism."

18. Mackenzie, "General History," 52. For arguments that the author of "A General History" was Roderick McKenzie, the cousin of Alexander Mackenzie, see Alexander Mackenzie's letter of November 7, 1806, to Roderic McKenzie, in R. McKenzie, "'Reminiscences,'" 1:51; Bigsby, *Shoe and the Canoe*, 1:115; and Daniells's introduction to *Voyages from Montreal*, vii. In the introduction to *The Journals and Letters of Alexander Mackenzie*, Lamb comments, "That Roderic assisted Mackenzie is entirely likely" (33). For a similar portrayal of French Canadian voyageurs from an HBC officer, see LAC, MG19 E1, 536.

19. Bakhtin, *Dialogic Imagination*, 263–64, 288.

20. Ginzburg, "Inquisitor as Anthropologist," 158.

21. Harmon, *Sixteen Years*, March 6, 1802, 55.

22. Muir, *Ritual in Early Modern Europe*, 3–4. See also Podruchny, "Baptizing Novices."

23. Ross, *Fur Hunters*, 2:234–37.

24. Dugas, *Un Voyageur des pays d'En-Haut*, 27. Original French: "Pour les uns, c'était le désir de jouir de la liberté illimitée qu'ils croyaient entrevoir dans les déserts de l'Ouest."

25. For an example of men from many different parishes making up a post community, see TBR, S13, George Nelson's journal "No. 5," 13–14 (my sequential pagination) or 197–98 (Nelson's pagination). In one of the few examples where brothers were posted to the same area, they did not get along with one another. See MRB, MC, C.13, November 26, 1799, 5 (my pagination).

26. Henry (the Younger), *New Light*, July 20, 1806, 1:333; Harmon, *Sixteen Years*, August 18, 1808, 113.

27. J. E. Foster, "Wintering"; and Devine, "Les Desjarlais."

28. Podruchny, "Un homme-libre"; and Peers, *Ojibwa of Western Canada*, 66, 69, 104–6.

29. For example, see Way, "Evil Humors and Ardent Spirits"; Peck, "Manly Gambles"; and Bederman, *Manliness and Civilization*, 17.

30. See the classic work of Turner, *Ritual Process*.

31. The concept was first suggested by Van Gennep in his *Rites of Passage*. The concept was further developed by Turner, *Ritual Process*, 94–95; and Turner, *Blazing the Trail*, 48–51.

32. For a theoretical discussion and cross-cultural comparisons of communitas, or the development of community in liminal spaces, see Turner, *Ritual Process*, 96–97, 125–30; and Turner, *Blazing the Trail*, 58–61.

33. Devine, *People Who Own Themselves*. Allaire found that in the period before the Seven Years' War, chain migration among servants was minimal ("Les Engagés de la Fourrure," iv, 148–49). This was not the case among traders in the first half of the eighteenth century. Dechêne found an overwhelming pattern of kin groups working in the trade and sharing trading permits; see her *Habitants and Merchants*, 120.

34. Peterson, "People In Between."

2. Leaving Home

1. John [Jean] Mongle, Fort Colville, to Marie St. Germain, Maskinongé, April 12, 1830, in HBCA, B.134/c/13, fol. 32. See also Beattie and Buss, *Undelivered Letters*, 295–96.

2. Because of the typical variability of spelling in the eighteenth and nineteenth centuries, Jean Mongle appears in various records as John, Monge, Mongell, Mongel, Mongall, Mongal, and

Monde. For information on the family, see Beattie and Buss, *Undelivered Letters*, 293–98, 453. All quotations of these letters are consistent with their publication in Beattie and Buss.

3. The Hessians were German soldiers whose services were purchased by the British to fight in the American Revolutionary War. See Vickerson, "Genealogy and the Hessian Soldiers." See also Dohla, *Hessian Diary*.

4. Roderick McKenzie hired a Jean Mongle from L'Assomption in 1814, and McTavish, McGillivray and Co. hired a Jean Mongle from L'Assomption in 1816. It is unclear whether this was the same man. Both partnerships belonged to the NWC. See the notarial records of J.-G. Beek, September 6, 1814, and January 13, 1816 in ANQM, CN 601 S29.

5. HBCA, F.4/32, fol. 749; and F.4/40, fol. 125.

6. Campagna, *Repertoire des Mariages de Maskinongé*, 228, 282.

7. HBCA, B.239/g/10, fol. 44, fol. 70; and B.45/a/1, fol. 3.

8. HBCA, B.45/a/1, fols. 20–22.

9. HBCA, E.31/2/2, fols. 24–25d.

10. The letter then sat untouched in the HBCA for over 150 years until the late 1990s when then keeper of the HBCA, Judith Beattie, and scholar Helen Buss began to research the writers of these letters, which they published as *Undelivered Letters*. I thank Beattie for drawing my attention to these letters at an early stage in my research and sharing her information with me.

11. HBCA, B.134/c/13, fol. 30; and Beattie and Buss, *Undelivered Letters*, 297–98.

12. Original: "[U]ne grande miserre à la remerCie de tout le monde" and "prier vos honneurs d['']avoir la Bonté d['']examiner Les Compte pour voir s['']ils lui revient quelquechose a seul fin de pouvoir me soulager et en meme temps pour prier humBlement vos honneurs d['']avoir quelque egard a ma miserre." Beattie and Buss, *Undelivered Letters*, 297–98.

13. Although Allaire found between 12.9 percent and 34.8 percent of fur trade servants came from the towns of Montreal, Trois-Rivières, and Quebec in the first half of the eighteenth century, he asserts that recruits were overwhelmingly rural in origin. See his "Les Engagés de la Fourrure," 180–86, 214.

14. See the work of Innis, particularly *Fur Trade in Canada*, 383–402.

15. Eccles, "Fur Trade and Eighteenth-Century Imperialism," 342.

16. Lunn, "Illegal Fur Trade."

17. Dechêne, *Habitants and Merchants*, 90–96, 107–25.

18. Dechêne, *Habitants and Merchants*, 96.

19. For a broad overview, see Rich, *Fur Trade and the Northwest*, 19–129.

20. Devine, "Fur Trade Diaspora."

21. Igartua, "Change in Climate"; and Rich, *Fur Trade and the Northwest*, 131–34, 138. Historian Fernand Ouellet asserts that French Canadians dominated the fur trade bourgeois until 1774, in *Economic and Social History of Quebec*, 79–83. The ethnicities, religions, business ties, social connections, and kinship networks among the Montreal fur trade bourgeois deserve fresh examinations to test the interpretations of Igartua and Ouellet.

22. Campbell, *North West Company*, 19, 33–34, 93. See also Davidson, *North West Company*; and LAC, MG19 B4.

23. Pendergast, "XY Company"; Rich, *Fur Trade and the Northwest*, 191, 195. For a general overview, see also Rumilly, *La compagnie du Nord Ouest*.

24. Keith, *North of Athabasca*, 28–30, 32–33.

25. Rich, *Fur Trade and the Northwest*, 189–90.

26. Nute, *Calendar of the American Fur Company's Papers*; DeVoto, *Across the Wide Missouri*; Chittenden, *American Fur Trade*; Terrell, *Furs by Astor*; Lavender, *Fist in the Wilderness*; Phillips, *Fur Trade*; and Jung, "Forge, Destroy, and Preserve," 255–320.

27. Rich, *Fur Trade and the Northwest*, 239–43.

28. Burley, *Servants of the Honourable Company*, 91–95.

29. Greer, "Fur-Trade Labour," 206–7; Greer, *Peasant, Lord, and Merchant*, 187–88; and Burley, *Servants of the Honourable Company*, 95.

30. Letter of Benjamin and Joseph Frobisher to General Haldimand, October 4, 1784, in Wallace, *Documents*, 73–74.

31. HBCA, F.4/32, fol. 749; and F.4/40, fol. 125.

32. Heriot, *Travels through the Canadas*, 246–48.

33. Mackenzie, "General History," 33.

34. London, PRO, Board of Trade Papers, Lt. Governor Milnes to Hobart, October 30, 1802, List of Departments in the North West Company Supplied by McTavish, Frobisher & Co. The list is reproduced in Davidson, *North West Company*, appendix 1, 279–81.

35. T. Douglas, *Sketch of the British Fur Trade*, 39.

36. On the move of the trading post and community from Michilimackinac to Mackinac Island, see Armour, *Colonial Michilimackinac*, 80–82. On the continued outfitting of voyageurs at Mackinac Island around 1817–18 and later, see Phillips, *Fur Trade*, 2:365–69.

37. Letter of Benjamin and Joseph Frobisher to General Haldimand, October 4, 1784, in Wallace, *Documents*, 73–74.

38. MHS, P791, folder 7, North West Company Letters, 1798–1816, Dominique Rousseau and Joseph Bailley v. Duncan McGillivray (originals from the Judicial Archives of Montreal).

39. Of 106 engagements for Sorel men between 1790 and 1799, Greer found that 99 specified the destinations. Of these, 52 were for trips to Grand Portage, and another 13 were for trips to other Great Lakes bases. Thus, two-thirds of the engagements were made for pork eaters. Greer, "Fur-Trade Labour," 202.

40. Mackenzie, "General History," 51.

41. For one example, see Back, *Narrative of the Arctic Land Expedition*, May 20, 1833, 37.

42. On a journey from Montreal to Fort Wedderburn on Lake Athabasca, Robert Seaborne Miles exchanged his crew for a fresh one at Rivière La Pluie on July 8, 1818. OA, MU 1391, 18.

43. Mackenzie, "General History," 51–52.

44. Mackenzie, "General History," 34. Also note that it is not clear from engagement records if French Canadian men entering the service for the first time could choose to become northmen immediately.

45. See Trudel, *Seigneurial Regime*; and Harris, *Seigneurial System*.

46. Greer, *Peasant, Lord, and Merchant*, xi–xii.

47. Dechêne, *Habitants and Merchants*, 195–96.

48. Allaire, "Fur Trade Engagés," 20. Similarly, in the seventeenth century Dechêne finds that more than half of all voyageurs came from the island of Montreal, while 30 percent came from the parishes surrounding Trois-Rivières. Most of the remaining voyageurs came from areas around Varennes and Châteauguay (*Habitants and Merchants*, 119).

49. Ouellet, "Dualité économique," 268–70.

50. Greer, "Fur-Trade Labour," 198–200.

51. In the period from 1701 to 1740, Allaire identifies Varennes, Saint-Sulpice, Repentigny,

Lachenaie, L'Assomption, Boucherville, Longueuil, Laprairie, and Châteauguay. Allaire, "Fur Trade Engagés," 20–21.

52. Greer, "Fur-Trade Labour," 200–201; and Greer, *Peasant, Lord, and Merchant*, 177–93.

53. Greer, "Fur-Trade Labour," 204; and Greer, *Peasant, Lord, and Merchant*, 181.

54. Greer, "Fur-Trade Labour," 204; and Greer, *Peasant, Lord, and Merchant*, 181.

55. Greer, "Fur-Trade Labour," 206.

56. Gâerin, *Trois types de l'habitation*, 99–107.

57. A close look at the parish registers might reveal some local and curé attitudes toward voyageurs. Genealogist Ellen Paul has closely examined the parish registers of l'Assomption to trace the life of a voyageur who returned from fur trade service and settled there. Paul, "Voyageur at Home."

58. Allaire, "Fur Trade Engages," 19–20; Charbonneau, Desjardins, and Beauchamp, "Le comportement démographique," 125–26; Dechêne, *Habitants and Merchants*, 120; and Devine, *People Who Own Themselves*.

59. Greer, "Fur-Trade Labour," 203–4.

60. Dechêne, *Habitants and Merchants*, 118–19.

61. Greer, "Fur-Trade Labour," 200, 204–9; and Dechêne, *Habitants and Merchants*, 123–24.

62. TBR, S13, George Nelson, Tête au Brochet, to his parents, December 8, 1811, 7.

63. Van Kirk, "George Nelson's 'Wretched' Career."

64. TBR, S13, George Nelson, Tête au Brochet, to his parents, December 8, 1811, 7. For examples of voyageurs entering the trade to make money, see also Harmon, *Sixteen Years*, May 24, 1800, 17.

65. Ross, *Fur Hunters*, 1:117; for a similar view, see Landmann, *Adventures and Recollections*, 1:310.

66. Greer, *Peasant, Lord, and Merchant*, 88.

67. Ross, *Fur Hunters*, 2:237.

68. Lande, *Development of the Voyageur Contract*, 41.

69. Lande, *Development of the Voyageur Contract*, 48–57; and HBCA, F.3/1. See also Greer, "Fur-Trade Labour," 200.

70. Lande, *Development of the Voyageur Contract*, 41–42.

71. McDonell, "Diary," 67–68.

72. Duckworth, *English River Book*, 146–47.

73. HBCA, F.3/1, fols. 37 and 37b, Joseph Frobisher to Simon McTavish, Montreal, January 7, 1792.

74. Greer, "Fur-Trade Labour," 200, 203; and Greer, *Peasant, Lord, and Merchant*, 181, 183.

75. Mackenzie, "General History," 52; Henry (the Younger), *New Light*, July 1, 1804, 1:247; and "Documents relating to the Engagement of Jean Batiste Cadot, Jr., with the NWC, 1795," in Wallace, *Documents*, 92.

76. Franchère, *Journal of a Voyage*, May 24, 1810, 44; LAC, MG19 A41; Landmann, *Adventures and Recollections*, June 3, 1800, 2:167–68; and LAC, MG24 H1, 45.

77. HBCA, F.3/1, fol. 126, John Gregory to Simon McTavish, Montreal, March 16, 1793.

78. LAC, MG19 A5, Montreal, July 26, 1788, Joseph Frobisher to John Collins, Esq., 63.

79. HBCA, F.3/1, fols. 27, a and b, Joseph Frobisher to Simon McTavish, Montreal, November 24, 1791.

80. HBCA, F.3/1, fol. 30b, John Gregory to Simon McTavish, Montreal, November 24, 1791.

81. HBCA, F.3/1, fols. 37 a and b, 41 a and b, 42, and 43, Joseph Frobisher to Simon McTavish,

Montreal, January 7, 1792, John Gregory to Simon McTavish, Montreal, February 18, 1792, and Joseph Frobisher to Simon McTavish, Montreal, February 18, 1792.

82. McDonell, "Diary," June 1, 1793, 72.

83. Lefroy, *In Search of the Magnetic North*, letter to Sophia (sister), Fort Frances on Rainy Lake, June 15, 1843, 37.

84. LAC, MG19 C1, vol. 8, reel C–15638, October 20, 1804, 13; OA, MU 572, vol. 2, Donald McIntosh, Michipicoten, to Duncan Clark, Pic, August 24, 1825, 2–3; and Ross, *Fur Hunters*, 1:118–19.

85. OA, MU 572, vol. 2, R. McKenzie, Pic, to Duncan Clark, Long Lake, May 1, 1825, 1, 3.

86. For a brief overview of master-servant law in a colonial setting, see Hay and Craven, "Master and Servant."

87. These studies are mainly of the ancien régime. Dechêne, *Habitants and Merchants*, 217–26; and Charbonneau, Desjardins, and Beauchamp, "Le comportement démographique," 120–33.

88. Allaire, "Les engagements"; and Greer, "Fur-Trade Labour," 197–214.

89. Dechêne, *Habitants and Merchants*, 117.

90. Ouellet, "Dualité économique," 294–95; and Allaire, "Les engagements."

91. Journals and letters include frequent mention of the arrangement of engagements at the interior posts. For a few examples, see LAC, MG19 C1, vol. 1, August 9, 1797, April 7, 1798, and May 14, 1798, 3, 53, 60; LAC, MG19 C1, vol. 4, April 2, 1790, 50; LAC, MG19 C1, vol. 5, April 2, 1790, 15; TBR, S13 George Nelson's Journal, January 29–June 23, 1815, March 19, 1815, 20–21; Henry (the Younger), *New Light*, May 15, 1801, May 1, 1803, and May 6, 1804, 1:180–81, 1:211, 1:243, and March 2 and September 18, 1810, 2:590–91, 2:628; Faries, "Diary," December 26, 1804, and February 24, 1805, 223, 230; Harmon, *Sixteen Years*, July 16, 1800, 23; Fraser, "First Journal," April 13, 1806, 109; and Heriot, *Travels through the Canadas*, 254–55.

92. See Massicotte, "Répertoire des Engagements."

93. My translation. Original: "Avoir bien et duement soin, pendant les routes, et étant rendu aux dits lieux, des Marchandises, Vivres, Pelleteries, Ustensiles, et de toutes les choses nécessaires pour le voyage; servir, obéir et exécuter fidèlement tout ce que les dits Sieurs Bourgeois, ou tout autre représentant leurs personnes, auquels ils pourraient transporter le présent engagement, lui commanderont de licite et honnête, faire leur profit, éviter leur dommage, les en avertir s'il vient à sa connaissance; et généralement tout ce qu'un bon et fidèle engagé doit et est obligé de faire, sans pouvoir faire aucune traite particulière; s'absenter ni quitter le dit service, sous les peines portée par les loix de cette Province, et de perdre ses gages." PAM, MG1 C1, fol. 33, contract form for McTavish, McGillivrays & Co.

94. Franchère, *Journal of a Voyage*, 181–82.

95. Lande, *Development of the Voyageur Contract*, 41–42.

96. For examples, see Joseph Defont's 1809 contract with the NWC, PAM, MG1 C1, fol. 32, and the contract of Louis Santier of St. Eustache with Parker, Gerrard, Ogilvy, & Co. as a milieu to transport goods between Montreal and Michilimackinac, April 21, 1802, LAC, MG19 A51.

97. Mackenzie, "General History," 34; and Heriot, *Travels through the Canadas*, 248.

98. Cox, *Adventures on the Columbia River*, 305.

99. McDonell, "Diary," 95.

100. Cox, *Adventures on the Columbia River*, 305.

101. LAC, MG19 C1, vol. 7, October 12, 1798, and March 2, 1799, 9, 39.

102. Henry (the Younger), *New Light*, July 23, 1800, 1:10.

103. OA, reel MS65, Donald McKay, Journal from January 1805 to June 1806, June 27, 1805,

22 (my pagination); MRB, MC C.24, February 11, 1801, 21; LAC, MG19 C1, vol. 6, May 14, 1800, 21; LAC, MC, MG19 C1, vol. 7, December 26, 1798, January 5, 1799, and March 2, 1799, 23, 25, 39; and Keith, *North of Athabasca*, 97.

104. MRB, MC C.24, January 21, 1801, 18.

105. LAC, MG19 B6, February 3, 1803, Montreal.

106. LAC, MC MG19 C1, vol. 15, June 27, 1800(?), 8; and Henry (the Younger), *New Light*, March 30, 1814, 2:862. For examples of men hired to fish, see Fraser, "First Journal," April 24, 1806, 113; and OA, MU 2199, Edward Umfreville, June 28–30, 1784, and July 11, 1784, 10, 16.

107. Greer, "Fur-Trade Labour," 206–8.

108. For example, after the 1821 merger, balances in men's accounts were paid to them or their families or their friends in Montreal. HBCA, F.4/61, fol. 29. Also see HBCA, E.31/2/2, Lebrun, Hercule, from brother Charles M., Maskinongé, April 18, 1831 ("deceased"), fols. 15–18; Mongall, Thomas, from wife, Marie St. Germain, Maskinongé, April 20, 1830, fols. 24–25; and St. Pierre, Olivier, from wife, Nelly, Trois-Rivières, March 28, 1831, fols. 30–31.

109. Mackenzie, "General History," 52.

110. For another example, see HBCA, E.31/2/2, McKissee, [John], from friend Andre Blais, York, April 12, 1833, fols. 19–20.

111. HBCA, E.31/2/2, Lebrun, Felix, from brother David, Maskinongé, April 17, 1831, and friend David Sigard, Maskinongé, April 20, 1831 ("deceased"), fols. 11–14; Lebrun, Hercule, from brother Charles M., Maskinongé, April 18, 1831 ("deceased"), fols. 15–18; and Mongall (Mongle), Thomas, from wife, Marie St. Germain, Maskinongé, April 20, 1830, fols. 24–25. On "plumes," see Lebrun, Hercule, from brother Charles M., Maskinongé, April 18, 1831 ("deceased"), fols. 15–18. Also see Beattie and Buss, eds., *Undelivered Letters*, 293–97, 303–9, For an example of a clerk sending buffalo robes, moccasins, and money to Canada, see OA, NWCC, MU 2198, item 1. 2–3, Donald McIntosh, Michipicoten, to sister Christy McDonald, Cornwall, August 12, 1816.

112. HBCA, E.31/2/2, McKissee, [John], from friend Andre Blais, York, April 12, 1833, fols. 19–20, and Rogue, Amable, from mother, Marianne, Maskinongé, April 15, 1830, fols. 26–27.

113. McCullough, *Money and Exchange*, 17–19, 67–81.

114. McCullough, *Money and Exchange*, 228–29.

115. McDonell, "Diary," 93.

116. Heriot, *Travels through the Canadas*, 254; and MRB, MC, C.27, 3, 23.

117. OA, MU2199, "Account of the Athabasca Indians," 51; Mackenzie, "General History," 34; and Landmann, *Adventures and Recollections*, 1:305.

118. The same pattern operated at higher ranks: junior clerks were paid a smaller annual salary than senior bourgeois and did not hold shares in the partnerships that made up the Montreal fur trading companies. Partners were granted voting privileges in business meetings, in addition to their company shares and higher salaries. OA, MU2199, "Account of the Athabasca Indians," 51.

119. Wallace, *Documents*, 213–15.

120. Wallace, *Documents*, 272.

121. Heriot, *Travels through the Canadas*, 246.

122. TBR, S13, George Nelson, Tête au Brochet, to his parents, 8 December 1811, 8–9.

123. Mackenzie, "General History," 52.

124. Minutes of the Meetings of the NWC at Grand Portage and Fort William, 1801–7, with Supplementary Agreements, in Wallace, *Documents*, July 16, 1808, 256.

125. Agreement of McTavish, Frobisher and Company, 1799, with Statement of Accounts, in Wallace, *Documents*, 104, 268.

126. For examples, see the contracts of Pierre Forcier and Joseph Longueil, in LAC, MG19 A51.

127. For hunting, see LAC, MG19 C1, vol. 1, January 26, 1798, and March 25, 1798, 37, 50. For guiding and interpreting, see LAC, MG19 C1, vol. 1, March 20, 1798, 49; and LAC, MG19 C1, vol. 55, July 11, 1784, 16.

128. Mackenzie, "General History," 51.

129. MRB, MC, C.11, Sunday, September 12, 1802, 6. See also Keith, *North of Athabasca*, 173.

130. TBR, S13, George Nelson's Coded Journal, May 12, 1821, 19–20. See also Podruchny, "Un homme-libre."

131. John Thomson, "Journal, Mackenzies River alias Rocky Mountain, 1800–1," February 16, 1801, 23. See also Keith, *North of Athabasca*, 152.

132. Fraser, "First Journal," May 19, 1806, 121.

133. MRB, MC, C.7, January 17, 1794, 7.

134. MRB, MC, C.28, April 8, 1808, 30. See also Keith, *North of Athabasca*, 336. For a second among many examples, see OA, MU1391, May 31, 1818, 4.

135. Ross, *Adventures of the First Settlers*, 114. For other examples, see Ross, *Fur Hunters*, 1:118–19; Nelson, *My First Years*, August 25, 1803, 104; and OA, MU1391, June 6 and 9, 1818, and July 8, 1818, 7–8, 18.

136. Faries, "Diary," December 20 and 21, 1804, 223.

137. LAC, MG19 B1, vol. 1, William McGillivray to P. Grant, Grand Portage, August 2, 1800, 155.

138. TBR, S13, George Nelson's journal, September 1, 1808–March 31, 1810, January 19, 1809, 16 (my pagination).

139. TBR, S13, George Nelson's journal and reminiscences, a reminiscence of September 13, 1802; and Henry (the Younger), *New Light*, October 26, 1805, 1:269.

140. Ross, *Fur Hunters*, 55.

141. HBCA, A.16/54.

142. LAC, MG19 C1, vol. 1, 10, 44, and 62; and LAC, MG19 C1, vol. 7, January 5, 1799, 25.

143. OA, MU 842, March 3, 1819, 35.

144. Rochefoucauld Liancourt, *Voyage dans les États-Unis d'Amérique*, 2:225, cited by T. Douglas, *Sketch of the British Fur Trade*, 36–37.

145. T. Douglas, *Sketch of the British Fur Trade*, 32–47. See also MRB, MC, C.17, August 3, 1804, 4, 11–29.

146. Nelson, *My First Years*, 97–98.

147. TBR, S13, George Nelson, Tête au Brochet, to his parents, December 8, 1811, 7–9.

148. OA, MU2199, "Account of the Athabasca Indians," 3; Ross, *Fur Hunters*, 2:235–38; Henry (the Younger), *New Light*, October 3, 1803, 1:225; Cox, *Adventures on the Columbia River*, 305–8; and Ross, *Adventures of the First Settlers*, 169–71.

149. HBCA, B.42/a/136a, fol. 19.

150. Cox, *Adventures on the Columbia River*, August 16, 1817, 287.

151. Rediker, *Between the Devil*, 146–49.

152. HBCA, E.31/2/2, Grenier, Joseph, from parents Joseph & Marie, Ruisseau des chenes, April 20, 1831 ("deceased"), fols. 7–10; and Lebrun, Hercule, from brother Charles M., Maskinongé, April

18, 1831 ("deceased"), fols. 15–18. See also Beattie and Buss, *Undelivered Letters*, 286–92, 303–9.

153. Greer, "Pattern of Literacy in Quebec," 330–31.

154. Franchère, *Voyage to the Northwest Coast*, June 5, 1814, 241.

155. Harrison, *Until Next Year*.

156. HBCA, E.31/2/2, Grenier, Joseph, from parents Joseph & Marie, Ruisseau des chenes, April 20, 1831 ("deceased"), fols. 7–10. See also Beattie and Buss, *Undelivered Letters*, 286–92.

157. HBCA, E.31/2/2, St. Pierre, Olivier, from wife Nelly, Trois-Rivières, March 28, 1831, fols. 30–1. See also Beattie and Buss, *Undelivered Letters*, 299–302.

158. HBCA, E.31/2/2, Benoit, Francois, from mother Marianne Dorgue, St. Ours, April 23, 1830, fols. 1–2.

159. My translation. Original: "Enfin je rond Le Silence Je te Crie pour a savoir tes nouvelles." HBCA, E.31/2/2, Boimier, Isidore, from brother Charles, Mascouche, April 28, 1823, fols. 3–4.

160. My translation. Original: "Je teprie Chér enfant c? toute foi tu ne Peus Pas dèsendre cette année ges Pére au moins que tu aurat la bonté de nous Ecrire cette au tonne Par les voyageur qui vons décendre." HBCA, E.31/2/2, Benoit, Francois, from mother Marianne Dorgue, St. Ours, April 23, 1830, fols. 1–2. See also Rogue, Amable, from mother Marianne, Maskinongé, April 15, 1830, fols. 26–27.

161. HBCA, E.31/2/2, Benoit, Francois, from mother Marianne Dorgue, St. Ours, April 23, 1830, fols. 1–2; Grenier, Joseph, from parents Joseph & Marie, Ruisseau des chenes, April 20, 1831 ("deceased"), fols. 7–10; Lebrun, Felix, from brother David, Maskinongé, April 17, 1831, and friend David Sigard, Maskinongé, April 20, 1831 ("deceased"), fols. 11–14; Lebrun, Hercule, from brother Charles M., Maskinongé, April 18, 1831 ("deceased"), fols. 15–18; and Rogue, Amable, from mother Marianne, Maskinongé, April 15, 1830, fols. 26–27. See also Beattie and Buss, *Undelivered Letters*, 303–9.

162. HBCA, E.31/2/2, St. Pierre, Olivier, from wife Nelly, Trois-Rivières, March 28, 1831, fols. 30–31; and Grenier, Joseph, from parents Joseph & Marie, Ruisseau des chenes, April 20, 1831 ("deceased"), fols. 7–10. See also Beattie and Buss, *Undelivered Letters*, 286–92, 299–302.

163. HBCA, E.31/2/2, Boimier, Isidore, from brother Charles, Mascouche, April 28, 1823, fols. 3–4; and Rogue, Amable, from mother Marianne, Maskinongé, April 15, 1830, fols. 26–27.

164. On the reporting of births, see HBCA, E.31/2/2, Lebrun, Felix, from brother David, Maskinongé, April 17, 1831; and friend David Sigard, Maskinongé, April 20, 1831 ("deceased"), fols. 11–14. For news that a family member had died, see Benoit, Francois, from mother Marianne Dorgue, St. Ours, April 23, 1830, fols. 1–2; and Boimier, Isidore, from brother Charles, Mascouche, April 28, 1823, fols. 3–4. For news of marriages in the parish, see Lebrun, Hercule, from brother Charles M., Maskinongé, April 18, 1831 ("deceased"), fols. 15–18; and St. Pierre, Olivier, from wife Nelly, Trois-Rivières, March 28, 1831, fols. 30–31. For reports on houses and roads in the parish, see Lebrun, Hercule, from nephew, Olivier Fizette, Maskinongé, March 12, 1831 ("deceased"), fols. 15–18. See also Beattie and Buss, *Undelivered Letters*, 303–9.

165. HBCA, E.31/2/2, Rogue, Amable, from mother Marianne, Maskinongé, April 15, 1830, fols. 26–27; and McKissee, [John], from friend Andre Blais, York, April 12, 1833, fols. 19–20.

166. HBCA, E.31/2/2, Lebrun, Felix, from brother David, Maskinongé, April 17, 1831; and friend David Sigard, Maskinongé, April 20, 1831 ("deceased"), fols. 11–14. See also Beattie and Buss, *Undelivered Letters*, 303–9.

167. HBCA, E.31/2/2, Lebrun, Felix, from brother David, Maskinongé, April 17, 1831; and friend David Sigard, Maskinongé, April 20, 1831 ("deceased"), fols. 11–14; Lebrun, Hercule, from brother

Charles M., Maskinongé, April 18, 1831 ("deceased"), fols. 15–18; and Mauraux, Francois, from Uncle Manuelle Preville, Maskinongé, April 11, 1834, fols. 21–23. See also Beattie and Buss, *Undelivered Letters*, 303–9.

168. HBCA, E.31/2/2, St. Pierre, Olivier, from wife Nelly, Trois-Rivières, March 28, 1831, fols. 30–31. See also Beattie and Buss, *Undelivered Letters*, 299–302.

169. HBCA, E.31/2/2, Lebrun, Hercule, from brother Charles M., Maskinongé, April 18, 1831 ("deceased"), fols. 15–18; and Rose, David, from brother Jacques, Maskinongé, April 14, 1834, fols. 28–29. See also Beattie and Buss, *Undelivered Letters*, 303–9.

170. Original: "je ta sur [t'assure] Cher Enfant que tu nous cause beaucoupe d'ennui et de chagrin sur nos vieu jour de voir notre cher Enfan que nous avons tems [tant] eu de peine à Ellevé et croyant avoir du Soulagement et la consolation de lui et a present de le voir si Elloignée[.] Cher Enfan nous atû [as-tu] oublier et a tu perdu le Souvenir de notre tendress enver toi dans ta jeunesse[?] Croi moi Cher Joseph [his son], moi et ta peauvre mère te Disirons bein de te revoir en cor [encore] une foi a vant [avant] que de mourrir parce que si tu ne dessent [descends] pas bien vite tu pouroit bien pas nous voir vivant parce que nous tasurons que nos peauvre cheveux on biens blanchie de pui que tes [t'es] partie d'avec nous[.] Prand donc courage revien don nous voir Encor une foi nous te recevrons les bras oûvert et ton arrivée pouroit petaitre bien nous faire vivre ~~qu'el~~ [crossed out] quelques année de plus par la joi que tu nous Causerai de te revoir et ta peauvre Grande mère Sicard qui est agé apresent de Quatrevingt Neuf ans[.] Elle dit toujour quelle demande à Dieu de te revoir devant que de mourire et Elle tams brasse biens et Ell prie Dieu pour toi que Dieu te fase Connoitre le Devoir que tu doit a ton cher Père et Mère." HBCA, E.31/2/2, Grenier, Joseph, from parents Joseph & Marie, Ruisseau des chenes, April 20, 1831 ("deceased"), fols. 7–10. See also Mauraux, Francois, from Uncle Manuelle Preville, Maskinongé, April 11, 1834, fols. 21–23; and Benoit, Francois, from mother Marianne Dorgue, St. Ours, April 23, 1830, fols. 1–2. See also Beattie and Buss, *Undelivered Letters*, 288–89.

171. Original: "je ne Croÿ Pas que tu doute de ma Peine et de mon annui [ennui] et de mon inquietude[.] sÿ je navais Pas Craint Les reproche Jamais je naurais Consentie a ton Depart. Je nest [n'ai] aucune Consolation--toujour dans la Peine et Lannui[.] Plus je vie et Plus je manui et Plus ma Peine est Grande[.] Cante [Quand] je Pensse quil faut que je ~~pens~~ [crossed out] Passe encore deux ans sans avoire le Plessire [plaisir] de te voire je m[']en deespere [desespère] que ce tems sera Long mais infin il faut que je me Conforme a La Volontez de Dieu et vive dans Lesperance que tu viendra ausitot ton tem[p]s fini[.]" HBCA, E.31/2/2, St. Pierre, Olivier, from wife Nelly, Trois-Rivières, March 28, 1831, fols. 30–31. See also Beattie and Buss, *Undelivered Letters*, 299–300. See also Mongall, Thomas, from wife Marie St. Germain, Maskinongé, April 20, 1830, fols. 24–25.

172. HBCA, E.31/2/2, St. Pierre, Olivier, from wife Nelly, Trois-Rivières, March 28, 1831, fols. 30–31. See also Beattie and Buss, *Undelivered Letters*, 299–302.

173. HBCA, E.31/2/2, Rose, David, from brother Jacques, Maskinongé, April 14, 1834, fols. 28–29.

174. Greer, "Fur-Trade Labour," 202.

3. Rites of Passage

1. Pond, "Narrative," 29–30.
2. See Hardin, "'Ritual' in Recent Criticism."
3. Turner, "Social Dramas," 155–56.

4. Turner, *Ritual Process*, 96, 131–32.

5. Muir, *Ritual in Early Modern Europe*, 6.

6. Muir, *Ritual in Early Modern Europe*, 5.

7. Beaudoin, *L'Été dans la culture Québécoise*, 168.

8. Mackenzie, "General History," 35–36; see also LAC, MG19 A17, June 5, 1791, 15; and Henry (the Elder), *Travels and Adventures*, 16; Heriot, *Travels through the Canadas*, 248; and R. McKenzie, "'Reminiscences,'" 1:7. See also Podruchny, "*Dieu*, *Diable* and the Trickster."

9. McDonell, "Diary," May 27, 1793, 69; see also Pond, "Narrative," 29–30; and Nelson, *My First Years*, 35–36.

10. Ross, *Adventures of the First Settlers*, 171–72.

11. See Hamelin, *Histoire du Catholisme Québécois*; Moir, *Church and State in Canada*; and Jaenen, *Role of the Church*.

12. Hubert, *Sur la terre*; and Moogk, *La Nouvelle France*, 235–64.

13. See Ginzburg, *Cheese and the Worms*.

14. See K. Thomas, *Religion and the Decline of Magic*.

15. Hubert, *Sur la terre*, 40–41.

16. McBrien, "Roman Catholicism," 12:442.

17. McDonell, "Diary," August 11, 1793, 99–100.

18. See Podruchny, "Baptizing Novices."

19. Rediker asserts that sailors stripped baptism of its Christian meaning and used it to serve the ends of occupational solidarity. Rediker, *Between the Devil*, 189.

20. Henry (the Elder), *Travels and Adventures*, 25–26; Harmon, *Sixteen Years*, April 30, 1800, 11–12; Heriot, *Travels through the Canadas*, 251–52; OA, MU 1956, ca. July 23, 1813, 13–14; and OA, MU 1391, Wednesday, June 3, 1818, 6. See also map in Morse, *Fur Trade Canoe Routes*, 68.

21. Troyes, *Journal de l'Expedition*, May 15, 1686, 37 (my translation). The original French is "Nos françois ont coustume de baptiser en cet endroit ceux qui n'y ont point encore passé."

22. Geological Survey of Canada, "Chalk River."

23. OA, MU 2199, Edward Umfreville, July 22, 1784, 25; McDonell, "Diary," August 11, 1793, 99–100; and Henry (the Younger), *New Light*, July 24, 1800, 1:11. See also Nute, *Voyageur's Highway*, 48–49 and the map on 4; and Nute, *Voyageur*, 66–67.

24. Lefroy, *In Search of the Magnetic North*, Lefroy to Isabella, McKenzie's River, Fort Simpson, April 29, 1844, 116–17; and "Canada: Écoulement Fluvial."

25. Mackenzie, *Voyages from Montreal*, 89–90.

26. Franklin, *Narrative of a Journey*, 118–20.

27. Although I have not been able to find evidence for points of ritual baptism in the districts of the Saskatchewan, Missouri, Columbia, and Fraser rivers, it is possible that voyageurs ritually marked the boundaries of these regions as well.

28. For an excellent example, see Natalie Zemon Davis, "Women on Top," in Davis, *Society and Culture*.

29. *DCB* 7:552.

30. Lev. 14:4, 6, 49, 52; and Num. 19:6.

31. Heriot, *Travels through the Canadas*, 251–52.

32. Harmon, *Sixteen Years*, 12.

33. The Swiss artist Karl Bodmer, who traveled in the Upper Missouri District in the 1830s,

portrays Aboriginal men shooting guns in a ceremonial fashion in his painting "Buffalo Dance of the Mandan." In *Karl Bodmer's America*, 16–17.

34. On Aboriginal cultural borrowings by French Canadians, both material and ideological, see Delâge, "L'influence des Amérindiens."

35. For an explanation of en dérouine, see McLeod, "Diary," 144n31. For examples, see MRB, MC, C.24, December 21, 1800, 12; Nelson, *My First Years*, mid-November 1802, 65–66; and Faries, "Diary," November 19, 1804, 219.

36. For a few examples, see Franklin, *Narrative of a Journey*, February 8 and 16, 1820, 109, 112–13; OA, MU 842, September 27, 1818, 3; MRB, MC, C.13, January 1, 1800, 11 (my pagination); Henry (the Younger), *New Light*, January 1, 1801, and January 1, 1802, 1:162, 192; Franchère, *Journal of a Voyage*, 107–8; and Mackenzie, *Voyages from Montreal*, January 1, 1793, 252.

37. Podruchny, "Festivities, Fortitude and Fraternalism," 43.

38. Deloria, *Playing Indian*, 2, 14, 17–20, 25–27, 68.

39. Troyes, *Journal de l'Expedition*, May 15, 1686, 37 (my translation). Original French: "On voit du costé du nord, suivant la route, une hautte montagne dont la roche est droite et fort escarpée, le milieu en paroist noir. Cela provient peut estre de ce que les sauvages y font leaurs sacrifices jettant des flèches par dessus, au bout desquelles il attahent un petit bout de tabac. Nos françois ont coustume de baptiser en cet endroit ceux qui n'y ont point encore passé. Cette roche est nommée l'oiseau par les sauvages et quelques uns de nos gens ne voulant perdre l'ancienne coustume se jetterent de l'eau, nous fumes campés au bas du portage."

40. Sullivan, *Native American Religions*, 8, 25, 28. For an Ojibwe example, see Vecsey, *Traditional Ojibwa Religion*, 108. For Plains Cree examples, see Mandelbaum, *Plains Cree*, 186, 191, 199–203, 227–29. For comparisons of the Plains Cree with other Algonquian groups, see Mandelbaum, *Plains Cree*, 309–10. For Siouan examples, see DeMallie and Parks, introduction; and Looking Horse, "Sacred Pipe," 3–5, 67–73.

41. Meyer and Thistle, "Saskatchewan River Rendezvous Centers."

42. The role of women in fur trade society has been explored extensively. See Van Kirk, *"Many Tender Ties"*; and Brown, *Strangers in Blood*.

43. For a similar example among American whalers, see Creighton, *Rites and Passages*, 117.

44. Harmon, *Sixteen Years*, 12.

45. Rediker, *Between the Devil*, 186. See also Dening, *Mr. Bligh's Bad Language*, 71, 76–78; and Creighton, *Rites and Passages*, 117–23.

46. Harmon, *Sixteen Years*, Wednesday, April 30, 1800, 12. For other, more general comparisons of voyageurs to sailors, see Lefroy, *In Search of the Magnetic North*, Lefroy to sister Fanny, Fort William, Lake Superior, May 30, 1843, 16. For mention of voyageurs participating in the baptism at the equator while sailing on the Tonquin, see Gabriel Franchère, *Voyage to the Northwest Coast*, October 22, 1810, 16.

47. Kalm, *Voyage*, 222–23, 428.

48. For examples and discussion of the contracts, or engagements, see Lande, *Development of the Voyageur Contract*.

49. LAC, MG19 B1, William McGillivray to Peter Grant, Grand Portage, August 10, 1800, 165.

50. Cox, *Adventures on the Columbia River*, 308.

51. LAC, MG19 C1, vol. 15, July 20, 1800(?), 9–11.

52. LAC, MG19 C1, vol. 6, October 13, 1800, 55, and December 23, 1800, 73. See also Keith, *North of Athabasca*, 115, 122.

53. LAC, MG19 C1, vol. 8, November 29, 1804, 24–25. See also Keith, *North of Athabasca*, 193, 387.

54. TBR, S13, George Nelson's "Journal from Bas De La Rivière to Cumberland House, 1819–?" September 9, 1819, 6 (my pagination); Ross, *Fur Hunters*, 1:303; McDonell, "Diary," 92; OA, MU 1956, 16, 23; and TBR, S13 George Nelson's journal, November 3, 1807–August 31, 1808, June 13, 1808, 39.

55. Ross, *Fur Hunters*, 1:303; McDonell, "Diary," 92.

56. Ballantyne, *Hudson Bay*, 200.

57. Cox, *Adventures on the Columbia River*, 263.

58. Landmann, *Adventures and Recollections*, spring 1789, 1:310.

59. Dugas, *Un Voyageur des pays d'En-Haut*, 27.

60. Harmon, *Sixteen Years*, August 18, 1808, 113; Lefroy, *In Search of the Magnetic North*, Lefroy to Sabine, Fort Simpson, McKenzie's River, March 27, 1844, 99; MRB, MC, C.13, July 31, 1800, 60–61 (my pagination); and Henry (the Younger), *New Light*, August 26, 1800, 1:66. For a discussion of food preferences and customary complaining about provisions in the fur trade, see Vibert, *Traders' Tales*, 94–113.

61. Vibert, *Traders' Tales*, 179–80.

62. TBR, S13, George Nelson's diary of events, June 20, 1822 (no page numbers); Mackenzie, "General History," 52–53; and Franchère, *Journal of a Voyage*, 180–81.

63. D. Thompson, *Narrative*, 319. For similar comments, see Harmon, *Sixteen Years*, March 7, 1804, 75.

64. Lefroy, *In Search of the Magnetic North*, Lefroy to Isabella, McKenzie's River, Fort Simpson, April 29, 1844, 116–17.

65. McGillivray, *Journal*, August 18, 1794, 11.

66. Mackenzie, *Voyages from Montreal*, June 13, 1793, 325–26.

67. For a discussion of the NWC's first efforts to find an overland route to the Pacific coast, see Mackie, *Trading beyond the Mountains*, 7–12.

68. Podruchny, "Festivities, Fortitude, and Fraternalism."

69. Lytwyn, "Transportation in the Petit Nord." Alexander Mackenzie marks the portage over this height of land as 679 paces ("General History," 57).

70. Harmon, *Sixteen Years*, May 24, 1800, 17.

71. Fraser, "First Journal," May 29–31, 1806, 126; Landmann, *Adventures and Recollections*, 1:309; and Ballantyne, *Hudson Bay*, 76.

72. Pond, "Narrative," 31.

73. Cox, *Adventures on the Columbia River*, 149.

74. Cox, *Adventures on the Columbia River*, 248.

75. Nelson, *My First Years*, 41n28.

76. MRB, MC, C.1, 28.

77. Ross, *Fur Hunters*, 1:301.

78. MRB, MC, C.29, 26.

79. Kohl, *Kitchi-Gami*, 29–34.

80. McDonell, "Diary," August 21, 1793, 103.

81. Cox, *Adventures on the Columbia River*, June 29, 1812, 73.

82. McDonell, "Diary," 97n61; and Kohl, *Kitchi-Gami*, 59.

83. Heriot, *Travels through the Canadas*, 252.

84. Kohl, *Kitchi-Gami*, 336; and Roger Roulette, personal communication with author, July 2003.

85. Kohl, *Kitchi-Gami*, 336; and Lefroy, *In Search of the Magnetic North*, Fort Simpson, March 28, 1844, to his mother, 103.

86. McLeod, "Diary," 141n23; and Davidson, *North West Company*, 77.

87. Laura Murray argues that Harmon's particular ideas of "conversation" prevented him from genuine communication with voyageurs and Aboriginal peoples. See her "Fur Traders in Conversation."

88. Harmon, *Sixteen Years*, July 9, 1800, October 28, 1800, April 4, 1801, May 2, 1801, and March 6, 1802, 22, 37, 45–46, 47, 55.

89. Bakker, *Language of Our Own*, 3. See also Laverdure and Allard, *Michif Dictionary*.

90. Bakker, *Language of Our Own*, 4.

91. Cox, *Adventures on the Columbia River*, 77, 278.

92. OA, MU 2199, Edward Umfreville, July 12–13, and 22, 1784, 17–19, 25.

93. Cox, *Adventures on the Columbia River*, 237, 239, 252–53.

94. TBR, S13, George Nelson's diary of events, July 23, 24, and 27, 1822, 6, 11, and August 18–20, 1822.

95. Such as Derreaud's Rapid, named after a voyageur of that name who broke his canoe in it. McDonell, "Diary," June 24, 1783, 84.

96. Mackenzie, *Voyages from Montreal*, June 5, 1789, 138–39.

97. Cox, *Adventures on the Columbia River*, 306.

98. Cox, *Adventures on the Columbia River*, 307.

99. Kohl, *Kitchi-Gami*, 184.

100. For some examples of scholarship exploring this theme, see Turner, *Ritual Process*, chap. 3; Babcock, *Reversible World*; Burke, *Popular Culture*; and Davis, "Reasons of Misrule."

101. Harmon, *Sixteen Years*, 12.

102. Heriot, *Travels through the Canadas*, 251–52.

103. OA, MU 2199, Edward Umfreville, Thursday, July 22, 1784, 25.

104. Rediker, *Between the Devil*, 187; and Dening, *Mr. Bligh's Bad Language*, 77–78.

105. MRB, MC C.24, April 12, 1801, 32.

106. Regarding the flying of flags, see Henry (the Younger), *New Light*, October 17, 1800, 1:121. Regarding Sunday labor, see Cox, *Adventures on the Columbia River*, 307; and Lefroy, *In Search of the Magnetic North*, Lefroy to his mother, Savanne River, en route, June 6, 1843, contd. to July 1, 22.

107. Ballantyne, *Hudson Bay*, 219–20.

108. Alexander Henry the Younger wrote that he allowed his men to observe the Sabbath, which probably meant that they demanded the rite. See *New Light*, September 21, 1800, 1:101 and September 16, 1810, 2:627.

109. TBR, S13, George Nelson's journal, November 3, 1807–August 31, 1808, December 25, 1807, 14.

110. Harmon, *Sixteen Years*, December 25, 1802, December 25, 1803, and December 25, 1806, 65, 71, 102–3.

111. OA, MU 1956, 7.

112. Ross, *Fur Hunters*, 2:239.

113. Ross, *Fur Hunters*, 2:244–47, 248.

114. Nelson, *My First Years*, 37–38; and Kohl, *Kitchi-Gami*, 262–63. This anecdote is part of a much

longer story about Jean Cadieux and his song "The Little Rock." See chap. 4, 206–7.

115. Ross, *Fur Hunters*, 2:244–47, 248.

116. Cox, *Adventures on the Columbia River*, 173–75.

117. LAC, MG19 A17, 29–30.

118. Nelson, *My First Years*, 39.

119. For an extensive discussion of the mingling of stories about windigos and werewolves, see Podruchny, "Werewolves and Windigos."

120. TBR, S13, George Nelson's journal and reminiscences, fall 1803, 51. See also Nelson, *My First Years*, 153.

121. See Ahenakew, "Cree Trickster Tales"; Radin and Reagan, "Ojibwa Myths and Tales"; Radin, *Trickster*; Makarius, "Crime of Manabozo"; Vecsey, *Traditional Ojibwa Religion*, 84–100; Carroll, "Trickster as Selfish Buffoon"; and Louis Bird, personal communication with author, spring 2000; and see http://www.uwinnipeg.ca/academic/ic/rupert/bird/bio2.html.

122. Cox, *Adventures on the Columbia River*, 161–62; Gates, *Five Fur Traders*, 71n10; Harmon, *Journal of Voyages*, 6, 9; McDonell, "Diary," July 5, 1793, 90; and Harmon, *Sixteen Years*, May 15 and 16, 1800, 15.

123. Harmon, *Sixteen Years*, Saturday, May 24, 1800, 17.

124. Ross, *Fur Hunters*, 2:204; and Franchère, *Journal of a Voyage*, May 25, 1814, 164.

125. McDonell, "Diary," June 24, 1793, 87; Landmann, *Adventures and Recollections*, 1:307; and R. McKenzie, "'Reminiscences,'" 1:8–9.

126. McDonell, "Diary," June 24, 1783, 84.

127. Cox, *Adventures on the Columbia River*, 145; and Harmon, *Sixteen Years*, May 11, 1812, 152.

128. MRB, MC, C113, December 17, 1799, 8–9 (my pagination).

129. McDonell, "Diary," May 27, 1793, 69.

130. Ross, *Fur Hunters*, 2:125.

131. TBR, S13, George Nelson's journal, November 3, 1807–August 31, 1808, July 14, 1808, 47.

132. James McKenzie, Extracts from his journal, 1799–1800, Athabasca District, in Masson, *Les Bourgeois*, February 11, 1800, 2:385–86.

133. TBR, S13, George Nelson's Journal, September 1, 1808–March 31, 1810, September 3, 1809, 36 (my pagination).

4. It Is the Paddle That Brings Us

1. Barbeau, *Jongleur Songs*, 138–41, my translation. See also *Guide des parcours canotables du Québec*, vol. 2.

2. Kohl, *Kitchi-Gami*, 254.

3. French title is "Mon Canot d'Écorce." See Massicotte and Barbeau, "Chants populaires du Canada," 78–79. English translation taken from Nute, *Voyageur*, 28–30.

4. French title is "Petit Roche." Barbeau, "La Complainte de Cadieux." This is part of the story mentioned in chapter 3 of the Virgin Mary appearing to guide a canoe over rapids to escape the Iroquois.

5. French titles are "À la claire fountaine" and "Voici Le Printemps." See Nute, *Voyageur*, 105–7, 110–11. See also Gibbon, *Canadian Folk Songs*.

6. See Wood, *The Degradation of Work?*; Kusterer, *Know-How on the Job*; Heron and Storey, *On the Job*; and Radforth, "Shantymen."

7. Greer, *Peasant, Lord, and Merchant*, 33.

8. Landmann, *Adventures and Recollections*, 1:309.

9. Rochefoucauld Liancourt, *Travels through the United States*, 293.

10. Cox, *Adventures on the Columbia River*, 202.

11. Back, *Narrative of the Arctic Land Expedition*, 33.

12. McKenny, *Sketches of a Tour*, 210; and Ballantyne, *Hudson Bay*, 255.

13. Kennicott, "Robert Kennicott," 193, as cited by Nute, *Voyageur*, 104.

14. Jameson, *Winter Studies*, 3:321.

15. Rochefoucauld Liancourt, *Travels through the United States*, 293.

16. Barbeau, "Ermatinger Collection of Voyageur Songs," 147. Grace Lee Nute cited some alternate endings to the songs "À la Claire Fontaine" and "J'ai Trop Grand Peur des Loups [I am very afraid of those Wolves]" that do not necessarily tell us anything in particular about voyageurs, but they make clear that voyageurs could easily change parts of the lyrics. Nute, *Voyageur*, 107–8.

17. Moore, *Epistles, Odes, and Other Poems*, 231. In a letter to his mother, dated September 16, 1804, Moore wrote, "[T]ell Kate I have learnt some of the '*Chansons des Voyageurs*' in coming down the St. Lawrence, which I hope before three months, at the utmost, to sing for her." See letter 98 in Moore, *Letters*, 80.

18. Moore, *Rapids*.

19. Frank B. Mayer, "Frank B. Mayer and the Treaties of 1851" (Mayer's diary, July 23–August 23), in Mayer, *With Pen and Pencil*, 220–21.

20. Chicago, Newberry Library, Oversize Ayer Art, Mayer Sketchbook #43, 49. For another mention of "chansons du nord," see Mayer, "Frank B. Mayer and the Treaties of 1851," 232.

21. Now known as the Library and Archives Canada. See LAC, R7712-0-7-E.

22. In "The Ermatinger Collection of Voyageur Songs," Barbeau cites Ermatinger, "Edward Ermatinger's York Factory Express Journal."

23. Kohl, *Kitchi-Gami*, 254–55.

24. Kohl, *Kitchi-Gami*, 257.

25. Béland, *Chansons de voyageurs*.

26. LaRue, "Les chansons populaires." See also Nute, *Voyageur*, 151–53.

27. In its first four years Fort William was called Fort Kaministiquia because it was built on the Kaministiquia River, but it was renamed to honour of William McGillivray, who replaced Simon McTavish as the head of the North West Company in 1804. Campbell, *North West Company*, 128, 138, 160.

28. Lytwyn, "Transportation in the Petit Nord"; Innis, *Fur Trade in Canada*, 222; Skinner, "Sinews of Empire," 200–205; and Rich, *Fur Trade and the Northwest*, 188.

29. For a detailed description of this route, see Morse, *Fur Trade Canoe Routes*, 48–70.

30. For drainage systems, see "Canada: Écoulement Fluvial." For fur trade routes in the interior, see Ray, Moodie, and Heidenreich, "Rupert's Land"; Moodie, Lytwyn, Kaye, and Ray, "Competition and Consolidation"; and Moodie, Kaye, and Lytwyn, "Fur Trade Northwest to 1870."

31. Lytwyn, *Fur Trade of the Little North*, v; and Lytwyn, "Transportation in the Petit Nord."

32. For a detailed description of canoe routes in the area between Lake Superior and Lake Winnipeg, see Nute, *Voyageur's Highway*, 11–18; and Skinner, "Sinews of Empire," 282–96.

33. Morse, *Fur Trade Canoe Routes*, 20.

34. Nute, *Voyageur*, 24.

35. MRB, MC, C.20, 7, Monk, "Description of Northern Minnesota," 33; and Curot, "Wisconsin Fur Trader's Journal," May 18 and 20, 1804, 468.

36. See Kemp, "Impact of Weather and Climate."

37. P. Grant, "Sauteux Indians about 1804," 2:313–14.

38. Skinner, "Sinews of Empire," 217.

39. McDonell, "Diary," July 5, 1793, 90 and 72n12.

40. Morse, *Fur Trade Canoe Routes*, 20.

41. Rich, *Fur Trade and the Northwest*, 189.

42. Heriot, *Travels through the Canadas*, 246–48.

43. Landmann, *Adventures and Recollections*, 1:167–69.

44. MacGregor, *John Rowand*, 3.

45. Henry (the Younger), *New Light*, 2:509.

46. TBR, S13, George Nelson's diary of events, June 3–July 11, 1822, June 20, 1822.

47. Nute, *Voyageur*, 29–31. Her translation to English. Original French title: "Mon Canot D'Écorce." Original French lyrics: "Dans mon canot d'écorce, assis à la fraiche' du / temps, Où j'ai bravé tout' les tempêtes les grandes eaux / du Saint Laurent; Car j'ai bravé tout' les tempêstes les / grandes eaux du Saint Laurent. Mon canot est fait d'écorce fines / Qu'on pleume sur les bouleaux blancs; / Les coutures sont faites de racines, / Les avirons de bois blancs. / Je prends mon canot, je le lance / A travers les rapides, les bouillons. / Là, à grands pas il s'avance. / Il ne laisse j mais le courant. / C'est quand je viens sur le portage, je prends mon canot sur mon dos. / Je le renverse dessus ma tête: c'est ma cabane pour la nuit. / J'ai parcouru le long des rives, tout le long du fleuve Saint-Laurent / J'ai connu les tribus sauvage et leurs languages différents. / Tu es mon compagnon de voyage!/ Je veux mourir dans mon canot. Sur le tompeau, près du rivage, / Vous renversez mon canot. / Le laboureur aime sa charrue, le chasseur son fusil, son chien: / Le musicien aime sa musique; moi, mon canot, c'est [tout] mon bien!"

48. Mackenzie, "General History," 35; Innis, *Fur Trade in Canada*, 222; and Delâge, "L'influence des Amérindiens," 111.

49. LAC, MG24 H1, 3.

50. McKenny, *Sketches of a Tour*, July 8, 1826, 201; and Innis, *Fur Trade in Canada*, 22.

51. On purchasing canoes, see Mackenzie, "General History," 53; Henry (the Younger), *New Light*, July 26, 1800, 1:14; and Landmann, *Adventures and Recollections*, June 3, 1800, 2:168.

52. McGillivray, *Journal*, August 2, 1794, 6.

53. OA, MU 572, Duncan Clark Papers, vol. 2, R. McKenzie, Pic, to Duncan Clark, Long Lake, May 1, 1825, 3 (in the note at the bottom).

54. Fraser, "First Journal," May 21–22, 1806, 122.

55. Nelson, *My First Years*, September 3, 1803, 105.

56. TBR, S13, George Nelson's journal, August 29, 1805–March 8, 1806, September 12, 1805, 2 (my pagination).

57. For a description of canoe construction, see Franks, *Canoe and White Water*, 9; and Kent, *Birchbark Canoes*, 116–47.

58. Harmon, *Sixteen Years*, July 15, 1800, 23. On a trip from Grand Portage to Fort des prairies (Fort Charlotte) in summer 1800, two canoes carried a ton and a half burden each, staffed with six men.

59. Landmann, *Adventures and Recollections*, spring 1798, 1:303; LAC, MG24 H1, 1; McKenny, *Sketches of a Tour*, 199–200; Morse, *Fur Trade Canoe Routes*, 22–4; and Franks, *Canoe and White Water*, 18–20.

60. P. Grant, "Sauteux Indians about 1804," 2:313–14.

61. Mackenzie, "General History," 35, 54. For a detailed discussion of bills of lading, see B. M. White, "Montreal Canoes and Their Cargoes"; and Winterburn, "Lac La Pluie Bills of Lading, 1806–1809."

62. McDonell, "Diary," May 1793, 67–68 and 88n45; and Mackenzie, "General History," 35.

63. Mackenzie, "General History," 35, 54. Also see Weld, *Travels through the States*, 1:319.

64. Landmann, *Adventures and Recollections*, 1:303–4. See also TBR, S13, George Nelson's journal "No. 1," 7.

65. McDonell, "Diary," May 1793, 67–68; and OA, MU 1391, May 17, 1818, 1.

66. Harmon, *Sixteen Years*, April 29–30, 1800, 11–12.

67. Landmann, *Adventures and Recollections*, 1:304–5.

68. Heriot, *Travels through the Canadas*, 1790, 246–48.

69. Nelson, *My First Years*, July 13, 1803, 96; and Landmann, *Adventures and Recollections*, spring 1798, 1:304–5.

70. Franchère, *Journal of a Voyage*, May 24, 1810, 44.

71. Franchère, *Voyage to the Northwest Coast*, June 20, 1814, 272.

72. TBR, S13, George Nelson's diary of events on a journey, June 3, 1822; Harmon, *Sixteen Years*, July 26, 1808, 111; and TBR, S13, George Nelson's journal, August 29, 1805–March 8, 1806, August 29, 1805, 1 (my pagination).

73. For examples, see Nelson, *My First Years*, July 13, 1803, and May 23, 1804, 95–96, 167–68. Michilimackinac to Rivière des Saulteaux, July 1803, in a "Michilimackinac canoe," one clerk, one interpreter, three men; return trip from Rivière des Saulteaux to Grand Portage, May 1804, in two canoes, ten people, four men, one clerk, two women, two children, and one Aboriginal person.

74. TBR, S13, George Nelson's diary of events, June 20, 1822.

75. Ross, *Fur Hunters*, 1:78.

76. Cox, *Adventures on the Columbia River*, June 29, 1812, and August 5, 1814, 72, 160.

77. Franchère, *Voyage to the Northwest Coast*, April 4, 1814, 199.

78. Cox, *Adventures on the Columbia River*, 236–37.

79. Henry (the Younger), *New Light*, August 21, 1800, 1:49–52.

80. TBR, S13, George Nelson's coded journal, April 17–October 20, 1821, May 30, 1821, 24–26.

81. In September 1800 six canoes set out from Fort Chipweyan, three bound for the Mackenzie River, one for Marten Lake, and two for Slave Lake; each canoe had four to five men. LAC, MG19 C1, vol. 6, September 29, 1800, 50; and MRB, MC, C.26, September 29, 1800, 1. See also Keith, *North of Athabasca*, 112, 129–30. For other examples, see Henry (the Younger), *New Light*, July 8 and September 24, 1810, 2:610, 629–30. Barry Gough translates *ducent* as conductor, bowman, or headman. See his edition of Henry (the Younger), *Journal*, 1:23n42.

82. For example, in May 1813 Stuart, six Canadians, and two Aboriginal people embarked aboard two canoes, with a small assortment of goods (for pocket money) and provisions for a month and a half, to find a water route to the Columbia and to build up the coastal trade. Harmon, *Sixteen Years*, May 13, 1813, 259.

83. MRB, MC, C.5, July 26 and August 7, 1806, 75, 79; Henry (the Younger), *New Light*, July 7 and 14, 1806, 1:185–88, 304; and Larocque, "Yellowstone Journal," 184.

84. Mackenzie, "General History," 135–36, 265, 325–26.

85. Fraser, "First Journal," April 13, 1806, and May 11, 14, and 17, 1806, 109, 118–20.

86. Mackenzie, "General History," 54.

87. Henry (the Younger), *New Light*, August 11, 1800, 1:30–31.

88. For one example, see McGillivray, *Journal*, August 24, 1794, 12.

89. TBR, S13, George Nelson's diary of events, June 22 and 23, 1822.

90. Ballantyne, *Hudson Bay*, 245.

91. TBR, S13, George Nelson's journal, November 3, 1807–August 31, 1808, June 28 and 30 and July 1–7, 1808, 44–46.

92. TBR, S13, George Nelson's journal, September 1, 1808–March 31, 1810, September 1–2, 1808, 1 (my pagination).

93. Harmon, *Sixteen Years*, July 22 and 25, 1800, 25–26. For other examples, see Henry (the Younger), *New Light*, July 26, 1800, 1:14; Cox, *Adventures on the Columbia River*, July 30, 1817, 280; and TBR, S13, George Nelson's diary of events, June 17, 1822.

94. TBR, S13, George Nelson's journal, September 1, 1808–March 31, 1810, June 25 and 29 and July 4, 1809, 26–27 (my pagination).

95. OA, MU 572, Duncan Clark Papers, vol. 2, R. McKenzie, Fort William, to Duncan Clark, Pic, June 11, 1825, 1–3.

96. McDonell, "Diary," June 1, 1793, 72.

97. Franchère, *Journal of a Voyage*, May 24, 1810, 44.

98. Landmann, *Adventures and Recollections*, June 3, 1800, 2:167–68.

99. McDonell, "Diary," June 27, 1783, 88.

100. TBR, S13, George Nelson's journal and reminiscences, December 1, 1825–September 13, 1836, August 12, 1803, 35.

101. See appropriate entries in Trigger, *Northeast*. On the Christian reserves that came to be called the Seven Nations, see Sawaya, *La Fédération*; Delâge, "Les Iroquois chrétiens; Trigger, *Natives and Newcomers*, 292–96; Richter, *Ordeal of the Longhouse*, 119–28; and Dechêne, *Habitants and Merchants*, 6–8.

102. Perrot, *Indian Tribes*, 1:174–75, 210–20; Dechêne, *Habitants and Merchants*, 10; and Greer, *People of New France*, chapter on "French and Others."

103. See Dechêne, *Habitants and Merchants*, 117–24; Greer, *Peasant, Lord, and Merchant*, 177–93; Charbonneau, Desjardins, and Beauchamp, "Le comportement démographique"; and Skinner, "Sinews of Empire," 345–71.

104. Cox, *Adventures on the Columbia River*, September 15, 1817, 299–300.

105. McDonell, "Diary," June 1, 1793, 72.

106. MHS, P791, folder 7, 1–2, NWC Letters, 1798–1816, Dominique Rousseau and Joseph Bailley v. Duncan McGillivray (originals from the Judicial Archives of Montreal); MRB, MC, C.24, May 6, 1801, 36; and Henry (the Younger), *New Light*, June 28, 1803, 1:219.

107. OA, MU 1391, June 6, 1818, 7.

108. TBR, S13, George Nelson's "Journal from Bas De La Rivière to Cumberland House, 1819–?" September 1–4, 1819, 4–5 (my pagination).

109. Mayer, *With Pen and Pencil*, 232.

110. Back, *Narrative of the Arctic Land Expedition*, 38–9.

111. Pond, "Narrative," 30.

112. For one example, see LAC, MG19 C1, vol. 14, April 7 and 8, 1800, 22.

113. LAC, MG19 C1, vol. 14, April 9, 1800, 22; Nelson, *My First Years*, May 23, 1804, 157–58; TBR, S13, George Nelson's journal, November 3, 1807–August 31, 1808, June 27 1808, 44; LAC, MG19 C1, vol. 6, August 6, 1800, 48; and Keith, *North of Athabasca*, 111.

114. Henry (the Younger), *New Light*, August 14, 1800, 1:35–36; LAC, MG19 C1, vol. 6 , May 16, 1800, 21; and Keith, *North of Athabasca*, 97.

115. LAC, MG19 C1, vol. 6, October 9, 1800, 54; Keith, *North of Athabasca*, 114; and TBR, S13, George Nelson's journal, November 3, 1807–August 31, 1808, June 13, 1808, 39–40.

116. OA, MU 1956, 9, recorded starting out at 4 a.m.; TBR, S13, George Nelson's "Journal from Bas De La Rivière to Cumberland House, 1819–?" September 4, 1819, 5 (my pagination), recorded starting off in the middle of the night; TBR, S13, George Nelson's diary of events, June 18, 1822; and Henry (the Younger), *New Light*, September 3, 1808, 2:486, recording starting out at 4 a.m.

117. Lefroy, *In Search of the Magnetic North*, Lefroy to Julia, Lac des Chats, Ottawa River, May 6, 1843, and Lefroy to Younghusband, Sault Ste. Marie, May 20, 1843, 10, 13.

118. OA, MU 1391, June 3–9, 1818, 5–8.

119. Fraser, "First Journal," May 30 to June 5, 1806, 126–28.

120. Landmann, *Adventures and Recollections*, 2:309.

121. Ross, *Fur Hunters*, 1:303. Landman records a case where voyageurs paddled for twenty-five hours straight, ostensibly because the shores were too infested with snakes for the crew to stop and camp (in *Adventures and Recollections*, 2:69–70).

122. Wallace, *Documents*, Benjamin and Joseph Frobisher to General Haldimand, October 4, 1784, 73–74.

123. Ray, *Indians in the Fur Trade*, 128–34.

124. Sprenger, "Métis Nation," 128, 131.

125. McGillivray, *Journal*, September 18, 1794, 23–24.

126. Henry (the Younger), *New Light*, September 1, 1808, 2:485.

127. Fraser, "Journal of a Voyage," May 22, 1808, 1; and Henry (the Younger), *New Light*, August 22, 1800, 1:58.

128. McDonell, "Diary," 77; McGillivray, *Journal*, lii; and TBR, S13, George Nelson's diary of events, Monday, June 17, 1822.

129. Henry (the Younger), *New Light*, August 30, 1808, 2:482.

130. OA, MU 842, September 23 and 24, 1818, 2; TBR, S13, George Nelson's journal, September 1, 1808–March 31, 1810, September 15, 1808, 3 (my pagination); and Harmon, *Sixteen Years*, October 16, 1800, 35.

131. TBR, S13, George Nelson's diary of events, June 9 and 10, 1822.

132. TBR, S13, George Nelson's diary of events, June 9, 1822; and Fraser, "First Journal," April 24, 1806, 113.

133. Henry (the Younger), *New Light*, August 26, 1800, 1:66. See also Vibert, *Traders' Tales*, 173–80.

134. Henry (the Younger), *New Light*, September 5, 1800, 1:85; and Harmon, *Sixteen Years*, October 15, 1800, 35; and TBR, S13, George Nelson's diary of events, June 26, 1822.

135. LAC, MG19, C1, vol. 1, August 22, 1797, 5.

136. Cox, *Adventures on the Columbia River*, 242.

137. McGillivray, *Journal*, September 12, 1794, 22.

138. Fraser, "First Journal," April 17, 1806, 111.

139. For examples of purchasing food from Aboriginal peoples, see Fraser, "First Journal," April 17 and 23, 1806, 111–12.

140. Henry (the Younger), *New Light*, August 26, 1800, 1:62; and TBR, S13, George Nelson's "Journal from Bas De La Rivière to Cumberland House, 1819–?" September 4, 1819, 5 (my pagination).

141. OA, MU 1391, June 6, 1818, 7.

142. Henry (the Younger), *New Light*, September 5 and 6, 1800, 1:85.

143. Henry (the Younger), *New Light*, September 5, 1800, 1:85.

144. TBR, S13, George Nelson's diary of events, July 7, 1822.

145. Fraser, "First Journal," Thursday, April 24, 1806, 113; and LAC, MG19 A9, vol. 5, June 3, 1808, 31.

146. TBR, S13, George Nelson's diary of events, June 21, 1822; and LAC, MG19 A9, vol. 5, June 2, 1808, 20.

147. Fraser, "First Journal," April 21 and June 7 and 23, 1806, 112, 129, 132.

148. TBR, S13, George Nelson's journal, 29 August 1805–8 March 1806, September 6 and 8, 1805, 2 (my pagination); and LAC,MG19 C1, vol. 2, October 11, 1803, 10.

149. OA, MU 842, September 24, 1818, 2.

150. For instances of eating in canoes, see Nelson, *My First Years*, 41–42; and McGillivray, *Journal*, September 18, 1794, 23–24. Reports of eating while performing other activities appear in OA, MU 1956, July 8 and 22, 1813, 7, 10.

151. Ross, *Fur Hunters*, 1:302.

152. TBR, S13, George Nelson's diary of events, June 28, 1822; Ross, *Fur Hunters*, 1:302–3; and Heriot, *Travels through the Canadas*, 1791, 252.

153. Fraser, "First Journal," May 29, 1806, 126.

154. For mealtimes of twenty minutes, see Ross, *Fur Hunters*, 1:302. For mealtimes of one and a half hours, see Fraser, "First Journal," June 25, 1806, 103.

155. D. Thompson, "Journal, November 1797," December 10, 1797, 103.

156. Henry (the Younger), *New Light*, September 2, 1808, 2:486.

157. Both of these positions were referred to as the *bout*, but the term has also been used to refer to paddlers in general.

158. Ross, *Fur Hunters*, 2:186.

159. TBR, S13, George Nelson's journal, August 29, 1805–March 8, 1806, August 29, 1805, 1 (my pagination); OA, reel MS65, Donald McKay, journal from January 1805 to June 1806, June 29 and July 11, 1805, 22, 24 (my pagination); TBR, S13, George Nelson's journal, November 3, 1807–August 31, 1808, June 19, 1808, 42; and TBR, S13, George Nelson's journal, September 1, 1808–March 31, 1810, September 1, 1808, 1 (my pagination).

160. TBR, S13, George Nelson's diary of events, July 10, 1822.

161. OA, MU 1956, July 22, 1813, 9.

162. For an example of engaging a freeman as a guide, see OA MU 2199, Edward Umfreville, June 28, 1784, 10. For examples of engaging Aboriginal people as guides, see Nelson, *My First Years*, August 30 and September 3, 1803, 105; Mackenzie, *Voyages from Montreal*, June 24 and July 8, 1789, 150, 173; Ross, *Fur Hunters*, 1:63–65; and Fraser, "First Journal," May 15, 1806, 120.

163. See chapter 2.

164. P. Grant, "Sauteux Indians about 1804," 2:313–14.

165. Nelson, *My First Years*, August 22, 1803, 103; and Fraser, "First Journal," July 7, 1806, 139–40.

166. Nelson, *My First Years*, 41–42.

167. MRB, MC, C.26, September 4, 1800, 2.

168. Heriot, *Travels through the Canadas*, 247; and P. Grant, "Sauteux Indians about 1804," 2:313.

169. Kohl, *Kitchi-Gami*, 255–56.

170. Creighton, *Rites and Passages*, 131.

171. Franklin, *Narrative of a Journey*, March 6, 1820, 116.

172. Cox, *Adventures on the Columbia River*, September 12, 1817, 298; Ross, *Fur Hunters*, 1:302–3; Franchère, *Voyage to the Northwest Coast*, July 14, 1814, 264; and Lefroy, *In Search of the Magnetic North*, Lefroy to his mother, Fort Chipewyan, Lake Athabasca, September 30, 1843, to January 2, 1844, 63.

173. See the sketch of a sail in use on a York boat in Morse, *Fur Trade Canoe Routes*, 45.

174. P. Grant, "Sauteux Indians about 1804," 2:314. Also see Nelson, *My First Years*, 41–42.

175. TBR, S13, George Nelson's diary of events, June 13, 1822. See also Ross, *Fur Hunters*, 2:238–39.

176. Morse, *Fur Trade Canoe Routes*, 66.

177. Henry (the Younger), *New Light*, August 30, 1808, 2:482.

178. For examples of pipes referring to small parts of a day's journey, see Fraser, "First Journal," May 29–31, 1806, 126; Landmann, *Adventures and Recollections*, 1:309; Ballantyne, *Hudson Bay*, 76; and Jameson, *Winter Studies*, 3:319–20.

179. Kohl, *Kitchi-Gami*, 59.

180. McDonell, "Diary," 97n61.

181. P. Grant, "Sauteux Indians about 1804," 2:313–14.

182. MacDonald, *Peace River*, 44.

183. Nute, *Voyageur*, 47.

184. *JR*, 7:111, Paul Le Jeune, Relation of 1634.

185. See Leblanc, "*Une jolie cincture*", 30, 34–36, 41–57.

186. MRB, MC, C.6, 34–36.

187. Landmann, *Adventures and Recollections*, 1:305. See also Heriot, *Travels through the Canadas*, 251.

188. P. Grant, "Sauteux Indians about 1804," 2:313–14.

189. Lefroy, *In Search of the Magnetic North*, Lefroy to his mother, Savanne River, en route, June 6, 1843, 22.

190. TBR, S13, George Nelson's diary of events, June 27, 1822.

191. P. Grant, "Sauteux Indians about 1804," 2:313.

192. Mackenzie, "General History," 51.

193. MRB, MC, C.7, May 30, 1795, 36.

194. Lefroy, *In Search of the Magnetic North*, Lefroy to his mother, Savanne River, en route, June 6, 1843, 19.

195. McGillivray, *Journal*, July 21, 1794, 3; and Henry (the Younger), *New Light*, July 23, 1800, 1:10.

196. Nelson, *My First Years*, September 16, 1803, 110; TBR, S13, George Nelson's diary of events, June 22 and July 4, 1822; and OA, MU 1956, July 18 and 23, 1813, 4–7, 12.

197. Morse, *Fur Trade Canoe Routes*, 7; and Skinner, "Sinews of Empire," 221.

198. Lefroy, *In Search of the Magnetic North*, Lefroy to Sophia, Norway House, August 8, 1843, 47–48.

199. P. Grant, "Sauteux Indians about 1804," 2:313–14.

200. Landmann, *Adventures and Recollections*, 1:308.

201. Fraser, "Journal of a Voyage," June 1, 1808, 6–7.

202. Lefroy, *In Search of the Magnetic North*, Lefroy to Sophia, Norway House, August 8, 1843, 47.

203. Lefroy, *In Search of the Magnetic North*, Lefroy to Sophia, Norway House, August 8, 1843, 47.

204. P. Grant, "Sauteux Indians about 1804," 2:313–14.

205. For one example, see Fraser, "First Journal," May 27 and 28, 1806, 124–25.

206. Weld, *Travels through the States*, 1:319; and McDonell, "Diary," Monday, September 16, 1793, 112.

207. Fraser, "First Journal," May 30 and July 6, 1806, 126, 139.

208. TBR, S13, George Nelson's journal, September 1, 1808–March 31, 1810, June 25, 1809, 26 (my pagination).

209. For a few of the many examples of stopping to gum the canoes, see OA, MU 1956, July 18, 1813, 7; Henry (the Younger), *New Light*, September 3, 1808, 2:486; Nelson, *My First Years*, August 7, 1803, 101; and TBR, S13, George Nelson's diary of events, June 7 and 14, 1822.

210. Heriot, *Travels through the Canadas*, 1790, 247.

211. Nelson, *My First Years*, September 21, 1803, 111.

212. TBR, S13, George Nelson's "Journal from Bas De La Rivière to Cumberland House, 1819–?" September 4, 1819, 5 (my pagination); and McDonell, "Diary," June 6, 1793, 76.

213. Henry (the Younger), *New Light*, July 24, 1800, 1:12.

214. LAC, MG19 C1, vol. 1, August 24, 1797; and Henry (the Younger), *New Light*, August 14, 1800, 1:35–36.

215. Henry (the Younger), *New Light*, July 22, 24–26 and August 3, 8–9, 16, 22, 25, 1800, 1:10–11, 13–14, 20, 28–29, 38, 57, 62.

216. OA, MU 2199, Umfreville, June 22, 1784, 7.

217. Fraser, "First Journal," May 22–25, 29, 30 and June 1, 3, 1806, 122–27.

218. Nelson, *My First Years*, 35–36.

219. Henry (the Younger), *New Light*, July 27 and 29, 1800, 1:14–15.

220. MRB, MC, C.7, May 30, 1795, 36; TBR, S13, George Nelson's diary of events, June 7, 1822; and Fraser, "First Journal," April 23–26 [skipped 25] and May 7 and 11, 1806, 113–14, 116, 118.

221. Henry (the Younger), *New Light*, August 17, 1800, 1:39–40.

222. Nute, *Voyageur*, 151–53. My translation; French lyrics: "Quand un chrétien se détermine / A voyager, / Faut bien penser qu'il se destine / A des dangers. / Mille fois à ses yeux la mort / Par son image, / Mille fois il maudit son sort / Dans le cours du voyage. / Ami, veux-tu voyager sur l'onde / De tous les vents? / Les flots et la tempête grondent / Cruellement. / Les vagues changent tous les jours, / Et il est écrit: / Que l'image de ton retour / Est l'image de ta vie. / Quand tu seras sur ces traverses, / Pauvre affigé, / Un coup de vent vient qui t'exerce / Avec danger. / Prenant et poussant ton aviron / Contre la lame, / Tu es ici près du démon, / Qui guette ta pauvre âme. / Quand tu seras sur le rivage, / Las de nager, / Si tu veux faire un bon usage / De ce danger, / Va prier Dieu dévotement, / Avec Marie. / Mais promets--lui sincèrement / De réformer ta vie. / Si, le soir, l'essaim de mouches / Pique trop fort, / Dans un berceau tu te couches, / Pense à la mort. / Apprends que ce petit berceau / Te fait comprendre / Que c'est l'image du tombeau, / Où ton corps doit se rendre. / Si les maringouins te réveillent / De leurs chansons, / Ou te chatouillent l'oreille / De leurs aiguillons. / Apprends, cher voyageur, alors, / Que c'est le diable / Qui chante tout autour de ton corps / Pour avoir ta pauvre âme. / Quand tu seras dans ces rapides / Très-dangereux, / Ah! prie la Vierge Marie, / Fais-lui des vœux. / Alors lance-toi dans ce flots / Avec hardiesse, / Et puis dirige ton

canot / Avec beaucoup d'adresse. / Quand tu seras dans les portages, / Pauvre engagé, / Les sueurs te couleront du visage, / Pauvre affigé. / Loin de jurer, si tu me crois, / Dans la colère, / Pense à Jésus portant sa croix, / Il a monté au Calvaire. / Ami, veux-tu marcher par terre, / Dans ces grands bois, / Les sauvages te feront la guerre, / En vrais sournois. / Si tu veux braver leur fureur, / Sans plus attendre, / Prie alors de tout ton cœur, / Ton ange de te défendre."

223. John Henry Lefroy records several near disasters in his travels through Rupert's Land with voyageurs in the 1840s. For one example, see Lefroy, *In Search of the Magnetic North*, Lefroy to his mother, Savanne River, en route, June 6, 1843, 24–25. See also OA, MU 1956, July 18, 1813, 6; and Harmon, *Sixteen Years*, August 5, 1800, 28.

224. TBR, 917.11 F671; and LAC, MG19, A9, Simon Fraser Collection, vol. 6. Published in Masson, *Les Bourgeois*, vol. 1; and in Fraser, *Letters and Journals*, June 1, 1808, 6–7.

225. Fraser, "Journal of a Voyage," June 4, 1808, 10.

226. Fraser, "Journal of a Voyage," June 9, 1808, 12.

227. McGillivray, *Journal*, September 10, 1794, 21.

228. Henry (the Younger), *New Light*, September 1–3, 1808, 2:485–86.

229. Kohl, *Kitchi-Gami*, 257–61.

230. Rediker, *Between the Devil*, 189.

231. Radforth, "Shantymen," 225.

232. Barbeau, "La Complainte de Cadieux," 163; and Nute, *Voyageur*, 148–50.

233. Duncan, *Travels through Part of the United States and Canada*, 2:121–22; see also Heriot, *Travels through the Canadas*, 247.

5. The Theater of Hegemony

1. Ballantyne, *Hudson Bay*, 191–92.

2. See Greer, *Patriots and the People*, 107–13; Hall, *Archaeology of the Soul*, 107–8; and Ridington and Hastings, *Blessing for a Long Time*, 1–3, 53–54, 66–67, 68–106.

3. Gramsci, *Selections from the Prison Notebooks*; and Thurston, "Hegemony."

4. For a discussion of cultural hegemony and the consent of the masses to be ruled, see Lears, "Concept of Cultural Hegemony," 568–70.

5. Edith Burley also found that the relationship between masters and servants in the HBC was constantly subject to negotiation. Burley, *Servants of the Honourable Company*, 110–11.

6. E. P. Thompson, *Customs in Common*, 85–86.

7. E. P. Thompson, *Customs in Common*, 7.

8. E. P. Thompson, *Customs in Common*, 8, 46.

9. Franklin, *Narrative of a Journey*, October 2, 1819, 40; Kane, *Wanderings*, 236; Nute, *Voyageur*, 67; and Nute, *Voyageur's Highway*, 49.

10. Ross, *Adventures of the First Settlers*, May 2, 1811, 78–79.

11. Greer, *Patriots and the People*, 107–13.

12. Van Gennep, *Le Folklore du Daphiné*, 1:300–301. Also cited in Greer, *Patriots and the People*, 111. For the European roots to maypole ceremonies in Canada, Greer cites Arnold Van Gennep, *Manuel de folklore français contemporain*, vol. 1, pt. 4, 1516–75; and Ozouf, *La fête révolutionnaire*, 293.

13. Greer, *Patriots and the People*, 112.

14. See, for example, Brown, "Dwellings and Households along the Berens River [1935–36]," in Hallowell, *Ojibwa of Berens River*, 102–7.

15. Kohl, *Kitchi-Gami*, 10.

16. Ridington and Hastings, *Blessing for a Long Time*, xvii.

17. Henry (the Younger), *New Light*, 1:269 and 2:507, 640, 662.

18. Hind, *Narrative of the Canadian Red River*, 489.

19. Nute, "Journey for Frances," *The Beaver* (Summer 1954), 17. For the rest of the published excerpts of Frances Simpson's diary, see *The Beaver* (December 1953), 50–59, and (March 1954), 12–17.

20. Van Kirk, *"Many Tender Ties,"* 204.

21. Kane, *Wanderings*, 236.

22. Nevins, *Narrative*, 90–91.

23. McDonell, "Diary," August 16, 1793, 102.

24. Franklin, *Narrative of a Journey*, 40.

25. Ross, *Fur Hunters*, 2:242.

26. Morris, *Treaties of Canada*, 157.

27. G. M. Grant, *Ocean to Ocean*, 196.

28. Nute, *Voyageur's Highway*, 49.

29. LAC, MG21, Add. MSS-21661–21892, cited by Innis, *Fur Trade in Canada*, 221.

30. *Ordinances and Acts of Quebec and Lower Canada*, 36 George III, chap. 10, May 7, 1796. See also Wicksteed, *Table*.

31. Hogg and Shulman, "Wage Disputes," 129.

32. For one example, see Montreal, McCord Museum of Canadian History, M17607, M17614, Deposition of Basil Dubois, June 21, 1798, and Complaint of Samuel Gerrard, of the firm of Parker, Gerrard, and Ogilvie against Basil Dubois.

33. ANQM, TL32 S1 SS1, Robert Aird vs. Joseph Boucher, April 1, 1785, JP Pierre Foretier; Atkinson Patterson vs. Jean-Baptiste Desloriers dit Laplante, April 21, 1798, JP Thomas Forsyth; and Angus Sharrest for McGillivray & Co. vs. Joseph Papin of St. Sulpice, June 14, 1810, JP J.-M. Mondelet. These cases were compiled by Don Fyson as part of a one-in-five sample of the whole series.

34. ANQM, TL16 S4 /00005, 37, March 27, 1784, JPs Hertelle De Rouville and Edward Southouse; and TL16 S4 /00002, no page numbers, April 2, 1778, JPs Hertelle De Rouville and Edward Southouse.

35. The JPs were William McGillivray, Duncan McGillivray, Sir Alexander Mackenzie, Roderick McKenzie, and John Ogilvy. Campbell, *North West Company*, 136–37.

36. LAC, MG19 B1, 131, William McGillivray to Thomas Forsyth, Esq., Grand Portage, June 30, 1800.

37. LAC, MG19 B1, 131, William McGillivray to Thomas Forsyth, Esq., Grand Portage, June 30, 1800.

38. LAC, MG19 B1, 152–53, William McGillivray to McTavish, Frobisher, and Company, Grand Portage, July 28, 1800.

39. LAC, MG19 B1, 40, D. Sutherland to Henry Harou, May 15, 1803.

40. ANQM, TL16 S3 /00001, 41, 314–25, July 3, 1770, and July 3, 1778, JPs Hertelle De Rouville and Edward Southouse; and TL16 S3 /00008, no page numbers, January 13, 1786, JPs Hertelle De Rouville and Edward Southouse; October 6, 1786 (followed by several other entries later in the month), JPs John Fraser, Edward Southouse, and Hertelle De Rouville; October 27, 1786, JPs Edward Southouse and Hertelle De Rouville; and Henry (the Younger), *New Light*, March 27, 1814, 2:860–61.

41. Hogg and Shulman, "Wage Disputes," 128, 132, 135–40, 141–43.

42. See Podruchny, "Festivities, Fortitude and Fraternalism."

43. Reed, *Masters of the Wilderness*, 69. Reed's piece on the Beaver Club is almost entirely a quotation of Brian Hughes describing the stories he was told by his grandfather, James Hughes, who was a Beaver Club member.

44. Brennan, *Public Drinking*, 8; and Rice, *Early American Taverns*, 88.

45. Montreal, McCord Museum of Canadian History, M144450, *Rules and Regulations of the Beaver Club: Instituted in 1785*, 3; and Montreal, McCord Museum of Canadian History, M14449, 3.

46. For an example of a Beaver Club menu, see Benoît, "Wintering Dishes." For mention of Beaver Club glass and silverware, see Watson, "First Beaver Club," 337.

47. For example, see Harmon, *Sixteen Years*, 197–98.

48. Montreal, McCord Museum of Canadian History, M144450, *Rules and Regulations*, 3; and Reed, *Masters of the Wilderness*, 68.

49. Reed, *Masters of the Wilderness*, 68.

50. OA, MU 1146, Moffatt, Fort William, to George Gordon, Monontagué [*sic*], July 25, 1809. See also Hamilton, "Fur Trade Social Inequality," 135–36. Burley found a similar pattern in the HBC; see her *Servants of the Honourable Company*, 122–23.

51. LAC, MG19 A17, 119–21.

52. Ross, *Fur Hunters*, 1:301–2.

53. Tyrrell, *Journals*, journal 3, "A Journal of the most remarkable Transactions and Occurrences from York Fort to Cumberland House, and from said House to York Fort from 9th Septr 1778–15th Septr 1779 by Mr Philip Turnor," July 15, 1779, 252.

54. As described by Vibert, *Traders' Tales*, 110–12.

55. Harris, *Resettlement of British Columbia*, 43.

56. As described by Hamilton, "Fur Trade Social Inequality," 137–38, 261–63.

57. For examples, see Henry (the Younger), *New Light*, July 23, 1800, and May 6, 1804, 1:10, 243; Harmon, *Sixteen Years*, July 19, 1807, 105; and Cox, *Adventures on the Columbia River*, September 19, 1817, 304–5.

58. For an example of completing a house, see TBR, S13, George Nelson's Journal, August 29, 1805–March 8, 1806, October 10, 1805. For examples of erecting flagstaffs, see LAC, MG19 C1, vol. 14, November 11, 1799, 3a; LAC, MG19 C1, vol. 6, October 11, 1800, 54; Keith, *North of Athabasca*, 114; Henry (the Younger), *New Light*, October 28, 1801, 1:191; and LAC, MG19 C1, vol. 12, attributed to John Sayer, November 21, 1804, 28. (A published version of this journal can be found in Gates, *Five Fur Traders*, 249–78; Gates attributes the journal to Thomas Connor.)

59. LAC, MG19 C1, vol. 7, February 10, 1799, 30; LAC, MG19 C1, vol. 6, February 28 and 29, April 7, and May 16, 1800, 1, 2, 12, 21; Henry (the Younger), *New Light*, September 4, 1800, 1:78; MRB, MC, C.26, January 11, February 7 and 22, 1801, 20, 22, 25; and MRB, MC, C.28, October 2 and 3, 1807, 8. See also Keith, *North of Athabasca*, 86, 87, 93, 97, 150, 152, 154, 311–12.

60. LAC, MG19 C1, vol. 7, October 12, 18, and 27, 1798, 8, 11–12, 15; and LAC, MG19 C1, vol. 14, October 19, 1799, 3. Voyageurs' Aboriginal wives and families are discussed in chapter 8.

61. Heron, *Booze*, 34.

62. In 1797 Charles Chaboillez commented at a portage that "after they had finished according to custom gave the People each a Dram." LAC, MG19 C1, vol. 1, August 11, 1797, 3. For other ex-

amples see LAC, MG19 C1, vol. 9, November 10, 1805; MRB, MC, C.1; Mackenzie, *Voyages from Montreal*, June 13, 1793, 325; and McGillivray, *Journal*, July 25, 1794, 5.

63. Henry (the Younger), *New Light*, July 23, 1800, 1:10.

64. MRB, MC, C.26, February 5 and 24, 1801, 22, 27. See also Keith, *North of Athabasca*, 152, 155.

65. Ca. June 20, 1807, described in TBR, S13, George Nelson's journal "No. 5," 186.

66. LAC, MG19 C1, vol. 1, August 29, 1797, 6; Henry (the Younger), *New Light*, September 26, 1800, 2:98; LAC, MG19 C1, vol. 13, October 9, 1804, 22; and Fraser, "First Journal," July 8, 1806, 140.

67. MRB, MC, C.26, October 10, 1798, 6; and Henry (the Younger), *New Light*, September 9 and 10, 1800, 1:91, 93.

68. LAC, MG19 C1, vol. 13, October 12, 1804, 22.

69. Mackenzie, *Voyages from Montreal*, June 13, 1793, 322–26.

70. Cox, *Adventures on the Columbia River*, 111–13, 173–76.

71. MRB, MC, C.26, January 1, 1801, 19. See also Keith, *North of Athabasca*, 148. I could not find any evidence of voyageurs giving one another gifts. Bourgeois may not have found this practice noteworthy or perhaps were not aware of their men's relationships with one another.

72. For some examples see Ray, *Indians in the Fur Trade*, 137–42; B. M. White, "'Give us a little milk,'" 61–62; and R. White, *Middle Ground*, 113–15.

73. MRB, MC, C.26, October 13, 18, 22, 29, and 30, 1800, 6–8. See also Keith, *North of Athabasca*, 136–38.

74. MRB, MC, C.24, November 30, 1800, 6.

75. E. P. Thompson, *Customs in Common*, 67.

76. MRB, MC, C.1, 38–39.

77. Henry (the Younger), *New Light*, July 28, 1804, 1:247–48.

78. TBR, S13, George Nelson's journal "No. 5," 2 (my sequential pagination)/186 (Nelson's pagination).

79. TBR, S13, George Nelson's journal, January 29–June 23, 1815, February 10, 1815, 8.

80. Mentioned in Henry (the Younger), *New Light*, July 1, 1804, 1:247.

81. LAC, MG19 A7, D. Sutherland to Monsr. St. Valur Mailloux, Montreal, November 10, 1802, November 29, 1802, and December 20, 1802, 18–19, 25–26. My translation.

82. For one example of men demanding their pay be doubled for extra duties, see LAC, MG C1, March 20, 1798, 49.

83. MRB, MC, C.27, April 5, 1819.

84. MRB, MC, C.29, 42–44; TBR, S13, George Nelson's journal, November 30, 1815–January 13, 1816, December 31, 1815, January 1 and 7, 1816, 92–94, 97; LAC, MG19 B1, William McGillivray to Murdock Cameron, Montreal, May 10, 1799, and May 23, 1802, 44–45, 183; and R. McKenzie, "'Reminiscences,'" Alexander Mackenzie to Roderick McKenzie, Rivière Maligne, September 1, 1787, 1:20.

85. Extracts from a Letter of Andrew Graham, Master at York Fort, to the Governor and Committee of the HBC, dated York Fort, August 26, 1772, in Wallace, *Documents*, August 26, 1772, 43.

86. TBR, S13, George Nelson's journal, April 1, 1810–May 1, 1811, June 18 and 20, 1810, 13–14 (my pagination); TBR, S13, George Nelson's Journal and reminiscences, September 13, 1836; and MRB, MC, C.13, July 31, 1800, 60–61 (my pagination).

87. Henry (the Younger), *New Light*, Sunday, April 17, 1814, 2:890.

88. TBR, S13, George Nelson's journal, January 29–June 23, February 7, 1815, 3.

89. HBCA, B.89/a/2, June 15 and 21, 1810, fols. 2, 3.

90. LAC, MG19 C1, vol. 3, 8–15; and TBR, S13, George Nelson, January 29–June 23, 1815, April 8, 1815, 30–32.

91. See entries November 2 and December 1–30, 1818, OA, MU 842, 10–11, 18–23.

92. LAC, MG19 C1, vol. 15, June 26, 1800, 7.

93. MRB, MC, C.8, March 5, 1806, 125. See also Keith, *North of Athabasca*, 228.

94. On a trip from Athabasca to the Mackenzie River, see LAC, MG19 C1, vol. 6, September 29, 1800, 50. James Porter quotes the man as saying, "Se Je avait Point des gages que le Diable ma aport Se Vous ma forcer EmBarker." John Thomson recorded that this man, named Bernier, gave further trouble to Porter on the trip. Thomson's interpretation of Bernier's swearing is "swearing the Devil myte take him if he had stirred a Step." See entries September 29 to October 4, 1800, MRB, MC, C.26, 1–2. See also Keith, *North of Athabasca*, 112, 130–31.

95. OA, MU 2199, Edward Umfreville. For other examples of theft, see MRB, MC, C24; OA, MU 1956; and LAC, MG19 C1, vol. 2, October 11, 1803.

96. Nelson, *My First Years*, 34–35.

97. Henry (the Younger), *New Light*, August 6, 1800, 1:25.

98. Burley, *Servants of the Honourable Company*, 139–44.

99. Mackenzie, "General History," 34. On the HBC prohibition of private trading, see Burley, *Servants of the Honourable Company*, 24–25. However, Burley suggests that the lack of reporting on this offense may indicate that the officers tacitly allowed their men to do so (144–52).

100. Described by Ross, *Fur Hunters*, 1:159.

101. MHS, P791, folder 7, NWC Letters, 1798–1816, Dominique Rousseau and Joseph Bailley v. Duncan McGillivray (originals from the Judicial Archives of Montreal), 2.

102. Campbell, *North West Company*, 155.

103. Minutes of the Meetings of the NWC at Grand Portage and Fort William, 1801–7, with Supplementary Agreements (originals in Montreal, Sulpician Library, Baby Collection), in Wallace, *Documents*, July 15, 1806, 216.

104. For an example see MRB, MC, C.7, December 5 and 6, 1793, 4.

105. Burley, *Servants of the Honourable Company*, 153–54; and Harris, *Resettlement of British Columbia*, 45–46.

106. For example, see MRB, MC C.24, January 2, 1801, 15.

107. Mackenzie, *Voyages from Montreal*, June 15, 1793, 329.

108. Mackenzie, *Voyages from Montreal*, June 29, 1793, 373–74.

109. MRB, MC, C.12; the account is published in Wood and Thiessen, *Early Fur Trade*, 221–95.

110. MRB, MC C.24, November 22, 1800.

111. Nelson mentioned that fear of starvation bolstered clerks' limited authority with voyageurs. TBR, S13, George Nelson's journal "No. 1," November 17, 1809, 43.

112. TBR, S13, George Nelson's journal, January 29–June 23, 1815, February 10, 1815, 8; and Faries, "Diary," April 2, 1805, 235.

113. TBR, S13, George Nelson's coded journal, April 17–October 20, 1821, May 10, 1821, 14–15. Constant had been threatening to desert the service for years, and he did make arrangements with another bourgeois, William Connolly, to leave the service. See Nelson's coded journal entries for May 10 and 24, 1821, 14–15, 20.

114. Faries, "Diary," August 26, 1804, 206.

115. Henry (the Younger), *New Light*, October 9, 1800, 1:114.

116. Henry (the Younger), *New Light*, September 18–19, 1800, 1:100.

117. Cox, *Adventures on the Columbia River*, 166–67.

118. Rochefoucauld Liancourt, *Voyages dans l'Amerique*, 2:225; and T. Douglas, *Sketch of the British Fur Trade*, 32–47.

119. TBR, S13, George Nelson's journal, January 29–June 23, 1815, March 9, May 23 and 24, 1815, 17–18, 40–41.

120. LAC, RG7 G15C, vol. 2, CO42, vol. 100, Sheriff Edward Gray to Attorney General James Monk, June 9, 1794; J. Reid to same, June 12, 1794; T. A. Coffin to James McGill, July 21, 1794; cited in Greenwood, *Legacies of Fear*, 80, 285.

121. LAC, MG23 GII10, vol. 9, 4613–14, Jonathan Sewell to Lieutenant Colonel Beckworth, July 28, 1795. Donald Fyson brought this reference to my attention.

122. For example, in late December 1744, French and Swiss soldiers at Louisbourg on Isle Royale mutinied because they were dissatisfied with poor rations and meager pay. Greer, *Soldiers of Isle Royale*, 41–51.

123. Crowley, "'Thunder Gusts,'" 11–31, 105–6, 114–17; and Hardy and Ruddel, *Les Apprentis Artisans*, 74–80.

124. Wallot, *Un Québec qui Bougeait*, 266–67.

125. McGillivray, *Journal*, 6–7.

126. MRB, MC, C.12, 72, 77–8.

127. MRB, MC, C.5, July 26 and August 7, 1806.

128. Burley, *Servants of the Honourable Company*, 118–20.

129. Ross, *Fur Hunters*, 2:236–37.

130. Nelson, *My First Years*, January 31, February 14, 15, and 17, 1804, 143, 148.

131. LAC, MG19 C1, vol. 7, November 18–20, 1798, 19–20.

132. LAC, MG19 C1, vol. 7, January 4, 1799, 23–24.

133. MRB, MC, C.5, July 23, 1806, 50.

6. Rendezvous

1. Cox, *Adventures on the Columbia River*, 2:287.

2. Pond, "Narrative," 47.

3. For the central position of Grand Portage and Fort William in the Montreal fur trade, see Gilman, *Grand Portage Story*; and Morrison, *Superior Rendezvous-Place*.

4. TBR, S13, George Nelson's journal "No. 1," 15–16. See also Nelson, *My First Years*, 42.

5. A voyageur quoted in Ross, *Fur Hunters*, 2:236–37.

6. TBR, S13, George Nelson's journal and reminiscences, 32; and Henry (the Younger), *New Light*, August 30, 1808, 2:482.

7. Turner, "Variations of a Theme," 57.

8. Bakhtin, *Rabelais and His World*, 4, 5–6.

9. Bakhtin, *Rabelais and His World*, 7.

10. Le Roy Ladurie, *Carnival in Romans*, xiv–xv.

11. For example, see Hutchenson, *Theory of Parody*.

12. For example, see Bristol, *Carnival and Theater*.

13. Davis, *Society and Culture*, 97.

14. Nelson, *My First Years*, 32–33.

15. Nelson, *My First Years*, 32–33; see also LAC, MG19 A17, June 15, 1791, 15.

16. Dugas, *Un Voyageur*, 25, 30 (my translation). Original French: "Pendant quinze jours, c'était, pour ces vieux loups du Nord, une suite de fêtes et de divertissements; ils invitaient tous leurs amis, et faisaient bombance; on aurait dit qu'ils tenaient à dépenser jusqu'à leur dernier sou, et à partir le gousset complètement vide. La boisson coulait à flots; le soir il y avait bal. . . . Le jour du départ, une foule de personnes se rendaient à Lachine pour être témoins du spectacle."

17. Back, *Narrative of the Arctic Land Expedition*, 31–32.

18. LAC, MG24 H1, 2.

19. Landmann, *Adventures and Recollections*, April 25, 1798, 1:295–96, 302.

20. For one example of muskets being fired at departure, see Franklin, *Narrative of a Journey*, February 8, 1820, 109. Muskets were fired on both arrival and departure on February 16, 1820, 112–13.

21. Dugas, *Un Voyageur*, 27 (my translation). Original French: "La vie sauvage leur souriait; il leur semblait que là-bas, débarrassés de tout frein, vêtus comme l'Indien, couchant avec lui sous la tente, et chassant comme lui pour vivre."

22. For the influence of Aboriginal cultures on French Canada, see Delâge, "L'influence des Amérindiens," 103–91.

23. Deloria, *Playing Indian*, 5.

24. Deloria, *Playing Indian*, 11–20.

25. Henry (the Younger), *New Light*, July 20, 1800, 1:8. Similarly, at York Factory, the main administration post of the HBC, the departure of ships for England was always marked by a celebration. Payne, *Most Respectable Place*, 87.

26. Cox, *Adventures on the Columbia River*, September 19, 1817, 304–5.

27. Mackenzie, "General History," 52; and Nelson, *My First Years*, 40–42.

28. OA, MU 2199, Edward Umfreville, July 24, 1784, 26; and MRB, MC, C.28, October 2 and 3, 1807, 8. See also Keith, *North of Athabasca*, 311–12.

29. Fingard, *Jack in Port*, 8, 74–75; and Radforth, "Shantymen," 221.

30. Creighton, *Rites and Passages*, 140.

31. TBR, S13, George Nelson's diary of events on a journey from Cumberland House to Fort William, June 19, 1822; and McDonell, "Diary," 92.

32. Ross, *Fur Hunters*, 1:303–4.

33. OA, MU 842, September 27, 1818, 3.

34. Nelson, *My First Years*, August 22, 1803, 103; and LAC, MG19 A9, Simon Fraser Collection, vol. 3, Fraser to Mr. McDougall, Sturgeon Lake, August 6, 1806, 15.

35. Lefroy, *In Search of the Magnetic North*, Lefroy to his mother, Toronto, November 20, 1844, 136; and Ballantyne, *Hudson Bay*, 212.

36. LAC, MG19 A17, 37. For an example of rendezvous at Mackinaw, see Pond, "Narrative," 47.

37. Cox, *Adventures on the Columbia River*, 287.

38. TBR, S13, George Nelson's journal, September 1, 1808–March 31, 1810, September 14, 1809, 37 (my pagination); Nelson, *My First Years*, July 13, 1803, 95–97; and Harmon, *Sixteen Years*, 115.

39. TBR, S13, George Nelson's journal from Bas De La Rivière to Cumberland House, 1819–?, June 6, 1819, 11 (my pagination).

40. Lefroy, *In Search of the Magnetic North*, Lefroy to Fanny, Cross Lake, Saskatchewan, August 17, 1843, 54.

41. OA, MU 1391, June 6, 1818, 7; and Bigsby, *Shoe and the Canoe*, 1:141.

42. Creighton, *Rites and Passages*, 82.

43. Perrot, *Indian Tribes*, 1:174–75, 210–20; Dechêne, *Habitants and Merchants*; and Greer, *People of New France*, chapter on "French and Others."

44. See H. H. Tanner, *Settling of North America*, 28–29.

45. Milloy, *Plains Cree*, 11, 17, 51–52, 54; and Peers, *Ojibwa of Western Canada*, 30.

46. Meyer and Thistle, "Saskatchewan River Rendezvous Centers."

47. Lytwyn, "Anishinabeg and the Fur Trade," 32.

48. Lefroy, *In Search of the Magnetic North*, Lefroy to Isabella, Lake Athabasca, Christmas Day, 1843, 84.

49. For examples of All Saint's Day, see LAC, MG19 C1, vol. 12, November 1, 1804, 25; MRB, MC, C.28, November 1, 1807, 12; and Keith, *North of Athabasca*, 316. For examples of St. Andrew's Day, see OA, reel MS65, Donald McKay, Journal from January to December 1799, November 30, 1799, 43 (my pagination); and MRB, MC, C.24, Sunday, November 30, 1800, 6. For examples of celebrating Easter, see LAC, MG19 C1, vol. 1, April 8, 1798, 53; LAC, MG19 C1, vol. 14, April 12, 1800, 23; and OA, MU 842, April 11, 1819, 43.

50. Morton, "Chief Trader Joseph McGillivray"; and Payne, *Most Respectable Place*, 65, 87–92.

51. For an example of celebrating Palm Sunday, see OA, MU 842, April 4, 1819, 42. For examples of celebrating the King's birthday, see TBR, S13, George Nelson's journal, April 1, 1810–May 1, 1811, June 4, 1810, 11 (my pagination); and Landmann, *Adventures and Recollections*, 2:167–68. For an example of celebrating Epiphany, see Henry (the Younger), *New Light*, January 6, 1801, 1:165.

52. For comments on New Year's celebrations as a French Canadian custom, see Harmon, *Sixteen Years*, January 2, 1801, 41; see also Grenon, *Us et coutumes du Québec*, 153–68; Lamontagne, *L'hiver dans la culture québécoise*, 101–3; and Provencher, *Les Quatre Saisons*, 449–57, 463–70.

53. Landmann, *Adventures and Recollections*, 1:239–40.

54. Henry (the Younger), *New Light*, January 1, 1803, 1:207.

55. OA, reel MS65, Donald McKay, Journal from January 1805 to June 1806, December 25, 1805, 47 (my pagination); TBR, S13, George Nelson's journal, November 3, 1807–August 31, 1808, December 25, 1807, 14; November 1, 1807, 7; and Henry (the Younger), *New Light*, November 1, 1810, 2:660.

56. OA, reel MS65, Donald McKay, journal from January to December 1799, December 24, 1799, 46 (my pagination); TBR, S13, George Nelson's journal, November 3, 1807–August 31, 1808, December 25, 1807, 14; George Nelson's journal, April 1, 1810–May 1, 1811, December 23, 1810, 39 (my pagination).

57. OA, MU 842, December 23 and 30, 1818, 22–23.

58. Faries, "Diary," December 25–28, 1804, and January 1, 1805, 223–24.

59. Henry (the Younger), *New Light*, January 1, 1801, 1:162–63; and Harmon, *Sixteen Years*, January 1, 1811 and 1812, 136, 147–48.

60. OA, reel MS65, Donald McKay, Journal from August 1800 to April 1801, December 25, 1800, 17.

61. LAC, MG19 C1, vol. 12, January 1, 1805, 35.

62. LAC, MG19 C1, vol. 14, January 1, 1800, 9; Faries, "Diary," January 1, 1805, 224; LAC, MG19 C1, vol. 8, January 1, 1805, 37; and Keith, *North of Athabasca*, 197.

63. MRB, MC, C.13, January 1, 1800, 11 (my pagination); Henry (the Younger), *New Light*, January 1, 1801 and 1802, 1:162, 192; TBR, S13, George Nelson's journal, November 30, 1815–January

13, 1816, Monday, December 25, 1815, 91; George Nelson's journal and reminiscences, 84; and Franchère, *Journal of a Voyage*, 107–8.

64. Mackenzie, *Voyages from Montreal*, January 1, 1793, 252. On other comments of the long-standing custom, see MRB, MC, C.28, January 1, 1808, 20; Keith, *North of Athabasca*, 326; and Franklin, *Narrative of a Journey*, January 1, 1802, 53.

65. For drams, see LAC, MG19 C1, vol. 1, November 1 and December 25, 1797, 17, 27; MRB, MC, C.24, December 25, 1800, 13; LAC, MG19 C1, vol. 6, December 25, 1800, 72; vol. 8, December 25, 1804, 34; and MRB, MC, C.28, December 25, 1807, 20; see also Keith, *North of Athabasca*, 122, 196, 325. For large quantities of alcohol, see LAC, MG19 C1, vol. 7, December 25, 1798, 23; MRB, MC, C.13, December 25, 1799, 10 (my pagination); Harmon, *Sixteen Years*, December 25, 1801, 52; and LAC, MG19 C1, vol. 12, November 1 and December 25, 1804, 25, 34.

66. Harmon, *Sixteen Years*, January 1, 1802, 53.

67. TBR, S13, George Nelson's journal, November 30, 1815–January 13, 1816, December 25, 1815, 91.

68. MRB, MC, C.7, January 1, 1794 and 1795, 6, 23; OA, MG19, C1, vol. 1, January 1, 1798, 29; LAC, MG19, C1, vol. 7, January 1, 1799, 24; and vol. 12, January 1, 1805, 35.

69. Mackenzie, *Voyages from Montreal*, January 1, 1793, 252; Henry (the Younger), *New Light*, December 25, 1800, 1:161; LAC, MG19 C1, vol. 9, January 1, 1806, 21; Cox, *Adventures on the Columbia River*, 305–6; and MRB, MC, C.8, January 1, 1806, 10.

70. Franchère, *Journal of a Voyage*, 107. See also LAC, MG19 A14, January 1, 1806, 6.

71. Henry (the Younger), *New Light*, 2:781.

72. OA, reel MS65, Donald McKay, journal from August 1800 to April 1801, December 25, 1800, 17; and TBR, S13, George Nelson's journal, September 1, 1808–March 31, 1810, January 1, 1809, 14 (my pagination).

73. MRB, MC, C.13, January 1, 1800, 11 (my pagination).

74. OA, MG19, C1, vol. 1, January 1, 1798, 29; Harmon, *Sixteen Years*, January 2, 1801, 40; and Montreal, McCord Museum, M 22074, James Keith, Fort Chipewyan to McVicar, January 31, 1825, 2.

75. Faries, "Diary," December 25–27, 1804, 223.

76. Morton, "Chief Trader Joseph McGillivray"; and Burley, *Servants of the Honourable Company*, 133.

77. Henry (the Younger), *New Light*, January 1, 1802 and 1803, 1:192, 207; Harmon, *Sixteen Years*, January 1, 1811, 136; and Faries, "Diary," January 1, 1805, 224.

78. McGillivray, *Journal*, Fort George, January 26, 1795, 51.

79. Harmon, *Sixteen Years*, January 2, 1801, December 25, 1805, 40, 99; TBR, S13, George Nelson's journal, April 1, 1810–May 1, 1811, December 1810 to January 1811, 39 (my pagination); and George Nelson's journal, September 1, 1808–March 31, 1810, January 1, 1809, 14 (my pagination).

80. Bahktin, *Rabelais and His World*, 7.

81. Kane, *Wanderings of an Artist*, 261–63.

82. Lefroy, *In Search of the Magnetic North*, Lefroy to Sophia, Fort Chipewyan, Athabasca, January 1, 1844, 91–93.

83. Cox, *Adventures on the Columbia River*, July 31, 1817, 280.

84. Podruchny, "Festivities, Fortitude and Fraternalism," 41.

85. Payne, *Most Respectable Place*, 89, citing Ballantyne, see next note.

86. Ballantyne, Hudson Bay, 164–65.

87. Radforth, "Shantymen," 231–32.

88. Creighton, *Rites and Passages*, 136.

89. See also Van Kirk, "*Many Tender Ties*," 126–29.

90. For examples of balls at Great Lakes posts, see Pond, "Narrative," Mackinaw, 47; and OA, MU 1146, Frederick Goedike, Batchiwenon, to George Gordon, Michipicoten, February 11, 1812, 1–3. For examples of balls at interior posts, see TBR, S13, George Nelson's journal, November 3, 1807–August 31, 1808, Fort Alexandria, June 18, 1808, 42; and Ross, *Adventures of the First Settlers*, Spokane House, summer 1812, 212.

91. Harmon, *Sixteen Years*, Grand Portage, July 4, 1800, 22.

92. TBR, S13, George Nelson's coded journal, June 28, 1821, 29; Henry (the Younger), *New Light*, September 6, 1810, 2:626; and Faries, "Diary," December 16, 1804, February 24, March 31, April 28, May 12 and 17, 1805, 222, 230, 234–35, 238, 240–41.

93. For an example of NWC and HBC men dancing together at Fort George, see McGillivray, *Journal*, March 22, 1795, 66. For an example of NWC and XYC men dancing together, see Faries, "Diary," January 11, 1805, 224–25. For an example of NWC, XYC, and HBC men dancing together at Rivière Souris, Fort Assiniboine, see Harmon, *Sixteen Years*, May 27, 1805, 89–90.

94. Henry (the Younger), *New Light*, January 27, 1810, 2:584.

95. Brennan, *Public Drinking*. For a discussion of how drinking can be understood as part of the social order, see M. Douglas, *Constructive Drinking*.

96. Heron, *Booze*, 17.

97. For one of many examples of bourgeois drunkenness and brawling, see TBR, S13, George Nelson's journal and reminiscences, 57.

98. MRB, MC, C.24, January 2, 1801, 15; and OA, MU 842, March 3, 1819, 34–35.

99. See Podruchny, "Festivities, Fortitude and Fraternalism."

100. Burley, *Servants of the Honourable Company*, 134–35; and Noel, *Canada Dry*, 189–93.

101. Rediker, *Between the Devil*, 192.

102. For two examples see Cox, *Adventures on the Columbia River*, June 29, 1812, and July 30, 1817, 74, 280. However, Alexander Mackenzie characterized it as a regular occurrence, in his "General History," 17–18.

103. LAC, MG19 B1, A. McKenzie to John Layer [Sayer?], Grand Portage, August 9, 1799, 87. For another example of drunk voyageurs preventing a departure, see LAC, MG19 C1, vol. 12, September 20, 1804, 17.

104. Nelson, *My First Years*, 100–101, August 5, 1803.

105. Regarding posts known for heavy drinking, see MRB, MC, C.7, October 27, 1793, 2.

106. MRB, MC, C.7, December 14, 1794, 22; LAC, MG19, C1, vol. 14, November 11–12, 1799, 3a; MRB, MC, C.26, October 10, 1800, 9; and Keith, *North of Athabasca*, 133.

107. Mackenzie, *Voyages from Montreal*, June 15, 1793, 329.

108. For an example of drinking when supplies arrived, see Henry (the Younger), *New Light*, March 7, 1814, 2:851. For examples of drunkenness during parties, see McGillivray, *Journal*, March 22, 1795, 66; Faries, "Diary," January 11–12, 1805, 224–25; and Harmon, *Sixteen Years*, May 27, 1805, 89–90. For examples of heavy drinking at a rendezvous, see Nelson, *My First Years*, 42–43; and Mackenzie, "General History," 1789, 52.

109. Ross, *Fur Hunters*, 2:249–50.

110. LAC, MG19 B1, Alexander Mackenzie to the proprietors of the NWC, Grand Portage, June 16, 1799, 71.

111. TBR, S13, George Nelson's journal and reminiscences, 57.

112. Payne, *Most Respectable Place*, 83.

113. TBR, S13, George Nelson's journal "No. 5," June 1807–October 1809, 20–21 (my sequential pagination)/204–5 (Nelson's pagination).

114. Bourdieu, "Forms of Capital," 242. See also Bourdieu, *Logic of Practice*, 112–21; and Bourdieu and Wacquant, *Invitation to Reflexive Sociology*, 119.

115. In his discussion of the cargoes carried in canots du maître, Bruce M. White notes only the basic necessities of food, clothing, and alcohol as equipment for voyageurs, in his "Montreal Canoes," 185–87.

116. For an example of playing cards, see Harmon, *Sixteen Years*, November 16, 1800, 37. For an example of playing a game called "La Mouche" with cards and chips, see TBR, S13, George Nelson's journal and reminiscences, 63. On gambling as a widespread practice, see Cox, *Adventures on the Columbia River*, 306.

117. Payne, *Most Respectable Place*, 69.

118. OA, reel MS65, Donald McKay, Journal from August 1800 to April 1801, Sunday, December 28, 1800, 17.

119. For an example of voyageurs playing Aboriginal games, see Kohl, *Kitchi-Gami*, 82. On voyageurs tattooing themselves, see MRB, MC, C.24, January 22–23, 1801, 19. On Cree tattooing, see Dr. Richardson's account in Franklin, *Narrative of a Journey*, 67.

120. Franklin, *Narrative of a Journey*, 63, 68.

121. Ross, *Fur Hunters*, 2:236–37.

122. Henry (the Younger), *New Light*, August 11, 1800, 1:30–31; McGillivray, *Journal*, August 18, 1794, 11–12; and TBR, S13, George Nelson's diary of events, July 9, 1822, July 21–August 22, 1822, August 19, 1822.

123. Landmann, *Adventures and Recollections*, 1:167–69.

124. Payne, *Most Respectable Place*, 68–69.

125. Henry (the Younger), *New Light*, May 6, 1804, 1:243; and MRB, MC, C.24, April 10, 1801, 31.

126. LAC, MG19, C1, vol. 14, April 11, 1800, 23. For another example of brawling referred to as a sport or competition, see TBR, S13, George Nelson's journal, April 1, 1810–May 1, 1811, May 13, 1810, 7 (my pagination), which mentions two voyageurs fighting "rough and tumble" and a "pitch battle."

127. OA, MU 1146, Athabasca River, May 3, 1819, 69.

128. Payne, *Most Respectable Place*, 69; and J. E. Foster, "Paulet Paul."

129. TBR, S13, George Nelson's diary of events, June 21, 1822. For other examples see diary entries for July 4 and 9, and August 6, 1822; Mackenzie, *Voyages from Montreal*, 251–52; Ross, *Fur Hunters*, 1:303 and 2:179, 186; Heriot, *Travels through the Canadas*, 246–47; and Extracts from a Letter of Andrew Graham, Master at York Fort, to the Governor and Committee of the HBC, dated York Fort, August 26, 1772, in Wallace, *Documents*, 43.

130. TBR, S13, George Nelson's journal, "No. 5," 28–29 (my sequential pagination)/212–13 (Nelson's pagination).

131. For examples of the pervasiveness of joking, see Ross, *Fur Hunters*, 2:243; OA, MU 1146, Lake Nippissing, June 6, 1818, 7; and Henry (the Younger), *New Light*, October 1, 1803, 227. For examples of teasing, see Henry (the Younger), *New Light*, September 10, 1800, 93; TBR, S13, George Nelson's diary of events, June 20, 1822; George Nelson's journal "No. 5," summer 1807, 4 (my sequential pagination)/188 (Nelson's pagination); and Lefroy, *In Search of the Magnetic North*, Fort

Simpson, McKenzie's River, June 5, 1844, 121. For an example of a bourgeois teasing a voyageur, see MRB, MC, C.13, January 31, 1800, 17 (my pagination).

132. LAC, MG19 C1, vol. 14, December 4, 1799, 5–6.

133. Franklin, *Narrative of a Journey*, Fort Chipewyan, March 26, 1820, 127–28. For other examples see Henry (the Younger), *New Light*, March 30, 1803, 1:210, and February 13, 1811, 2:699.

134. Henry (the Younger), *New Light*, January 6, 1801, 1:166.

135. Bakhtin, *Rabelais and His World*, 18–19.

136. It was common among many Aboriginal groups to sacrifice dogs and then ritually consume them, especially before battle, but many also incorporated dogs into their diets when other meat was unavailable. For some examples see Honigman, "West Main Cree," 220; Henning, "Plains Village Tradition," 233; Gunnerson, "Plains Village Tradition," 240; Swagerty, "History of the United States Plains," 258; and Schwartz, *History of Dogs*.

137. For a reproduction see Darnton, *Great Cat Massacre*, 74.

138. Darnton, *Great Cat Massacre*, 77–78.

139. MRB, MC, C.24, April 10, 1801, 31.

140. Henry (the Younger), *New Light*, October 2, 1800, 1:109–10.

141. Henry (the Younger), *New Light*, August 19, 1804, 1:249.

142. Nelson never knew if his men were responsible for these strange occurrences, but it seems highly probable, especially considering Nelson's fear of night in the early part of his career. TBR, S13, George Nelson's journal and reminiscences, fall 1803, 52; Nelson, *My First Years*, May 18, 1804, 157; and TBR, S13, George Nelson's journal "No. 5," 15 (my sequential pagination)/199 (Nelson's pagination).

143. OA, MU 842, Monday, November 2, 1818, 10–11.

144. Suggested by Darnton, *Great Cat Massacre*, 101.

145. Henry (the Younger), *New Light*, September 2 and 3, 1800, 1:76.

146. Ross, *Adventures of the First Settlers*, May 2, 1811, 78–79.

147. TBR, 917.11 F671, June 20, 1808, 22.

148. Cox, *Adventures on the Columbia River*, August 31, 1814, 164. For an example of voyageurs joking with an elderly Aboriginal woman, see Henry (the Younger), *New Light*, January 1, 1801, 1:163.

149. TBR, S13, George Nelson's journal and reminiscences, fall 1803, 51.

150. TBR, S13, George Nelson's journal, September 1, 1808–March 31, 1810, January 10, 1810, 48 (my pagination).

151. Lambert, *Travels through Canada*, 1:173.

152. Cox, *Adventures on the Columbia River*, 306. Also see Ross, *Fur Hunters*, 1:304.

153. TBR, S13, George Nelson's journal "No. 5," 30 (my sequential pagination)/214 (Nelson's pagination).

154. For a few examples see TBR, S13, George Nelson's diary of events, June 18, 1822; Nelson, *My First Years*, 35–36; and Cox, *Adventures on the Columbia River*, 167.

155. See Podruchny, "Festivities, Fortitude and Fraternalism," for a discussion of bourgeois efforts to reconcile what they perceived as "rough" and "gentle" forms of masculinity.

156. Moogk, "'Thieving Buggers'"; and Bakhtin, *Rabelais and His World*, 5, 16–17.

157. Rediker, *Between the Devil*, 166.

158. Near Michilimackinac in 1799 Landmann's crew became ill and could not proceed. A passing canoe of French Canadians delayed their voyage to help the brigade, a sacrifice that they cheerfully made. Landmann, *Adventures and Recollections*, 2:117–18.

159. In July 1800 in the Rainy Lake District Daniel Harmon's brigade stopped to provide drams to the crew of the Athabasca brigades who were on their way to Grand Portage because they had been starving on much of their journey out. Harmon, *Sixteen Years*, July 25, 1800, 26.

160. Henry (the Younger), *New Light*, February 26, 1810, 2:589–90. For another example of men working together and protecting one another from hostile Aboriginal people, see Cox, *Adventures on the Columbia River*, 111–14.

161. Cox, *Adventures on the Columbia River*, 81–82, 213–14.

162. Cox, *Adventures on the Columbia River*, May 5, 1817, 240; Franchère, *Journal of a Voyage*, May 25, 1814, 164; and McKenzie, "'Reminiscences,'" 1:7–9.

163. For an Ojibwe example, see Kohl, *Kitchi-Gami*, 72–76.

164. Ross, *Fur Hunters*, 1:303–4.

165. For an example of men quarreling, see LAC, MG19 C1, vol. 14, November 14, 1799, 3a. For an example of men quarreling over trapping territory, see Henry (the Younger), *New Light*, October 31, 1800, 1:132–33.

166. LAC, MG19 C1, vol. 14, October 25, 1799, 3; MRB, MC, C.13, January 22, 1800, 16 (my pagination); and Faries, "Diary," August 1, 1804, 197.

167. Henry (the Younger), *New Light*, November 6, 1800, 1:135.

168. TBR, S13, George Nelson's journal, January 29–June 23, 1815, April 8, 1815, 30–32.

169. Henry (the Younger), *New Light*, May 1, 1803, 211.

170. LAC, MG19 C1, vol. 6, March 8, 1800, 4.

171. Ross, *Fur Hunters*, 1:139–40; and Fraser, "First Journal," July 1, 1806, 136–37.

172. Ross, *Fur Hunters*, 1:60; and Cox, *Adventures on the Columbia River*, 1817, crossing The Dalles, 245.

173. Maynard, "Rough Work"; and Blye, "Hegemonic Heterosexual Masculinity."

174. Gilbert, "Buggery and the British Navy"; Maynard, "Making Waves"; T. D. Moodie, "Migrancy and Male Sexuality"; and Chauncey, "Christian Brotherhood."

175. Maynard, "Rough Work," 169.

176. Gagnon, *Plaisir d'Amour*, 12–23.

177. Ross, *Fur Hunters*, 1:303–4.

178. Brown, *Strangers in Blood*, 87–88.

179. Burley, *Servants of the Honourable Company*, 129–30.

180. Harriet Whitehead, "The Bow and the Burden Strap." For a critique of Whitehead's imposition of a two-gender model on Aboriginal societies, see Roscoe, "How to Become a Berdache." See also Williams, *Spirit and the Flesh*. On lesbianism see Allen, "Lesbians in American Indian Cultures."

7. En Dérouine

1. PAM, MG1 C1–1, Fort William [Kaministiquia] Post Records, 1803, folder 39(B), fols. 98–99, my emphasis.

2. Also spelled as drouine, drouyn, deroüinne, deroine, deroinne, dorwine, or dourouine.

3. Vézina, "Les mauvais renards et la garce." For other descriptions of trading en dérouine, see McLeod, "Diary," 144n31; and J. E. Foster, "Wintering."

4. Wallace, *Documents*, Letter of Benjamin and Joseph Frobisher to General Haldimand, Octo-

ber 4, 1784, 74. For a similar comment see Lefroy, *In Search of the Magnetic North*, Lake Athabasca, to Anne, January 1, 1844, 89.

5. The tedium of post life is conveyed very well in OA, reel MS65, Donald McKay, Journal from January 1805 to June 1806.

6. For portraits of many of the posts, see Losey, *Let Them Be Remembered*; and Voorhis, *Historic Forts*.

7. Campbell, *North West Company*, 138, 160.

8. Innis, *Fur Trade in Canada*, 232–35.

9. For an exhaustive list of fur trade posts and their approximate life spans and size, see Moodie, Lytwyn, and Kaye, "Trading Posts"; and Moodie, Kaye, and Lytwyn, "Fur Trade Northwest."

10. Keith, *North of Athabasca*, 14, 18–19.

11. Keith, *North of Athabasca*, 19.

12. Henry (the Younger), *New Light*, September 9 and 10, 1800, 1:78.

13. For a description of the annual round of agriculture and house construction and maintenance on habitant farms, see Greer, *Peasant, Lord, and Merchant*, 28–32, 195–98.

14. Wallace, *Documents*, 170–290. On the management of the NWC, see Rich, *Fur Trade and the Northwest*, 189–90.

15. TBR, S13, George Nelson's journal "No. 5," 12 (my sequential pagination)/196 (Nelson's pagination); and George Nelson's journal, September 1, 1808–March 31, 1810, September 22 and 24, 1808, 4–5, 38, (my pagination).

16. TBR, S13, George Nelson's journal, July 13, 1803–June 25, 1804, October 2 and 12, 1803, 12–13. See also Nelson, *My First Years*, 115–16.

17. MRB, MC, C.26, October 13 and 14, 1800, 6. See also Keith, *North of Athabasca*, 136.

18. LAC, MG19 C1, vol. 14, October 20, 1799, 3.

19. Henry (the Younger), *New Light*, September 9 and 10, 1800, 1:91–93.

20. LAC, MG19 C1, vol. 7, October 15, 1798, 10. For another example see OA, MU 842, Diary of George Nelson, 9, 10, 12, 17, 19, and October 26 and November 23, 1818, 6–9, 15.

21. Wallace, *Documents*, 170–290.

22. Van Kirk, *"Many Tender Ties,"* 28–52; and Brown, *Strangers in Blood*, 89–96, 107–10.

23. McGillivray, *Journal*, October 7, 1794, 32.

24. LAC, MG19 A17, 54.

25. Harmon, *Sixteen Years*, January 4, 1801, 41.

26. Francis and Payne, *Narrative History*, xv, 43.

27. Harris, *Resettlement of British Columbia*, 39.

28. Mackenzie, *Voyages from Montreal*, December 23, 1792, 251.

29. Moogk, *Building a House*, 27, 32, 34, 36, 60.

30. Ens, *Homeland to Hinterland*, 26–27; and Harris, *Resettlement of British Columbia*, 36, 39.

31. MRB MC C. 7, October 1, 1794, 17; and TBR, S13, George Nelson's journal, September 1, 1808–March 31, 1810, May 17, 21, and 26, 1809, 22–23 (my pagination).

32. Faries, "Diary," December 10 and 19, 1804, 18, January 30 and 31, 1805, 221–22, 226–27.

33. LAC, MG19 C1, vol. 1, September 28, 1797, 11. One bourgeois commented on October 9, 1804, that his men were employed clearing land for building along the Snake River. LAC, MG19 C1, vol. 12, 22. In October 1807 George Nelson noted that his men began to clear a place for building along the Rivière Dauphin. TBR, S13, George Nelson's journal, November 3, 1807–August 31, 1808, 3.

34. For a general history of the fur trade at Fort Temiscamingue and a biographical sketch of

Donald McKay, see Mitchell, *Fort Timiskaming and the Fur Trade*, 235–36.

35. See entries for July 29, August 5, 17, and 20, 1805, in OA, reel MS65, Donald McKay, journal from January 1805 to June 1806, 27–30 (my pagination).

36. OA, reel MS65, Donald McKay, Journal from January 1805 to June 1806, April 8 and May 22, 1805, 9–11, 14 (my pagination).

37. OA, MU 842, October 9, 10, 12, 17, 19, and 26 and November 23, 1818, 6–9, 15. See another example where an old house was turned into a shop for a new post. TBR, S13, George Nelson's journal, September 1, 1808–March 31, 1810, October 1, 1808, and September 8, 1808, 6 (my pagination).

38. LAC, MG19 C1, vol. 1, November 8, 1797, 18.

39. MRB, MC, C.26, September 16, 18–20, and 22, 1800, 7. For another example of shop construction, at Fort George, see McGillivray, *Journal*, October 10, 1794, 32.

40. TBR, S13, George Nelson's journal, August 29, 1805–March 8, 1806, September 19 and October 10, 1805, 3–4 (my pagination). Also see Nelson's description of post construction at Rivière Dauphin, TBR, S13, George Nelson's journal, April 1, 1810–May 1, 1811, September 28 and October 3, 1810, 28–29 (my pagination).

41. TBR, S13, George Nelson's journal, November 3, 1807–August 31, 1808, early November [which was really October, mistake on Nelson's part] 1807, 3, 6 , 9, 10, 16, and November 18, 1807, 3–5.

42. Faries, "Diary," March 25, 1805, 234; Henry (the Younger), *New Light*, October 16–20, 1809, 552–54; TBR, S13, George Nelson's journal, November 3, 1807–August 31, 1808, November [which was really October, Nelson's mistake] 3 and 6, 1807, 3–4; George Nelson's Journal, September 1, 1808–March 31, 1810, September 8 and October 12, 1808, 6–7 (my pagination); and Nelson's "Journal of Daily Occurrencies--Commencing 15th Septr. 1804," 17, 19, 27 and 30 October 1804, 23–24.

43. LAC, MG19 C1, vol. 12, October 25–27, 30–31, 1804, 23–24; LAC, MG19 A14, reel M-130, January 25, 1806, 16; and TBR, S13, George Nelson's journal, September 1, 1808–March 31, 1810, October 1 and December 9, 1808, 6, 13 (my pagination).

44. For example, see OA, reel MS65, Donald McKay, Journal from January to December 1799, November 8, 1799, 40 (my pagination).

45. For example, see Henry (the Younger), *New Light*, July 17, 1810, 2:614–15.

46. See entries from October 21 to November 4, 1805, MRB, MC, C.8, 6–7; see also Keith, *North of Athabasca*, 220–21.

47. LAC,MG19 A14, January 15, 1806, 12.

48. "Old Godin" seems to have been primarily responsible for shingles at the Rainy Lake post in the winter of 1804–5. Faries, "Diary," December 19, 1804, January 18 and 31, 1805, 222, 226–27.

49. For examples of laying floors, see Nelson, *My First Years*, March 8, 1804, 151; and TBR, S13, George Nelson's journal, November 3, 1807–August 31, 1808, November [actually October, Nelson's error]16 and 18, 1807, 5. For examples of whitewashing, see OA, reel MS65, Donald McKay, Journal from January to December 1799, November 18, 1799, 41; OA, MU 842, January 22, 1819; and Faries, "Diary," November 16, 1804, 219.

50. For examples of chimney building, see Henry (the Younger), *New Light*, July 1810, 2:614–15; and Fairies, "Diary," October 12, 1804, 214. For examples of chimney repair, see LAC, MG19 C1, vol. 1, March 13, 1798, 48; MG19 C1, vol. 8, October 10, 1798, 6; and MG19 A14, December 20–21, 27, and 29, 1805, 2–4.

51. Henry (the Younger), *New Light*, September 28, 1800, 1:104.

52. For example see OA, MU 842, October 17, 1818, 7; and Faries, "Diary," May 1, 1805, 239.

53. OA, MU 842, October 17, 1818, 7; MRB, MC, C.24, November 25, 1800, 5.

54. See entries between October 21 and November 18, 1799, OA, reel MS65, Donald McKay, Journal from January to December 1799, 38–41 (my pagination). For another example of cellar construction, see Henry (the Younger), *New Light*, July 1810, 2:614–15.

55. OA, S13, George Nelson's journal, November 3, 1807–August 31, 1808, December 11, 1807, 13.

56. LAC, MG19 C1, vol. 12, November 21, 1804, 28; LAC, MG19, C1, vol. 6, October 11, 1800, 54; MRB, MC, C.26, October 30, 1800, 8; see also Keith, *North of Athabasca*, 114, 138; and Henry (the Younger), *New Light*, October 1, 13, and 28 1801, 1:188, 191. For an example of flying the flag on Sundays, see MRB, MC, C.26, October 17, 1800, 121.

57. Harris, *Resettlement of British Columbia*, 39, 57.

58. Henry (the Younger), *New Light*, September 10–12, 20–21, 1800, 1:93–95, 100–101. For other examples see Harmon, *Sixteen Years*, June 11, 1801, and June 2, 1803, 49, 67.

59. Harris, *Resettlement of British Columbia*, 35–36.

60. Ross, *Fur Hunters*, 1:83.

61. McDonell, "Diary," 93.

62. OA, MU 842, November 18–19, 1818, 14; and Henry (the Younger), *New Light*, October 19, 1800, 1:122.

63. For one example at Fort Vermilion, see Henry (the Younger), *New Light*, August 31, 1810, 2:622.

64. Faries, "Diary," September 26–27 and October 29, 1804, 212, 216; and Fort Alexandria, before departure to Tête au Brochet, see OA, MU 842, September 21, 1818, 1.

65. Henry (the Younger), *New Light*, October 13, 1801, September 19, 1807, 1:191, 424.

66. MRB, MC, C.24, February 26 and March 25, 1801, 23, 28; and MRB, MC C.28, October 16–17, 21, and 24, 1807, 10–11. See also Keith, *North of Athabasca*, 314–15.

67. Henry (the Younger), *New Light*, October 10, 1807, 1:425.

68. OA, reel MS65, Donald McKay, Journal from January to December 1799, November 8, 1799, 40 (my pagination).

69. See entries from September 28 to October 10, 1804, in Faries, "Diary," 212–14.

70. For an example of bourgeois expecting their voyageurs to be jacks of all trades, see OA, MU 572, vol. 2, to Duncan Clark, Pic, from Donald McIntosh, Michipicoten, July 8, 1825, 1.

71. See entries for October 20, 22, 28, 29, and 31, 1804, in Faries, "Diary," 215–17.

72. MRB, MC, C.24, March 2–5, 1801, 24.

73. MRB, MC, C.24, November 25, 1800, 5; and LAC, MG19 A14, December 20, 1805; see also January 22, 1806, which records that Mayace and La Gard were sent for wood to make a table, 1, 15.

74. For examples of tables and chairs, see Faries, "Diary," January 31, 1805, 227; OA, reel MS65, Donald McKay, journal from January to December 1799, November 29, 1799, 43 (my pagination); MRB, MC, C.24, November 25, 1800, 5; LAC, MG19 C1, vol. 7, October 23, 1798, 14; and MRB, MC, C.26, January 21 and February 5 and 9, 1801, 21–23; see also Keith, *North of Athabasca*, 150, 152. For examples of beds and bedframes, see Faries, "Diary," October 20, 1804, 215; OA, MU 842, October 20, 1818, 7; and TBR, S13, George Nelson's journal, September 1, 1808–March 31, 1810, January 24, 1809, 16 (my pagination).

75. On shovels, see Henry (the Younger), *New Light*, September 10, 1800, 1:93. On wheelbarrows, see Faries, "Diary," November 23 and December 17 and 19, 1804, 220–22. On fish baskets,

see OA, MU 842, October 15, 1818, 6–7. On wedges, see MRB, MC, C.26, February 12, 1801, 23; see also Keith, *North of Athabasca*, 152.

76. Mention of a cooper is found at Rainy Lake Post, in Faries, "Diary," November 16 and 26, 1804, 219–20; and Franchère, *Journal of a Voyage*, January 1, 1812, 108.

77. Faries, "Diary," November 26, 1804, 220; and Franchère, *Journal of a Voyage*, January 1, 1813, 108.

78. Lynn Louise Morland found that some voyageurs at Michilimackinac became part-time artisans, but always as a supplement to their fur trading. Morland, "Craft Industries at Fort Michilimackinac," 143.

79. Henry (the Younger), *New Light*, March 30, 1803, 1:210.

80. See mentions of a blacksmith shop at Fort Vermilion in Henry (the Younger), *New Light*, November 22, 1809, and August 31, 1810, 2:572, 622; and Franchère, *Journal of a Voyage*, January 1812, 108.

81. Henry (the Younger), *New Light*, January 28, 1814, 2:825.

82. Henry (the Younger), *New Light*, October 24, 1800, 1:124.

83. For a couple of examples, see Harmon, *Sixteen Years*, July 30, 1801, 50; and Henry (the Younger), *New Light*, October 1, 1801, 188.

84. For a few examples, see MRB, MC, C.7, November 18 and 22, 1794, 20–21; OA, reel MS65, Donald McKay, Journal from January to December 1799, November 9, 1799, 40 (my pagination); Henry (the Younger), *New Light*, October 22 and 23, 1800, 1:122–23; Faries, "Diary," October 20, 29, and 31, 1804, and November 26, 1804, 215–20; and OA, MU 842, October 31, 1818, 10.

85. See entries between October 28 and December 17, 1805, in OA, reel MS65, Donald McKay, Journal from January 1805 to June 1806, 39–46, (my pagination). See also Faries, "Diary," January 30, 1805, 227.

86. Faries, "Diary," March 10–11, 1805, 232.

87. MRB, MC, C.28, November 6, 1807, 12; see also Keith, *North of Athabasca*, 317; and Faries, "Diary," December 1, 1804, and March 21, 1805, 220, 233.

88. For examples see MRB, MC, C.28, October 14, 1807, and mid-June 1808, 9, 41; see also Keith, *North of Athabasca*, 313, 345; and Faries, "Diary," December 7, 15, and 17, 1804, 221–22.

89. Henry (the Younger), *New Light*, September 9 and 24, 1800, 1:91, 102.

90. MRB, MC, C.28, March 29, 1808, 29; see also Keith, *North of Athabasca*, 334; and LAC, MG19 A.14, December 20, 1805, January 15–16, 1806, 1, 11–12. In another example a voyageur named Coutu mended his clothes; see Faries, "Diary," October 20, 1804, 215. Most clothing was brought from Canada, but some clothing was obtained from Aboriginal peoples and made by Aboriginal women, especially moccasins; see Van Kirk, "*Many Tender Ties*", 54.

91. For a couple of examples, voyageurs Lisé and Cloutier baked five and four loaves of bread, respectively, and helped McKay organize the cellar, while voyageurs Faries and Le Blanc cleaned potatoes; see OA, reel MS65, Donald McKay, journal from January to December 1799, June 21 and November 19, 1799, 31, 41 (my pagination). Voyageurs melted and boiled buffalo fat to put into pemmican, and Plante hung up the meat and tongues, which he had salted ten days earlier; see MRB, MC, C.24, March 3–4, 1801, 24.

92. For a few examples, see LAC, MG19 C1, vol. 7, October 26, 1798, 14; Henry (the Younger), *New Light*, September 17, 1800, February 25, 1801, 1:99, 171; and TBR, S13, George Nelson's journal, November 3, 1807–August 31, 1808, August 18, 1808, 56.

93. The Swampy Cree who settled near HBC posts on the shores of Hudson Bay are most com-

monly referred to as the homeguard. Ray, *Indians in the Fur Trade*, 85; and Francis and Morantz, *Partners in Furs*, 41. Many later homeguard were Aboriginal peoples of mixed descent.

94. Ross, *Fur Hunters*, 2:6. In another example an Aboriginal man signed a contract for six years at the rate of 300 livres per annum. Fraser, "First Journal," May 17, 1806, 120.

95. Carol Judd has found that the HBC began to hire Aboriginal people in the 1770s on a casual basis without formal contracts to perform specific tasks, which could normally be performed in a single season. Judd, "Native Labour," 306.

96. On hiring individual Aboriginal people, see LAC, MG19 C1, vol. 12, October 2, 1804, 20; LAC, MG19 A9, vol. 3, Simon Fraser to McDougall, Naugh-al-chum, August 31, 1806, 23; Fraser, "First Journal," June 21, 1806, 132; and Henry (the Younger), *New Light*, September 16, 1800, 1:98. On employing Aboriginal people as hunters, see TBR, S13, George Nelson's journal and reminiscences, August 12, 1803, 35–36; Henry (the Younger), *New Light*, September 5–6, 1800, 1:85; and McGillivray, *Journal*, Fort George, October 10, 1794, 52.

97. McLeod, "Diary," 55; and LAC, MG19 A9, vol. 3, Simon Fraser to McDougall, Naugh-al-chum, August 31, 1806, 23–25.

98. LAC, MG19 A14, December 22–24, 26, 1805, and January 2 and 22 and February 12, 1806, 2–4, 6, 15, 25–26.

99. Fraser, "First Journal," May 11–12, 1806, 118.

100. LAC, MG19 C1, Vol. 5, April 12, 1790, 17; OA, MU 572, vol. 2, R. McKenzie, Pic, to Duncan Clark, Long Lake, May 1, 1825, 1, 3; Nelson, *My First Years*, July 27, 1803, 99–100; and Henry (the Younger), *New Light*, July 26–27, August 9, 1800, and September 16, 1800, 1:14–15, 30, 98.

101. Henry (the Younger), *New Light*, February 12, 1810, 2:584; and Kohl, *Kitchi-Gami*, 122–23.

102. OA, MU 2199, Edward Umfreville, June 16, 20–23, and 27–28 and July 10, 13, and 17, 1784, 5–10, 16, 19, 21.

103. Mackenzie, *Voyages from Montreal*, June 24, 1789, July 8–9, 1789, July 27, 1789, and August 11, 1789, 150, 173, 175, 211, 223; Ross, *Fur Hunters*, 2:63–65; LAC, MG19 A9, vol. 3, Simon Fraser to Mr. McDougall, Sturgeon Lake, August 6, 1806, 14; Fraser, "First Journal," May 15, 1806, 120; and Nelson, *My First Years*, August 12 and 30 and September 3, 1803, 97, 105.

104. Mackenzie, *Voyages from Montreal*, early June 1789 and May 9, 1793, 135, 265; TBR, S13, George Nelson's journal and reminiscences, August 12, 1803, 35–36; and Nelson, *My First Years*, July 21, 1803, 99.

105. Judd found the same pattern with the HBC. Judd, "Native Labour," 306.

106. MRB, MC, C.26, December 17 and 27, 1800, 17–19; Keith, *North of Athabasca*, 167–68; and LAC, MG19 A9, vol. 3, Simon Fraser to Mr. McDougall, Sturgeon Lake, August 6, 1806, and Simon Fraser to McDougall, Naugh-al-chum, August 31, 1806, 15–16, 23–25.

107. MRB, MC, C.28, August 10, 1807, 2; and Keith, *North of Athabasca*, 304n9.

108. OA, MU2199, Edward Umfreville, June 28 and July 10, 1784, 10, 16.

109. Henry (the Younger), *New Light*, winter 1799, Rivière Terre Blanche, near Fort Dauphin, 1:2–3.

110. MRB, MC, C.24, November 16, 1800, 3.

111. TBR, S13, George Nelson's journal, January 29–June 23, 1815, February 11, 1815, 8; and Van Kirk, "*Many Tender Ties*", 58–59.

112. For examples, see OA, MU 842, November 11, 1818, 13; Henry (the Younger), *New Light*, October 19, 1800, 1:122; and Faries, "Diary," December 16, 17, 20, and 23, 1804, and February 3, 1805, 222–23, 227.

113. Faries, "Diary," February 16 and 22, 1805, 229–30. Steel traps for beaver originated in 1797 and spread slowly westward because steel was heavy to transport. See Innis, *Fur Trade in Canada*, 263–64.

114. For one example, see "The Beaver Trap is repaired & sent down--," in OA, MU 572, vol. 2, R. McKenzie, Fort William, to Duncan Clark, Pic, July 18, 1825, 1.

115. LAC, MG19 C1, vol. 1, January 21, 1798, 36; LAC, MG19 A14, January 31, 1806, 19; and Henry (the Younger), *New Light*, September 11, 1800, 1:95.

116. LAC, MG19 C1, vol. 1, November 20, 1797, and January 14, 1798, 20, 34; and TBR, S13, George Nelson's journal, November 3, 1807–August 31, 1808, November 20, 1807, December 26, 1807, and January 2, 1808, 9, 14–15.

117. MRB, MC, C.26, October 14 and 15, 1800, 6; and see also Keith, *North of Athabasca*, 136. See also Nelson, *My First Years*, October 2 and 12, 1803, 115–16; and TBR, S13, George Nelson's journal, September 1, 1808–March 31, 1810, September 9, 1808, 2 (my pagination).

118. MRB, MC, C.24, November 16–17, 1800, January 4, 1801, and February 1–2, 1801, 3, 15, 20. For another example, see LAC, MG19 A14, January 14, 1806, 11.

119. LAC, MG19 C1, vol. 4, February 26, 1790, 11–12, 27–28; and MRB, MC, C.26, December 10–11, 1800, and January 11, 1801, 14, 20–21. For another example of reporting bad news see MRB, MC, C.28, January 8, 1808, 21; see also Keith, *North of Athabasca*, 144, 150, 326–27.

120. For one example, see Faries, "Diary," March 19, 1805, 233.

121. OA, MU 842, December 9, 1818, 18.

122. MRB, MC C.13, July 31, 1800, 61 (my pagination).

123. Faries, "Diary," November 19 and 20, 1804, December 1, 5, and 5, 1804, January 12, 1805, and March 1805, 219–21, 225, 231–32.

124. T. Douglas, *Sketch of the British Fur Trade*, 50.

125. OA, MU 842, October 20 and December 9, 1818, 7–8, 18. For other examples, see TBR, S13, George Nelson's journal, November 3, 1807–August 31, 1808, August 24, 1808, 57; George Nelson's journal, September 1, 1808–March 31, 1810, August 26 and September 1, 1809, 35–36; George Nelson's journal, January 29–June 23, 1815, January 29 and February 2, 1815, 1; George Nelson's journal, November 30, 1815–January 13, 1816, January 2, 1816, 95; and George Nelson's coded journal, April 27, 1821, 10.

126. For an example see William McGillivray sending Cadotte and Bellangé to fetch furs. LAC, MG19 C1, vol. 4, February 26, 1790, 11–12.

127. For examples, see MRB, MC, C.24, December 21, 1800, 12. For other examples, see TBR, S13, George Nelson's journal "No. 1," mid-November 1802, 30; and Faries, "Diary," November 19, 1804, 219.

128. TBR, S13, George Nelson's journal, November 3, 1807–August 31, 1808, November 20, 1807, December 26, 1807, and January 2, 1808, 9, 14–15; and Henry (the Younger), *New Light*, September 21, 1800, 1:101. For other examples, see LAC, MG19 C1, vol. 1, October 29, November 7 and 9, 1797, 16–18; MRB, MC, C.24, February 1–2 and 6, 1801, 20; and Larocque, "Journal of an Excursion," June 11, 1805, 164.

129. MRB, MC, C.26, December 11, 1800, 14. See also Keith, *North of Athabasca*, 144–45.

130. For an example of men trading with the English, see LAC, MG19 C1, vol. 1, March 13, 1798, 48. For examples of men trading with freemen, see Henry (the Younger), *New Light*, July 11 and 24, 1808, 1:431, 434, and February 26, 1810, 2:589.

131. MRB, MC C.7, February 17, 1794 (no page number).

132. LAC, MG19 C1, vol. 3, November 25, 1804, 8.

133. MRB, MC, C.1, 60–61.

134. LAC, MG19 C1, vol. 1, January 6 and April 7, 1798, 31, 53.

135. TBR, S13, George Nelson's journal "No. 7," 278–79.

136. MRB, MC, C.26, October 10, 1800, and February 7, 1801, 9, 22; LAC, MG19 C1, vol. 6, April 11, 1800, 13; LAC, MG19 C1, vol. 8, January 22, 1805, 44; MRB, MC, C.28, November 9, 1807, 14; MRB, MC. C.8, December 13, 1805, 9; see also Keith, *North of Athabasca*, 133, 152, 94, 200, 318, 223; OA, reel MS65, Donald McKay, Journal from January 1805 to June 1806, April 20, 1805, 10 (my pagination); Faries, "Diary," February 12, 1805, 229; and MRB, MC, C.24, February 18–19, 1801, 22.

137. Sending men out to stay at Aboriginal lodges was regularly reported in fur trade journals. For some examples, see OA, reel MS65, Donald McKay, journal from January to December 1799, May 29, 1799, 26–27 (my pagination); LAC, MG19 C1, vol. 14, October 19, 1799, 3; MRB, MC, C.24, January 3, 1801, 15; Faries, "Diary," October 8, 1804, 213; TBR, S13, George Nelson's journal, August 29, 1805–March 8, 1806, December 4, 1805, 7 (my pagination); George Nelson's journal, September 1, 1808–March 31, 1810, early February 1810, 50 (my pagination); and LAC, MG19 C1, vol. 9, January 7, 1806, 22.

138. For an example of bringing Aboriginal people back to the post, see LAC, MG19 C1, vol. March 8, 1800, 4; see also Keith, *North of Athabasca*, 89. For an example of voyageurs trading with Aboriginal people when they were sent out to stay with them, see TBR, S13, George Nelson's journal, November 3, 1807–August 31, 1808, November 20, 1807, 9. For examples of encouraging Aboriginal people to bring meat and furs to the posts, see LAC, MG19 A14, December 22, 23, and 26, 1805, 2, 4; and LAC, MG19 C1, vol. 8, October 20, 1804, 13; see also Keith, *North of Athabasca*, 187.

139. MRB, MC, C.24, December 11, 1800, 9.

140. For an example of a voyageur taking "his turn," see MRB, MC, C.24, November 18, 1800, 3.

141. For one example, see MRB, MC, C.24, January 16, 1801, 18.

142. For examples, see MRB, MC, C.24, December 3, 1800, 6; MRB, MC. C.8, October 27, 1805, 6; see also Keith, *North of Athabasca*, 220–21; and TBR, S13, George Nelson's journal, "Journal from Bas De La Rivière to Cumberland House, May 23, 1819, 8 or b8.

143. TBR, S13, George Nelson's journal, January 29–June 23, 1815, April 30, 1815, 36.

144. TBR, S13, George Nelson's journal, September 1, 1808–March 31, 1810, December 12, 1808, 13.

145. LAC, MG19 C1, vol. 7, October 12, 18, 19, and 21, November 18, and December 13, 1798, 8–13, 19, 22.

146. TBR, S13, George Nelson's journal, April 1, 1810–May 1, 1811, September 24, 1810, 27 (my pagination).

147. MRB, MC, C.26, November 6, 18, and 21, 1800, December 15, 1800, and February 16, 1801, 9–12, 16, 23–24. See also Keith, *North of Athabasca*, 139–42, 146, 152–53.

148. MRB, MC. C.26, February 19 and 20, 1801, 24. See also Keith, *North of Athabasca*, 153.

149. TBR, S13, George Nelson's journal, September 1, 1808–March 31, 1810, October 16, 1809, 39 (my pagination).

150. Henry (the Younger), *New Light*, September 3 and 4, 1800, October 15, 1800, and October 3, 1803, 1:77–8, 120, 225–27. For other examples, see Nelson, *My First Years*, August 7 and 15, 1803, 101–2; and OA, MU 842, October 20, November 2 and 9, 1818, 7–8, 11–12.

151. LAC, MG19 C1, vol. 9, September 18 and 29, and October 7, 1805, 4–5, 9, 12. For another example, see LAC, MG19 C1, vol. 4, April 2, 1790, 15.

152. LAC, MG19 A14, February 6, 7, 19, and 24, 1806, 24–25, 28, 31–33. La Malice and Lammalice are probably the same person.

153. TBR, S13, George Nelson's journal, September 1, 1808–March 31, 1810, June 1, 1809, 24 (my pagination); George Nelson's journal, April 1, 1810–May 1, 1811, August 13 and 17, 1810, 22 (my pagination); and George Nelson's journal, January 29–June 23, 1815, February 25, 1815, 12. For other examples, see and LAC, MG19 A17, 30–31; Henry (the Younger), *New Light*, October 17, 1800, and January 4, 1803, 1:121, 207; and LAC, MG19 C1, vol. 1, January 15, 1798, 35.

154. LAC, MG19 C1, vol. 6, October 20, 1800, 57; for other examples, see MRB, MC, C.26, October 4 and 10, 1800, 2, 3; see also Keith, *North of Athabasca*, 116, 132–33; TBR, S13, George Nelson's journal, November 3, 1807–August 31, 1808, June 30, 1808, 44; George Nelson's coded journal, June 4, 1821, 25–26; Henry (the Younger), *New Light*, May 12 and 19, 1801, 1:180, 182; and MRB, MC, C.24, May 15, 1801, 37.

155. Keith, *North of Athabasca*, 127.

156. Harmon, *Sixteen Years*, September 21, 1805, 97.

157. Nelson, *My First Years*, February 24, 1804, 149.

158. Nelson, *My First Years*, October 19 and 20, 1803, December 25, 1803, and January 6, 1804, 120–21, 137–39. For another example, see MHS, P849, Joseph Guy to his father Pierre Guy, Mackinac, August 15, 1805.

159. OA, reel MS65, Donald McKay, journal from January 1805 to June 1806, August 30, 1805, 31 (my pagination); and Journal from January to December 1799, November 19, 1799, 41 (my pagination).

160. LAC, MG19 A17, 26.

161. LAC, MG19 A9, vol. 2, Simon Fraser to McDougall, Naugh-al-chum, August 31, 1806, and Simon Fraser to "my dear Stuart, Naukazeleh," September 29, 1806, 22, 29; and R. McKenzie, "'Reminiscences,'" Alexander Mackenzie to Roderick McKenzie, October 1, 1787, Île a la Crosse, 1:20.

162. R. McKenzie, "'Reminiscences,'" 1:11–12.

163. Henry (the Younger), *New Light*, September 19, 1800, 1:100.

164. HBCA, A.11/4, Thomas Hutchins to London Committee, Albany Fort, Hudson Bay, July 5, 1775, fol. 29.

165. One example is the daughter (Magdalaine) of voyageur André Poitras and his Cree wife. She married bourgeois John McDonell. See Van Kirk, *"Many Tender Ties,"* 269n46; and Brown, *Strangers in Blood*, 101–3.

166. OA, MU 572, vol. 2, R. McKenzie, Pic, to Duncan Clark, Long Lake, May 1, 1825, 2. For another example, see TBR, S13, George Nelson's journal "No. 1," 21.

167. MRB, MC, C.26, February 22, 1801, 26; see also Keith, *North of Athabasca*, 154–55. For other examples, see LAC, MG19 A9, vol. 14, January 26, 1800, 13; and Henry (the Younger), *New Light*, August 19 and 30, 1800, 1:47, 73.

168. See LAC, MG19 A14, December 26, 1805, January 2 and 22, 1806, and February 12, 1806, 1–4, 6, 15, 25–26.

169. LAC, MG19 A9, vol. 6, March 1–2 and 7, 1800, 3. See also Keith, *North of Athabasca*, 88–89.

170. LAC, MG19 C1, vol. 4, January 1, 1790, 5.

171. Henry (the Younger), *New Light*, July 20, 1806, 1:333.

172. Harmon, *Sixteen Years*, August 18, 1808, 113.

173. Nelson, *My First Years*, January 31 and February 14, 1804, 143, 148.

174. TBR, 917.11 F671, June 16 and 19, 1808, 19–12.

175. TBR, 917.11 F671, June 20, 1808, 22.

176. OA, reel MS65, Donald McKay, Journal from January to December 1799, November 8, 1799, 40 (my pagination); and Henry (the Younger), *New Light*, July 27, 1800, 1:14–15.

177. TBR, S13, George Nelson's journal and reminiscences, August 12, 1803, 50.

178. LAC, MG19 C1, vol. 12, November 25, 1804, 29; Tanner, *A Narrative of the Captivity*, 80–81; MRB, MC, C.26, February 16, 1801, 23–24; see also Keith, *North of Athabasca*, 152–53; Cox, *Adventures on the Columbia River*, 145; MRB, MC, C.13, December 6, 1799, and January 14–15, 1800, 6, 14 (my pagination); TBR, S13, George Nelson's journal "No. 7," 283–84; and LAC, MG19 A.17, 65–66. For examples of Aboriginal peoples providing medical aid to bourgeois and voyageurs, see TBR, S13, George Nelson's journal "No. 1," 37–38 (for a report of the same incident, see George Nelson's journal and reminiscences, 29); George Nelson's journal and reminiscences, 66; George Nelson's journal "No. 5," Tête au Chien, September 12, 1807, 6–7, 9–10 (my sequential pagination)/190–91, 193–94 (Nelson's pagination); and Ross, *Fur Hunters*, 1:139–40. For examples of Aboriginal peoples requesting medical aid, see MRB, MC, C.28, August 28, 1807, 4; see also Keith, *North of Athabasca*, 307; and Cox, *Adventures on the Columbia River*, 126.

179. Cox, *Adventures on the Columbia River*, 126.

180. MRB, MC, C.26, February 16, 1801, 23; see also Keith, *North of Athabasca*, 152–53.

181. TBR, S13, George Nelson's journal "No. 5," 25–26 (my sequential pagination)/209–10 (Nelson's pagination); George Nelson's journal and reminiscences, fall 1803, 53–54; and Harmon, *Sixteen Years*, September 3, 1808, 114.

182. TBR, S13, George Nelson's journal, November 30, 1815–January 13, 1816, December 14, 1815, 87.

183. OA, MU 842, February 4, 1819, 31. For another example, see TBR, S13, George Nelson's journal "No. 1," 39.

184. OA, MU 842, February 4, 1819, 30–31; TBR, S13, George Nelson's coded journal, May 11, 1821, 15; and George Nelson's journal "No. 7," 278–79.

185. LAC, MG19 C1, vol. 9, September 24, 1805, and January 4, 1806, 6–7, 22.

186. HBCA, B.89/a/2, June 9, 15, and 23, 1810, fols. 1–2, 4.

187. Mackenzie, "General History," February 2, 1793, 263.

188. MRB, MC, C.27, June 3, 1822, n.p.

189. MRB, MC, C.24, November 28 and December 1, 1800, 5–6.

190. MRB, MC, C.1, 60.

191. Henry (the Younger), *New Light*, September 4, 1808, 2:495. Aboriginal peoples also vied with one another to become middlemen and control the trade. In the first quarter of the eighteenth century, Crees and Assiniboines assumed control of the trade out of York Factory until the companies began to move inland and make contact with interior peoples. See Ray, *Indians in the Fur Trade*, 53, 59, 61.

192. MRB, MC, C.27, April 5, 1819, 2.

193. TBR, S13, George Nelson's journal, November 3, 1807–August 31, 1808, June 17 and August 1, 1808, 41–42, 51–52; and George Nelson's journal "No. 5," June 1808, 16–18 (my sequential pagination)/200–202 (Nelson's pagination). See also Peers, *Ojibwa of Western Canada*, 68, 85–88; Tanner, *Narrative of the Captivity*, 156–58; and Edmunds, *Shawnee Prophet*, 39, 51.

194. Henry (the Younger), *New Light*, April 1 and May 23, 1810, 593, 2:599–600; Cox, *Adventures on the Columbia River*, June 23, 1817, 262; and MRB, MC, C.27, W. F. Wentzel to R. McKenzie, Mackenzie River Department, Great Bear Lake, February 28, 1814, 1.

195. Henry (the Younger), *New Light*, September 23, 1804, 1:251, and November 28, 1809, and January 22, 1810, 2:573, 580; Harmon, *Sixteen Years*, April 10 and September 21, 1805, 87–88, 97–98; LAC, MG19 A.17, 59–61; TBR, S13, George Nelson's journal "No. 1," 28–29; and McGillivray, *Journal*, October 17 and 20, 1794, 36.

196. Henry (the Younger), *New Light*, 1:292–93; MRB, MC C.5, July 11, 1806, 3; and John McDonell's "The Red River," in Wood and Thiessen, *Early Fur Trade*, 82.

197. Henry (the Younger), *New Light*, 1:85; and TBR, S13, George Nelson's journal "No. 7," 283–84, describes a case where Aboriginal people were displeased with voyageurs for killing and eating a bear.

198. TBR, S13, George Nelson's coded journal, April 17, 1821, 1–2.

199. B. M. White, "Skilled Game of Exchange."

200. MRB, MC, C.7, May 2, 1795, 33; Ross, *Fur Hunters*, 2:74–87; and Charles Chaboillez, "Journal for the Year 1797," December 1797, 24.

201. LAC, MG19 C1, vol. 1, December 1, 1797, 21.

202. TBR, S13, George Nelson's diary of events, June 30, 1822; George Nelson's journal and reminiscences, August 1803, 39; Henry (the Younger), *New Light*, September 1, 1800, 1:75 and January 27, 1810, February 10–11, 1810, 2:582, 584; and MRB, MC, C.24, February 20, 1801, 22.

203. B. M. White, "Fear of Pillaging."

204. TBR, S13, George Nelson's journal "No. 1," 32–37; George Nelson's journal "No. 7," 286–88; Henry (the Younger), *New Light*, September 6–7, 9–12, 23, 29 and October 2, 1800, 1:85–86, 90–93, 95, 102, 107–9; and D. Thompson, "Journal, November 1797," December 16, 1797, 105.

205. TBR, S13, George Nelson's journal "No. 7," 286–88.

206. Voyageur Paradix was neither liked nor respected by the Aboriginal peoples, but Nelson provides no clues as to his brutal behavior toward the Aboriginal peoples. OA, MU 842, February 4, 1819, and February 23, 1819, 31, 33.

207. Henry (the Younger), *New Light*, February 26, 1810, 2:589–90.

208. TBR, S13, George Nelson's diary of events, June 24, 1822; and OA, MU 842, February 5, 1819, 31.

209. Henry (the Younger), *New Light*, September 9, 1808, 2:499. Further detail is provided by Henry (the Younger), *Journal*, 2:361n38.

210. T. Douglas, *Sketch of the British Fur Trade*, 48–50.

211. See Ray, *Indians in the Fur Trade*, 117–24.

212. On Aboriginal food cycles, see Ray, *Indians in the Fur Trade*, 27–48.

213. Harmon, *Sixteen Years*, July 25, 1802, and February 22, 1804, 60, 72. In another example George Nelson also describes a desperate search for provisions one winter, when he dragged his men around against their will looking for Aboriginal people until they finally found some with provisions. TBR, S13, George Nelson's journal and reminiscences, 70.

214. Henry (the Younger), *New Light*, 1:101; and TBR, S13, George Nelson's journal, April 1, 1810–May 1, 1811, April 3, 13, 16, and 21, 1810, 2–5 (my pagination).

215. MRB, MC, C.26, December 10, 1800, 14; see also Keith, *North of Athabasca*, 144. In other examples voyageur La France accompanied two young Aboriginal boys bringing skins, oats, and bear meat to the Rainy Lake post; Faries, "Diary, " February 12, 1805, 229. Voyageur Jolibois ac-

companied some Aboriginal peoples with meat to the post at Great Bear Lake; MRB, MC, C.8, May 18, 1806, 16; see also Keith, *North of Athabasca*, 233.

216. LAC, MG19 C1, vol. 1, January 21 and February 21, 1798, 36, 44. For other examples see LAC, MG19 A14, January 31, 1806, 19; OA, MU 842, October 18, 1818, 7; and Henry (the Younger), *New Light*, August 26, September 11 and 16, 1800, 1:62, 65–66, 95, 98.

217. LAC, MG19 A14, December 26, 1805, 3. See also entries for December 22–23 and 26, 1805, January 2 and 22, 1806, February 12 and 22, 1806, 2, 4, 6, 15, 25–26, 31.

218. LAC, MG19 C1, vol. 12, October 2, 1804, 20.

219. LAC, MG19 C1, vol. 3, June 21, 1806, 132.

220. Mackenzie, *Voyages from Montreal*, 135–36.

221. Henry (the Younger), *New Light*, 1:2–3. For other examples of masters becoming frustrated with Aboriginal hunters, see MRB, MC, C.24, November 16 and 19, 1800, 3–4; and McGillivray, *Journal*, October 10 and 20, 1794, and January 27, 1795, 32–33, 36, 52.

222. Ross, *Fur Hunters*, 2:11.

223. Henry (the Younger), *New Light*, November 20, 1809, 2:572. Sylvia Van Kirk asserts that Aboriginal women were especially important to traders because they could process and prepare meat. Van Kirk, "*Many Tender Ties*", 56–57.

224. See entries between November 10, 1794, and February 11, 1795, in MRB, MC, C.7, 20–26. For other examples of hunting, see LAC, MG19 C1, vol. 1, September 24, 1797, October 6, 1797, January 12, 1798, and March 25, 1798, 10, 12–13, 33, 50; and MRB, MC, C.24, December 20 and 27, 1800, January 4 and 18, 1801, and February 18, 1801, 12, 14–15, 18, 22.

225. Mackenzie, *Voyages from Montreal*, June 9 and 11, 1789, 140, 143.

226. OA, reel MS65, Donald McKay, journal from August 1800 to April 1801, November 10 and December 25, 1800, 10, 17 (my pagination).

227. TBR, S13, George Nelson's journal, November 3, 1807–August 31, 1808, December 23, 1807, 13.

228. Henry (the Younger), *New Light*, September 23, 1800, 1:102; Ross, *Fur Hunters*, 1:26–27; and Harmon, *Sixteen Years*, September 2, 1810, 126.

229. Snares were most often used to catch hares. OA, reel MS65, Donald McKay, journal from January to December 1799, December 24, 1799, and February 17, 1806, 46, 58; and MRB, MC, C.26, October 20 and 22, 1800, 7; see also Keith, *North of Athabasca*, 137.

230. Van Kirk, "*Many Tender Ties*," 58–59.

231. Lefroy, *In Search of the Magnetic North*, Fort Chipewyan, Athabasca, January 1, 1844, Lefroy to Sophia, 93. For an example of the high frequency of hauling meat, see MRB, MC, C.24, November 24–25, 1800, December 20, 1800, January 3–4, 1801, February 7, 12, and 28, 1801, 5, 12, 15, 21, 23.

232. LAC, MG19 C1, vol. 7, October 19, 1798, 12.

233. MRB, MC, C.7, November 18, 1794, 20; LAC, MG19 C1, vol. 7, October 27, 1798, 16; and Henry (the Younger), *New Light*, October 15, 1801, 1:191.

234. For examples of men retrieving meat from Aboriginal hunters, see McGillivray, *Journal*, October 20, 1794, and January 27, 1795, 36, 52; and LAC, MG19 A14, December 21 and 27, 1805, and January 2, 1806, 1, 4, 6. For examples of men retrieving meat from Aboriginal caches, see LAC, MG19 C1, vol. 1, October 2, 7, 8, and 22, 1797, 11, 13, 15; and TBR, S13, George Nelson's journal, April 1, 1810–May 1, 1811, December 16 and 20, 1810, 38–39 (my pagination).

235. For one example see LAC, MG19 C1, vol. 7, October 15 and 16, 1798, 10.

236. Henry (the Younger), *New Light*, September 16, 1800, 1:98; and LAC, MG19 C1, vol. 7, October 18, 1798, 11.

237. LAC, MG19 A14, January 5, 6, and 13 and February 2, 1806, 8, 10, 11, 21. In another case, at Dauphin River, a voyageur named Paradix was unable to locate an Aboriginal cache to which he had been sent to retrieve meat. TBR, S13, George Nelson's journal, September 1, 1808–March 31, 1810, February 12, 1809, 19 (my pagination). In another case at Tête au Brochet on November 24, 1818, the men had a good deal of trouble getting to the lodges and nearly lost Welles and two sleighs by sinking. OA, MU 842, 15.

238. TBR, S13, George Nelson's journal and reminiscences, 78.

239. For examples see TBR, S13, George Nelson's journal, September 1, 1808–March 31, 1810, October 14, 1808, December 12, 1808, and November 17, 1809, 7–9, 13, 43 (my pagination); OA, MU 842, October 20 and November 2, 1818, 7, 10; and TBR, S13, George Nelson's journal "No. 5," 24 (my sequential pagination)/208 (Nelson's pagination).

240. LAC, MG19 C1, vol. 6, February 18, 1800, 1. See also Keith, *North of Athabasca*, 86–87.

241. For examples see Mackenzie, *Voyages from Montreal*, June 11, 1789, 143; OA, reel 65, Donald McKay, journal from January to December 1799, May 29, 1799, 27 (my pagination); and journal from January 1805 to June 1806, February 18, 1806, 58 (my pagination); and LAC, MG19 C1, vol. 12, October 9, 1804, 22.

242. Faries, "Diary," October 11, 22, 28, and 31, 1804, November 8–9, 1804, December 10, 15, 18, and 19, 1804, 214–22.

243. MRB, MC, C.13, December 7, 1799, 6 (my pagination).

244. TBR, S13, George Nelson's journal, September 1, 1808–March 31, 1810, August 12, 1809, 32 (my pagination).

245. TBR, S13, George Nelson's journal, August 29, 1805–March 8, 1806, mid-October 1805, October 23, 1805, 4–5 (my pagination).

246. For examples, see LAC, MG19 C1, vol. 6, October 30, 1800, 60; see also Keith, *North of Athabasca*, 117; and TBR, S13, George Nelson's journal, April 1, 1810–May 1, 1811, October 22 and November 18, 1810. See also Van Kirk, *"Many Tender Ties,"* 56.

247. TBR, S13, George Nelson's coded journal, April 28, 1821, 10.

248. TBR, S13, George Nelson's journal, January 29–June 23, 1815, May 24, 1815, 41.

249. MRB, MC, C.13, November 12, 1799, 3 (my pagination).

250. Faries, "Diary," March 25 and 30, and April 2–4, 7, 1805, 233–36.

251. Nelson, *My First Years*, April 6 and May 18, 1804, 154, 157.

252. For examples of making nets, floats, and fish houses, see TBR, S13, George Nelson's journal, November 3, 1807–August 31, 1808, October [Nelson mistakenly recorded November] 21 and December 11, 1807, 6, 13; and George Nelson's journal, April 1, 1810–May 1, 1811, October 3, 1810, 29 (my pagination). For an example of mending nets, see Nelson, *My First Years*, March 10, 1804, 151. For examples of caching and drying, see TBR, S13, George Nelson's journal, April 1, 1810–May 1, 1811, Friday, April 13, 1810, 3 (my pagination); and OA, MU 842, October 20 and November 2, 1818, 7–8, 10.

253. Van Kirk, *"Many Tender Ties,"* 56.

254. For an example of planting a garden, see Henry (the Younger), *New Light*, June 1810, 2:604–5. See also Faries, "Diary," November 23, 1804, 220. Much of the historiography of the fur trade portrays agriculture as a signal of the decline of trade. D. W. Moodie, however, points out that ag-

riculture was an important part of provisioning strategies for fur trade companies. D. W. Moodie, "Agriculture in the Fur Trade."

255. For a discussion of limited agriculture and gardening at fur trade posts, see L. H. Thomas, "History of Agriculture"; and D. W. Moodie, "Agriculture in the Fur Trade." Agriculture played an even greater role in provisioning after the 1821 merger. The new HBC encouraged farmers in the Red River settlement to produce surplus to trade to the company and also established "experimental" farms to discover the most productive crops and provision the workforce directly. See HBCA, A.6/24, fols. 22, 22d, March 9, 1836. The HBC also established a provisioning farm at Puget Sound. See Gibson, *Farming the Frontier*.

256. For examples see MRB, MC, C.7, October 6, 1794, 17; MRB, MC, C.28, mid-May 1808, 34; see also Keith, *North of Athabasca*, 339–40; TBR, S13, George Nelson's journal, September 1, 1808–March 31, 1810, mid-April 1809, 21 (my pagination); Henry (the Younger), *New Light*, October 6, 9, and 14, 1809, and mid-June 1810, 2:549, 552, 604–5; Harmon, *Sixteen Years*, April 29, 1804, May 1807, and October 10, 1808, 80, 103, 118; and Faries, "Diary," Monday, October 8, 1804, 213.

257. For an example of the annual cycle of garden maintenance, see OA, reel MS65, Donald McKay, journal from January 1805 to June 1806, May 6, 1805, June 17 and 20, 1805, October 21–22, 1805, April 3, 1806, and May 16, 1806, 12, 18–19, 37, 68, 76 (my pagination). On weeding see, for example, TBR, S13, George Nelson's journal, November 3, 1807–August 31, 1808, July 5, 1808, 45.

258. For one example see TBR, S13, George Nelson's coded journal, May 14, 1821, 16.

259. For examples see Harmon, *Sixteen Years*, June 2, 1803, 67; TBR, S13, George Nelson's coded journal, April 17–October 20, 1821, May 14 and 25, 1821, 16, 22–25; Faries, "Diary," September 29, 1804, October 10–11, 1804, November 23, 1804, and April 18, 1805, 212, 214, 220, 237, 240; and OA, reel MS65, Donald McKay, journal from January to December 1799, May 29 and November 19, 1799, 27, 41 (my pagination).

260. TBR, S13, George Nelson's Journal, August 29, 1805–March 8, 1806, September 17, 1805, 3 (my pagination); and OA, MU 842, September 21, 1818, 1.

261. For examples of making hay, see Henry (the Younger), *New Light*, August 31, 1807, and October 10, 1807, 1:424–25, and August 29, 1810, 2:622.

262. For example, see MRB, MC, C.7, La Grasse, November 18, 1793, 3.

263. For examples, see Henry (the Younger), *New Light*, August 22, 1800, 1:58; and MRB, MC, C.28, October 11, 1807, 9; see also Keith, *North of Athabasca*, 313.

264. For example, see Mackenzie, *Voyages from Montreal*, June 11, 1789, 143.

265. Faries, "Diary," April 18, 1805, 237; Henry (the Younger), *New Light*, September 17, 1800, 1:99; and Van Kirk, "*Many Tender Ties*," 58–59.

266. In the Cordillera region, Cole Harris has also found that posts were linked by local, regional, and external circulation. Harris, *Resettlement of British Columbia*, 39–41.

267. For an example of making packs at the Swan River post, see Harmon, *Sixteen Years*, May 26, 1801, 48. For an example of making packs at Grand Portage in 1789, see Mackenzie, "General History," 52.

268. For one example, see TBR, S13, George Nelson's coded journal, May 14, 1821, 16.

269. For a few examples, see OA, reel MS65, Donald McKay, journal from January to December 1799, March 4, 1799, 9 (my pagination); Nelson, *My First Years*, August 1, 1803, 100; and Fraser, "First Journal," April 13, 1806, 109–45.

270. Faries, "Diary," November 8, 1804, December 19 and 20, 1804, April 7, 8, 11, and 17, 1805, 218, 222, 236–37.

271. TBR, S13, George Nelson's journal, November 3, 1807–August 31, 1808, February 20, 1808, 19; and George Nelson's journal, September 1, 1808–March 31, 1810, November 23, 1808, February 11, 1809, and August 26, 1809, 12, 19, 35 (my pagination).

272. MRB, MC, C.24, November 18, 1800, and February 7, 1801, 3, 21; and MRB, MC, C.7, January 28, February 7, November 14, December 17 and 23, 1794, 8, 20, 22–23.

273. For examples, see LAC, MG19 C1, vol. 7, March 28, 1799, 44; LAC, MG19 C1, vol. 14, April 3, 1800, 21–22; Faries, "Diary," August 27, 1804, 206; Harmon, *Sixteen Years*, late March and early April 1809, 120; TBR, S13, George Nelson's journal, November 3, 1807–August 31, 1808, late March and early April 1808, 28; and George Nelson's journal, September 1, 1808–March 31, 1810, April 22 and August 1, 1809, 21, 31 (my pagination).

274. LAC, MG19 C1, vol. 4, April 12, 1790, 17.

275. Nelson, *My First Years*, July 27, 1803, 99–100.

276. TBR, S13, George Nelson's journal, "Journal from Bas De La Rivière to Cumberland House, 1819–?" May 15, 1819, 5–6 or b6 (my pagination).

277. OA, MU 572, vol. 2, R. McKenzie, Pic, to Duncan Clark, Long Lake, May 1, 1825, 3.

278. For examples of men making canoes, see LAC, MG19 C1, vol. 1 April 2, 1798, 52; LAC, MG19 C1, vol. 7, March 28, 1799, 44; and Henry (the Younger), *New Light*, May 19, 1804, 1:244. On Aboriginal women making canoes for traders, see Van Kirk, "*Many Tender Ties*," 61; and TBR, S13, George Nelson's journal, September 1, 1808–March 31, 1810, August 1 and 13, 1809, 31–33 (my pagination).

279. For examples, see OA, reel MS65, Donald McKay, Journal from January to December 1799, April 20, 1799, 17 (my pagination); LAC, MG19 C1, vol. 1, May 14, 1798, 60; LAC, MG19 C1, vol. 14, Friday and Monday, April 3 and 6, 1800, 22; LAC, MG19 C1, vol. 12, April 16, 1805, 62; LAC, MG19 C1, vol. 2, August 10, 1805, 5; and TBR, S13, George Nelson's journal, September 1, 1808–March 31, 1810, September 3, 1808, and April 22, 1809, 6 and 21.

280. TBR, S13, George Nelson's journal, "Journal from Bas De La Rivière to Cumberland House, 1819–?" May 22, 1819, 8 or b8.

281. For examples of Amelle's work on canoes, see entries in Faries, "Diary," October 10 and 31, 1804, November 19, 1804, December 22, 1804, and April 16, 1805, 214, 217, 219, 221, 223, 237.

282. MRB, MC, C.24, March 18, 19, 23, and 25, 1801, 27–28. For another example, see McGillivray, *Journal*, January 31, 1795, 52–53.

283. For examples see OA, reel MS65, Donald McKay, Journal from January 1805 to June 1806, June 3 and September 13–14, 1805, 16 and 32 (my pagination); and Henry, *New Light*, 2: 9 October 1809, 549.

284. Henry (the Younger), *New Light*, August 19, 1800, July 7, 1806, 1:47, 285.

285. For a few examples, see Henry (the Younger), *New Light*, October 12, 1800, and January 27, 1810, 1:117, 582, and early June 1810, 2:602.

286. McDonell, "Diary," September 16, 1793, 112.

287. TBR, S13, George Nelson's journal, August 29, 1805–March 8, 1806, December 4–5, 1805, 7–8 (my pagination).

288. MRB, MC, C.8, November 14, 1805, 7; see also Keith, *North of Athabasca*, 222; and Faries, "Diary," December 8, 1804, 221. See also Van Kirk, "*Many Tender Ties*," 54–55.

289. George Nelson records that he spent much time making snowshoes because he was determined to learn to make them properly. OA, MU, 842, January 2, 1819, 23.

290. Voyageur Roy procured wood for snowshoe frames. MRB, MC, C.24, January 19 and Feb-

ruary 7, 1801, 18, 21; and LAC, MG19 A14, December 20 and 29, 1805, January 6 and 21, 1806, 1, 5, 8, 14. For examples of obtaining the other materials from Aboriginal people, see OA. MU 842, December 1, 1818, 17; and TBR, S13, George Nelson's journal, November 3, 1807–August 31, 1808, December 26, 1807, and January 2,1808, 14–15. For descriptions of babiche, see McDermott, *Mississippi Valley French*, 18.

291. LAC, MG19 C1, vol. 7, October 24 and 26, 1798, 14. For other examples of men seeking wood for sleds, see MRB, MC, C.24, November 25, 1800, and January 19, 1801, 5, 18; OA, reel MS65, Donald McKay, Journal from January 1805 to June 1806, January 11, 1806, 51; LAC, MG19 A14, December 20, 1805, and January 21, 1806, 1, 14; Faries, "Diary," November 16 and 19, 1804, 219; and OA, MU 842, November 7 and 9, 1818, 11–12.

292. OA, reel MS65, Donald McKay, journal from January 1805 to June 1806, February 18, 1806, 58 (my pagination); and LAC, MG19 C1, vol. 7, October 27, 1798, 16.

293. TBR, S13, George Nelson's journal, September 1, 1808–March 31, 1810, November 24, 1808, 12 (my pagination).

294. Henry (the Younger), *New Light*, November 24, 1800, and October 30, 1801, 1:155, 191.

295. Henry (the Younger), *New Light*, October 3, 1803, 1:227; and Lefroy, *In Search of the Magnetic North*, Lefroy, Fort Chipweyan, Lake Athabasca, to Anne, January 1, 1844, 89.

296. For an example of this problem, see TBR, S13, George Nelson's journal, August 29, 1805–March 8, 1806; see entries from late October to mid-December 1805, 5–7 (my pagination).

297. TBR, S13, George Nelson's journal, November 3, 1807–August 31, 1808, January 24, 1808, 17. For another example of becoming lost, see OA, MU 842, March 10–13, 1819, 36–38.

298. MRB, MC, C.24, December 28, 1800, 14. For another example, see TBR, S13, George Nelson's journal, November 3, 1807–August 31, 1808, August 1, 1808, 51–52. See also Harris, *Resettlement of British Columbia*, 39.

299. MRB, MC, C.7, September 7, 1794, 17. For another example, see Faries, "Diary," December 15, 1804, 222.

300. Nelson, *My First Years*, August 10, 1803, 101–2.

301. Harrison, *Until Next Year*, introduction.

302. OA, MU 572, vol. 2, Donald McIntosh, Michipicoten, to Duncan Clark, Pic, July 8, 1825, 1.

303. OA, MU 572, vol. 2, R. McKenzie, Fort William, to Duncan Clark, Pic, July 18, 1825, 1. For other examples, see R. McKenzie, Pic, to Duncan Clark, Long Lake, May 1, 1825, 1; and Donald McIntosh, Michipicoten, to Duncan Clark, Pic, August 24, 1825, 1.

304. Montreal, McCord Museum, M 22074, May 21, 1815, 1.

305. Harmon, *Sixteen Years*, August 18, 1805, 95.

306. Fraser, "First Journal," April 13, 1806. Also see Nelson, *My First Years*, August 1, 1803, 100.

307. For a couple of examples, see TBR, S13, George Nelson's journal, September 1, 1808–March 31, 1810, December 24, 1808, and February 12, 1809, 14, 19 (my pagination).

308. For one example, see Harmon, *Sixteen Years*, May 26, 1801, 48.

309. LAC, MG19 C1, vol. 6, February 18, 1800, to February 14, 1801, July 10, 1800, 42; see also Keith, *North of Athabasca*, 109; and TBR, S13, George Nelson's journal, November 30, 1815–January 13, 1816, December 23, 1815, 90. For other examples, see LAC, MG19 C1, vol. 1, April 4, 1798, 52; and MRB, MC, C.7, November 3, 1793, 2.

310. TBR, S13, George Nelson's journal, August 29, 1805–March 8, 1806, September 10, 1805, 2 (my pagination); and Kohl, *Kitchi-Gami*, 122–23.

311. Henry (the Younger), *New Light*, February 12, 1810, 2:584.

312. MRB, MC, C.28, December 10, 1807, 18; see also Keith, *North of Athabasca*, 323.

313. MRB, MC, C.26, February 28, 1801, 28; see also Keith, *North of Athabasca*, 156. For other examples, see Henry (the Younger), *New Light*, November 25 and 28, 1800, 1:155–66; OA, MU 842, December 4, 1818, 17; and MRB, MC, C.24, December 17 and 25, 1800, and Friday, January 30, 1801, 10–13, 20. For other examples, see OA, reel MS65, Donald McKay, Journal from January 1805 to June 1806, July 23, 1805, 25 (my pagination); and TBR, S13, George Nelson's journal, September 1, 1808–March 31, 1810, November 29, 1809, 44 (my pagination).

314. For examples of the sending and receiving of letters, see MRB, MC, C.7, December 5, 1793, February 8, 1794, October 8, 1794, October 18, 1794, and May 2, 1795, 4, 8, 17, 19, 33.

315. TBR, S13, George Nelson's journal, September 1, 1808–March 31, 1810, September 9, 1808, 2.

316. For examples, see Henry (the Younger), *New Light*, April 11, 1806, 1:275; and TBR, S13, George Nelson's journal, April 1, 1810–May 1, 1811, April 7, 1810, 2.

317. Ross, *Fur Hunters*, 1:304.

318. Harmon, *Sixteen Years*, January 4, 1801, 42.

319. For examples, see MRB, MC, C.24, January 4, February 7 and 12, 1801, 15, 21; MRB, MC, C.28, April 8, 1807, 30; see also Keith, *North of Athabasca*, 336; and LAC, MG19 C1, vol. 9, December 18 and 22, 1805, 20.

320. LAC, MG19 C1, vol. 1, February 3, 1798, 39. See also TBR, S13, George Nelson's journal, September 1, 1808–March 31, 1810, November 14, 1808, 11–12 (my pagination).

321. LAC, MG19 C1, vol. 7, November 3 and 5, 1798, February 10, 1799, and April 9, 1799, 17, 30, 49.

322. Harmon, *Sixteen Years*, September 29, 1801, 51.

323. Harmon, *Sixteen Years*, September 3, 1806, 101.

8. Tender Ties

1. Ross, *Fur Hunters*, 1:296–97. Ross is referring to "different classes of people in the employ of the Company," which includes voyageurs.

2. Harmon, *Sixteen Years*, December 28, 1801, 52–53. Harmon is referring specifically to his interpreter Payet, but he generalizes to all men working in the trade, including voyageurs and probably clerks and bourgeois as well.

3. Van Kirk, *"Many Tender Ties"*; Brown, *Strangers in Blood*; and Peterson, "People In Between."

4. Thorne, *Many Hands of My Relations*; Sleeper-Smith, *Indian Women and French Men*; and Murphy, *Gathering of Rivers*.

5. Brown, "Partial Truths," 62.

6. For a few broad overviews of gender in Europe, see King, *Women of the Renaissance*, 38, 47–48; and Fletcher, *Gender, Sex and Subordination*, 101–279.

7. Bosher, "Family in New France," 1–13.

8. Noel, "New France," 18–40.

9. Greer, *People of New France*, 60–64.

10. Landes, *Ojibwa Woman*; Leacock, "Montagnais Women"; Leacock, "Women in Egalitarian Societies"; Anderson, *Chain Her by One Foot*; and M. H. Foster, "Of Baggage and Bondage."

11. For overviews, see Bonville, "Gender Relations"; and Shoemaker, *Negotiators of Change*, introduction, 2–7.

12. McGillivray, *Journal*, October 10, 1794, 33–34; and TBR, S13, George Nelson's Journal, July 13, 1803–June 25, 1804, 9. See also Nelson, *My First Years*, 107.

13. Smits, "'Squaw Drudge'"; Weist, "Beasts of Burden"; and Van Kirk, *"Many Tender Ties,"* 17–19.

14. Buffalohead, "Farmers, Warriors, Traders," 237–38. See also Vibert, *Traders' Tales*, 127–29.

15. Greer, *People of New France*, 61, 64–70; and Noel, *Women in New France*, 17–19.

16. Brown, "Partial Truths," 68.

17. TBR, S13, George Nelson's journal "No. 5," 22–23 (my sequential pagination)/206–7 (Nelson's pagination).

18. Brown, "Partial Truths," 76.

19. Cox, *Adventures on the Columbia River*, 231.

20. Ross, *Fur Hunters*, 1:296.

21. Henry (the Younger), *New Light*, November 26, 1802, 1:206.

22. MRB, MC, C.13, November 18, 1799, 4 (my pagination).

23. Henry (the Younger), *New Light*, August 6, 1800, 1:25; and HBCA, B.42/a/136a, fol. 19.

24. For examples of complaints, see Henry (the Younger), *New Light*, August 6, 1800, 1:25; and MRB, MC, C.26, February 22, 1801, 26. See also Keith, *North of Athabasca*, 154–55. One voyageur tried to blackmail Ross into giving him a horse to pay for a bride; Ross, *Adventures of the First Settlers*, 200–201.

25. Cox, *Adventures on the Columbia River*, 308.

26. TBR, S13, George Nelson's journal and reminiscences, 72.

27. Fraser, "First Journal," April 16 and 18, 1806, 110–11.

28. McGillivray, *Journal*, March 8, 1795, 60–61.

29. TBR, S13, George Nelson's journal, November 3, 1807–August 31, 1808, December 8, 1807, 12.

30. Henry (the Younger), *New Light*, August 29, 1800, and January 1, 2, and 30, 1801, 71–73, 163, 169.

31. Brown, "Fur Trade as Centrifuge," 206.

32. TBR, S13, George Nelson's journal "No. 5," 41 (my sequential pagination)/225 (Nelson's pagination).

33. TBR, S13, George Nelson's coded journal, May 11, 1821, 15.

34. Mackenzie, *Voyages from Montreal*, February 2, 1793, 263.

35. Larocque, "Journal of an Excursion," August 19, 1805, 184.

36. LAC, MG19 C1, vol. 8, January 13, 1805, 41–42. See also Keith, *North of Athabasca*, 198–99.

37. Larocque, "Journal of an Excursion," August 19, 1805, 184. For another example, see Henry (the Younger), *New Light*, August 29, 1800, 1:71.

38. Sleeper-Smith, *Indian Women and French Men*, 5–6.

39. Fur, "'Some Women Are Wiser,'" 82.

40. LAC, MG19 C1, vol. 1, October 24, 1797, January 7, 1798, and February 21, 1798, 15, 32, 44; OA, MU 842, October 18, 1818, 7; and Faries, "Diary," April 18, 1805, 237.

41. Tanner, *Narrative of the Captivity*, 86; and Peers, *Ojibwa of Western Canada*, 36. See also Fierst, "Strange Eloquence."

42. Unfortunately in this instance Net-no-kwa decided to follow her son in joining another group of Aboriginals and thus needed to be free of her cargo. She sold her furs quickly at a loss. Tanner, *Narrative of the Captivity*, 51–52.

43. Peers suggests age was one of the sources of Net-no-kwa's authority. Peers, *Ojibwa of Western Canada*, 57.

44. Peterson, "People In Between," 60–64.

45. Buffalohead, "Farmers, Warriors, Traders," 238, 240–41.

46. Cooper, "Native Women."

47. TBR, S13, George Nelson's journal, November 3, 1807–August 31, 1808, Friday, November 20, 1807, 9.

48. Devens, *Countering Colonization*, 15–18.

49. MRB, MC, C.12, 19; and Van Kirk, *"Many Tender Ties,"* 65. Aboriginal husbands and wives often worked together as guides. See OA, MU 2199, Edward Umfreville, June 22 and July 17, 1784, 7, 21. Aboriginal women sometimes moved far beyond these roles to become diplomatic emissaries between traders and Aboriginals, as did Thanadelthur; Van Kirk, *"Many Tender Ties,"* 66–71.

50. MRB, MC, C.7, February 27, 1794, 10.

51. Van Kirk, "Thanadelthur"; and McCormack, "Many Faces of Thanadelthur."

52. Van Kirk, *"Many Tender Ties,"* 5; Brown, *Strangers in Blood*, 81; and Sleeper-Smith, *Indian Women and French Men*, 4–6.

53. See, for example, Rich, "Trade Habits"; and Ray and Freeman, *"Give Us Good Measure."*

54. For some examples, see R. White, *Middle Ground*; B. M. White, "Skilled Game of Exchange"; and Peers, *Ojibwa of Western Canada*.

55. Landes, *Ojibwa Woman*, 119–20.

56. Brown, *Strangers in Blood*, 88.

57. On berdaches, see Whitehead, "Bow and the Burden Strap"; Roscoe, "How to Become a Berdache"; Williams, *Spirit and the Flesh*; Allen, "Lesbians in American Indian Cultures"; and Callender and M. Kochems, "North American Berdache."

58. Landes, *Ojibwa Woman*, 119–20; and Peers, *The Ojibwa of Western Canada*, 45.

59. Greer, *Peasant, Lord, and Merchant*, 50–51.

60. Gagnon, *Plaisir d'Amour*.

61. MRB, MC, C.5, July 23 and 26, 1806, 47, 70; Lewis, *History of the Expedition*, January 16, 1805, 1:215; and Ross, *Adventures of the First Settlers*, 93.

62. MRB, MC, C.7, March 26, 1795, 29; and McDonell, "Extracts," 1:293.

63. MRB, MC, C.7, April 5, 1795, 30.

64. Van Kirk, *"Many Tender Ties,"* 25–26.

65. Cooper, "Native Women," 104–5.

66. See Alexander Henry the Younger's "Report of North West Population 1805," in his *Journal*, 1:188. He found a 2.25:1 ratio of Aboriginal women to Aboriginal men.

67. Brown, *Strangers in Blood*, 88. Sherry Ortner and Harriet Whitehead assert that in "prestige societies" often the erotic pleasure, passion, and images of male and female bodies dissolve in the face of economics, rank, and male honor. Ortner and Whitehead, "Introduction."

68. Cox, *Adventures on the Columbia River*, September 15, 1817, 300.

69. MRB, MC, C.27, March 27, 1807, 17; and Cox, *Adventures on the Columbia River*, summer 1812, 83.

70. Henry (the Younger), *New Light*, November 1, 1810, 2:660.

71. Lewis, *History of the Expedition*, 2:271.

72. Henry (the Younger), *New Light*, April 19, 1814, 2:890–91.

73. Ross, *Fur Hunters*, 2:128; and Henry (the Younger), *New Light*, October 24, 1803, 1:228.

74. Henry, *New Light*, January 12, 1804, 1:235.

75. MRB, MC, C.7, March 26, 1795, 29; and McDonell, "Extracts," 1:293.

76. Tyrrell, *Journals*, 446n, 449.

77. Brown, *Strangers in Blood*, 84.

78. The term *pillage* meant to rob, but it sometimes had sexual connotations and was a polite word for rape. McGillivray, *Journal*, October 23, 1794, 37. For another example, see J. McKenzie, "Journal, 1799."

79. TBR, S13, George Nelson's journal, "Journal from Bas De La Rivière to Cumberland House, 1819–?" May 13, 1819, 5 (my pagination); and George Nelson's coded journal, April 20, 1821, 5.

80. Ross, *Fur Hunters*, 1:23–24.

81. TBR, S13, George Nelson's Journal, September 1, 1808–March 31, 1810, January 10, 1810, 48 (my pagination).

82. McKenzie, "Journal, 1799," February 9 and 10, 1800, 2:385 (page missing from the original James McKenzie's Journal, 1799–1800, MRB, MC, C.13).

83. Fraser, "First Journal," May 17 and 19, 1806, 120–21; and MRB, MC, C.24, May 8, 1801, 36. For another example, see Faries, "Diary," May 10, 1805, 240.

84. Franchère, *Journal of a Voyage*, 182; and Kohl, *Kitchi-Gami*, 3. See also Giraud, *Le métis canadien*; Peterson, "People In Between"; and Peterson and Brown, *New Peoples*.

85. MRB, MC, C.7, April 29, 1795, 32.

86. Minutes of the Meetings of the NWC at Grand Portage and Fort William, 1801–7, with Supplementary Agreements, in Wallace, *Documents*, 211.

87. Van Kirk, "*Many Tender Ties*," 92.

88. Minutes of the Meetings of the NWC at Grand Portage and Fort William, 1801–7, with Supplementary Agreements, in Wallace, *Documents*, 262; Van Kirk, "*Many Tender Ties*," 39–40, 92; Brown, "Fur Trade as Centrifuge," 202, 205; Brown, *Strangers in Blood*, 97; and Brown, "Partial Truths."

89. HBCA, B.22/a/6, November 13, 1798, fol. 9.

90. HBCA, B.89/a/2, June 13, 1810, fol. 2; and Harmon, *Sixteen Years*, May 19, 1803, and April 29, 1804, 66–67, 80.

91. Ross, *Fur Hunters*, 1:17, 23–24, and 2:7; Mackenzie, *Voyages from Montreal*, early June 1789, 135; TBR, S13, George Nelson's journal, September 1, 1808–March 31, 1810, September 9, 1808, 2; and Henry (the Younger), *New Light*, August 21, 1800, 1:50–52, and October 3, 1803, 2:26–27.

92. Fraser, "First Journal," May 17 and 19, 1806 120–21.

93. LAC, MG19 A9, vol. 2, Simon Fraser to James McDougall, [Natleh ?] January 31, 1807; Simon Fraser to my dear friend (John Stuart), [Natleh ?] February 1, 1807.

94. My translation; italics in original. Original: "La façon de ces pays est que lorsqu'on avait envie d'avoir une femme, *on allait demander au père s'il voulait nous la donner, et si le père voulait donner sa fille, on allait leur acheter quelque chose par reconnaissance. Ordinairement, c'était la façon du pays de donner un présent au père de la fille donnée en marriage.* Ce n'était pas loisible d'avoir plus d'une femme. . . . J'ai souvant vu faire des mariages dans ce pays, et je parle de cette coutume avec connaissance." From "Connolly vs. Woolrich," 227–28.

95. My translation; italics in original. Original: "Un homme par là [dans le pays d'en haut]

ne pouvait pas prendre plus d'une femme, nous regardions cette union comme l'union de mari et femme par ici [Canada], [illegible] et une aussi sacrée. J'ai été marié là moi-même à la façon du pays. J'ai vécu vingt-trois ans avec elle, et elle est morte il y a huit ans passés. *Quand on voulait se marier dans le Nord Ouest, il fallait demander au père et à la mère [illegible] qu'on voulait avoir, et s'ils consentaient, on demandait après au bourgeois permission de se marier, et c'était la toute là cérèmonie; et aprés cela, nous [illegible] considèrions comme mari et femme légitimes comme ici, comme si nous étés mariés à l'église.*" From "Connolly vs. Woolrich," 227–28.

96. "Johnstone et al. vs. Connolly," 280–81.

97. "Johnstone et al. vs. Connolly," 287–88. See also Brown, *Strangers in Blood*, 94–95; and Van Kirk, "*Many Tender Ties*," 117, 121.

98. Greer, *Peasant, Lord, and Merchant*, 48–49.

99. Palmer, *Journal of Travels*, September 21, 1817, 217.

100. Original in French: "J'étais moi-même mariée dans le Nord-Ouest. La façon est qu'on couche avec les hommes. Je ne saisd pas si on est obligé de faire des présents pour se marier." From "Johnstone et al. vs. Connolly," 287.

101. TBR, S13, George Nelson's journal "No. 5," 22–23 (my sequential pagination)/206–7 (Nelson's pagination); and Henry (the Younger), *New Light*, November 10, 1809, 2:571.

102. Van Kirk found the same patterns; see "*Many Tender Ties*," 36–37.

103. Cox, *Adventures on the Columbia River*, 128–29.

104. My translation; emphasis in original. Original French of Joseph Mazurette: A La façon du pays quand un bourgeois ou un engagé voulait une femme, il allait trouver les parents de la fille qu'il aimait, leur demandait s'ils voulaient lui donner leur fille pour sa femme, et s'ils consentaient, il s'habillait, la prenait pour sa femme et ils vivaient ensemble comme tels. Ce n'était pas permis de prendre *plus d'une femme dans le pays*. Cette sorte de mariage était respectée solennellement. . . . Presque toutes les nations sont pareilles, quant aux coutumes. On ne se joue pas d'une femme sauvage comme on veut. On sait en user à l'égard des femmes comme par ici. . . . Il y aurait du danger d'avoir la tête cassée, si l'on prend dans ce pays, sans le consentement des parents. C'est le père et la mère qui donnent les femmes, et s'ils sont morts, ce sont les plus proches parents. [Question.—Quand vous parlez d'avoir, de prendre ou payer pour une femme, en quel sens parlez-vous? Est-ce comme mari et femme pour toujours ou que pour le moment?] Réponse.—Pour toujours, Monsieur." From "Johnstone et al. vs. Connolly," 280–81.

105. Editor Barry Gough asserts that "women 'of' white men" were called "White." In Henry (the Younger), *Journal*, 1:188.

106. Brown, *Strangers in Blood*, 87–88.

107. Van Kirk, "*Many Tender Ties*," 53, 54–59, 61–65.

108. MRB, MC, C.24, March 17, 1801, 27; LAC, MG19 C1, vol. 10, January 20, 1804, 30; and LAC, MG19 C1, vol. 6, March 9, June 2, and October 14, 1800, 4, 27, 56. See also Keith, *North of Athabasca*, 89, 101–2, 115.

109. Sleeper-Smith, *Indian Women and French Men*, 4.

110. MRB, MC, C.26, February 22, 1801, 25–26. See also Keith, *North of Athabasca*, 155.

111. Van Kirk, "*Many Tender Ties*," 84–85.

112. MRB, MC, C.7, April 2 and 11, 1795, 30; HBCA, B.89/a/2, June 13, 1810, fol. 2.

113. TBR, S13, George Nelson's journal, September 1, 1808–March 31, 1810, September 1, 1809, 36 (my pagination); and George Nelson's journal, April 1, 1810–May 1, 1811, September 24, 1810, 27 (my pagination).

114. Van Kirk, "*Many Tender Ties*," 65–73; see also Lefroy, *In Search of the Magnetic North*, Lefroy, Lake Superior to Fanny, Montreal, October 22, 1844, 132, and Lefroy, Fort Chipewyan to Isabella, McKenzie's River, Fort Simpson, April 29, 1844, 112–13, 119; HBCA, B.89/a/2, December 11, 1810, and March 1, 1811, fols. 18, 26; and LAC, MG19 C1, vol. 6, June 2, 1800, 27. See also Keith, *North of Athabasca*, 101.

115. OA, MU 1391, June 26, 1818, 13.

116. HBCA, B.39/a/16, July 8, 1820, fol. 7; Nelson, *My First Years*, September 16, 1803, 110; and TBR, S13, George Nelson's journal and reminiscences, fall 1803, 49.

117. Nelson, *My First Years*, January 14 and 31, and February 14, 1804, 139–40, 143, 148.

118. Van Kirk, "*Many Tender Ties*," 46–47.

119. Brown, *Strangers in Blood*, xxi, 51. Sleeper-Smith in *Indian Women and French Men* does not specify that she is writing about fur trade elites, but on page 30 she distinguishes the term "French trader," used throughout the book, from "canoemen or voyageurs," implying that the traders were masters in the trade.

120. Brown, *Strangers in Blood*, 82, 89, 96. Brown's recent article "Partial Truths" further supports this assertion.

121. "Johnstone et al. vs. Connolly," 287.

122. Ross, *Fur Hunters*, 2:234–37.

123. Henry (the Younger), *New Light*, May 12, 1803, 1:211.

124. Harmon, *Sixteen Years*, October 10, 1805, 98. In the end, however, Harmon decided to keep his country wife and children when he returned to Vermont. See Harmon, *Sixteen Years*, February 28, 1819, 194–95; and Van Kirk, "*Many Tender Ties*," 138–39.

125. Nelson, *My First Years*, June 29, 1804, 170–71.

126. Cox, *Adventures on the Columbia River*, 312; and Van Kirk, "*Many Tender Ties*," 50.

127. Van Kirk, "*Many Tender Ties*," 46.

128. See the example of Desrocher in TBR, S13, George Nelson's journal, April 1, 1810–May 1, 1811, September 24, 1810 and January 1811, 27, 42 (my pagination). See the example of Brunet's wife in Nelson, *My First Years*, October 16, 1803, 116. See also LAC, MG19 A9, vol. 2, Simon Fraser to James McDougall, [Natleh ?] January 31, 1807, and Simon Fraser to my dear friend (John Stuart), [Natleh ?] February 1, 1807.

129. Van Kirk, "*Many Tender Ties*," 40.

130. For examples of Aboriginal men sexually assaulting the wives and daughters of voyageurs, see LAC, MG19 A17, 123–25; and OA, MU 842, February 5, 1819, 31.

131. MRB, MC, C.7, May 30, 1795, 36.

132. Tyrrell, *Journals*, 449.

133. OA, MU 842, April 16, 1819, 45; and MRB, MC, C.28, June 19, 1808, 43. See also Keith, *North of Athabasca*, 347.

134. Peers, *Ojibwa of Western Canada*, 56–59. For instances of Algonquian women committing suicide, see Henry (the Younger), *New Light*, October 22 and 27, 1804, 1:252, and September 3, 1808, 2:486–87; Harmon, *Sixteen Years*, February 19, 1803, and January 27, 1811, 66, 136–37.

135. TBR, S13, George Nelson's journal, April 1, 1810–May 1, 1811, July 9, 1810, 17 (my pagination); for an example of a voyageur giving his wife a black eye, see Faries, "Diary," September 1, 1804, 207.

136. Cooper, "Native Women," 100.

137. TBR, S13, George Nelson's journal and reminiscences, 72; Henry (the Younger), *New Light*, March 3, 1806, 1:274; and MRB, MC, C.8, February 28, 1806, 12.

138. See also Keith, *North of Athabasca*, 227–28.

139. TBR, S13, George Nelson's journal, September 1, 1808–March 31, 1810, October 29 and November 5, 1809, 41 (my pagination).

140. Henry (the Younger), *New Light*, May 7, 1802, 1:197; and Cox, *Adventures on the Columbia River*, 310–11.

141. Harmon, *Sixteen Years*, 62–63, 98, 194.

9. Disengagement

1. Dugas, *Un Voyageur*, 107, my translation.

2. TBR, S13, George Nelson's journal, July 13, 1803–June 25, 1804, August 2, 1803, 4. See also Nelson, *My First Years*, 100.

3. Some scholars are beginning to study this question. See, for example, Englebert, "Storm before the Calm."

4. For examples, see ANQM, CE601 S11, 1965, 6884.

5. LAC, RG7 G15C, vol. 2, CO42, vol. 100, Sheriff Edward Gray to Attorney General James Monk, June 9, 1794; J. Reid to same, June 12, 1794; T. A. Coffin to James McGill, July 21, 1794; cited in Greenwood, *Legacies of Fear*, 80, 285.

6. LAC, MG23 G1110, vol. 9, 4613–14, Jonathan Sewell to Lieutenant Colonel Beckworth, July 28, 1795. Donald Fyson brought this reference to my attention.

7. HBCA, E31/2/2, fols. 1–2, Marianne Duque, mere, St. Ours, to Francois Benoit, fils, voyageur des pays d'en Haut, au soin de Mr athanas Felix. Original French: "Je profite de locaasion de Mr Athanase felix Pour tapprendre L'Etat de macente qui nes Pas bien," and "Je dezire bien de te pri et faire tous ton Posible Pour desendre que Jai la consolassion de te voir avant que je meur."

8. The voyageurs' loneliness was often expressed in their songs. See Kohl, *Kitchi-Gami*, 258–60. Clerks and bourgeois often recorded their feelings of being homesick. See Nelson, *My First Years*, May 23, 1804, 157–58; TBR, S13, George Nelson's journal "No. 1," 10; and George Nelson's journal and reminiscences, 22–23. See also Cox, *Adventures on the Columbia River*, 130–31, 198–99, 218; Harmon, *Sixteen Years*, April 4, 1801, September 29, 1801, and June 21, 1803, 45–46, 51, 67–68; and Franchère, *Voyage to the Northwest Coast*, July 26 and September 6, 1810, 3, 10–11.

9. For example, Vivier in LAC, MG19 C1, vol. 7, Sunday, November 18, 1798, to Tuesday, November 20, 1798, 19–20.

10. MRB, MC, C.27, 3.

11. OA, MU 2199, box 4, no. 1 (photostat of original), "An Account of the Athabasca Indians by a Partner of the North West Company, 1795," revised 4 May 1840 (forms part of the manuscript titled "Some Account of the North West Company", by Roderick McKenzie, director of the NWC. Original at MRB, MC, C.18, reel 22. Photostat can also be found at LAC, MG19 C1, vol. 55, reel C-15640), 3–4.

12. Morice, *Dictionnaire historiques*, 243; HBCA, B.177/a/1, June 1791; HBCA, B.105/a/4, June 1, 1797; HBCA, B.22/a/5, August 27, 1797; and TBR, S13, George Nelson's journal, November 3, 1807–August 31, 1808, 2, 6.

13. MRB, MC, C.29, 6.

14. Cox, *Adventures on the Columbia River*, 306–7.

15. Ross, *Fur Hunters*, 1:284–85.

16. Mayer, *With Pen and Pencil*, 229.

17. Henry (the Younger), *New Light*, November 28 to December 1, 1800, 1:157–58.

18. LAC, MG18 C5.

19. Franchère, *Journal of a Voyage*, 182; and Kohl, *Kitchi-Gami*, 3, 168–70, 212–13.

20. Osborne, "Migration of Voyageurs," 123–24.

21. Ross, *Fur Hunters*, 2:243.

22. Dugas, *Un Voyageur*, 105–8.

23. Henry (the Younger), *New Light*, Sunday, July 20, 1806, 1:333.

24. Rochefoucauld Liancourt, *Travels through the United States*, 296–97.

25. Cox, *Adventures on the Columbia River*, June 23, 1817, 262.

26. TBR, S13, George Nelson's journal and reminiscences, "St. Judes, Dec 1st 1825," 82.

27. Henry (the Younger), *New Light*, July 13, 1810, 2:613. On Desjarlais as the sovereign of Red Deer Lake, see Franchère, *Voyage to the Northwest Coast*, June 5, 1814, 214. For more information on freeman Antoine Desjarlais, see Devine, *People Who Own Themselves*, 82, 84–86, 92, 95–97; and Devine, "Les Desjarlais."

28. Ross, *Fur Hunters*, 1:291–92.

29. Regarding Boucher, see Henry (the Younger), *New Light*, 1:219; and Franchère, *Voyage to the Northwest Coast*, 264. Some referred to the trader as Jean-Marie Boucher. See Morrison, *Superior Rendezvous Place*, 42. On Constant, see Podruchny, "Un homme-libre."

30. Ross, *Fur Hunters*, 1:293.

31. PAM, MG2 A1–1, "Actual Number of Free Canadians with Their Indian Wives," 18–19, 506–7.

32. Minutes of the Meetings of the NWC at Grand Portage and Fort William, 1801–7, with Supplementary Agreements, in Wallace, *Documents*, 272.

33. Devine, "Les Desjarlais," especially 130–32.

34. Winnipeg, Société historique de Saint-Boniface, Catholic Parish Records, microfilm 2936, Saint-Augustin-de-Desmaures, ZQ-1–348. Thanks to Harry Duckworth, Alfred Fortier, and William Benoit for helping me find this source.

35. HBCA, B.177/a/1, James Sutherland's Red Lake journal of 1790–91. See also item no. 16 in the collection of historic document dealer Warren Baker, Montreal; this document concerns a suit that Charles Racette, voyageur, brought against Angelique Blondeau, widow of Gabriel Cotte, and includes a declaration by Racette dated April 4, 1796, and a two-page holograph account by Racette, undated; also includes undated notes on depositions by two other voyageurs, Alexis Carpentier and Jac. Desnoyers; and a writ of appeal by Auldjo, Jordan and Claus (probably executors to Gabriel Cotte's estate), dated February 24, 1797. Thanks to Harry Duckworth for sharing these references.

36. HBCA, B.22/a/6, 1798–1799, Robert Goodwin, September 1–2, 1797.

37. TBR, S13, George Nelson's journal and reminiscences, "St. Judes, Dec 1st 1825," 82.

38. HBCA, B.22/a/6, 1798–1799, Robert Goodwin, September 2, 1797.

39. TBR, S13, George Nelson's journal, November 3, 1807–August 31, 1808, 2, 6, 36, 44; and George Nelson's journal, September 1, 1808–March 31, 1810, September 14, 1808, and September 14, 1809.

40. Morice, *Dictionnaire historiques*, 243.

41. TBR, S13, George Nelson's journal, November 3, 1807–August 31, 1808, May 14 and 22, 1808,

31, 34; George Nelson's journal, September 1, 1808–March 31, 1810, September 14, 1809; George Nelson's journal, April 1, 1810–May 1, 1811, July 9, 1810; George Nelson's journal and reminiscences, "St. Judes, Dec 1st 1825," 82; and Cox, *Adventures on the Columbia River*, July 15, 1817, 276.

42. TBR, S13, George Nelson's coded journal, May 10 and 24, 1821, 14–15, 20.

43. MRB, MC, C.13, July 31, 1800, 61 (my pagination).

44. Cox, *Adventures on the Columbia River*, 171–72.

45. TBR, S13, George Nelson's journal "No. 5," 32 (my sequential pagination)/216 (Nelson's pagination); George Nelson's journal "No. 7," 280; Harmon, *Sixteen Years*, January 4, 1801, 41; and Henry (the Younger), *New Light*, September 18, 1810, 2:628.

46. Devine, "Les Desjarlais," 133.

47. Sprague and Frye, *Genealogy of the First Métis Nation*, 15; Thistle, *Indian-European Trade Relations*, 73; and Devine, "Les Desjarlais," 135–36, 139.

48. TBR, S13, George Nelson's coded journal, May 9 and 21, 1821, 12, 20.

49. TBR, S13, George Nelson's journal, April 1, 1810–May 1, 1811, July 7, 1810, 16 (my pagination).

50. MRB, MC, C.7, November 6, 1793; MRB, MC, C.24, November 28, 1800, and Wednesday, May 6, 1801, 5, 36; and Harmon, *Sixteen Years*, July 16, 1800, 23. For an example of engaging freemen for two and three years see MRB, MC, C.24, January 21–22, 1801, 18–19. For an example of engaging freemen for a season, see Henry (the Younger), *New Light*, September 21, 1809, 2:546.

51. For one example, see MRB, MC, C.24, March 27 and April 11, 1801, 29, 31.

52. La Fraise did not know how to write and so needed assistance in his clerical duties. MRB, MC, C.12; this account is published in Wood and Thiessen, *Early Fur Trade*. It is uncertain if he had any relation to the coureur de bois Joseph La France taken into custody by the British at York Fort in 1742. See H. H. Tanner, "Career of Joseph La France."

53. OA, MU 2199, Edward Umfreville, June 10, 11, 28–30, and July 15, 1784, 10, 16, 20.

54. MRB, MC, C.24, March 27, 1808, 29; TBR, S13, George Nelson's journal, August 29, 1805–March 8, 1806, September 10, 1805, 2 (my pagination); and HBCA, B.89/a/2, June 22, 1810, fol. 4.

55. TBR, S13, George Nelson's "Journal from Bas De La Rivière to Cumberland House, 1819–?" September 1, 3, and 4, 1819, 4–5 (my pagination); and Cox, *Adventures on the Columbia River*, June 23, 1817, 262.

56. TBR, S13, George Nelson's journal, August 29, 1805–March 8, 1806, August 29–30 and September 10, 1805, 1–2 (my pagination).

57. For examples of freemen selling food to traders, see Franchère, *Voyage to the Northwest Coast*, June 5, 1814, 240–41; OA, MU 1391, June 6 and 16, 1818, 7, 10; and TBR, S13, George Nelson's "Journal from Bas De La Rivière to Cumberland House, 1819–?" September 4, 1819, 5 (my pagination). For examples of freemen hunting for a post, see MRB, MC, C.24, May 6, 1801, 36; and Henry (the Younger), *New Light*, September 21, 1809, 2:546 (and following). For examples of freemen trading furs with a post, see Henry (the Younger), *New Light*, May 15, 1806, and November 28, 1809, 2:119, 574; and MRB, MC, C.24, November 28, 1800, and May 6, 1801, 5, 36.

58. TBR, S13, George Nelson's coded journal, May 20, 21, and 25, 1821, 18–20, 22.

59. MRB, MC, C.24, May 6, 1801, 36.

60. Henry (the Younger), *New Light*, November 30, 1803, and October 26, 1805, 1:231, 269.

61. Nelson, *My First Years*, August 13, 1803, 102.

62. TBR, S13, George Nelson, Tête au Brochet, to his parents, 9.

63. For an example of two freemen traveling together, see Nelson, *My First Years*, August 7,

1803, 101. For an example of four freemen and their families living together, see Cox, *Adventures on the Columbia River*, July 15, 1817, 276.

64. Alexander Henry the Younger mentioned a "canotée" of freemen traveling together in one instance and an unspecified number of freemen living together in another instance. Henry (the Younger), *New Light*, March 19, 1814, 2:856, and July 9, 1806, 1:289–90. George Nelson refers to meeting four canoes of freemen traveling together. TBR, S13, George Nelson's journal, November 3, 1807–August 31, 1808, June 4, 1808, 37.

65. TBR, S13, George Nelson's journal, January 29–June 23, 1815, April 8, 1815, 30.

66. Henry (the Younger), *New Light*, August 31, 1807, 1:424.

67. Devine, "Les Desjarlais," 134.

68. See entry for July 1, 1833, in Back, *Narrative of the Arctic Land Expedition*, 64. Historian Paul Thistle found that Cree families began to garden in The Pas in the 1830s, in his *Indian-European Trade Relations*, 82–83.

69. Winnipeg, Provincial Archives of Manitoba, Church Missionary Society, C.1/M.2, 551–52.

70. Association de la Propagation de la foi (Diocèse de Québec), *Notice sur les Missions*, Joseph E. Darveau, St. François-Xavier, December 7, 1843, 92.

71. Thistle, *Indian-European Trade Relations*, 73.

72. Peers, *Ojibwa of Western Canada*, 69, 104–5.

73. TBR, S13, George Nelson's journal and reminiscences, "St. Judes, Dec 1st 1825," 82.

74. Franchère, *Voyage to the Northwest Coast*, June 25, 1814, 256.

75. HBCA, D.3/3, January 31, 1822, fol. 20.

76. McLean, *Notes of a Twenty-Five Years' Service*, 1:134.

77. Devine, "Les Desjarlais," 141–44.

78. Ross, *Fur Hunters*, 2:234–37.

10. Conclusion

1. Nelson, *My First Years*, 38.

2. See the extensive collection of the Archives de Folklore at the Université Laval, Québec. For published examples, see Barbeau, "Field of European Folk-Lore"; Bolduc, "Contes Populaires Canadiens"; Massicotte and Barbeau, "Chantes Populaire du Canada"; Barbeau, *Quebec*; Barbeau, *Jongleur Songs of Old Quebec*; and Fowke, *Folktales of French Canada*.

3. There has been a growing interest in the cultural history of French Canada in the past couple of decades. For examples related to oral traditions, see Crowley, "'Thunder Gusts'"; Greer, *Patriots and the People*, 52–86; and Moogk, *La Nouvelle France*, 145–48, 247–49.

4. TBR, S13, George Nelson's journal "No. 1," 12. See also Henry (the Younger), *New Light*, 1:100, 297; TBR, S13, George Nelson's journal and reminiscences, 32; and Ross, *Fur Hunters*, 2:237.

5. See Bouchard, *Genèse des nations*; Bouchard, "Le Québec comme collectivité neuve"; and Lamonde, *Ni Avec Eux Ni Sans Eux*, 13–42.

6. Giraud, *Le métis canadien*; Peterson, "People In Between"; and Pannekoek, "Metis Studies."

7. See the bibliography in Barkwell, Dorion, and Préfontaine, *Metis Legacy*.

Bibliography

Unpublished Sources

Chicago

NEWBERRY LIBRARY

Oversize Ayer Art. Mayer Sketchbook no. 43, Minnesota.

London

PUBLIC RECORD OFFICE (PRO)

Board of Trade Papers. B.T. 1, vol. 20, no. 93.

Montreal

ARCHIVES NATIONALES DE QUÉBEC, DÉPÔT DE MONTRÉAL (ANQM)

CE601 S11. Sainte-Anne-du-Bout-de-l'Île, 1703–1899. Microfilm reels 50–53.

CN601 S29. John-Gerbrand Beek (notaire), 1781–1822.

TL16 S3 /00001. CPCM, Cour du vendredi (matières civiles inférieurs).

TL16 S4 /00002. CPCM, Cour du samedi (matières civiles supérieurs).

TL16 S4 /00005. CPCM, Cour du samedi (matières civiles supérieurs).

TL16 S3 /00008. CPCM, Cour du samedi (matières civiles supérieurs).

TL32 S1 SS1. Court of Quarter Sessions of the District of Montreal.

MCCORD MUSEUM OF CANADIAN HISTORY

M14449. Beaver Club Minute Book, 1807–27, original. Photostats and typescripts can also be obtained at MRB and LAC.

M144450. *Rules and Regulations of the Beaver Club: Instituted in 1785* (Montreal: W. Gray, 1819).

M17607. North West Company Papers, deposition of Basil Dubois, June 21, 1798.

M17614. North West Company Papers, complaint of Samuel Gerrard, of the firm of Parker, Gerrard, and Ogilvie against Basil Dubois.

M22074. Robert McVicar correspondence.

RARE BOOKS AND SPECIAL COLLECTIONS DIVISION OF MCGILL UNIVERSITY LIBRARIES (MRB)

Masson Collection (MC)

C.1. Microfilm reel 55. Duncan Cameron, "The Nipigon Country," with extracts from his journal in the Nipigon, 1804–5. Also found in OA, in photostat, MU 2198 box 3, item 3; and in triplicate typescript, MU 2200, box 5, a–c.

C.5. Microfilm reel 5, abridged version on microfilm reel 6. Alexander Henry the Younger, travels in the Red River Department, 1806.

c.6. John Johnston, description of the country around Lakes Superior & Huron, with a letter to R. Mackenzie, ca. 1799.

c.7. Microfilm reel 4. Journal of John McDonell, Assiniboines-Rivière Qu'Appelle, 1793–95. Typescript copy in LAC MC MG19 C1, vol. 54, microfilm reel C–15640.

c.8. Microfilm reel 14. Alexander Mackenzie, journal of Great Bear Lake, March 1806.

c.11. Microfilm reel 52. W. Ferdinand Wentzel, "Journal kept at Slave Lake," 1802.

c.12. Microfilm reel 6. Charles McKenzie, "Some Account of the Missouri Indians in the years 1804, 5, 6 & 7," addressed to Roderick McKenzie, 1809, 41. Photostat and typescript copies in LAC MC MG19 C1, vol. 59, microfilm reel C–15640 and OA NWCC MU2204, vol. 3 and MU2200 box 5–4 (a).

c.13. James McKenzie's journal, 1799–1800.

c.17. Liste des effets donnés pour des vivres et depenses du Fort du Lac de Flambeau, août 3, 1804.

c.20. Microfilm reel 22. "Some account of the Department of Fond du Lac or Mississippi by George Monk."

c.24. Microfilm reel 2. Archibald Norman McLeod, journal kept at Alexandria, 1800.

c.26. Microfilm reel 15. John Thomson, "Journal, Mackenzies River alias Rocky Mountain, 1800–1801."

c.27. Microfilm reel 13, 2. Athabasca Department, Great Slave Lake, W. F. Wentzel to Roderick McKenzie, Letters Inward, 1807–24.

c.28. Microfilm reel 13. W. Ferdinand Wentzel, "A Continuation of the Journal of the Forks, Mackenzie River, for Summer 1807," August 1807–June 1808.

c.29. Microfilm reel 23. Samuel Hull Wilcocke, "Mort de B Frobisher, Difficultés de Nord Ouest, 1819."

Ottawa

LIBRARY AND ARCHIVES CANADA (LAC)

MG18 C5. Claude-Godefroy Coquart, Jesuit, Mémoire de Coquart adressé à François Bigot sur les postes du Domaine du Roi: La Malbaie, Tadoussac, Île-Jérémie et Chicoutimi, 5 avril 1750.

MG19 A5. McTavish, Frobisher & Co., originals, 1784–1804, vol. 3, "Letter Book of Joseph Frobisher, of the North West Company containing letters written by him from April 15th 1787 until October 20th 1788. From the Frobisher Documents in the possession of McGill University Library Montreal."

MG19 A7. Alexander Mackenzie, Letterbook of Sir Alexander Mackenzie and Company, 1802–9, vol. 1. Copies. Originals in the Seminaire de Québec.

MG19 A9. Simon Fraser Collection.

Vol. 2. Simon Fraser's letters to James McDougall, 1806–7, and to John Stuart, 1807. Originals in Provincial Archives of British Columbia.

Vol. 3. Simon Fraser's letters from the Rocky Mountains to proprietors of the NWC, 1 August 1806–10 February 1807. Copied in 1858 from Bancroft Library, no. 18, series C, at the University of California, Berkeley. Can also be found in appendix C, *Public Archives Report for 1929*, 147–59.

Vol. 5. "Second Journal of Simon Fraser," May–June 1808. Copied from the Bancroft Collection, Pacific Coast MSS at the University of California, Berkeley; originals in the Provincial Archives of British Columbia.

MG19 A14. Microfilm reel M–130. John Stuart, journal kept at North West Company Rocky Mountain House, 1805–6. Original in Provincial Archives of British Columbia.

MG19 A17. Autobiographical notes of John McDonald of Garth, 1791–1815, written in 1859. Photostat. Original in MRB MS 406 and typescript in OA MU 1763.

MG19 A35. Simon McGillivray Papers. Vol. 7, memoranda IV, 1815.

MG19 A41. Microfilm reel A–676. James Keith Papers. Memorandum book of James Keith, 1811–21, A2.

MG19 A51. Contrats d'engagements.

MG19 B1. North West Company letterbook, 1798–1800, vol. 1.

MG19 B4. Reproduction of "Sketch of Fur Trade, 1809: Some Account of the Trade of the North West Company," by William McGillivray; original in Library of the Royal Colonial Institute, London.

MG19 B6. McKenzie, Oldham & Company, originals, 1805, T. Pothier to McKenzie, Oldham & Co.

MG19 C1. Masson Collection (MC).

Vol. 1. Microfilm reel C–15638. Charles Chaboillez, "Journal for the Year 1797."

Vol. 2. Microfilm reel C–15638. Michel Curot, "Journal, Folle Avoine, Rivière Jaune, Pour 1803 & 1804."

Vol. 3. Microfilm reel C–15638. François-Antoine Larocque, "Missouri Journal, Winter 1804–5."

Vols. 4 and 5. Microfilm reel C–15638. William McGillivray, handwritten transcript of "Rat River Fort near Rivière Malique," September 9, 1789–June 13, 1790. Each version is written in a different hand.

Vol. 6. Microfilm reel C–15638. James Porter, journal kept at Slave Lake, February 18, 1800–February 14, 1801.

Vol. 7. Microfilm reel C–15638. John Thomson, "A Journal kept at Grand Marais ou Rivière Rouge, 1798."

Vol. 8. Microfilm reel C–15638. W. Ferdinand Wentzel, "A Journal kept at the Grand River, Winter 1804 & 1805."

Vol. 9. Microfilm reel C–15638, 16. Unidentified North West Company wintering partner, "Journal for 1805 & 6, Cross Lake."

Vol. 10. Microfilm reel C–15638. J. Dufant, "Journal--Commencé le 7e octobre, continué par J. Dufant," at Fort des Épinettes, near Fort Dauphin, October 7, 1803–May 17, 1804.

Vol. 12. Microfilm reel C–15638. Attributed to John Sayer in the LAC Finding Aid 797, 2, "Journal of Daily Occurrencies--Commencing 15th Septr. 1804," September 15, 1804–April 27, 1805, with some account of 1791–93.

Vol. 14. Microfilm reel C–15638. "Journal of the Rocky Mountain Fort, Fall 1799," author unknown.

Vol. 15. Microfilm reel C–15638. Fragment of a journal, attributed to W. Ferdinand Wentzel, kept during an expedition from June 13–August 20, 1800(?).

Vol. 32a. Microfilm reel C–15638. Correspondence between Alexander Mackenzie and Roderick McKenzie, 1785–1820.

Vol. 54. Microfilm reel C–15640. Journal of John McDonell, Assiniboines-Rivière Qu'Appelle, 1793–95, typescript.

Vol. 55. Microfilm reel C–15640. Edward Umfreville, "Journal of a Passage in a Canoe from Pais Plat in Lake Superior to Portage de L'Isle in Rivière Ouinipique," June–July 1784.

Vol. 59. Microfilm reel C–15640. Charles MacKenzie, "Some Account of the Missouri Indians in the years 1804, 5, 6 & 7," addressed to Roderick McKenzie, 1809.

MG19 E1. Selkirk Papers. Microfilm reel C–1. Vol. 2, Colin Robertson, "Suggestions for the Consideration of the Honourable Hudson Bay Company," 1812.

MG21 Add. MSS 21661–21892. Haldimand Papers. "Memorandum for Sir Guy Carleton," January 20, 1778.

MG23 GII10. Jonathan Sewell Papers.

MG24 H1. William Bentinck Papers. Journals kept during a trip from Montreal to Niagara and the return trip, 1800, and from Montreal to Washington and the return trip in 1801, copies.

R7712–0–7–E. Ermatinger Estate Fonds. Series 2, Edward Ermatinger, vol. 4, French Canadian folk songs.

RG7 G15C. "Civil Secretary's Letter Books, 1788–1829."

St. Paul

MINNESOTA HISTORICAL SOCIETY (MHS)

P791. Folder 7. Grace Lee Nute Papers.

P849. Marjorie Gourdeau Gerin-Lajoie Collection. Box 4, letters (in French) by Joseph Guy to his father Pierre Guy II and his brother Louis. Originals in Université de Montréal, Baby Collection, correspondence G.

P1571. Edward Umfreville, journal, 1784. Photostat and typescript; original at McGill University.

Toronto

ONTARIO ARCHIVES (OA)

MU 572. Duncan Clark Papers.

MU 842. Diary of George Nelson, in the service of the North West Company at Tête au Brochet, 1818–19.

MU 1146. George Gordon Papers.

MU 1391. Hudson's Bay Company Collection. Robert Seaborne Miles's journal, 1818–19.

MU 1956. Angus Mackintosh Papers. Box 4, Journal from Michilimackinac to Montreal via the French River, summer 1813, ca. July 23, 1813.

Microfilm reel MS65. Donald McKay, journal from January to December 1799, Company of Temiscamingue.

Microfilm reel MS65. Donald McKay, journal from August 1800 to April 1801, Company of Temiscamingue.

Microfilm reel MS65. Donald McKay, Journal from January 1805 to June 1806, Company of Temiscamingue.

MU 2198. North West Company Collection (NWCC). Donald McIntosh, Michipicoten, to Christy McIntosh, Cornwall, 1816.

MU 2199. North West Company Collection (NWCC).

Edward Umfreville, "Journal of a Passage in a Canoe from Pais Plat in Lake Superior to Portage de L'Isle in Rivière Ouinipique," June to July 1784 (photostat of original). Part of the manuscript titled "Some Account of the North West Company," by Roderick McKenzie, director of the North West Company. Typescripts also in the OA NWCC MU 2200, box 5, nos. 2 (a), (b), and (c). Photostats and typescripts also in LAC MC vol. 55, microfilm reel C–15640; MRB MC C.17; and the MHS P1571.

"An Account of the Athabasca Indians by a Partner of the North West Company, 1795," revised May 4, 1840. Part of the manuscript titled "Some Account of the North West Company," by Roderick McKenzie, director of the North West Company. Typescripts also in the OA NWCC MU 2200, box 5, nos. 2 (a), (b), and (c). Photostats and typescripts also in LAC MC vol. 55, microfilm reel C–15640; MRB MC C.17; and the MHS P1571.

TORONTO METROPOLITAN REFERENCE LIBRARY BALDWIN ROOM (TBR)

917.11 F671. Simon Fraser, "Journal of a voyage from the Rocky Mountains to the Pacific Ocean, Performed in the year 1808." Photostat and typescript also available; photostat of the transcription of the journal at the University of California at Berkeley, Bancroft Library, no. 18, series C, in the Pacific Coast MSS.

S13. George Nelson Collection.

Journal "No. 1," written as a reminiscence, describing a journey from Montreal to Grand Portage, and at Folle Avoine, April 27, 1802–April 1803.

Journal, July 13, 1803–June 25, 1804.

Journal, August 29, 1805–March 8, 1806.

Journal "No. 5," June 1807–October 1809, written as a reminiscence, dated February 7, 1851.

Journal, November 3, 1807–August 31, 1808.

Journal, September 1, 1808–March 31, 1810, titled "Journal for 1808 &c &c &c."

Journal, April 1, 1810–May 1, 1811.

Tête au Brochet, to his parents, December 8, 1811.

Journal "No. 7," describing the Lake Winnipeg district in 1812, written as a reminiscence, March 1812.

Journal, January 29–June 23, 1815, titled "A Daily Memoranda of my, my men, & my Neighbors' transactions, as far as can be necessary, in Manitonamingon Lake, for NWC."

Journal, November 30, 1815–January 13, 1816 (parts of the journal in code).

"Journal from Bas De La Rivière to Cumberland House, 1819–?" also titled "Journal B," May 1–June 8, 1819, August 16–September 15, 1819. This journal is a continuation of Nelson's journal found in OA MU 842.

Coded journal, April 17–October 20, 1821, titled "A continuation of My Journal at Moose Lake."

Diary of events on a journey from Cumberland House to Fort William, part in code, June 3–July 11, 1822.

Journal and reminiscences, December 1, 1825–September 13, 1836.

Winnipeg

HUDSON'S BAY COMPANY ARCHIVES (HBCA)

A.6/24. Microfilm reel 41. London outward correspondence, 1836–38.

A.11/4. Microfilm reel 138. London inward correspondence from the HBC posts, 1775–83, Albany Fort. No. 105.

A.16/54. North West Company Collection (NWCC). Microfilm series I, reels 317–18. Servant's Accounts, Montreal, 1810–26.

B.22/a/5. Microfilm reel 1M17. John Mackay's Brandon House journal of 1797–98.

B.22/a/6. Microfilm reel 1M17. Robert Goodwin, Brandon House post journal, 1798–99.

B.39/a/16. Microfilm reel 1M22. Fort Chipewyan, post journal, 1820–21, titled "Journal of Transactions & occurrences at Fort Wedderburn Athabasca Lake, Kept by William Brown Commencing June 6th 1820, and Ending February 10th 1821. Volume 1st."

B.42/a/136a. Microfilm reel 1M34. Fort Churchill post journal, 1810–11, author not listed.

B.45/a/1. Microfilm reel 1M37. Fort Colville (Columbia River) post journal, 1830–31.

B.89/a/2. Microfilm reel 1M63. Peter Fidler, Ile à la Crosse post journal, 1810–11.

B.105/a/4. Microfilm reel 1M67. John Mackay's Lac La Pluie journal of 1796–97.

B.134/c/13. Microfilm reel 1M283–4, Montreal, inward correspondence.

B.177/a/1. Microfilm reel 1M119. James Sutherland's Red Lake (NW Ontario) journal of 1790–91.

B.239/g/10. Microfilm reel 1M801. York Factory, abstracts of servants' accounts.

D.3/3. Microfilm reel addenda M1. Governor George Simpson's journal, 1821–22.

E.31/2/2. Unallocated correspondence and employees' private letters, undelivered, 1823–92, voyageurs, 1823–50.

F.3/1. Microfilm reel 5M1–2. North West Company, miscellaneous papers, 1791–99.

F.4/32. North West Company ledger, 1812–21.

F.4/40. North West Company account book, 1820–21.

F.4/61. Microfilm reel 5M13. North West Company miscellaneous accounts, 1808–27.

PROVINCIAL ARCHIVES OF MANITOBA (PAM)

C.1/M.2. Church Missionary Society. Microfilm reel A-78, John Smithurst's Report of Cumberland House, August 1841.

MG1 C1. Fort William Collection.

MG2 A1–1. Lord Selkirk Papers.

SOCIÈTÈ HISTORIQUE DE SAINT-BONIFACE

Catholic Parish Records. Microfilm reel 2936. Saint-Augustin-de-Desmaures, ZQ-1–348.

Published Sources, Dissertations, and Papers in Circulation

Ahenakew, Reverend Edward. "Cree Trickster Tales." *Journal of American Folklore* 42, no. 166 (October–December 1929): 309–53.

Allaire, Gratien. "Les engagements pour la traité des fourrures: Évaluation de la documentation." *Revue d'histoire de l'amérique française* 34 (June 1980): 3–26.

———. "Les Engagés de la Fourrure, 1701–1745: Une Étude de Leur Motivation." PhD diss., Concordia University, Montreal, 1981.

———. "Fur Trade Engages, 1701–1745." In *Rendezvous: Selected Papers of the Fourth North American Fur Trade Conference*, edited by Thomas C. Buckley, 15–26. St. Paul MN: The Conference, 1984.

Allen, Paula Gunn. "Lesbians in American Indian Cultures." In *Hidden from History: Reclaiming the Gay and Lesbian Past*, edited by Martin Bauml Duberman, Martha Vicinus, and George Chauncey Jr., 106–17. New York: New American Library, 1989.

Anderson, Karen. *Chain Her by One Foot: The Subjugation of Women in Seventeenth-Century New France*. London: Routledge, 1991.

Armour, David. *Colonial Michilimackinac*. Mackinac Island MI: Mackinac State Historic Parks, 2000.

Association de la Propagation de la foi (Diocèse de Québec). *Notice sur les Missions de Diocèse de Québec, 1839–75*. Quebec, 1845.

Babcock, Barbara A., ed. *The Reversible World: Symbolic Inversion in Art and Society*. Ithaca NY: Cornell University Press, 1978.

Back, Captain George. *Narrative of the Arctic Land Expedition to the Mouth of the Great Fish River and along the Shores of the Arctic Ocean, in the Years 1833, 1834, and 1835*. London: John Murray, 1836. Reprint, Edmonton: Hurtig, 1970.

Bakhtin, Mikhail. *The Dialogic Imagination*. Edited by Michael Holmquist. Translated by Caryl Emerson and Michael Holmquist. Austin: University of Texas Press, 1981.

———. *Rabelais and His World*. Translated by Hélène Iswolsky. Bloomington: Indiana University Press, 1984. Originally published in Russian in 1965.

Bakker, Peter. *A Language of Our Own: The Genesis of Michif, the Mixed Cree-French Language of the Canadian Métis*. New York: Oxford University Press, 1997.

Ballantyne, Robert M. *Hudson Bay; or, Every-Day Life in the Wilds of North America during Six Years' Residence in the Territories of the Honourable Hudson's Bay Company*. London: William Blackwood & Sons, 1848. Reprint, Edmonton: Hurtig, 1972.

Barbeau, Marius. "La Complainte de Cadieux, Coureur de Bois (ca. 1709)." *Journal of American Folklore* 67 (April–June 1954): 163–83.

———. "The Ermatinger Collection of Voyageur Songs (ca. 1830)." *Journal of American Folklore* 67 (April–June 1954): 147–61.

———. "The Field of European Folk-Lore in America." *The Journal of American Folk-Lore* 32, no. 124 (April–June 1919): 185–97.

———. *Jongleur Songs of Old Quebec*. Translated by Sir Harold Boulton and Sir Ernest MacMillan. Toronto: Ryerson Press; New Brunswick NJ: Rutgers University Press, 1962.

———. *Quebec: Where Ancient France Lingers*. Toronto: Macmillan, 1936.

Barkwell, Lawrence J., Leah Dorion, and Darren R. Préfontaine, eds. *Metis Legacy: A Metis Historiography and Annotated Bibliography*. Winnipeg: Pemmican Publications, 2001.

Beattie, Judith Judson, and Helen M. Buss, eds. *Undelivered Letters to Hudson's Bay Company Men on the Northwest Coast of America, 1830–57*. Vancouver: University of British Columbia Press, 2003.

Beaudoin, Thérèse. *L'Été dans la culture Québécoise, XVIIe–XIXe siècles*. Québec: Institut québécois de recherche sur la culture, documents de recherche no. 10, 1987.

Bederman, Gail. *Manliness and Civilization: A Cultural History of Gender and Race in the United States, 1880–1917*. Chicago: University of Chicago Press, 1995.

Béland, Madeleine. *Chansons de voyageurs, coureurs de bois et forestiers*. Quebec: Presses de l'Université Laval, 1982.

Benoît, Jehane. "Wintering Dishes." *Canadian Collector* (May/June 1985): 25–27.

Bigsby, John J. *The Shoe and the Canoe or Pictures of Travel in the Canadas*. 2 vols. London: Chapman & Hall, 1850.

Binnema, Theodore, Gerhard Ens, and R. C. MacLeod, eds. *From Rupert's Land to Canada: Essays in Honour of John E. Foster*. Edmonton: University of Alberta Press, 2001.

Blye, Frank. "Hegemonic Heterosexual Masculinity." *Studies in Political Economy* 24 (1987): 159–70.

Bodmer, Karl. "Buffalo Dance of the Mandan" (painting). In *Karl Bodmer's America*, introduced by H. Goetzmann, plate 18. Lincoln: Joslyn Art Museum and University of Nebraska Press, 1984.

Bolduc, Evelyn. "Contes Populaires Canadiens (troisième série)." *Journal of American Folk-Lore* 32, no. 123 (January–March 1919): 90–167.

Bonville, Nancy. "Gender Relations in Native North America." *American Indian Culture and Research Journal* 13, no. 2 (1989): 1–28.

Bosher, John. "The Family in New France." In *In Search of the Visible Past*, edited by Barry Gough, 1–13. Waterloo ON: Wilfred Laurier University Press, 1991.

Bouchard, Gérard. *Genèse des nations et cultures du Nouveau Monde: Essai d'histoire comparée*. Montreal: Boréal, 2000.

———. "Le Québec comme collectivité neuve: Le refus de l'américanité dans le discourse de la survivance." In *Québécois et Américains: La culture québécoise aux XIXe et XXe siécles*, edited by Yvan Lamonde and Gérard Bouchard, 15–60. Quebec: Fides, 1995.

Bourdieu, Pierre. "The Forms of Capital." In *Handbook of Theory and Research for the Sociology of Education*, edited by John G. Richardson, 241–58. New York: Greenwood Press, 1986.

———. *The Logic of Practice*. Translated by Richard Nice. Stanford CA: Stanford University Press, 1980.

Bourdieu, Pierre, and Loïc J. D. Wacquant. *An Invitation to Reflexive Sociology*. Chicago: University of Chicago Press, 1992.

Bourgeault, Ron C. "The Indian, the Métis and the Fur Trade: Class, Sexism and

Racism in the Transition from 'Communism' to Capitalism." *Studies in Political Economy: A Socialist Review*, no. 12 (Fall 1983): 45–80.

Brennan, Thomas. *Public Drinking and Popular Culture in Eighteenth-Century Paris*. Princeton NJ: Princeton University Press, 1988.

Bristol, Michael D. *Carnival and Theater: Plebian Culture and the Structure of Authority in Renaissance England*. New York: Routledge, 1985.

Brown, Jennifer S. H. "Fur Trade as Centrifuge: Family Dispersal and Offspring Identity in Two Company Contexts." In *North American Indian Anthropology: Essays on Society and Culture*, edited by Raymond J. DeMallie and Alfonso Ortiz. Norman: University of Oklahoma Press, 1994.

———. "Partial Truths: A Closer Look at Fur Trade Marriage." In Binnema, Ens, and MacLeod, *From Rupert's Land to Canada*, 59–80.

———. *Strangers in Blood: Fur Trade Company Families in Indian Country*. Vancouver: University of British Columbia Press, 1980.

Brown, Jennifer S. H., and Elizabeth Vibert, eds. *Reading beyond Words: Contexts for Native History*. Peterborough ON: Broadview Press, 1996.

Buffalohead, Priscilla K. "Farmers, Warriors, Traders: A Fresh Look at Ojibway Women." *Minnesota History* 48, no. 5 (Spring 1983): 236–44.

Bumsted, J. M. *A History of the Canadian Peoples*. Toronto: Oxford University Press, 1998.

Burke, Peter. *Popular Culture in Early Modern Europe*. New York: New York University Press, 1978.

Burley, Edith I. *Servants of the Honourable Company: Work, Discipline, and Conflict in the Hudson's Bay Company, 1770–1879*. Toronto: Oxford University Press, 1997.

Callender, Charles, and Lee M. Kochems. "The North American Berdache." *Current Anthropology* 24, no. 4 (1983): 443–56.

Campagna, F. Dominique. *Répertoire des Mariages de Maskinongé, 1728–1966*. N.p.: Académie Pierre-Boucher, 1966.

Campbell, Marjorie Wilkins. *The North West Company*. New York: St. Martin's Press; Toronto: Macmillan, 1957. Reprint, Vancouver: Douglas & McIntyre, 1983.

"Canada: Écoulement Fluvial." *L'Atlas National du Canada*. 5th ed. Ottawa: Environment Canada; Energy, Mines and Resources, 1993.

Carroll, Michael P. "The Trickster as Selfish Buffoon and Culture Hero." *Ethos* 12, no. 2 (Summer 1984): 105–31.

Charbonneau, Hubert, Bertrand Desjardins, and Pierre Beauchamp. "Le comportement démographique des voyageurs sous le régime français." *Histoire sociale/Social History* 11, no. 21 (May 1978): 120–33.

Chauncey, George, Jr. "Christian Brotherhood or Sexual Perversion? Homosexual Identities and the Construction of Sexual Boundaries in the World War I Era." In *Hidden from History: Reclaiming the Gay and Lesbian Past*, edited by Martin Bauml Duberman, Martha Vicinus, and George Chauncey Jr., 294–317. New York: New American Library, 1988.

Chittenden, Hiram Martin. *The American Fur Trade of the Far West*. 3 vols. New York: F. P. Harper, 1902. Reprint, Lincoln: University of Nebraska Press, 1986.

"Connolly vs. Woolrich, Superior Court, Montreal, 9 July 1867." *Lower Canada Jurist* 11:197–265.

Cooper, Carol. "Native Women of the Northern Pacific Coast: An Historical Perspective, 1830–1900." *Journal of Canadian Studies* 27, no. 4 (Winter 1992–93): 44–75.

Cox, Ross. *Adventures on the Columbia River, including the Narrative of a Residence of Six Years on the Western Side of the Rocky Mountains, among Various Tribes of Indians Hitherto Unknown: Together with a Journey across the American Continent.* 2 vols. London: Henry Colburn & Richard Bentley, 1831. Published in one volume in 1832 by J. & J. Harper, New York.

Creighton, Margaret S. *Rites and Passages: The Experience of American Whaling, 1830–1870.* Cambridge: Cambridge University Press, 1995.

Crowley, Terence. "'Thunder Gusts': Popular Disturbances in Early French Canada." *Canadian Historical Association Historical Papers* (1979): 11–31.

Curot, Michel. "A Wisconsin Fur Trader's Journal, 1803–4." In *Collections of the State Historical Society of Wisconsin*, 20:396–471. Madison: Wisconsin Historical Society, 1911.

Daniells, Roy. Introduction. In Mackenzie, *Voyages from Montreal on the River St. Laurence.*

Darnton, Robert. *The Great Cat Massacre and Other Episodes in French Cultural History.* New York: Vintage Books, 1985.

Davidson, Gordon Charles. *The North West Company.* Berkeley: University of California Press, 1918.

Davis, Natalie Zemon. "The Reasons of Misrule: Youth Groups and Charivaris in Sixteenth-Century France." *Past & Present* 50 (February 1971): 41–75.

———. *Society and Culture in Early Modern France.* Stanford CA: Stanford University Press, 1965.

Dechêne, Louise. *Habitants and Merchants in Seventeenth-Century Montreal.* Montreal: McGill–Queen's University Press, 1992. First published as *Habitants et marchands de Montréal au XVIIe siècle* (Paris: Editions Plon, 1974).

Delâge, Denys. "L'influence des Amérindiens sur les Canadiens et les Français au temps de la Nouvelle-France." *Lekton* 2, no. 2 (Autumn 1992): 103–91, 280–91.

———. "Les Iroquois chrétiens des 'réductions,' 1667–1770. I. Migration et rapports avec les Français. II. Rapports avec la Ligue iroquoise, les Britanniques et les autres nations autochones." *Recherches amérindiennes au Québec* 21, nos. 1–2, 3 (1991): 59–70, 39–50.

Deloria, Philip J. *Playing Indian.* New Haven CT: Yale University Press, 1998.

DeMallie, Raymond J., ed. *Plains.* Vol. 13 of *Handbook of North American Indians*, edited by William C. Sturtevant. Washington DC: Smithsonian Institution, 2001.

DeMallie, Raymond J., and Douglas R. Parks. Introduction. In *Sioux Indian Religion: Tradition and Innovation.* Norman: University of Oklahoma Press, 1987.

Dening, Greg. *Mr. Bligh's Bad Language: Passion, Power and Theatre on the Bounty.* Cambridge: Cambridge University Press, 1992.

Devens, Carol. *Countering Colonization: Native American Women and Great Lakes Missions, 1630–1900*. Berkeley: University of California Press, 1992.

Devine, Heather. "Les Desjarlais: The Development and Dispersion of a Proto-Métis Hunting Band, 1785–1870." In Binnema, Ens, and MacLeod, *From Rupert's Land to Canada*, 129–58.

———. "A Fur Trade Diaspora: Canadien Merchant Families in St. Louis after the British Conquest." Paper presented at the Canadian Historical Association Annual Meeting, University of Manitoba, Winnipeg, June 2004.

———. *The People Who Own Themselves: Aboriginal Ethnogenesis in a Canadian Family 1660–1900*. Calgary: University of Calgary Press, 2004.

DeVoto, Bernard A. *Across the Wide Missouri*. Boston: Houghton Mifflin, 1947, reprint, 1987.

Dictionary of Canadian Biography (DCB).

Dohla, Johann Conrad. *A Hessian Diary of the American Revolution by Johann Conrad Dohla*. Translated, edited, and with an introduction by Bruce E. Burgoyne. Norman: University of Oklahoma Press, 1990.

Douglas, Mary, ed. *Constructive Drinking: Perspectives on Drink from Anthropology*. Cambridge: Cambridge University Press, 1987.

Douglas, Thomas, Earl of Selkirk. *A Sketch of the British Fur Trade in North America; with Observations Relative to the North-West Company of Montreal*. 2nd ed. London: James Ridgway, 1816.

Duckworth, Harry, ed. *The English River Book: A North West Company Journal and Account Book of 1786*. Montreal: McGill-Queen's University Press, 1990.

Dugas, Georges. *Un Voyageur des pays d'En-Haut*. St. Boniface MB: Editions des Plaines, 1981. First published in 1890.

Duncan, John M. *Travels through Part of the United States and Canada in 1818 and 1819*. 2 vols. Glasgow: Wardlaw & Cunninghame, 1823.

Eccles, W. J. "The Fur Trade and Eighteenth-Century Imperialism." *William and Mary Quarterly*, 3rd ser., 40, no. 3 (July 1983): 341–62.

Edmunds, R. David. *The Shawnee Prophet*. Lincoln: University of Nebraska Press, 1983.

Englebert, Robert. "The Storm before the Calm: Desertion, Corporate Competition, and Voyageur Identity during the Fur Trade Wars, 1814–1822." Master's paper, Department of History, University of Ottawa, 2004.

Ens, Gerhard J. *Homeland to Hinterland: The Changing Worlds of the Red River Métis in the Nineteenth Century*. Toronto: University of Toronto Press, 1997.

Ermatinger, C. O., ed. "Edward Ermatinger's York Factory Express Journal Being a Record of Journeys Made between Fort Vancouver and Hudson Bay in the Years . . . 1827–1828." *Proceedings and Transactions of the Royal Society of Canada*, 3rd ser., section 2 (1912): 67–132.

Faries, Hugh. "The Diary of Hugh Faries." In Gates, *Five Fur Traders of the Northwest*, 189–241.

Fierst, John T. "Strange Eloquence: Another Look at *The Captivity and Adventures of John Tanner*." In Brown and Vibert, *Reading beyond Words*, 220–41.

Fingard, Judith. *Jack in Port: Sailortowns of Eastern Canada*. Toronto: University of Toronto Press, 1982.

Fletcher, Anthony. *Gender, Sex and Subordination in England, 1500–1800*. New Haven CT: Yale University Press, 1995.

Foster, John E. "Paulet Paul: Métis or 'House Indian' Folk Hero?" *Manitoba History*, no. 9 (Spring 1985): 2–7.

———. "Wintering, the Outsider Adult Male and the Ethnogenesis of the Western Plains Métis." *Prairie Forum* 19, no. 1 (Spring 1994): 1–13.

Foster, Martha Harroun. "Of Baggage and Bondage: Gender and Status among Hidatsa and Crow Women." *American Indian Culture and Research Journal* 17, no. 2 (1993): 121–52.

Fowke, Edith. *Folktales of French Canada*. Toronto: NC Press, 1979.

Franchère, Gabriel. *Journal of a Voyage on the North West Coast of North America during the Years 1811, 1812, 1813 and 1814*. Toronto: Champlain Society, 1969.

———. *A Voyage to the Northwest Coast of America*. Edited by Milo Milton Quaife. Chicago: R. R. Donnelley & Sons, 1954.

Francis, Daniel. *Battle for the West: Fur Traders and the Birth of Western Canada*. Edmonton: Hurtig, 1982.

Francis, Daniel, and Toby Morantz, *Partners in Furs: A History of the Fur Trade in Eastern James Bay, 1600–1870*. Montreal: McGill-Queens Press, 1983.

Francis, Daniel, and Michael Payne. *A Narrative History of Fort Dunvegan*. Winnipeg: Watson & Dwyer, 1993.

Francis, R. Douglas, Richard Jones, and Donald B. Smith. *Origins: Canadian History to Confederation*. 3rd ed. Toronto: Harcourt & Brace, 1996.

Franklin, Captain John. *Narrative of a Journey to the Shores of the Polar Sea in the Years 1819, 20, 21 and 22*. London: J. M. Dent & Sons, 1819.

Franks, C. E. S. *The Canoe and White Water: From Essential to Sport*. Toronto: University of Toronto Press, 1977.

Fraser, Simon. "First Journal of Simon Fraser from April 12th to July 18th, 1806." In appendix B, *Public Archives Report for 1929*, 109–45. Ottawa, 1930. (Transcript from a copy at University of California at Berkeley, Bancroft Collection, Pacific Coast MSS, series C, no. 16; copy also at LAC, MG19 A9, Simon Fraser Collection, vol. 4; originals at the Provincial Archives of British Columbia.)

———. "Journal of a Voyage from the Rocky Mountains to the Pacific Coast, 1808." In Masson, *Les Bourgeois de la Compagnie du Nord-Ouest*, 1:155–221.

———. *The Letters and Journals of Simon Fraser, 1806–1808*. Edited by W. Kaye Lamb. Toronto: Macmillan, 1960.

Friesen, Gerald. *The Canadian Prairies: A History*. Toronto: University of Toronto Press, 1987.

Fur, Gunlög. "'Some Women Are Wiser Than Some Men': Gender and Native American History." In *Clearing a Path: Theorizing the Past in Native American Studies*, edited by Nancy Shoemaker, 73–103. New York: Routledge, 2002.

Gâerin, Lâeon. *Trois types de l'habitation Canadien-français*. 18–. CIHM 05769. Canadian Institute for Historic Microreproductions.

Gagnon, Serge. *Plaisir d'Amour et Crainte de Dieu*. Quebec: Les presses de l'Université Laval, 1990.

Gates, Charles M., ed. *Five Fur Traders of the Northwest*. St. Paul: Minnesota Historical Society, 1965.

Geological Survey of Canada. "Chalk River." Map 1132A. Surficial Geology, Ottawa, 1962.

Gibbon, J. Murray. *Canadian Folk Songs: Old and New*. London: J. M. Dent & Sons, 1927.

Gibson, James R. *Farming the Frontier: The Agricultural Opening of the Oregon Country, 1786–1846*. Vancouver: University of British Columbia Press, 1985.

Gilbert, Arthur N. "Buggery and the British Navy, 1700–1861." *Journal of Social History* 10, no. 1 (Fall 1976): 72–98.

Gilman, Carolyn. *The Grand Portage Story*. St. Paul: Minnesota Historical Society, 1992.

Ginzburg, Carlo. *The Cheese and the Worms: The Cosmos of a Sixteenth-Century Miller*. Translated by Anne Tedeschi. Baltimore: Johns Hopkins University Press, 1980.

———. "The Inquisitor as Anthropologist." In *Clues, Myths, and the Historical Method*, translated by John and Anne C. Tedeschi. Baltimore: Johns Hopkins University Press, 1992.

Giraud, Marcel. *Le métis canadien*. 2 vols. Paris: Institut d' Ethnologie, 1945.

Goldring, Philip. *Papers on the Labour System of the Hudson's Bay Company, 1821–1900*. Manuscript Report Series, vol. 1, no. 362, Parks Canada. Ottawa: Ministry of Supply and Services, 1979.

Grabowski, Jan, and Nicole St-Onge. "Montreal Iroquois Engagés in the Western Fur Trade, 1800–1821." In Binnema, Ens, and MacLeod, *From Rupert's Land to Canada*, 23–58.

Gramsci, Antonio. *Selections from the Prison Notebooks*. Edited and translated by Quintin Hoare and Geoffrey Nowell Smith. New York: International Publishers, 1971.

Grant, George M. *Ocean to Ocean: Sanford Fleming's Expedition through Canada in 1872: Being a Diary Kept during a Journey from the Atlantic to the Pacific with the Expedition of the Engineer-in-Chief of the Canadian Pacific and Intercolonial Railways*. Toronto: J. Campbell et. al., 1873.

Grant, Peter. "The Sauteux Indians about 1804." In Masson, *Les Bourgeois de la Compagnie du Nord-Ouest*, 2:307–66.

Green, Gretchen. "A New People in an Age of War: The Kahnawake Iroquois, 1667–1760." PhD diss., College of William and Mary, Williamsburg VA, 1991.

Greenwood, F. Murray. *Legacies of Fear: Law and Politics in Quebec in the Era of the French Revolution*. Toronto: University of Toronto Press, 1993.

Greer, Allan. "Fur-Trade Labour and Lower Canadian Agrarian Structures." *Canadian Historical Association Historical Papers* (1981): 197–214.

———. *The Patriots and the People: The Rebellion of 1837 in Rural Lower Canada*. Toronto: University of Toronto Press, 1993.

———. "The Pattern of Literacy in Quebec, 1745–1899." *Histoire sociale/Social History* 9 (November 1978): 295–335.

———. *Peasant, Lord, and Merchant: Rural Society in Three Quebec Parishes, 1740–1840*. Toronto: University of Toronto Press, 1985.

———. *The People of New France*. Toronto: University of Toronto Press, 1997.

———. *The Soldiers of Isle Royale*. Parks Canada History and Archaeology 28. Ottawa: Minister of Supply and Services Canada, 1979.

Grenon, Hector. *Us et coutumes du Québec*. Montréal: La Presse, 1974.

Gross, Konrad. "The Voyageurs: Images of Canada's Archetypal Frontiersmen." In *A Talent(ed) Digger: Creations, Cameos, and Essays in Honour of Anna Rutherford*, edited by Hena Maes-Jelinek, Gordon Collier, and Geoffrey V. Davis, 411–21. Amsterdam: Rodopi, 1996.

Guide des parcours canotables du Québec. Vol. 2, *Nord du fleuve Saint–Laurent excluant le bassin de l'Outaouais*. Par la Fédération québécoise du canot et du kayak. Québec: Editions Broquet, 2001.

Gunnerson, James H. «Plains Village Tradition: Western Periphery.» In *Handbook of North American Indians*, vol. 13, *Plains*. Edited by DeMallie, 234–44.

Hall, Robert L. *An Archaeology of the Soul: North American Indian Belief and Ritual*. Urbana: University of Illinois Press, 1997.

Hallowell, A. Irving. *The Ojibwa of Berens River, Manitoba: Ethnography into History*. Edited by Jennifer S. H. Brown. Fort Worth: Harcourt Brace, 1992.

Hamelin, Jean. *Histoire du catholicisme Québécois*. 2 vols. Montreal: Boreal, 1984.

Hamilton, James Scott. "Fur Trade Social Inequality and the Role of Non-Verbal Communication." PhD diss., Simon Fraser University, Vancouver, 1990.

Hardin, Richard F. "'Ritual' in Recent Criticism: The Elusive Sense of Community." *Publication of the Modern Language Association* 98 (1983): 846–62.

Hardy, Jean-Pierre, and David-Thiery Ruddel. *Les Apprentis Artisans à Québec, 1660–1815*. Quebec: Les Presses de L'Université du Québec, 1977.

Harmon, Daniel W. *Journal of Voyages and Travels in the Interior of North America*. Trails Makers of Canada Series. Toronto: Courier, 1911.

———. *Sixteen Years in Indian Country: The Journal of Daniel Williams Harmon, 1800–1816*. Edited by W. Kaye Lamb. Toronto: Macmillan, 1957.

Harris, R. C. *The Resettlement of British Columbia: Essays on Colonialism and Geographical Change*. Vancouver: University of British Columbia Press, 1997.

———. *The Seigneurial System in Early Canada: A Geographical Study*. Kingston ON: McGill-Queen's University Press, 1984.

Harrison, Jane E. *Until Next Year: Letter-Writing and the Mails in the Canadas, 1640–1830*. Waterloo ON: Wilfrid Laurier University Press for the Canadian Postal Museum, 1997.

Hay, Douglas, and Paul Craven. "Master and Servant in England and the Empire: A Comparative Study." *Labour/Le Travail*, no. 31 (Spring 1993): 175–84.

Helm, June, ed. *Subarctic*. Vol. 6 of *Handbook of North American Indians, Volume 6, Subarctic*, edited by William C. Sturtevant. Washington DC: Smithsonian Institution, 1981.

Henning, Dale R. "Plains Village Tradition: Eastern Periphery and Oneota Tradition." In *Handbook of North American Indians*, vol. 13, *Plains*. Edited by DeMallie, 222–33.

Henry, Alexander (the Elder). *Travels and Adventures in Canada and the Indian Territories between the Years 1760 and 1776*. Edmonton: M. G. Hurtig, 1969.

Henry, Alexander (the Younger). *The Journal of Alexander Henry the Younger, 1799–1814*. Edited by Barry M. Gough. 2 vols. Toronto: Champlain Society, 1988.

———. *New Light on the Early History of the Greater Northwest: The Manuscript Journals of Alexander Henry*. Edited by Elliott Coues. 2 vols. Minneapolis: Ross & Haines; New York: F. Harper, 1897.

Heriot, George. *Travels through the Canadas, Containing a Description of the Picturesque Scenery on Some of the Rivers and Lakes; with an Account of the Productions, Commerce, and Inhabitants of Those Provinces*. Philadelphia: M. Carey, 1813.

———. *Travels through the Canadas: to which is subjoined a comparative view of the manners and customs of several of the Indian nations of North and South America*. London: Printed for Richard Phillips . . . by J. G. Barnard, 1805.

Heron, Craig. *Booze: A Distilled History*. Toronto: Between the Lines, 2003.

Heron, Craig, and Robert Storey, eds. *On the Job: Confronting the Labour Process in Canada*. Montreal: McGill-Queen's University Press, 1986.

Hind, Henry Youle. *Narrative of the Canadian Red River Exploring Expedition of 1857 and of the Assiniboine and Saskatchewan Exploring Expedition of 1858*. London: Longman, Green, Longman, & Roberts, 1860.

Hogg, Grace Laing, and Gwen Shulman. "Wage Disputes and the Courts in Montreal, 1816–1835." In *Class, Gender and the Law in Eighteenth- and Nineteenth-Century Quebec: Sources and Perspectives*. Edited by Donald Fyson, Colin M. Coates, and Kathryn Harvey, 127–43. Montreal: Montreal History Group, 1993.

Honigman, John J. "West Main Cree." In *Handbook of North American Indians*, vol. 6, *Subarctic*. Edited by Helm, 217–30.

Hubert, Ollivier. *Sur la terre comme au ciel: La gestion des rites par l'Église catholique de Québec (fin XVIIe–mi-XIXe siècle)*. Sainte-Foy QC: Les Presse de l'Université Laval, 2000.

Hutchenson, Linda. *A Theory of Parody: The Teachings of Twentieth-Century Art Forms*. New York: Methuen, 1985.

Igartua, José. "A Change in Climate: The Conquest and the *Marchands* of Montreal." *Canadian Historical Association Historical Papers* (1974): 115–34.

Innis, Harold Adams. *The Fur Trade in Canada: An Introduction to Canadian Economic History*. Toronto: University of Toronto Press, 1956. First published in 1930 by Yale University Press.

Jaenen, Cornelius J. *The Role of the Church in New France*. Toronto: McGraw-Hill Ryerson, 1976.

Jameson, Anna Brownell Murphy. *Winter Studies and Summer Rambles in Canada*. 3 vols. London: Saunder & Otley, 1838.

Jesuit Relations and Allied Documents, The (JR). Edited by Reuben Gold Thwaites. 73 vols. Cleveland: Burrows Brothers, 1896–1901. Reprint, New York: Pageant Books, 1959. Originally published 1610–1791.

"Johnstone et al. vs. Connolly, Cour d'Appel, Jugement Rendu le 7 septembre 1869." *La Revue Légale* 1:253–400.

Judd, Carol M. "Native Labour and Social Stratification in the Hudson's Bay Company's Northern Department, 1770–1870." *Canadian Review of Sociology and Anthropology* 17, no. 4 (November 1980): 305–14.

Jung, Patrick J. "Forge, Destroy, and Preserve the Bonds of Empire: Euro-Americans, Native Americans, and Métis on the Wisconsin Frontier, 1634–1856." PhD diss., Marquette University, Milwaukee, 1997.

Kalm, Pehr. *Voyage de Pehr Kalm au Canada en 1749*. Translated and annotated by Jacques Rousseau and Guy Béthune. Montreal: Pierre Tisseyre, 1977.

Kane, Paul. *Wanderings of an Artist among the Indians of North America from Canada to Vancouver's Island and Oregon through the Hudson's Bay Company's Territory and Back Again*. 1858. Toronto: Radisson Society, 1925.

Karamanski, Theodore J. "The Iroquois and the Fur Trade of the Far West." *The Beaver* (Spring 1982): 5–13.

Keith, Lloyd, ed. *North of Athabasca: Slave Lake and Mackenzie River Documents of the North West Company, 1800–1821*. Montreal: McGill-Queen's Press, 2001.

Kemp, David. "The Impact of Weather and Climate on the Fur Trade in the Canadian Northwest." *Thunder Bay Historical Museum Society Papers and Records* 8 (1980): 32–42.

Kennicott, Robert. "Robert Kennicott." *Transactions of the Chicago Academy of Sciences*, 1:133–226. Chicago: The Academy, 1869.

Kent, Timothy J. *Birchbark Canoes of the Fur Trade*. 2 vols. Ossineke MI: Silver Fox Enterprises, 1997.

King, Margaret L. *Women of the Renaissance*. Chicago: University of Chicago Press, 1991.

Kohl, Johann Georg. *Kitchi-Gami: Life among the Lake Superior Ojibway*. Translated by Lascelles Wraxall. Introduction by Robert E. Beider. St. Paul MN: Minnesota Historical Society Press, 1985. Originally published in Germany in 1859.

Kusterer, Ken C. *Know-How on the Job: The Important Working Knowledge of "Unskilled" Workers*. Boulder CO: Westview, 1978.

Lamb, W. Kaye. Introduction. In *The Journals and Letters of Alexander Mackenzie*. Cambridge: Hakluyt Society at the University Press, 1970.

Lambert, John. *Travels through Canada, and the United States of North America, in the years 1806, 1807, & 1808*. 1813. 2nd ed. London: C. Cradock and W. Joy, 1814.

Lamonde, Yvan. *Ni Avec Eux Ni Sans Eux: Le Québec et les États-Unis*. Montreal: Nuit blanche éditeur, 1996.

Lamontagne, Sophie-Laurence. *L'hiver dans la culture québécoise (xviie–xixe siècles)*. Quebec: Institut québécois de recherche sur la culture, 1983.

Lande, Lawrence M. *The Development of the Voyageur Contract (1686–1821)*. Montreal: McLennan Library, McGill University, 1989.

Landes, Ruth. *The Ojibwa Woman*. New York: AMS Press, 1969. First published in 1838 by Columbia University Press.

Landmann, George. *Adventures and Recollections of Colonel Landmann, Late of the Corps of Royal Engineers*. 2 vols. London: Colburn, 1852.

Larocque, François-Antoine. "Journal of an Excursion of Discovery to the Rocky Mountains by Mr. Larocque in the Year 1805 from the 2d of June to the 18th of October." In Wood and Thiessen, *Early Fur Trade*, 129–55.

———. "Yellowstone Journal." In Wood and Thiessen, *Early Fur Trade*, 156–220.
LaRue, F. A. H. "Les chansons populaires et historiques du Canada." *Foyer canadien* 1 (1865): 321–84.
Lavender, David S. *The Fist in the Wilderness*. Garden City NY: Doubleday, 1964.
Laverdure, Patline, and Ida Rose Allard. *The Michif Dictionary: Turtle Mountain Chippewa Cree*. Edited by John C. Crawford. Winnipeg: Pemmican Publications, 1983.
Leacock, Eleanor. "Montagnais Women and the Jesuit Program for Colonization." In *Women and Colonization: Anthropological Perspectives*, edited by Mona Etienne and Eleanor Leacock, 25–42. New York: Praeger, 1980.
———. "Women in Egalitarian Societies." In *Becoming Visible: Women in European History*, edited by Renate Bridenthal and Claudia Koonz, 11–35. Boston: Houghton Mifflin, 1977.
Lears, T. J. Jackson. "The Concept of Cultural Hegemony: Problems and Possibilities." *American Historical Review* 90, no. 3 (1985): 567–93.
Leblanc, Monique Genest. *"Une jolie cinture à flesche" Sa présence au Bas-Canada, son cheminement vers l'Ouest, son introduction chez les Amérindiens*. Sainte–Foy QC: Les Presses de l'Université Laval, 2003.
Lefroy, John Henry. *In Search of the Magnetic North: A Soldier-Surveyor's Letters from the North-West, 1843–1844*. Edited by George F. G. Stanley. Toronto: Macmillan, 1955.
Le Roy Ladurie, Emmanuel. *Carnival in Romans*. Translated by Mary Feeney. 1979. New York: George Braziller, 1980.
Lewis, Meriwether. *History of the Expedition under the Command of Captains Lewis and Clarke, to the Sources of the Missouri, across the Rocky Mountains, down the Columbia River to the Pacific in 1804–6*. 3 vols. Toronto: George N. Morang, 1814(?).
Looking Horse, Arval. "The Sacred Pipe in Mandan Life." In DeMallie, *Sioux Indian Religion*, 45–65.
Losey, Elizabeth Browne. *Let Them Be Remembered: The Story of the Fur Trade Posts*. New York: Vantage, 1999.
Lunn, Jean. "The Illegal Fur Trade out of New France, 1713–60." *Canadian Historical Association Report* (1939): 61–76.
Lytwyn, Victor P. "The Anishinabeg and the Fur Trade." In *Lake Superior to Rainy Lake: Three Centuries of Fur Trade History*, edited by Jean Morrison, 27–45. Thunder Bay ON: Thunder Bay Historical Museum Society, 2003.
———. *The Fur Trade of the Little North: Indians, Peddlars, and Englishmen East of Lake Winnipeg, 1760–1821*. Winnipeg: Rupert's Land Research Centre, 1986.
———. "Transportation in the Petit Nord." Plate 63 in *Historical Atlas of Canada*, vol. 1, *From the Beginning to 1800*, edited by R. Cole Harris. Toronto: University of Toronto Press, 1987.
MacDonald, Archibald. *Peace River: A Canoe Voyage from Hudson's Bay to Pacific in 1828*. Rutland VT: Charles E. Tuttle, 1971.
MacGregor, J. B. *John Rowand: Czar of the Prairies*. Saskatoon: Western Producer Prairie Books, 1978.

Mackenzie, Alexander. "A General History of the Fur Trade from Canada to the North-West." In Mackenzie, *Voyages from Montreal on the River St. Laurence*, 1–132.

———. *Voyages from Montreal on the River St. Laurence through the Continent of North America to the Frozen and Pacific Oceans in the Years 1789 and 1793 with a Preliminary Account of the Rise, Progress, and Present State of the Fur Trade of That Country*. London: R. Noble, Old Bailey, 1801.

Mackie, Richard Somerset. *Trading beyond the Mountains: The British Fur Trade on the Pacific, 1793–1843*. Vancouver: University of British Columbia Press, 1997.

Makahonuk, Glen. "Wage-Labour in the Northwest Fur Trade Economy, 1760–1849." *Saskatchewan History* 41, no. 1 (Winter 1988): 1–17.

Makarius, Laura. "The Crime of Manabozo." *American Anthropologist* 75, no. 3 (June 1973): 663–75.

Mandelbaum, David G. *The Plains Cree: An Ethnographic, Historical, and Comparative Study*. Regina SK: Canadian Plains Research Center, 1979.

Massicotte, E. Z. "Répertoire des Engagements pour l'Ouest Conservés dans les Archives Judiciaires de Montréal." In *Rapport de L'Archiviste de la Province de Québec Pour 1929–1930*, 191–466. Québec: Rédempti Paradis, 1930.

Massicotte, E. Z., and Marius Barbeau. "Chants populaires du Canada." *Journal of American Folklore* 32, no. 123 (January–March 1919): 1–89.

Masson, L. R, ed. *Les Bourgeois de la Companie du Nord-Ouest*. 2 vols. New York: Antiquarian Press, 1960. Originally edited in 1889–90.

Mayer, Frank B. *With Pen and Pencil on the Frontier in 1851: The Diary and Sketches of Frank Blackwell Mayer*. Edited by Bertha L. Heilbron. St. Paul: Minnesota Historical Society, 1986.

Maynard, Steven. "Making Waves: Gender and Sex in the History of Seafaring." *Acadiensis* 22, no. 2 (Spring 1993): 144–54.

———. "Rough Work and Rugged Men: The Social Construction of Masculinity in Working-Class History." *Labour/Le travail* 23 (Spring 1989): 159–69.

McBrien, Richard P. "Roman Catholicism." In *The Encyclopedia of Religion*, edited by Mircea Eliade, 12:429–45. New York: Macmillan, 1987.

McCormack, Patricia A. "The Many Faces of Thanadelthur: Documents, Stories, and Images." In Brown and Vibert, *Reading beyond Words*, 329–64.

McCullough, A. B. *Money and Exchange in Canada to 1900*. Toronto: Dundurn Press, 1984.

McDermott, John F. *Mississippi Valley French 1673–1850*. St. Louis: Washington University Studies, 1941.

McDonell, John. "The Diary of John Macdonell." In Gates, *Five Fur Traders of the Northwest*, 63–119.

———. "Extracts From Mr John McDonnell's Journal (1793–1795)." In Masson, *Les Bourgeois de la Compagnie du Nord-Ouest*, 1:283–95.

McGillivray, Duncan. *The Journal of Duncan McGillivray of the North West Company at Fort George on the Saskatchewan, 1794–5*. Edited by Arthur S. Morton. Toronto: Macmillan, 1929.

McKenny, Thomas L. *Sketches of a Tour to the Lakes, of the Character and Customs of the*

Chippeway Indians and of Incidents Connected with the Treaty of Fond du Lac. Baltimore: F. Lucas, 1827.

McKenzie, James. "Journal, 1799." In Masson, *Les Bourgeois de la Compagnie du Nord-Ouest*, 2:371–99.

McKenzie, Roderick. "'Reminiscences' by the Honorable Roderic McKenzie Being Chiefly a Synopsis of Letters from Sir Alexander Mackenzie." In Masson, *Les Bourgeois de la Compagnie du Nord-Ouest*, 5–66. (Based on the correspondence between Alexander Mackenzie and Roderick McKenzie, 1786–1816, LAC MC MG19 C1, vol. 32, 32A.)

McLean, John. *Notes of a Twenty-Five Years' Service in the Hudson's Bay Territory*. 2 vols. London: Richard Bentley, 1849. Toronto: Champlain Society, 1932.

McLeod, Archibald N. "The Diary of Archibald N. McLeod." In Gates, *Five Fur Traders of the Northwest*, 121–85.

Meyer, David, and Paul C. Thistle. "Saskatchewan River Rendezvous Centers and Trading Posts: Continuity in a Cree Social Geography." *Ethnohistory* 42, no. 3 (Summer 1995): 403–44.

Milloy, John S. *The Plains Cree: Trade, Diplomacy and War, 1790 to 1870*. Winnipeg: University of Manitoba Press, 1988.

Mitchell, Elaine Allan. *Fort Timiskaming and the Fur Trade*. Toronto: University of Toronto Press, 1977.

Moir, John S. *Church and State in Canada, 1627–1867*. Toronto: McClelland & Stewart, 1967.

Monk, George. "A Description of Northern Minnesota by a Fur Trade in 1807." Edited by Grace Lee Nute. *Minnesota History* 5 (1923): 28–39.

Moodie, D. W. "Agriculture in the Fur Trade." In *Old Trails and New Directions: Papers of the Third North American Fur Trade Conference*, edited by Carol M. Judd and Arthur J. Ray, 272–90. Toronto: University of Toronto Press, 1980.

Moodie, D. Wayne, Barry Kaye, and Victor Lytwyn. "The Fur Trade Northwest to 1870." Plate 17 in *Historical Atlas of Canada*, vol. 2, *The Land Transformed, 1800–1891*, edited by R. Louis Gentilcore. Toronto: University of Toronto Press, 1993.

Moodie, D. Wayne, Victor P. Lytwyn, and Barry Kaye. "Trading Posts, 1774–1821." Plate 62 in *Historical Atlas of Canada*, vol. 1, *From the Beginning to 1800*, edited by R. Cole Harris. Toronto: University of Toronto Press, 1987.

Moodie, D. Wayne, Victor P. Lytwyn, Barry Kaye, and Arthur J. Ray. "Competition and Consolidation, 1760–1825." Plate 61 in *Historical Atlas of Canada*, vol. 1, *From the Beginning to 1800*, edited by R. Cole Harris. Toronto: University of Toronto Press, 1987.

Moodie, T. Dunbar. "Migrancy and Male Sexuality in the South African Gold Mines." *Journal of Southern African Studies* 14, no. 2 (January 1988): 228–56.

Moogk, Peter N. *Building a House in New France*. Toronto: McClelland & Stewart, 1977.

———. *La Nouvelle France: The Making of French Canada--A Cultural History*. East Lansing: Michigan State University Press, 2000.

———. "'Thieving Buggers' and 'Stupid Sluts': Insults and Popular Culture in New France." *William and Mary Quarterly*, 3rd ser., 36 (1979): 524–47.

Moore, Thomas. *Epistles, Odes, and Other Poems*. Philadelphia: B. Graves, 1806.

———. *The Letters of Thomas Moore*. Edited by Wilfred S. Dowden. Vol. 1, *1793–1818*. Oxford: Clarendon Press, 1964.

———. *The Rapids; a Canadian Boat Song*. Philadelphia: G. E. Blake, 1806(?). (Score, 4 pp.)

Morice, A. G. *Dictionnaire historiques des Canadiens et des Métis Française de l'Ouest*. 2nd ed. Montreal: Granger Freres, 1912.

Morland, Lynn Louise. "Craft Industries at Fort Michilimackinac, an Eighteenth-Century Fur Trade Outpost." PhD diss., University of Pennsylvania, 1993.

Morris, Alexander. *The Treaties of Canada with the Indians of Manitoba and the North-West Territories, including the Negotiations on Which They Were Based*. Toronto: Belfords, Clarke, 1880.

Morrison, Jean. *Superior Rendezvous-Place: Fort William in the Canadian Fur Trade*. Toronto: Natural Heritage Books, 2001.

Morse, Eric W. *Fur Trade Canoe Routes of Canada/Then and Now*. Toronto: University of Toronto Press, 1969.

Morton, Anne. "Chief Trader Joseph McGillivray." Paper presented at the Rupert's Land Colloquium 1998, Winnipeg and Norway House, June 1998.

Muir, Edward. *Ritual in Early Modern Europe*. Cambridge: Cambridge University Press, 1997.

Murphy, Lucy Eldersveld. *A Gathering of Rivers: Indians, Métis, and Mining in the Western Great Lakes, 1737–1832*. Lincoln: University of Nebraska Press, 2000.

Murray, Laura J. "Fur Traders in Conversation." *Ethnohistory* 50, no. 2 (Spring 2003): 285–314.

Nelson, George. *My First Years in the Fur Trade: The Journals of 1802–1804*. Edited by Laura Peers and Theresa Schenck. St. Paul: Minnesota Historical Society Press, 2002.

Nevins, John Birkbeck. *A Narrative of Two Voyages to Hudson's Bay; With Traditions of the North American Indians*. London: Society for Promoting Christian Knowledge, 1847.

Newman, Peter C. *Company of Adventurers*. Vol. 2, *Caesars of the Wilderness*. Markham ON: Viking, 1987.

Nicks, John. "Orkneymen in the HBC, 1780–1821." In *Old Trails and New Directions: Papers of the Third North American Fur Trade Conference*, edited by Carol M. Judd and Arthur J. Ray, 102–26. Toronto: University of Toronto Press, 1980.

Nicks, Trudy. "The Iroquois and Fur Trade in Western Canada." In *Old Trails and New Directions: Papers of the Third North American Fur Trade Conference*, edited by Carol M. Judd and Arthur J. Ray, 85–101. Toronto: University of Toronto Press, 1980.

Noel, Jan. *Canada Dry: Temperance Crusades before Confederation*. Toronto: University of Toronto Press, 1995.

———. "New France: Les femmes favorisées." In *The Neglected Majority: Essays in Canadian Women's History*, edited by Alison Prentice and Susan Mann Trofimenkoff, 2:18–40. Toronto: McClelland & Stewart, 1985.

———. *Women in New France*. Historical Booklet no. 59. Ottawa: Canadian Historical Association, 1998.

Nute, Grace Lee. *Calendar of the American Fur Company's Papers*. 2 vols., Washington DC: U.S. GPO, 1945.

———. "Journey for Frances." *The Beaver* (Summer 1954), 12–18, (December 1953), 50–59, and (March 1954), 12–17.

———. *The Voyageur*. New York: Appleton, 1931.

———. *The Voyageur's Highway: Minnesota's Borderland*. St. Paul: Minnesota Historical Society, 1941.

Ordinances and Acts of Quebec and Lower Canada (1796), 36 George III. In *Ordinances Made and Passed by the Governor and Legislative Council of the Province of Quebec*. Quebec: P. E. Desbarats, 1825.

Ortner, Sherry B., and Harriet Whitehead. "Introduction: Accounting for Sexual Meanings." In *Sexual Meanings: The Cultural Construction of Gender and Sexuality*, edited by Sherry B. Ortner and Harriet Whitehead, 13–25. Cambridge: Cambridge University Press, 1981.

Osborne, A. C. "The Migration of *Voyageurs* from Drummond Island to Penetanguishene in 1828." *Ontario Historical Society Papers and Records* 3 (1901): 123–49.

Ouellet, Fernand. "Dualité économique et changement technologique au Québec (1760–1790)." *Histoire sociale/Social History* 9 (November 1976): 256–96.

———. *Economic and Social History of Quebec, 1760–1850*. Ottawa: Gage Publishing in association with the Institute of Canadian Studies, Carleton University, 1980. Originally published as *Histoire économique et sociale du Québec, 1760–1850* (Montreal: Fides, 1966).

Ozouf, Mona. *La fête révolutionnaire 1789–1799*. Paris: Gallimard, 1976.

Palmer, Bryan D. *Working-Class Experience: Rethinking the History of Canadian Labour, 1800–1991*. Toronto: McClelland & Stewart, 1992.

Palmer, John. *Journal of Travels in the United States of America and in Lower Canada, Performed in the Year 1817*. London: Sherwood, Neely, & Jones, 1818.

Pannekoek, Frits. "Metis Studies: The Development of a Field and New Directions." In Binnema, Ens, and MacLeod, *From Rupert's Land to Canada*, 111–28.

Paul, Ellen. "The Voyageur at Home: Parish Registers as a Tool in Understanding the Motivation and Formation of a Fur Trader." Paper presented at the Rupert's Land Colloquium, Winnipeg, 1998.

Payne, Michael. *The Most Respectable Place in the Territory: Everyday Life in Hudson's Bay Company Service, York Factory, 1788 to 1870*. Ottawa: Ministry of the Environment, Canadian Parks Service, 1989.

Peck, Gunther. "Manly Gambles: The Politics of Risk on the Comstock Lode, 1860–1880." *Journal of Social History* 26, no. 4 (1993): 701–23.

Peers, Laura. *The Ojibwa of Western Canada, 1780 to 1879*. Winnipeg: University of Manitoba Press, 1994.

Pendergast, Russell Anthony. "The XY Company 1798 to 1804." PhD diss., University of Ottawa, 1957.

Pentland, H. Clare. *Labour and Capital in Canada, 1650–1860*. Toronto: James Lorimer, 1981.

Perrot, Nicolas. *The Indian Tribes of the Upper Mississippi Valley and the Region of the Great*

Lakes. Edited and translated by Emma Helen Blair. 2 vols. Cleveland: Arthur H. Clark, 1911.

Peterson, Jacqueline. "The People In Between: Indian-White Marriage and the Genesis of a Métis Society and Culture in the Great Lakes Region, 1680–1830." PhD diss., University of Illinois at Chicago Circle, 1980.

Peterson, Jacqueline, and Jennifer S. H. Brown, eds. *The New Peoples: Being and Becoming Métis in North America*. Winnipeg: University of Manitoba Press, 1985.

Phillips, Paul Crisler. *The Fur Trade*. 2 vols. Norman: University of Oklahoma Press, 1961.

Podruchny, Carolyn. "Baptizing Novices: Ritual Moments among French Canadian Voyageurs in the Montreal Fur Trade, 1780–1821." *Canadian Historical Review* 83, no. 2 (June 2002): 165–95.

———. "Dieu, *Diable* and the Trickster: *Voyageur* Religious Syncretism in the *Pays d'en haut*, 1770–1821." In *Western Oblate Studies* 5, Proceedings of the Fifth Symposium on the History of the Oblates in Western and Northern Canada, edited by Raymond Huel and Gilles Lesage, 75–92. Winnipeg: Presses Universitaires de Saint-Boniface, 2000.

———. "Festivities, Fortitude and Fraternalism: Fur Trade Masculinity and the Beaver Club, 1785–1827." In *New Faces in the Fur Trade: Selected Papers of the Seventh North American Fur Trade Conference*, Edited by William C. Wicken, Jo-Anne Fiske, and Susan Sleeper-Smith, 31–52. East Lansing: Michigan State University Press, 1998.

———. "Un homme-libre se construit une identité: Voyage de Joseph Constant au Pas, de 1773 à 1853." *Cahiers franco-canadiens de l'Ouest, Numéro spécial sur la question métissage: entre la polyvalence et l'ambivalence identitaires* 14, nos. 1 and 2 (2002): 33–59.

———. "Unfair Masters and Rascally Servants? Labour Relations among Bourgeois, Clerks and Voyageurs in the Montréal Fur Trade, 1780–1821." *Labour/Le Travail: Journal of Canadian Labour Studies* 43 (Spring 1999): 43–70.

———. "Werewolves and Windigos: Narratives of Cannibal Monsters in French-Canadian Voyageur Oral Tradition." *Ethnohistory* 51, no. 4 (Fall 2004): 677–700.

Pond, Peter. "The Narrative of Peter Pond." In Gates, *Five Fur Traders of the Northwest*, 9–59.

Provencher, Jean. *Les Quatre Saisons dans la vallée du Saint-Laurent*. Montréal: Boréal, 1988.

Radforth, Ian. "The Shantymen." In *Labouring Lives: Work and Workers in Nineteenth-Century Ontario*, edited by Paul Craven, 204–76. Toronto: University of Toronto Press, 1995.

Radin, Paul. *The Trickster: A Study in American Indian Mythology*. 1956. New York: Schocken Books, 1972.

Radin, Paul, and A. B. Reagan. "Ojibwa Myths and Tales: The Manabozho Cycle." *Journal of American Folklore* 41, no. 159 (January–March 1928): 61–146.

Ray, Arthur J. *Indians in the Fur Trade: Their Roles as Hunters, Trappers and Middlemen in the Lands Southwest of Hudson Bay, 1660–1870*. Toronto: University of Toronto Press, 1974.

Ray, Arthur J., and Donald Freeman. "*Give Us Good Measure*": *An Economic Analysis of Relations between the Indians and the Hudson's Bay Company before 1763*. Toronto: University of Toronto Press, 1978.

Ray, Arthur J., D. Wayne Moodie, and Conrad E. Heidenreich. "Rupert's Land." Plate 57 in *Historical Atlas of Canada*, vol. 1: *From the Beginning to 1800*, edited by R. Cole Harris. Toronto: University of Toronto Press, 1987.

Rediker, Marcus. *Between the Devil and the Deep Blue Sea: Merchant Seamen, Pirates, and the Anglo-American Maritime World, 1700–1750*. Cambridge: Cambridge University Press, 1987.

Reed, Charles Bert. *Masters of the Wilderness*. Chicago: University of Chicago Press, 1914.

Rice, Kym. *Early American Taverns: For the Entertainment of Friends and Strangers*. Chicago: Regnery Gateway, 1983.

Rich, E. E. *The Fur Trade and the Northwest to 1857*. Toronto: McClelland & Stewart, 1967.

———. "Trade Habits and Economic Motivation among the Indians of North America." *Canadian Journal of Economics and Political Science* 26, no. 1 (1960): 35–53.

Richter, Daniel K. *The Ordeal of the Longhouse: The Peoples of the Iroquois League in the Era of European Colonization*. Chapel Hill: University of North Carolina Press, 1992.

Ridington, Robin, and Dennis Hastings (In'aska). *Blessing for a Long Time: The Sacred Pole of the Omaha Tribe*. Lincoln: University of Nebraska Press, 1997.

Rochefoucauld Liancourt, Duke de la. *Travels through the United States of North America, the Country of the Iroquois, and Upper Canada, in the Years 1795, 1796, and 1797; with an Authentic Account of Lower Canada*. Translated by H. Neuman. London: R. Phillips, 1799.

———. *Voyage dans les États-Unis d'Amérique, fait en 1795, 1796 et 1797 par La Rochefoucauld-Liancourt Paris*. 2 vols. Paris: Chez Du Pont, Imprimeur-Libraire, 1799–1800.

Roscoe, Will. "How to Become a Berdache: Toward a Unified Analysis of Gender Diversity." In *Third Sex, Third Gender: Beyond Sexual Dimorphism in Culture and History*, edited by Gilbert Herdt, 329–72. New York: Zone Books, 1994.

Ross, Alexander. *Adventures of the First Settlers on the Oregon or Columbia River: Being a Narrative of the Expedition Fitted Out by John Jacob Astor, to Establish the 'Pacific Fur Company' with an Account of Some Indian Tribes on the Coast of the Pacific*. Ann Arbor MI: University Microfilms, 1966. First published in 1849 by Smith, Elder, London.

———. *Fur Hunters of the Far West: A Narrative of Adventures in the Oregon and Rocky Mountains*. 2 vols. London: Smith, Elder, 1855.

Rumilly, Robert. *La compagnie du Nord Ouest, une épopée montréalaise*. 2 vols. Montreal: Fides, 1980.

Sawaya, Jean-Pierre. *La Fédération des Sept Feux de la Vallée du Saint-Laurent, xviie–xixe siècle*. Sillery QC: Septentrion, 1998.

Schwartz, Marion. *A History of Dogs in Early America*. New Haven CT: Yale University Press, 1997.

Shoemaker, Nancy, ed. *Negotiators of Change: Historical Perspectives on Native American Women*. New York: Routledge, 1995.

Skinner, Clairborne. "The Sinews of Empire: The Voyageurs and the Carrying Trade of the *Pays d'en Haut*, 1681–1754." PhD diss., University of Illinois at Chicago, 1991.

Sleeper-Smith, Susan. *Indian Women and French Men: Rethinking Cultural Encounter in the Western Great Lakes*. Amherst: University of Massachusetts Press, 2001.

Smits, David. "The 'Squaw Drudge': A Prime Index of Savagism." *Ethnohistory* 29, no. 4 (1982): 281–306.

Sprague, D. N., and R. P. Frye. *The Genealogy of the First Métis Nation: The Development and Dispersal of the Red River Settlement, 1820–1900*. Winnipeg: Pemmican Publications, 1983.

Sprenger, Herman. "The Métis Nation: Buffalo Hunting versus Agriculture in the Red River Settlement, 1810–1870." In *Native People, Native Lands: Canadian Indians, Inuit and Metis*, edited by Bruce Alden Cox, Carleton Library Series no. 142, 120–35. Ottawa: Carleton University Press, 1987.

Sullivan, Lawrence E., ed. *Native American Religions: North America*. New York: Macmillan, 1987.

Swagerty, William R. "History of the United States Plains until 1850." In *Handbook of North American Indians*, vol. 13, *Plains*. Edited by DeMallie, 256–79.

Swagerty, William R., and Dick A. Wilson. "Faithful Service under Different Flags: A Socioeconomic Profile of the Columbia District, Hudson's Bay Company and the Upper Missouri Outfit, American Fur Company, 1825–1835." In *The Fur Trade Revisited: Selected Papers of the Sixth North American Fur Trade Conference, Mackinac Island, Michigan, 1991*, edited by Jennifer S. H. Brown, W. J. Eccles, and Donald P. Heldman, 243–67. East Lansing: Michigan State University Press, 1994.

Tanner, Helen Hornbeck. "The Career of Joseph La France, *Coureur de Bois* in the Upper Great Lakes." In *The Fur Trade Revisited: Selected Papers of the Sixth North American Fur Trade Conference, Mackinac Island, Michigan, 1991*, edited by Jennifer S. H. Brown, W. J. Eccles, and Donald P. Heldman, 171–87. East Lansing: Michigan State University Press, 1994.

———, ed. *The Settling of North America: The Atlas of the Great Migrations into North America from the Ice Age to the Present*. New York: Macmillan, 1995.

Tanner, John. *A Narrative of the Captivity and Adventures of John Tanner during Thirty Years Residence among the Indians in the Interior of North America*. Minneapolis: Ross & Haines, 1956. First published in 1830 by G. & C. & H. Carvili, New York.

Terrell, J. U. *Furs by Astor*. New York: Morrow, 1963.

Thistle, Paul. *Indian-European Trade Relations in the Lower Saskatchewan River Region to 1840*. Winnipeg: University of Manitoba Press, 1986.

Thomas, Keith. *Religion and the Decline of Magic: Studies in Popular Beliefs in Sixteenth and Seventeenth Century England*. London: Weidenfeld & Nicholson, 1971.

Thomas, L. H. "A History of Agriculture on the Prairies to 1914." *Prairie Forum* 1, no. 1 (1976): 31–45.

Thompson, David. *David Thompson's Narrative, 1784–1812*. Edited by Richard Glover. Toronto: Champlain Society, 1962.

———. "Journal, November 1797." In Wood and Thiessen, *Early Fur Trade*, 93–128.

Thompson, E. P. *Customs in Common*. London: Merlin, 1991.

Thorne, Tanis C. *The Many Hands of My Relations: French and Indians on the Lower Missouri*. Columbia: University of Missouri Press, 1996.

Thurston, John. "Hegemony." In *Encyclopedia of Contemporary Literary Theory: Approaches, Scholars, Terms*, edited by Irena R. Makaryk, 549–50. Toronto: University of Toronto Press, 1993.

Trigger, Bruce G. *Natives and Newcomers: Canada's 'Heroic Age' Reconsidered*. Kingston ON: McGill-Queen's University Press, 1985.

———, ed. *Northeast*. Vol. 15 of *Handbook of North American Indians*, edited by William C. Sturtevant. Washington DC: Smithsonian Institution, 1978.

Troyes, Chevalier de. *Journal de l'Éxpedition du Chevalier de Troyes a la Baie d'Hudson, en 1686*. Edited by L'abbé Ivanhoe Caron. Beauceville QC: La Compagnie de 'L'Éclaireur,' 1918.

Trudel, Marcel. *The Seigneurial Regime*. Ottawa: Canadian Historical Association, 1956.

Turner, Victor. *Blazing the Trail: Way Makers in the Exploration of Symbols*. Tucson: University of Arizona Press, 1992.

———. *The Ritual Process: Structure and Anti-Structure*. Chicago: Aldine, 1969.

———. "Social Dramas and Stories about Them." In *On Narrative*, edited by W. J. T. Mitchell, 137–64. Chicago: University of Chicago Press, 1981. Reprint, New York: Aldine de Gruyter, 1995. Originally published in *Critical Inquiry* 7 (1980): 141–68.

———. "Variations of a Theme of Liminality." In Turner, *Blazing the Trail*, 48–65. Tucson: University of Arizona Press, 1992.

Tyrrell, J. B., ed. *Journals of Samuel Hearne and Philip Turnor*. Toronto: Champlain Society, 1934.

Van Gennep, Arnold. *Le Folklore du Daphiné (Isère): Étude descriptive et comparée de psychologie populaire*. 2 vols. Paris: Librarie Orientale et Américaine, 1932.

———. *Manuel de folklore français contemporain*. 4 vols. Paris: J. Picard, 1937–49.

———. *The Rites of Passage*. Translated by Monika B. Vizedom and Gabrielle L. Caffee. London: Routledge & Kegan Paul, 1909.

Van Kirk, Sylvia. "George Nelson's 'Wretched' Career, 1802–1823." In *Rendezvous: Selected Papers of the Fourth North American Fur Trade Conference*, edited by Thomas C. Buckley, 207–13. St. Paul MN: The Conference, 1984.

———. *"Many Tender Ties": Women in Fur-Trade Society, 1670–1870*. Winnipeg: Watson & Dwyer, 1980.

———. "Thanadelthur." *The Beaver* (Spring 1974): 40–45.

Vecsey, Christopher. *Traditional Ojibwa Religion and Its Historical Changes*. Philadelphia: American Philosophical Society, 1990.

Vézina, Robert. "Les mauvais renards et la garce: Description et origine du terme drouine." In *Le passage du Détroit: 300 ans de présence francophone / Passages: Three Centuries of Francophone Presence at Le Détroit*, edited by Marcel Bénéteau, 127–47. Windsor ON: Humanities Research Group, University of Windsor, 2003.

Vibert, Elizabeth. *Traders' Tales: Narratives of Cultural Encounters in the Columbia Plateau, 1807–1846*. Norman: University of Oklahoma Press, 1997.

Vickerson, Fred. "Genealogy and the Hessian Soldiers--Part 1." *The Global Gazette: Online Family History Magazine* 3, no. 4 (February 24, 1999), http://globalgazette.net/gazrr/gazrr23.htm.

Voorhis, Ernest. *Historic Forts and Trading Posts of the French Regime and of the English Fur Trading Companies*. Ottawa: Department of the Interior, 1930.

Wallace, W. Stewart, ed. *Documents Relating to the North West Company*. Toronto: Champlain Society, 1934.

Wallot, Jean-Pierre. *Un Québec qui bougeait: Trame socio-politique du Québec au tournant du XIXe siècle*. Montreal: Boréal, 1973.

Watson, Robert. "The First Beaver Club." *The Beaver* (December 1931): 334–7.

Way, Peter. "Evil Humors and Ardent Spirits: The Rough Culture of Canal Construction Laborers." *Journal of American History* 79 (March 1993): 1398–1400.

Weist, Katherine M. "Beasts of Burden and Menial Slaves: Nineteenth-Century Observations of Northern Plains Indian Women." In *The Hidden Half: Studies of Plains Indian Women*, edited by Patricia Albers and Beatrice Medicine, 29–107. Washington DC: University Press of America, 1983.

Weld, Isaac, Jr. *Travels through the States of North America, and the Provinces of Upper and Lower Canada, during the Years 1795, 1796, and 1797*. 4th ed. 2 vols. London: John Stockdale, 1807.

White, Bruce M. "The Fear of Pillaging: Economic Folktales of the Great Lakes Fur Trade." In *The Fur Trade Revisited: Selected Papers of the Sixth North American Fur Trade Conference, Mackinac Island, Michigan, 1991*, edited by Jennifer S. H. Brown, W. J. Eccles, and Donald P. Heldman, 199–216. East Lansing: Michigan State University Press, 1994.

———. "'Give Us a Little Milk': The Social and Cultural Meanings of Gift Giving in the Lake Superior Fur Trade." *Minnesota History* 48, no. 2 (1982): 60–71.

———. "Montreal Canoes and their Cargoes." In *Le Castor Fait Tout: Selected Papers of the Fifth North American Fur Trade Conference, 1985*. Edited by Bruce Trigger et. al., 164–92. Montreal: St. Louis Historical Society, 1987.

———. "A Skilled Game of Exchange: Ojibwa Fur Trade Protocol." *Minnesota History* 50, no. 6 (Summer 1987): 229–40.

White, Richard. *The Middle Ground: Indians, Empires, and Republics in the Great Lakes Region*. Cambridge: Cambridge University Press, 1991.

Whitehead, Harriet. "The Bow and the Burden Strap: A New Look at Institutionalized Homosexuality in Native North America." In *Sexual Meanings: The Cultural Construction of Gender and Sexuality*, edited by Sherry B. Ortner and Harriet Whitehead, 80–115. Cambridge: Cambridge University Press, 1981.

Wickstead, G. W. *Table of the Provincial Statutes and Ordinances in Force or Which Have Been in Force in Lower Canada*. Toronto, 1857.

Williams, Walter L. *The Spirit and the Flesh: Sexual Diversity in American Indian Culture*. Boston: Beacon Press, 1986.

Winterburn, Joseph D. "Lac La Pluie Bills of Lading, 1806–1809." In *Lake Superior to Rainy Lake: Three Centuries of Fur Trade History*, edited by Jean Morrison, 59–67. Thunder Bay ON: Thunder Bay Historical Museum Society, 2003.

Wood, Stephen, ed. *The Degradation of Work?: Skill, Deskilling and the Labour Process*. London: Hutchinson, 1982.

Wood, W. Raymond, and Thomas D. Thiessen. *Early Fur Trade on the Northern Plains: Canadian Traders among the Mandan and Hidatsa Indians, 1738–1818; The Narratives of John Macdonell, David Thompson, François-Antoine Larocque, and Charles McKenzie*. Norman: University of Oklahoma Press, 1985.

Woodcock, George. *A Social History of Canada*. Markham ON: Penguin, 1988.

Index

In many cases the first names of voyageurs and masters are unknown; all known names are listed. Page numbers in italics refer to illustrations.